The Imjin and Kapyong Battles

Korea, 1951

TWENTIETH-CENTURY BATTLES

Spencer C. Tucker, editor

The Imjin and Kapyong Battles

Korea, 1951

S. P. MacKenzie

INDIANA UNIVERSITY PRESS *Bloomington & Indianapolis*

This book is a publication of

INDIANA UNIVERSITY PRESS
601 North Morton Street
Bloomington, Indiana 47404–3797 USA

iupress.indiana.edu

Telephone orders 800-842-6796
Fax orders 812-855-7931

♾ The paper used in this publication meets the minimum requirements of the American National Standard for Information Sciences – Permanence of Paper for Printed Library Materials, ANSI Z39.48–1992.

Manufactured in the United States of America

Library of Congress Cataloging-in-Publication Data

Mackenzie, S. P.
The Imjin and Kapyong battles, Korea, 1951 / S.P. Mackenzie.
p. cm. – (Twentieth-century battles)
Includes bibliographical references and index.
ISBN 978-0-253-00908-1 (cloth : alk. paper) – ISBN 978-0-253-00916-6 (electronic book) 1. Imjin River, Battle of the, Korea, 1951. 2. Kapyong, Battle of, Korea, 1951. 3. Korean War, 1950–1953 – Participation, Australian. 4. Korean War, 1950–1953 – Participation, Canadian. I. Title.
DS918.2.I49M33 2013
951.904'242 – dc23

2012034927

1 2 3 4 5 18 17 16 15 14 13

Contents

For the British, the most celebrated action of the war . . .

BRITISH OFFICER on the Battle of the Imjin[1]

[T]he most significant and important battle for Australian troops in Korea . . .

AUSTRALIAN COMMENTATOR on the Battle of Kapyong[2]

The finest moment of the war for Canadians . . .

CANADIAN JOURNALIST on the Battle of Kapyong[3]

Preface

FOR SEVERAL DAYS AND NIGHTS IN THE FOURTH WEEK OF April 1951, two infantry brigades, one exclusively British and another dominated by contingents from the Commonwealth, each withstood repeated assaults by Chinese forces many times their size. Occurring simultaneously but in different locations along the Korean front, the engagements at the Imjin and Kapyong are remembered battles of a forgotten war. There were plenty of other major actions in which British and Commonwealth units fought with great doggedness and bravery against the odds in the Land of the Morning Calm, but these have mostly faded almost entirely from public consciousness. Not so the Imjin and Kapyong battles, which take pride of place in most popular histories and form the subject matter for impressive dioramas depicting the Last Stand on Gloster Hill during the Imjin battle, at the Imperial War Museum in London, and the defense of Hill 677 and of Hill 504 in, respectively, the Canadian War Museum in Ottawa and the Australian War Memorial in Canberra.[4]

The reasons for this prominence are not hard to discern. Both on the Imjin and at Kapyong infantry battalions – each theoretically numbering nearly a thousand soldiers organized into four rifle companies (130 men each) composed of three platoons (35 men each), plus assorted supporting sub-units, but at the time often several hundred men below establishment[5] – had made heroic stands in the face of vastly superior numbers of the enemy and, so it was often claimed, saved Seoul from being overrun by the Chinese and perhaps prevented the collapse of the entire U.N. war effort.

For the British, the Battle of the Imjin was a fight which had featured much stiff-upper-lip courage in the face of great adversity, including a number of instances of both physical and moral bravery chronicled in detail by participants and observers. It was also an engagement involving a widely reported Last Stand. "Here was a tale up there with Hastings, Rorke's Drift, or Arnhem," an enthusiastic journalist thought to himself fifty years on, "a stand against monumental odds, by men whose orders were simply to hold fast – the Thermopylae of the Korean War."[6] Surrounded, the officers and men of the Glosters, despite mounting losses and a steadily diminishing prospect of rescue, determinedly fought off successive Chinese assaults until casualties and a shortage of ammunition made further resistance impossible. In subsequent accounts of the battle it was always the doomed heroism and self-sacrifice of the "Glorious Glosters" that received the most attention, in part perhaps because it was they – along with an attached mortar troop – who were awarded a Presidential Unit Citation "for exceptionally outstanding performance of duty and extraordinary heroism in action."[7]

As to the outcome of the Battle of the Imjin, claims could be made that, despite the heavy losses incurred and the eventual retreat, the sacrifices of 29th Brigade in general and the Glosters in particular had not been in vain. The numerically superior enemy, after all, was thought to have suffered huge casualties while engaging the British across the Imjin, a figure of 10,000 or more killed, captured, and wounded becoming a standard estimate. In doggedly resisting the Chinese tide, moreover, 29th Brigade was said to have played a vital part in blunting the enemy advance on the South Korean capital. "The stand made by the Brigade had," as the official South Korean history based on British accounts put it, "completely frustrated the Chinese plan to break the United Nations front. For three days it had blocked all attempts to cut the road to Seoul and inflicted casualties on the enemy which brought his first spring offensive to a halt and resulted in his retreat."[8] Though virtually destroyed in the effort, the 1st Glosters had wrecked the enemy timetable for advance, thereby putting the South Korean capital out of reach and perhaps even forcing Peking to think seriously about starting peace talks.[9] Thus the Battle of the Imjin River, as well as containing incidents and attitudes in which the public might take enormous pride, was of great strategic significance.

Meanwhile for Australians and Canadians the pivotal moment in the Chinese spring offensive has long been seen as occurring at Kapyong seventy kilometers or so to the east of the Imjin battleground. Here too, repeated enemy attempts to break through in divisional strength had been thwarted by the heroic hilltop stands of, in this case, respectively an Australian infantry battalion and a Canadian infantry battalion from 27th British Commonwealth Brigade. Though at times surrounded and always in danger of being swamped by masses of Chinese troops, men from the Royal Australian Regiment and from Princess Patricia's Canadian Light Infantry, with support from other elements, had stood their ground until the enemy was too exhausted to continue. In the opinion of a leading Australian military historian writing toward the end of the twentieth century, it was here that the RAR "fought its greatest action of the war." Kapyong was also the "shining moment" for the PPCLI and indeed the nation's participation in the Korean War, according to the best-known popular interpreter of Canada's past in a book published shortly thereafter. Both battalions, as is always pointed out, received a Presidential Unit Citation for "extraordinary heroism and outstanding performance of combat duties."[10]

Moreover the outcome of the battle for the Kapyong Valley was of considerable strategic significance for the war itself. "After a night of heavy fighting during which their positions were overrun," reads a statement on a Commonwealth of Australia government website, "the Australians recaptured their positions and stalled the Chinese advance." Similar conclusions have been expressed in Canada with reference to Canadian actions at Kapyong. "The front held," as a Canadian Broadcasting Corporation television journalist put it almost fifty years after the event, "and Seoul was saved." While the emphasis might differ depending upon nationality, Australians and Canadians could agree that together their troops had prevented the enemy from retaking the capital of the Republic of Korea. "The Commonwealth Brigade had halted the might of the Chinese army and stopped them from streaming south and taking Seoul," as Australian TV documentary filmmaker Dennis K. Smith recently stated.[11]

In short, while the Imjin battle is the focal point for positive recollections of national military participation in Britain, the Kapyong battle serves a similar function in Australia and Canada. Yet though they took place at the same time, involved units that were often raised, trained, and armed along similar lines, and featured formations led by brigadiers from the same army, there have been few attempts to study these two much-storied battles from a comparative perspective.

In part this is a matter of the kind of national bias inherent in much popular history. If the intent is to celebrate the achievements of one's own soldiers, then stressing the contributions of other contingents tends to dilute the effect. Indeed, even with reference to Kapyong alone either 3RAR or 2PPCLI is the focus – rarely both – depending on whether the author is Australian or Canadian. Academic historians, while more capable of recognizing that the defeat of the Chinese spring offensive and the saving of Seoul was a combined effort by Eighth Army rather than just the result of heroic stands by a few exceptional battalions, also tend to work along national lines, not least in the composition of official histories.[12]

On occasion, however, explicit comparisons involving 27th Brigade at Kapyong and 29th Brigade at the Imjin have been made. This might be in order to suggest that British and Commonwealth forces were more adept at standing and fighting it out with the Chinese than retreat-prone South Korean and U.S. Army units.[13] It also could be in order to draw attention to supposed distinctions in combat performance between Commonwealth and British forces. Despite the unit citations, some veterans came to believe that undue praise was being lavished on those who had fought at the Imjin – particularly the Glosters – as compared to those who had made a stand at Kapyong. "I feel that the brigade [27BCB] never got the credit that they deserved at Kapyong," as a former soldier from the Middlesex regiment put it.[14] In the eyes of one Canadian veteran, the British on the Imjin had been incompetently led and poorly motivated compared to Commonwealth troops. "At Kapyong, the Australians, Canadians and New Zealanders were all volunteers, all with high morale," Robert Hepenstall claimed in his book on the Canadian army in Korea. British units on the Imjin such as the Glosters, on the other hand, were said to contain large numbers of reservists who "had a morale problem" and were not keen to fight. The fact that the Commonwealth units which had fought so much better at Kapyong apparently received second billing to the Glorious Glosters at the Imjin was, in the words of a Canadian journalist (and another veteran of Korea), due to "the power of British propaganda."[15]

That something had gone awry on the Imjin appears hard to dispute once the rhetoric of sacrifice is cast aside. Overall the 29th Brigade lost over a thousand men fighting on the line of the Imjin River, approximately ten times the losses suffered by the 27th Commonwealth Brigade defending the Kapyong Valley. Above all the 1st Glosters had been virtually wiped out in a stand on the Imjin that was subsequently made to seem inevitable and necessary but which in fact might have been avoided without too great a penalty. "Given the disparity between [British and] Commonwealth losses in the two engagements," as Jeffrey Grey of the Australian Defence Force Academy, one of the few academic historians to draw explicit parallels, rightly notes, "the question [why the difference?] seems worth asking."[16]

What, though, is the answer to the riddle of why losses were so much heavier for 29th Brigade on the Imjin than for 27th Brigade at Kapyong? Was it simply a matter of stark differences in leadership and morale, as some Anglophobe veterans loudly asserted? Or were the rather different higher U.S. command structures into which each brigade fitted at fault, as the Duntroon historian more cautiously suggests?[17]

These are certainly possibilities that deserve scrutiny, but several other potential factors also need to be explored. Were there significant differences in the terrain on which each battle was fought? Was one brigade better prepared than the other in terms of background, intelligence, weaponry, or other equipment? Did the enemy behave in ways which made it easier for one brigade to cope than the other? In recent years a quite comprehensive and realistic portrait of the complex and not always glorious events on the Imjin has emerged through the efforts of journalist Andrew Salmon.[18] A study of Kapyong with the same level of detail and forensic analysis has yet to be published, however;[19] and a greater understanding of each battle might be obtained through detailed comparison as opposed to just cautious academic hypothesis or, far worse, throwaway prejudicial assertion. Though analysis of Chinese actions and intentions is perforce limited by a one-party state which still guards its records closely (though dedicated scholars such as Xiaobing Li continue to make inroads), enough documentary material from Western archives and recollections by U.N. participants is available to build up a fairly detailed picture of events in the spring of 1951 as they affected 29th Brigade and 27th Brigade. By comparing and contrasting the Imjin and Kapyong battles a clearer picture of what happened, and above all why, should emerge for each of these twin engagements.

The course of events between 22 and 25 April 1951 along the Imjin River and down the Kapyong Valley will be explored in turn, followed by an examination of the aftermath. To fully understand what happened and why during those often chaotic and bloody nights and days, however, it is first necessary to scrutinize the nature and experience of the battalions involved in the months prior to the battle.

Acknowledgments

THIS BOOK WOULD NOT HAVE BEEN POSSIBLE WITHOUT HELP from the staff of the following libraries, archives, and other depositories: Archives New Zealand, Wellington; the Australian War Memorial, Canberra; the British Library, St. Pancras; the Directorate of History and Heritage, Department of National Defence, Ottawa; the George C. Marshall Library, Lexington, Va.; the Imperial War Museum, Lambeth; the Museum of the Gloucestershire Regiment, Gloucester; the National Archives, Kew; the National Archives and Records Administration, Archives II, College Park, Md.; the National Archives of Australia, Canberra; the National Army Museum, Chelsea; the National Library and Archives of Canada, Ottawa; the National Portrait Gallery, London; Robarts Library, University of Toronto; Thomas Cooper Library – particularly the inter-library loans department – at the University of South Carolina; the United States Army Military History Institute, Carlisle, Pa.; the University of Victoria, B.C.; and Veterans Affairs Canada, Ottawa. I must gratefully acknowledge Bob Gill for allowing me to publish an extract from a letter he wrote covering the 29th Brigade PUC ceremony, and F. E. Carter and Jim Jacobs for agreeing to let me print extracts from their unpublished war memoirs. All reasonable effort has been made to contact other potential copyright holders. The cartographic skills of Elbie Bentley allowed for the maps without which this book would be glaringly incomplete. I am also grateful for the help provided by Robert J. Sloan and the editorial staff at Indiana University Press and to series editor Spencer C. Tucker for agreeing that a published study of the Imjin and Kapyong battles would be worthwhile.

Note on Transliteration

SINCE THE 1980S CHINESE NAMES AND PLACES HAVE BEEN transliterated into English using pinyin in place of the older Wade-Giles system; thus, for instance, the founder of the People's Republic of China became Mao Zedong in place of Mao Tse-tung and the capital Beijing rather than Peking. The phonetic transliteration of Korean locations and names into English has if anything changed even more over the past sixty years as the McCune-Reischauer system was first modified and then, at the start of this century, supplanted in South Korea by Revised Romanization of Korean. Hence, for example, what started out as Kapyong became Kap'yong and is currently Gapyeong. In order to maintain consistency between direct quotations and the rest of the text, the spellings used by English-speaking participants at the time of the Korean War have been used throughout as far as possible. In addition, I have chosen to adopt the popular way of referring to the First Battalion, The Gloucestershire Regiment: "Glosters" rather than "Gloucesters."

Abbreviations

1A&SH – First Battalion, Argyll and Sutherland Highlanders

1GLOS – First Battalion, Gloucestershire Regiment

1KOSB – First Battalion, King's Own Scottish Borderers

1KSLI – First Battalion, King's Shropshire Light Infantry

1MX – First Battalion, Middlesex Regiment

1PPCLI – First Battalion, Princess Patricia's Canadian Light Infantry

1RNF – First Battalion, Royal Northumberland Fusiliers [5th Fusiliers]

1RUR – First Battalion, Royal Ulster Rifles

2PPCLI – Second Battalion, Princess Patricia's Canadian Light Infantry

3RAR – Third Battalion, Royal Australian Regiment

8RIH – Eighth King's Royal Irish Hussars

11LAA – 11 (Sphinx) Light Anti-Aircraft Battery, Royal Artillery

16FR – 16 Field Regiment, Royal New Zealand Artillery

27BCB – 27th British Commonwealth Brigade

28CB – 28th Commonwealth Brigade

29BIB – 29th British Independent Infantry Brigade Group

45FR – 45 Field Regiment, Royal Artillery

170IMB – 170 Independent Mortar Battery, Royal Artillery

AGPS – Australian Government Publishing Service

AIF – 2nd Australian Imperial Force [World War II]

ANZ – Archives New Zealand, Wellington

ANZAC – Australian and New Zealand Army Corps [World War I]

AT – anti-tank

AWM – Australian War Memorial, Canberra

BCT – Battalion Combat Team

Bde – Brigade

BLSA – British Library Sound Archive, St. Pancras

Bn – Battalion

CCF – Chinese Communist Forces

CIGS – Chief of the Imperial General Staff

CO – Commanding Officer

CP – Command Post

CPV – Chinese People's Volunteers

CSM – Company Sergeant Major

CTC – Civil Transportation Corps

DCM – Distinguished Conduct Medal

DSO – Distinguished Service Order

DHH – Directorate of History and Heritage, Department of National Defence, Ottawa

FM – Field Marshal

FOO – Forward Observation Officer

GCM – George C. Marshall Library, Lexington, Va.

GOC – General Officer Commanding

HMSO – Her Majesty's Stationery Office

HQ – Headquarters

i/c – in command

IO – Intelligence Officer

IWMDB – Department of Books, Imperial War Museum, Lambeth

IWMDD – Department of Documents, Imperial War Museum, Lambeth

IWMDS – Department of Sound, Imperial War Museum, Lambeth

LMG – Light Machine-Gun

MC – Military Cross

MM – Military Medal

MMG – Medium Machine-Gun

MO – Medical Officer

MP – Member of Parliament

MSR – Main Supply Route

NAA – National Archives of Australia, Canberra

NAM – National Army Museum, Chelsea

NARA – National Archives and Records Administration, Archives II, College Park, Md.

NCO – Non-Commissioned Officer

NKPA – North Korean People's Army

NLAC – National Library and Archives of Canada, Ottawa

OBE – Order of the British Empire

OC – Officer Commanding

PLA – People's Liberation Army

PUC – Presidential Unit Citation

RA – Royal Artillery

RAMC – Royal Army Medical Corps

RAP – Regimental Aid Post

RE – Royal Engineers

R&R – Rest and Recreation

RASC – Royal Army Service Corps

RCT – Regimental Combat Team

RNF – Royal Northumberland Fusiliers

RNZA – Royal New Zealand Artillery

ROK – Republic of Korea [army]

RSM – Regimental Sergeant Major

R/T – radio receiver/transmitter

RUR – Royal Ulster Rifles

SA – Small Arms

SOE – Special Operations Executive

TNA – The National Archives, Kew

UN – United Nations

USAF – United States Air Force

USAMHI – United States Army Military History Institute, Carlisle, Pa.

USGPO – United States Government Printing Office

USMC – United States Marine Corps

UVic – University of Victoria Library

VAC – Veterans Affairs Canada

VC – Victoria Cross

WD – War Diary

The Imjin and Kapyong Battles

Korea, 1951

Cor, they can have this country . . .

ROYAL MILITARY POLICEMAN, January 1951[1]

Korea? What's the matter with Korea? I like it . . .

BRIGADIER TOM BRODIE, December 1950[2]

Prologue

ON THE FACE OF THINGS NEITHER GREAT BRITAIN NOR ANY other British Commonwealth country had any obvious interests to protect in Korea in the middle of the twentieth century. The peninsula had been a part of the Japanese rather than the British empire prior to 1945, and subsequently had been divided into Soviet and American occupation zones that by the end of the decade had evolved into competing independent regimes north and south of the 38th Parallel, each claiming suzerainty over Korea as a whole. In late June 1950 the communists under Kim Il-sung in the north sought to resolve the issue definitively by launching a full-scale invasion of the south. Anxious to contain communist expansion, the Truman administration in the United States quickly and successfully convinced the Security Council of the United Nations – thanks to the absence of the representative of the Soviet Union, who was boycotting proceedings at the time – to authorize collective military action under U.S. command in support of the besieged Republic of Korea. Yet, though the United Kingdom had no direct stake in Korean affairs and was overburdened with other overseas commitments, it was accepted in London that as a Great Power and an ally of the United States, Great Britain was obliged not only to support resolutions at the U.N. but also do what it could to back up the ground forces immediately committed by Washington. As allies the governments of Australia, New Zealand, and then Canada, among others, also announced that they would send forces in support of the U.N. resolution.[3]

In 1950 the British Army was not in a position to commit men to Korea on any great scale. In the context of peace and a fragile economy over the previous five years, military spending had been severely curtailed. Arms and equipment for the most part dated from World War II and even with manpower needs being partially met through the introduction of National Service the force was overstretched by imperial policing and other overseas roles around the globe at the start of the new decade.[4] The armies of Commonwealth countries had all been drastically reduced in both size and capability in the war's aftermath, and it would take weeks or months to either build up an existing unit, such as the Third Battalion, Royal Australian Regiment (3RAR), or create entirely new ones, like the three special force infantry battalions raised in Canada or the "Kayforce" field artillery regiment from New Zealand.[5]

There did already exist on paper, however, a modest British imperial strategic reserve, 29th Independent Infantry Brigade Group. In late July 1950 the brigade headquarters at Colchester was put on notice that the brigade would be strengthened for deployment to Korea as quickly as possible. When the call to arms arrived, the designated fighting and support units were spread around the country and sadly lacking in a variety of essentials. Formations ranging from the infantry – the first battalions of the Royal Ulster Rifles (1RUR), the Royal Northumberland [5th] Fusiliers (1RNF), and the Gloucestershire Regiment (1GLOS) – to the tank squadrons of the 8th King's Royal Irish Hussars (8RIH), the crews of 45 Field Regiment (45FR), 170 Mortar Battery, and 11 (Sphinx) Light Anti-Aircraft Battery of the Royal Artillery, as well as component sub-units of the signals squadron, a mobile bath and laundry unit from the Royal Army Ordnance Corps and 57 Company Royal Army Service Corps, had to be brought together, greatly strengthened, and trained for war within three months.[6]

Time, indeed, was at a premium. In the weeks following the initial decision to mobilize 29th Brigade the situation in Korea deteriorated sharply, and additional emergency measures were taken. Two infantry battalions from the Hong Kong garrison were given a week's notice that they would be shipped to Pusan in late August 1950. A month later 3RAR, sent over from Japan, would join up with the Argyll and Sutherland Highlanders (1A&SH) and Middlesex Regiment (1MX) to form what was henceforth known as 27th British Commonwealth Brigade (27BCB). In early 1951 the brigade was significantly strengthened through the arrival and attachment of 16 Field Regiment, Royal New Zealand Artillery (16FR), and then the Second Battalion, Princess Patricia's Canadian Light Infantry (2PPCLI).[7]

In some ways the fact that the Korean War had broken out only five years after World War II had ended was a blessing for the units comprising the two brigades. Still largely organized, armed and equipped in the manner of the British Army, Commonwealth units, as had been the case in the previous war, could still operate alongside British units and within British-led formations with relative ease. As the contented British commander of a formation that included Australians, Canadians, Englishmen, New Zealanders, and Scots put it a few days before the Kapyong battle, 27th British Commonwealth Brigade was akin to a "miniature British Eighth Army of the last war."[8]

The proximity of World War II also meant that most of the senior officers had field leadership experience. Though the platoon subalterns were generally young and necessarily inexperienced, the commanding officers, like the brigade and battalion staffs and indeed most company commanders, had all led men against Axis forces and often been decorated for their services.[9] Deputy commander of 29th Brigade in Korea prior to taking over 27th Brigade in March 1951, Brian Burke had in the previous war led 25th Indian Brigade in Italy.[10] Tom Brodie, who commanded 29th Brigade, had among other things led a Chindit brigade into the jungles of Burma.[11] The battalion commanders also had plenty of honored wartime leadership experience. C. H. Nicholson, who took command of the Middlesex in early March 1951, had won an MC; Kingsley Foster of the Northumberlands had been mentioned twice in dispatches while leading the 7th Manchesters in Northwest Europe; J. P. "Fred" Carne of the Glosters had commanded a battalion of the King's African Rifles fighting the Japanese; and Gerald Rickord, who was in charge of the Ulsters when the Chinese struck in the third week of April, had led the battalion as part of a glider-borne force during the crossing of the Rhine.[12]

The supporting arms were also well served in terms of wartime experience. Most of the armor attached to 29th Brigade came from 8RIH, for example, the regiment in which the commanding officer and the second-in-command, J. W. "Jumbo" Phillips and Sir William Guy Lowther, along with subordinates such as Henry Huth and Peter Ormrod – the latter two respectively the commander and second-in-command of the tank squadron that would take part in the Imjin battle – had been promoted within the regiment as it had fought its way across Northwest Europe.[13]

The commanders of the Commonwealth units, mostly men who had gone back into civilian life but were specifically chosen to lead in Korea on the basis of their wartime record, were if anything even more experienced combat leaders. John Moodie, CO of 16 Field Regiment, had during World War II worked his way up in the Royal New Zealand Artillery to command 4 Field Regiment.[14] J. R. "Big Jim" Stone, leading 2PPCLI, had risen through the ranks to command the Loyal Edmonton Regiment during the hard-fought campaign in Italy, wining an MC and two DSOs in the process.[15] Bruce Ferguson, first 2i/c and then commander of 3RAR, also had a fine war record, having served on the staff and in the field – where he won an MC – with the AIF in the Middle East and New Guinea.[16] In addition, in most cases the Australian, Canadian, and New Zealander company commanders, all volunteers for Korea, possessed a good deal of combat experience.[17]

The officers at the top were often admired by those with whom they interacted. Brian Burke only led 27th Brigade for a matter of a month in Korea prior to its replacement by 28th Brigade, but quickly earned the respect of his battalion commanders.[18] In 29th Brigade, Tom Brodie, "a smallish, slim, very good looking man," according to a war correspondent, "immaculately turned out in any weather or situation," sometimes taciturn but with a fine memory for faces, made himself recognizable to regimental officers and the rank and file as he energetically visited units wearing his red-banded peaked service cap in all conditions, gesticulating with either a swagger stick, polo mallet, or tennis-racquet handle for emphasis. Exuding self-assurance – "I never knew him to show anything but supreme confidence in his own ability and that of his troops," a captain in the Ulsters remembered – he in turn inspired respect. Though he could be tolerant of war correspondents, Brodie was known for almost invariably bringing conversations with his subordinates to a decisive conclusion by barking out "ALL RIGHT, then." Even those who were in retrospect less than enthusiastic about his performance on the Imjin could admit, like another captain in the Ulsters, that "he was a nice guy";

or that, as one brigade staff officer grudgingly conceded, as a brigadier "he wasn't too bad."[19]

For the ordinary soldier, to be sure, the officer who mattered most was often the unit CO. Given their depth and breadth of wartime experience, it is not surprising to find that most commanding officers garnered a satisfactory degree of respect and, at least sometimes, personal loyalty.

The cavalry officers leading the Hussars in Korea, for instance, made a positive impression. They were, according to the reservist MO posted to the regiment prior to embarkation, "all very likeable people." More to the point, as a young troop officer explained, in spite of their huntin'-shootin'-fishin' mannerisms, "the squadron leaders, adjutant and colonel were all highly professional soldiers." Even a trooper who was far from happy at being recalled from civilian life to go to Korea with the regiment had to concede that in professional terms the officers "were all good regular army people."[20]

Some of the infantry battalion COs inspired great affection among their men. C. H. Nicholson, though coming from outside the regimental family, earned the respect of the Middlesex in the weeks prior to the Kapyong battle. "I like Nicholson," one of his subordinates wrote his predecessor, "we all do; and your Bn. appear to have accepted him."[21] Kingsley Foster was fondly described by one of his fusiliers as a "benevolent father" figure, someone whom the young men of the battalion were always keen to impress.[22] Though extremely taciturn – "one of the most silent individuals I have ever met," commented the senior Royal Engineers officer in the brigade[23] – the unflappable, pipe-smoking "Fred" Carne was well liked by the Glosters. "He was a very popular CO," remembered Private "Nick" Carter, "one of the old school, a very, very nice chap."[24]

Other battalion commanders produced more mixed reactions. "Big Jim" Stone, for instance, was known as a tough disciplinarian among the Other Ranks, and to the junior officers of 2PPCLI as unforgiving of mistakes. According to one disgruntled private, the CO "didn't give a shit" about the comfort of his men, while a subaltern found him "imperious and brusque."[25] There was, however, a method behind this tough approach to special-force soldiers who were tempted to behave in ways that were of no help to anybody. When in March 1951 several Canadian soldiers died after drinking the methyl alcohol compound used for heating ration cans, for instance, the CO had the entire battalion parade past the contorted bodies, to great inhibiting effect. "I had no sympathy for the mutterings of a few sensitive souls who chose to interpret Big Jim's dramatics as heartless," a corporal later reflected, noting that the "stark lesson would never be forgotten."[26]

Ferguson of 3RAR also gave some the impression of a rather aloof and harsh CO who "drove his subalterns mercilessly" and was seen as "a hard man" by the ordinary Digger; "we all hated his guts," a junior NCO later explained.[27] Again, though, a deep concern for the welfare of his men underlay this cold exterior. "I was immediately struck by how devoted he was to the battalion; absolutely devoted," remembered the MO. "It was almost as if he was hard, and harsh, and critical in an effort to teach you something," reflected a platoon commander.[28] Both COs were acknowledged, even by those who disliked them, to be skilled professionals. A lieutenant who did not get on well with Stone on a personal level nevertheless acknowledged that his CO "possessed a sterling reputation, and was a 'soldier's soldier,' brave beyond words in battle." Even the junior NCO in 3RAR who admitted to hating Ferguson conceded that "we knew that he knew what he was doing."[29]

The depth of combat leadership arising out of the recent global conflict that could be applied in Korea was matched by the amount of wartime kit – most of it of British design – that could be used to equip the two brigades. The effectiveness of some of the arms and equipment initially taken to the Land of the Morning Calm, however, was less clear-cut than was the case with command experience.

The troops of 27BCB, self-dubbed the Cinderella Brigade, were paupers in terms of vehicles and kit compared to 29th Infantry Brigade Group, known enviously as the Rolls Royce Brigade. Sent from Hong Kong as an emergency stopgap force, and initially consisting of only two understrength infantry battalions, the former had very little in the way of transport beyond used and soon-to-be worn-out Universal carriers – "absolutely hopeless" according to an Australian mortar platoon sergeant in the wake of 3RAR joining the brigade[30] – and the occasional elderly 15cwt truck or Land Rover.[31] The Cinderella Brigade had neither armor of its own, nor artillery until the arrival of the New Zealanders in January 1951 and occasionally thereafter when 16FR was detached for other duties. 27BCB therefore not only usually had to rely on the U.S. Army to assign transport units to move infantry over any distances, but also much of the time to attach tank and artillery units to provide supporting fire during battles.[32]

American trucks, half-tracks, artillery pieces, and tanks, to be sure, were more mechanically reliable and in certain aspects generally superior to their British counterparts – especially with respect to the provision of multiple machine-guns on armored vehicles. The Canadians, indeed, were fortunate in having been able to dispense with the small Universal carrier, better known as the Bren carrier ("an unreliable vehicle" in the words of a 2PPCLI captain[33]), in favor of the bigger and much more heavily armed M3 half-track courtesy of the U.S. Army shortly after they arrived in Korea in November 1950.[34]

Particular U.S. Army units sent at various points to assist the Commonwealth Brigade, such as Charlie Company of the 3rd Chemical Mortar Battalion attached to the Argylls, could become close at an individual level and militarily quite effective.[35] However, as troops in the brigade found to their discomfort, American firepower and transport were not always forthcoming when needed. Attached U.S. artillery observers, for example, might find themselves suddenly recalled to HQ even while a battle was in progress.[36] American armor also might abruptly be sent off on another mission, leaving British infantry without tank support.[37] Moreover, during the great retreat from North Korea after the Chinese intervened, it became uncomfortably apparent that at least some U.S. units, especially if they possessed vehicles, were liable to panic and "bug out" from the battle zone without regard for allied units.[38] By the spring of 1951, as the Kapyong battle would reveal, American servicemen were capable of both selfless heroism in support of allies and recklessly selfish behavior that put Commonwealth forces at considerable risk.

The 29th Brigade was, everyone agreed, much better equipped than 27th Brigade, insofar as it possessed its own fully integrated complement of British transport, artillery, and tanks. Yet even in the Rolls Royce Brigade not all equipment proved to be as flawless in design and operation as those whose lives could depend on it might have hoped.[39]

The most up-to-date fighting vehicles brought to Korea by 29th Brigade were the brand-new Centurion III tanks of the 8th King's Royal

Irish Hussars. These were the most advanced tanks in the British arsenal, well armored and equipped with a very accurate 20-pounder gun and highly advanced gun stabilizer. Though never used in its intended role as a means of foiling enemy armor – by the time the brigade arrived the North Korean force of T-34/85s supplied by the Soviet Union had been virtually wiped out and the newly emerging threat from the Chinese People's Volunteers did not include tanks – the Centurion would, especially during the later static phase of the war, prove immensely useful as a means of delivering accurate fire on precise targets across no-man's-land.[40]

During the more mobile phase that encompassed the April 1951 battles, however, the Centurion proved to have a number of drawbacks. Much of Korea was poor tank country, with paddy fields in the valleys that were, perforce, soft ground except in the dead of winter, bracketed all year round by hills with plenty of steep inclines. Roads were very few in number, badly maintained, and mostly narrow dirt tracks. The Centurion was eighteen feet wide and weighed over fifty tons, which meant that it was liable to get bogged down when traversing un-reconnoitered valley ground, to skid off the narrow roads when moving at any speed, throw tracks when climbing, get stuck in drainage ditches, and have difficulty negotiating tight turns (especially when the ground on either side – as was often the case – was either higher or lower than the pathway). "The Centurions fought in terrain for which they were never built," as the designated historian of the 8th Hussars put it. Crews eventually learned to tighten tracks and negotiate surprisingly steep angles, and the supporting fire offered by Centurions to infantry companies was always welcome, but there were still plenty of accidents in moments of high tension. Perhaps most problematic was the fact that the Centurion proved quite vulnerable to close-in infantry assault in the fluid phase of the war; it had a machine-gun mounted next to the main gun in the turret, but unlike the U.S. tanks supporting 27th Brigade, no hull-mounted machine-gun and, rather more significantly, no machine-gun on a swivel mount atop the turret of the kind that could be used to defeat infantrymen closing in with anti-tank explosive devices. "One machine gun on the Centurion was not enough," Lieutenant J. C. Butler complained to the War Office. Though some crews acquired more effective personal weapons, according to regulations all that tank commanders – who mostly operated with their hatches open so as to get a clearer idea of what was happening around them – had in the way of individual protection was a .38 caliber revolver and nine rounds of ammunition. These factors would create difficulties during the Imjin battle.[41]

For off-road work behind and in the combat zone, the 29th Brigade infantry battalions possessed two tracked vehicles. The first was the Bren carrier, which proved no more popular in 29th Brigade than in 27th Brigade. Designed in the 1930s, it could safely transport only a handful of men and with its narrow tracks proved unsuitable to the terrain in Korea. "It bogged down in mud," Brodie would later complain, "skidded on icy roads, and had insufficient clearance."[42] On the other hand, 29th Brigade, unlike 27th Brigade, did have the bigger and better Oxford carrier, designed to tow 17-pounder anti-tank guns. Powered by a 90 hp engine, it had fair cross-country performance, and could carry ten armed men at up to thirty miles per hour. Brodie liked the Oxfords, noting that compared to the Bren carriers they "were vastly superior in clearance and general mobility."[43] Little wonder that the Ulsters should use other vehicles to tow anti-tank guns and convert their Oxfords into personnel carriers. There were, however, relatively few Oxfords to spare; even the Ulsters could only muster about eight of them to equip their newly formed battle patrol, and Brodie stated at one point that he had a grand total of six at his disposal. Neither the Universal carrier nor the Oxford, moreover, came equipped with the standard swing-mount .30 and .50 caliber machine-guns of American design or the high armored compartment common to the half-tracks in both U.S. and Canadian service in Korea. Though the Fusiliers managed to mount either two Bren light machine-guns or a Vickers medium machine-gun on some of their Oxfords, and the Ulsters acquired some U.S. Browning medium machine-guns for the same purpose through unofficial channels, such upgrading was by no means universal and both British carriers remained comparatively underprotected against infantry assault. This too would become uncomfortably apparent at various stages in the Imjin battle.[44]

The 45 Field Regiment was equipped with a slightly more modern version of the 25-pounder field gun with which 16 Field Regiment went to war. In the hands of skilled crews this reliable artillery piece could attain a very high rate of fire and was easy to swing round to engage different lateral targets. This was definitely a good thing given the rather light shell the 25-pounder delivered when compared to other pieces of medium artillery such as the U.S. 105-mm howitzer.[45] For truly heavy supporting fire, both brigades would be dependent on the availability of American guns, especially the big 155-mm "Long Toms" and 8-inch howitzers. Like other U.S. support, heavy artillery fire was not always available, as would become apparent in April 1951.[46]

The six 17-pounder anti-tank guns with which 3RAR in 27th Brigade and all three British infantry battalions in 29th Brigade came equipped proved to be redundant in their primary role of defending against enemy armor. Though one of them, in service with the Glosters, did prove useful in killing a Chinese sniper during the Imjin battle, on the whole it might have been better if the Glosters and Northumberlands had followed the example of the Ulsters and ditched their anti-tank guns so as to free up more Oxford carriers for troop transport purposes. The large, long-barreled guns were heavy to manhandle and difficult to site among the steep hills of Korea. As an Australian NCO put it, the 17-pounder "really wasn't much good because of the conditions."[47]

The 11 Light Anti-Aircraft Battery, meanwhile, though also superfluous in its intended function due to the near total command of the skies the U.S. Air Force had established by the time 29th Brigade arrived in Korea, made itself useful on occasion by using its 40-mm Bofors guns in a direct-fire role in support of attacks or to provide additional defensive fire during ground operations. Unfortunately, due to a gross overestimation of the enemy air threat to the Han bridges, only a single troop of guns was near enough to the front to bolster the firepower available to the brigade during the Battle of the Imjin.[48]

The infantry battalions of 29th Brigade (as well as 2PPCLI and 3RAR in 27th Brigade) were also hastily trained in the use of the American 3.5-inch M20 "Super Bazooka" rocket launcher either before or after arriving in Korea. Though few in number and redundant in their anti-tank role, these were occasionally used with mixed results as anti-personnel weapons both on the Imjin and at Kapyong.[49]

Much more prevalent and useful for the infantry in early 1951 were the mortars which sent bombs against the enemy in parabolic arcs. The small 2-inch mortars with which most infantry companies in the two brigades were equipped "gave a big bang but weren't terribly effective" according to one officer, and were used primarily for flares.[50] Most support companies had six 3-inch mortars, but while able to give infantry a fair amount of much-appreciated close support, the maximum range of these mortars – 2,800 yards – was as much as 2,000 yards short of the enemy equivalent and the bombs were often poorly manufactured. There were also those who thought that given the wide frontages companies were routinely tasked with covering, six 3-inch tubes per battalion was insufficient.[51] Once again 2PPCLI was better off, having been issued with the American 60-mm mortar to replace the 2-inch type and 81-mm mortars to take the place of the 3-inch variety. The 81-mm, though weighing over a hundred pounds, could hurl a 7.5-lb bomb over a thousand yards farther than the 3-inch mortar.[52] Luckily, the infantry battalions in 29th Brigade could also call for support from the 4.2-inch mortars of 170 Battery, Royal Artillery, which could send 20-lb bombs up to 4,000 yards. "It was considered a close support weapon," a gunner in B Troop explained, "most appreciated by the infantry battalions to whom it was attached." The brigadier certainly valued them highly.[53]

Soldiers in both brigades would also rely on hand grenades. The No. 88 type was primarily used for generating smoke but contained phosphorous and could thereby burn skin on contact. More common was the tried-and-true No. 36 fragmentation grenade. Though comparatively heavy and therefore more limited in range than the lighter Russian-type stick grenades used by the Chinese in considerable quantity in Korea, the No. 36, when bursting, was far more lethal than enemy grenades (which relied primarily on their concussive effect). In grenade exchanges occurring when patrols bumped into the Chinese in open country the comparative weights could put British and Commonwealth soldiers at a disadvantage in terms of hurling distance; but the No. 36, either thrown or simply rolled, would prove extremely useful in dealing with massed Chinese infantry assaults as the enemy closed in on hill positions at the Imjin and Kapyong.[54]

The firearms used by British and Commonwealth infantry in Korea varied in quality and utility. Some types were as good as any in the world. Others possessed distinct shortcomings, especially in the Korean context.

The accurate and reliable Vickers .303 medium machine-gun, though antique in basic design, a bit heavy to manhandle, and lacking the punch of a heavy machine-gun, was nevertheless worth its weight in gold to

British and Commonwealth battalions. Apart from its poundage when carried the only trouble with the Vickers was that, in view of the vast number of Chinese infantry in Korea, the number allotted – three two-gun sections in each battalion organized as a medium machine-gun platoon – proved to be on the low side.[55] The infantry's standard light machine-gun, the Bren, issued on a scale of one per section, was also reliable and very well liked even though it had a comparatively slow rate of fire. "They never seized up," one 2PPCLI veteran remembered; "as long as you had rounds in it, you could fire it," recalled another. More of them, though, would have been useful than the standard single weapon per section, particularly given the controversial nature of both the submachine-gun and rifle.[56]

The submachine-gun that British and Canadian sections were issued for the Korean War was the 9-mm Sten with a 32-round magazine. Even though the infantry sections were equipped with the latest model of this simple weapon, first designed for cheap mass production during World War II, the Sten became awfully hot to handle if fired for very long and had a nasty tendency to jam when needed most. Though it had its defenders in relation to rifles and pistols, other soldiers described it as a "cumbersome," "useless," and "bloody hopeless" weapon, one Gloster going so far as to call it "a load of absolute rubbish."[57] The weaknesses of the Sten, which included a relatively slow rate of fire (550 rounds per minute), were highlighted by the uncomfortable fact that by the time of the April battles the Chinese had plenty of the superior "burp gun" (900 rounds per minute from a 50-round drum magazine).[58] Only the Diggers of 3RAR had a standard-issue alternative to the Sten. Also designed and manufactured during World War II, the Australian 9-mm Owen Gun, which held the same number of rounds in its magazine, was a bit bulkier but much more reliable than the British weapon. As with the Sten, however, users noticed that beyond a certain range the round-nosed bullets seemed to glance off the padded clothing the Chinese wore. Little wonder that soldiers should individually seek to obtain instead, by various means, a submachine-gun such as the U.S. Thompson: "a great personal weapon" in the opinion of Corporal Ken Campbell of 2PPCLI. "When you hit someone with a .45 slug, they stay down."[59]

Most prevalent of all was the standard-issue personal weapon of every British and Commonwealth infantryman, the .303 caliber Lee-Enfield rifle.[60] There were those who thought this bolt-action weapon, variants of which had equipped armies for nearly fifty years, was still a good weapon for Korea. Unlike automatic and semi-automatic weapons, its simple manual mechanism meant that it did not tend to jam even amid the dirt or snow of the Korean hills. "They served us well – extremely well," a regular from the Glosters later opined, stressing that the rifle was very accurate and that in trained hands the bullets in its ten-round magazine could be loosed off in very quick succession despite the user having to open and close the bolt each time.[61] There were also those, though, who after facing large numbers of Chinese at close quarters, thought the Lee-Enfield to have a too-sedate rate of fire even in the most experienced hands. Private "Lofty" Large let off steam about the comparative inadequacies of the Lee-Enfield in his war memoirs:

> The British Army had for many years been the victims of one of the greatest cons of all time. We were told time and again that well aimed single shots with bolt action rifles would beat "all comers." An enemy with automatic weapons could not sustain an attack because they would obviously run out of more ammunition than they could carry, etc.

Large continued:

> Before arriving in Korea we were told not to worry about mass attacks by the Chinese, as only one in ten had a rifle. This was basically true enough, but the other nine had Tommy guns, "Burp" guns or light machine guns. . . . The difference in fire power was such that I, personally, felt it was almost like trying to spit in someone's eye when he's spraying you with a fire hose.[62]

"We had no firepower compared to them," a third Gloster concurred.[63] Even his former comrade-in-arms who defended the Lee-Enfield had to concede that it might have been better on the Imjin if the battalion had possessed more automatic and semi-automatic weapons of the kind with which American units were equipped.[64]

Though the risk of jamming was greater, there were those who did their best through barter or even theft to acquire U.S. semi-automatics to fight with instead of the Lee-Enfield. According to Lieutenant-Colonel Stone, "a considerable number" soon began to appear in the hands of

2PPCLI soldiers. Edmund Ions, a junior officer with the Ulsters, acquired a .30 caliber M1 Carbine and happily confirmed that it was "lighter, handier, and almost as accurate" as the .303 and had a higher rate of fire. "I fell in love with it," David Green, a private in the Glosters, remembered of his own stolen M1 Carbine. "What a weapon it was!"[65]

Infantry officers, like tank commanders, were equipped with pistols as a last line of personal defense. The standard-issue six-shot Webley IV .38 caliber service revolver, with its trigger-finger operated mechanism, had an uncomfortably slow rate of fire, as an Australian officer discovered when it took him six pulls to loose off two shots at an approaching enemy soldier.[66] Only the officers of 2PPCLI were universally issued with an automatic, the excellent 9-mm Browning complete with a 13-round magazine.[67] Many infantry officers of all the Commonwealth contingents, though, eventually opted to carry a rifle or submachine-gun since even semi-automatic pistols were, as one company commander admitted, "virtually useless" in firefights where both accuracy and volume of fire counted.[68]

Whatever the comparative strengths and weaknesses of their various personal weapons, the officers and men of the two brigades seem to have been united in thinking that the steel helmet, whether the 1914 or the improved 1944 pattern, was superfluous. These were either carried on packs or discarded but almost never worn. As Lofty Large put it, "only one man in the Glosters wore a steel helmet," adding "don't know who he was, but I heard he existed."[69] In encounters with the enemy from the autumn of 1950 through into the spring of 1951 companies did not come under serious artillery, mortar, or even grenade fire, making the anti-shrapnel helmet seem pretty much redundant, something that could be discarded as excess weight or only used for other purposes such as holding shaving water. Second-Lieutenant Guy Temple of the Glosters commented later that "tin hats were unfashionable" among British troops in Korea because they were uncomfortable. The senior Royal Engineers officer remembered that "American regulations strictly enforced the wearing of this awkward headgear, but for the British troops the decision was left to each commander. We always opted for the more comfortable alternative." According to a corporal in the PPCLI "we threw away our helmets," while among the Australians sporting one on the head was viewed as a sign of virtual cowardice.[70]

The end result was that the vast majority of soldiers went into battle in April 1951 wearing an assortment of soft pieces of headgear that offered no protection from enemy mortar bomb splinters, not to speak of bullets ricocheting off rocks. Though one study suggested that wearing a helmet would not have done much to prevent the kind of head wounds sustained in the Korean fighting, a British private arriving six months after the spring battles was probably justified in commenting that it was "ridiculous" to discard them.[71]

Just as important as weapons and vehicles was radio communication within each brigade. Perhaps inevitably in terrain dominated by steep, rocky hills and narrow valleys, the available wireless sets did not always perform well. In the British and Australian battalions radio communication between sub-units was mainly by 88 Set. These, though they were comparatively light and portable, had a maximum range of only a few miles and had batteries that wore down quickly (and were sometimes difficult to replace in a timely fashion – so much so that 2PPCLI was forced to switch to the American walkie-talkie). According to a major in the Glosters, the 88 Set was "useless except under very favourable conditions and over very short distances."[72]

The 31 Set, used for communication between company and battalion headquarters, theoretically had about double the range of the 88 Set, but was also almost three times as heavy and, as a 27th Brigade report stated, "sometimes failed over ranges as small as one-quarter mile." Eric Hill, who operated the radio for A Company, 1GLOS, found that "you had to get in good positions to get any reception at all"; while John Bishop, a corporal in A Company, 2PPCLI, later commented that it "seldom worked when needed."[73] Hence, according to another private in the Glosters, during the Imjin battle "our radios were very unreliable." A lieutenant from the Ulsters agreed; during the fighting "they never bloody well worked."[74] The Canadians were somewhat better off than the other battalions in communication between battalion and company headquarters in that 2PPCLI had discarded the 31 Set in favor of the American SCR300 with its greater range and operating capability. According to the CO, "all worked well" and there was "no major problem in communications."[75]

Even the best weapons and equipment, of course, are only as good as the men using them. There exists in some quarters a belief that disgruntled recalled reservists and conscripted national servicemen in the ranks of British regiments significantly degraded the fighting quality of these units compared to Australian and Canadian battalions filled with volunteers.[76] It is therefore necessary to examine the composition of the British Commonwealth units concerned and the consequences in terms of discipline and morale before and after departure for Korea.

It was true enough that there were national servicemen among the first British troops sent to Korea. When David Wilson assumed command of A Company of the Argylls, for instance, he found that around half the Other Ranks were conscripts, something that appears to have been true for the rest of 1A&SH and 1MX as well.[77]

Some of the Middlesex national servicemen were, according to a couple of accounts, psychologically unprepared to risk their lives when the battalion departed from Hong Kong for Korea. Later there arrived casualty replacements who were disgruntled regulars or older reservists who were clearly unhappy at having been recalled to the colors.[78] On the other hand, to try to build up and then keep up the strength of the battalion, the Middlesex, like the Argylls, took in a fair number of eager volunteers from other regiments to add to the core of regular soldiers keen to show what they could do.[79] The national servicemen, moreover, were not necessarily reluctant warriors.[80] On arrival at Pusan in the latter part of August 1950 the men of both battalions certainly gave the impression that they were ready. "One felt that these two hard and professional battalions," remembered Alan Whicker, a British war correspondent depressed by the poor performance of the GI thus far, "their men lean and brown and cheerful after Hong Kong training, could see off the whole North Korean army on their own."[81] And while by no means able to accomplish the latter feat over the following months, they did win the respect of the hard men of 3RAR. The Argylls, as an Australian NCO put it, "were good to have alongside," adding "and so were the Middlesex."[82]

If the fighting spirit of 27th Brigade was not undermined by British national servicemen and recalled reservists, there remains the question of the effect of such men on the units of 29th Brigade. Did "the British at the Imjin have a morale problem" that severely compromised their fighting capacity?[83]

As in 27th Brigade, there were plenty of young soldiers and subalterns in 29th Brigade without combat experience who were keen to get some: "We couldn't wait to get out there," remembered Rifleman John Shaw, for example.[84] When the call came to prepare to go to Korea, though, the various components of the brigade were almost all seriously under strength for wartime conditions. Some soldiers – albeit some more willingly than others[85] – could be transferred from units outside the brigade. Others would be added through men whose service commitment had expired but who were willing to volunteer. However, the vast majority of the men brought into the brigade to bring it up to a war footing – in total seventy-five percent of strength[86] – were recalled reservists; that is, those who had served in the army and though now in civilian life could still be called up for an emergency.[87]

Some recalled servicemen, to be sure, quietly accepted their fate, and a few secretly were happy to rejoin an army from which absence had made the heart grow fonder.[88] Many, however, were seriously disgruntled. In some cases they were only weeks or even days away from the end of their reserve obligation when the call-up notice arrived on their doorstep. Going back into the army might mean giving up the relatively well-paid jobs that supported a wife and offspring, perhaps putting a mortgage or business in jeopardy, and certainly causing untold personal upheaval. In particular, men who had served in World War II often felt that they had already done their bit for King and Country. "We were right annoyed about it, really," as Private Sam Forward, sent to the Glosters only eleven weeks shy of the end of his reserve commitment and with two children to look after, bitterly remembered.[89] A significant number of those recalled to the colors were quickly released on medical or compassionate grounds – the Royal Engineers squadron, for example, processed 450 recalled reservists, of whom only 150 went to Korea[90] – but there were still plenty of men who felt that they were being treated unfairly.[91]

As a result reservists, on average in their late twenties according to the brigade major,[92] were often at first in a fractious, "Bolshie" frame of mind, resenting being back in the army in general and in particular being ordered about by comparatively inexperienced young regular officers and NCOs. As a private in the Glosters put it, "they all had a massive chip on their shoulder."[93] This could and did cause sporadic disciplinary problems as 29th Brigade prepared to go to Korea. A junior officer in the Ulsters, for instance, observed plenty of reservists who were "difficult to handle" and indeed "almost mutinous."[94] They could also be poor mentors to the younger soldiers. Frank Cottam, a regular platoon sergeant in the Glosters, remembered that "some of the reservists were so disillusioned with ever being called back that they were not necessarily a good example to anyone."[95] Other regulars agreed. "We revered the reservists when they first came," Vic Wear, a young soldier in the Northumberlands remembered, "but it turned out they were not as professional as we were."[96]

Moreover, it was not for nothing that the 29th became known as "the old man's brigade" or "the grandfathers' brigade," with its soldiers over the winter of 1950–51 in Korea "preoccupied with their varicose veins and other minor weaknesses," as one journalist put it.[97] Even after the most obviously unfit reservists had been weeded out before departure, the health of the some of the older men broke down in the harsh Korean winter.[98]

Recalled reservists certainly did not feel much affinity for the cause in which they were being required to fight. Very few soldiers even knew where Korea was, let alone cared about who controlled it. "Nothing; nothing whatsoever" was how Jack Arnall described his knowledge of the place and the U.N. cause when called up again to serve with 45 Field Regiment. "Quite candidly," Frank Brodie, sent as a reservist to bolster the ranks of the Ulsters, later explained, "I didn't think it was right that I should go out there to fight someone else's war."[99]

The sights of the Land of the Morning Calm did nothing to increase enthusiasm for the war after 29th Brigade disembarked from troopships at Pusan in November 1950. As units landed and moved northward by road and rail, the men of the brigade passed through a poverty-stricken, war-ravaged landscape. The towns and villages were ramshackle and dilapidated, the countryside desolate and dauntingly rugged, the weather a mixture of extremes. "It's the most terrible place I've ever seen in my life," exclaimed a reservist in the Glosters.[100] The smells of Korea were even worse. Pusan and other towns were rank with sewage, and hanging over everything in the countryside, except in the depths of winter, was a noxious and pervasive odor resulting from the universal practice of using human waste as manure in paddy fields.[101] As for the common people of Korea encountered, while there might be a good deal of sympathy for the plight of refugees fleeing southward, their clothing, language, customs, and habits were distinctly alien to insular Englishmen and Irishmen and likely did nothing to make the presence of the brigade appear more worthwhile. In a report to the Chiefs of Staff in the wake of a visit to Korea in early 1951, a senior general wrote that British soldiers, "although sympathetic to the South Koreans in their adversity, despise them and are not interested in this civil war."[102]

Though they were essential in fleshing out 29th Brigade, it would seem the reservists lacked motivation and might therefore prove as much a liability as an asset. "Morale was very low," a young lieutenant, whose platoon in D Company of the Glosters was composed almost entirely of such men, reflected on the situation the month before the Imjin battle, "and the mood was fairly bolshie."[103] Not at all keen to be sent back to war in the first place, reservists once in Korea could prove less than eager to put themselves in harm's way, sometimes even quietly disobeying orders which they thought too dangerous.[104] Between December 1950 and April 1951 almost two dozen soldiers drawn from the three infantry battalions were court-martialed for offenses ranging from disobedience and insubordination to outright desertion.[105]

There are, however, several factors that need to be taken into consideration before concluding, as claimed, that low morale among men dragooned into their units, in contrast to the high motivation of volunteers like the Australians and Canadians, lies at the root of the differences between the Imjin and Kapyong battles. By their very nature the reservists possessed valuable skills and experience, and once in the field there is evidence to suggest that they grumbled but still did what was necessary. Moreover, much of what is held against the reservists of 29th Brigade in terms of their outlook also applied to volunteers and indeed regulars in both brigades.

Only on very rare occasions did volunteers or regulars, any more than reservists or conscripts, want to go to Korea in order to turn back the communist tide. "I never met a soldier who cared a damn about the ideological aspect of the war," BBC war correspondent René Cutforth remarked.[106] As for the land over which the fighting was taking place, almost no one had heard of it or knew where it was, let alone the issues involved, when elements of the two brigades were first put on notice for shipment to Korea.[107] This was as true for Australian and Canadian volunteers as it was for the British (volunteer, regular, and conscript alike). Though some efforts were made before arrival to explain the need for the U.N. to defend against aggression, these occurred after men had joined up and seem to have had little impact. "The private soldiers I encountered in Korea had no real understanding of why they were there," Canadian journalist Pierre Berton later wrote of his visits to 2PPCLI.[108]

Many of the motives for enlisting among those who volunteered from civilian life to serve in Korea were common to men from Australia, Britain, Canada, and New Zealand. Most had to do with personal fulfillment rather than philosophical commitment. Some men who had been demobilized somewhere between 1945 and 1950 found civilian life not all that they had hoped it might be either professionally or personally. Tommy Prince, for example, a Native Canadian who had served with distinction in the Devil's Brigade in Italy, had seen his small business venture fail and volunteered for the Special Force and a familiar place in 2PPCLI. "Maybe it's just because I like a certain amount of excitement," explained the half-aboriginal Reg Saunders, who had seen more than his fair share of fighting the Japanese in New Guinea, reflecting on his decision to volunteer for K Force and thereby join 3RAR. John Martin, who was "bored to tears" in civilian life, liked the thought of a special gratuity for signing on again, but was especially attracted to the idea of getting back to the "shots of adrenalin and comradeship" he had experienced as a paratrooper, and ended up in the Northumberlands. "My first marriage had broken up," explained Alfred Holdham, who had served with SOE in the war, "so I volunteered for Korea"; he found himself among the Glosters. Len Opie, who had fought in New Guinea and signed on for the new war, remembered others in 3RAR "who were fleeing from alimony and angry wives."[109]

For the younger men there was the opportunity to escape a boring job, travel to an exotic land, and undertake the kind of adventure which every male a few years older seemed to have experienced but which they themselves had been denied. "Like most other volunteers for the Korean War," John Bishop, who left work at a logging camp and found himself in the ranks of 2PPCLI, later admitted, "I joined the Canadian Army's Special Force for reasons no nobler than the prospect of adventure and perhaps a chance to find a direction in my life."[110] A member of 3RAR recorded that there were young Australians aplenty who "wanted adventure" and were "sick of their civilian jobs." There was also the ANZAC tradition to live up to. K Force volunteers, as a senior Australian officer put it, were often "patriotic and adventurous young men" drawn by "stories of the Second World War."[111]

None of these volunteers were inspired by what they saw of Korea and its people any more than the conscripts were. Tom Muggleton of 3RAR doubtless summed up the feelings of many others when he described it as "a rotten place" to be. By the standards of the industrialized world "it was an incredibly backward country," wrote Hub Gray of 2PPCLI, adding feelingly, "frequently we wondered why the hell we had come to this Godforsaken country!"[112]

The motives of volunteers, in short, were usually personal in nature, and the mere fact of signing on did not guarantee a better soldier than a reservist or conscript. Australian and Canadian veterans at times lied about relevant prior experience when joining up, tended to think they knew more about soldiering than inexperienced postwar officers and NCOs, and sometimes disobeyed orders they did not like. "They feared neither God nor the Devil," as a young 3RAR subaltern put it.[113] More problematic were volunteers who were physically or mentally unfit to fight but who still found their way into the ranks of 2PPCLI due to a rushed processing procedure for the Special Force. There were petty criminals as well as "social misfits and drunkards," a few of whom stole, raped, and even committed murder while in Korea.[114]

It was true that the Commonwealth volunteers brought a good deal of relevant experience with them to 27th Brigade. Forty-two percent of 16 Field Regiment, for example, had been in the army while half of 2PPCLI soldiers had served in the world war; "they knew what the score was, they knew a lot more than we would ever learn," Canadian volunteer Stuart Reitsma observed. "These blokes we brought in off the street were magnificent men," Ben O'Dowd, a 3RAR officer, later wrote, explaining that this meant in effect that "training for Korea was done in World War Two."[115]

Experience, though, was something that the reservists of 29th Brigade also brought with them. They were veteran soldiers who knew their trades and could impart useful knowledge and skills to callow young men who had never heard a shot fired in anger. Major Patrick "Sam" Weller, for instance, in command of the Glosters' support company, thought that the reservists "were absolutely first class, because they had experience in the '39–'45 war and were able to give a lead and encouragement to the younger members of the battalion."[116] Tom Cunningham-Booth, the senior NCO in charge of the Fusiliers' command post in Korea, agreed: "I think we benefited from having reservists; they taught us things about survival that were helpful."[117]

It should also be borne in mind that most of the unfit, whether they had signed on or been compelled to go to Korea, were winnowed out before leaving for the war or in the first months in theater. Constant hill climbing and the extreme winter cold in Korea meant that those who by reason of age or health lacked the stamina to serve in the field were sent back. "Bad legs, wheezy lungs and faint and weak hearts were exposed and many sorry specimens of manhood were returned to Canada," as the CO of the Patricias explained.[118] Reservists could and did continue to grumble, the Ulsters, for example, taking to singing *The Red Flag*, but, just like everyone else, they eventually tended to knuckle down to the job at hand in Korea. As war correspondent René Cutforth observed:

> British soldiers, mostly Reservists dragged back for foreign service from civvy street in the most abrupt fashion (there was hardly a man in 29 Brigade who did not have some really complicated home problem concerned with his new lower standard of income), filled the air with complaints of the unfairness of life in general, the cold, the country and the horrors of war, expressed in a language of raucous obscenity, but they kept their fighting spirit, it seemed, in another compartment in their minds, and looked upon their job as soldiers with a professional eye. They soldiered well, no matter what.[119]

Morale in 3RAR, by most accounts, remained strong in Korea;[120] but this was true, for example, for many of the "Gloomy Glosters" also. "Morale was always very good," commented an RAMC corporal attached to A Company: "Always."[121]

It is thus incorrect to assume there was a simple dichotomy between colonial and metropolitan troops in terms of levels of motivation and kinds of behavior. The reality was rather more complex. Whatever the ratio of volunteers to conscripts, no battalion simply broke and ran in battle, and as we shall see, there would be isolated instances of cowardice even among the Diggers at Kapyong, just as there would be individual acts of extraordinary bravery by reservists at the Imjin.

It is safe to say that, in the rush to get fighting formations to Korea, no unit in either brigade was as prepared as it might have been. Though some of the officers and men might have a lot of relevant experience, opportunities for large-scale training were limited, not least because so much time and effort had to be devoted to bringing units up to strength and preparing for departure.[122] Memories of World War II aside, much of what all ranks in both brigades learned about fighting was acquired as a result of operational experience in Korea between the autumn of 1950 and the spring of 1951. First in the advance northward and then in the winter retreat southward, individual battalions and companies fought a succession of offensive, encounter, and defensive engagements with elements of either the North Korean or Chinese armies. Though events did not always play out as hoped and there were occasional mishaps, on the whole British and Commonwealth forces acquitted themselves well and significant lessons were learned. Some of the conclusions reached would prove useful; others were ignored or would create difficulties at Kapyong and the Imjin.[123]

Intelligence on the capabilities of the North Korean forces passed on before arrival in Korea was somewhat rudimentary at best and grossly inaccurate at worst.[124] By the time 29th Brigade arrived at Pusan the "Chinese People's Volunteers," in reality the battle-hardened People's Liberation Army, had intervened en masse to save the regime of Kim Il-sung. Unfortunately, intelligence on Chinese strength and capabilities was even sketchier than on the North Koreans, with British official assessments making sometimes dubious comparisons with the former Japanese foe and officers in the field confidently assuming that a mechanized British force was inherently superior to an Asiatic peasant army. As the senior Royal Engineers officer, Major Tony Younger, later put it, "we did not really believe that this [Chinese] intervention would be any problem." After all, Lieutenant Gordon Potts of the Ulsters later admitted somewhat ruefully, the general feeling among the officers was that the Chinese "were nowhere near as good as we were."[125]

Experience in the field did, to be sure, lead to some modification of opinion. As a company commander in the Argylls noted of the North Korean soldier, "he can fight very bravely indeed."[126] In significant encounters with the Chinese, such as parts of 27th Brigade experienced in the first days of November 1950 and elements of 29th Brigade underwent at the start of January 1951, it was clear that the CPV had the human resources and willpower to press home attacks at night and en masse. "I think our people in the companies were impressed with their tenacity," opined a 3RAR platoon commander. A company commander in the Middlesex agreed; the Chinese "proved to be both tough and resolute."[127] The ability of the enemy to infiltrate behind fixed positions by moving quickly on foot over unoccupied high ground was particularly impressive. An NCO in the Northumberlands admitted in the wake of the January encounter that he and others had underestimated the Chinese, who were in fact "very hardy" and "incredibly efficient" at infiltration; "they taught us a trick or two, I can tell you."[128] The full impact was felt by the Ulsters in the same period when they conducted a retreat at night down a valley floor and found themselves in a running fight with large numbers of Chinese who had got behind the forward positions. Charging down en masse from the high ground, the enemy managed to kill or capture well over a hundred soldiers. The Ulsters fought back fiercely, but the Chinese, directed by bugle calls and whistles, came on regardless. Mervyn McCord, a subaltern who survived the encounter, commented that "we must have killed and wounded hundreds of them – but it didn't stop them."[129]

For those willing to adjust, there were important lessons to be learned from these early encounters. At this stage in the war the Chinese had little in the way of field artillery and were at times even short of infantry weapons. If their huge numerical superiority and bravery in the attack were to be successfully countered, then defending troops would have to concentrate on the high features and prepare all-round defensive positions. Forces were too thin on the ground to hold a continuous front across hills and valleys alike – both brigades were routinely tasked by American corps and divisional commanders with covering frontages that, if it were not for manpower shortages and doubts about the reliability of other units, would have gone to an entire division, something which became almost a point of pride[130] – so the Chinese would inevitably get in behind. If the defenders were concentrated on the high ground, though, they would still dominate the valley floors; the CPV would be forced to assault rather than entirely bypass them, and superior U.N. firepower could prevail. Among those who developed a healthy respect for the Chinese and thought through the tactical implications was Brigadier Brodie, as Colonel Stone recorded in reference to a lunchtime conversation they had together shortly after the arrival of 2PPCLI in Korea. "It seems apparent that resolute men, dug in, in proper islands of defence can kill, at will, the hordes that rush the positions," he wrote. Infiltration between and behind hilltop positions had to be expected, but once all-round defense was prepared, "a defender's paradise" should result from the ensuing encounter as long as defending troops "realize that if they run, they will certainly die."[131]

At least one of the lessons drawn would, though, limit future effectiveness. In the same fighting retreat in which the Ulsters had been mauled a group of reconnaissance and artillery observation tanks dubbed "Cooperforce" had been overwhelmed and destroyed by Chinese infantry closing in with grenades and pole charges.[132] These vehicles were out-of-date Cromwells, but their loss appears to have augmented fears about the possibility of the state-of-the-art gun stabilizers of the new Centurions falling into the hands of an advancing enemy, and on instructions from London the Centurions were all ordered withdrawn from Korea. Thankfully this order was rescinded, but subsequent instructions were issued that only one squadron should be present in the front-line area at any one time once the brigade moved north of the Han. Thus when 29th Brigade joined the U.S. 3rd Division prior to the Imjin battle it was "with the restriction that two squadrons of the 8th Hussars could not be brought north of the HAN river."[133] This meant that only C Squadron would be available to support the infantry during the Imjin battle.

Moreover, in those units that had not faced large-scale assaults but instead met small units of the CPV when it was retreating between its fourth and fifth offensives and leaving only rear guards to delay the U.N. follow-up advance, the Chinese might not appear particularly formidable. It was true that they defended the hill features that battalions from the two brigades were tasked with taking, but the tendency seemed to be to break and run once British and Commonwealth forces had reached a certain point. As a private in 2PPCLI put it, "as soon as you hit 'em hard, they just disappeared."[134]

It is noteworthy that the first major encounter between the Glosters and the Chinese was of this kind. On 16 February 1951, Colonel Carne set in motion a set-piece attack on Hill 327 involving his C and D companies with plenty of fire support from USAF fighter-bombers firing rockets, three batteries of 45 Field Regiment, 11th Light Anti-Aircraft Battery, three mortar troops from 170 Battery, and the guns of the eighteen Centurion tanks of C Squadron, 8th Hussars. The Chinese defenders, operating from their well-camouflaged fortifications, at first fought fiercely, but then melted away or surrendered. The officers and men of Glosters thought they now had the full measure of the enemy. "We proved, I think, man for man," one private remembered, "[that] we were the equal of these Chinese."[135] This kind of action, however, was not a good predictor for CPV behavior during a full-scale offensive. Carne himself, who was heard to dismiss the enemy as "only little people, rabble,"[136] was confident enough to deploy his companies on widely separated secondary hills near the mouth of a valley rather than concentrating them on the main feature after 29th Brigade moved up to the Imjin in March.[137]

More generally, and even in the RUR, there was a sense that the Chinese, many of whom seemed to depend on picking up the weapons of those killed in front for personal armament and were directed in battle by such antiquated means as bugles and whistles, were, as a subaltern put it, just "unpleasant peasants" and that, as the adjutant claimed, "in a straight fight we felt we should always win." Many other ranks probably felt like the private in the Glosters who opined that "a first-class British infantry battalion" could never be defeated by "a rag, tag, and bobtail bunch of slope-headed slant-eyed sods from Shanghai."[138]

On the whole, British and Commonwealth soldiers were no more admiring of the "Gooks" – the local word for "man" but used generically and usually contemptuously to refer to all Koreans – than of the "Chinks"; indeed usually far less so.[139] On the other hand units did informally adopt a variety of orphans and other strays to help with everything from first aid to laundry, and there was appreciation for those whom Canadian troops, with a level of cultural insensitivity that was not unusual for the time and place, dubbed "rice burners"; that is, members of the Civil Transportation Corps. In a country with so few roads, many hills, and lots of displaced persons, it was practicable to use humans as pack animals in bringing supplies up from the valleys to the troops occupying the high ground. The companies of the CTC were made up of men too old or too young to fight in the South Korean army, and around the New Year each battalion received a company of roughly one hundred porters, which worked out to about nine Koreans per platoon. Wearing whatever clothing they brought or could scrounge, these porters, identified only by a numbered company disc and speaking little or no English, could carry heavy loads on A-frames strapped to their backs up steep hill slopes. As an officer from the Ulsters put it, "they became very much part and parcel of our operations."[140] On unfamiliar ground they might occasionally get lost, and not surprisingly some had an aversion to putting themselves directly in harm's way during engagements. Their efforts, though, were generally appreciated, since without them the other ranks would once more be doing the heavy lifting themselves. "I will take my hat off to the Korean porters," a private in the Glosters later commented; "they were fantastic... they were hard-working, they never complained." As a junior NCO in 2PPCLI explained, such men could carry loads "that would challenge most fit Canadian twenty-year-olds," adding, "I can't emphasize enough my respect for these unsung heroes."[141]

As U.N. forces in the west moved northward, a further foreign contingent was sent to 29th Brigade at the start of April 1951. This was the *Corps de Volontaires de la Corée,* the first national contingent from Belgium. These "bearded, wild-looking men," as an Ulsters subaltern put it, were in the words of a senior Glosters officer "some of the toughest soldiers we met in Korea." Wearing brown berets and somewhat piratical in appearance and manner, the men of the Belgian battalion (including a platoon from Luxembourg) were mostly equipped with British-style weapons and kit at this stage and were all enthusiastic volunteers led by experienced officers and NCOs. Though perhaps a little high-spirited – the distinguished commander of one company deciding to mortar with smoke bombs a party of Ulster officers on their way back to their positions after they had paid him a social call – the Belgians were in British eyes, as the senior Royal Engineers officer put it, "a robust and likeable bunch."[142] Their only drawback was relative lack of manpower; the Belgian battalion was only about half the size of any of the three British infantry battalions.[143]

As winter gave way to spring things seemed to be going quite well for the Eighth Army as it cautiously pushed northward past the 38th Parallel, with enemy resistance remaining limited and patchy. In the first weeks of April the military consensus in London was that the Chinese were unlikely to attack and that if this was indeed their intention then they would not be ready before the end of May.[144] There was, however, plenty of intelligence gleaned from aerial surveillance of roads and rail lines that the enemy was preparing to launch a new offensive. This was why Matthew Ridgway, the general in overall command, had issued orders for the preparation of a series of defense-in-depth lines of resistance behind the front; preparations continued under a new army commander, Lieutenant General James A. Van Fleet, after General Douglas McArthur was fired as supreme commander in the second week of April and Ridgway took his place in Tokyo.[145]

Exactly when and where the enemy would strike, however, remained unknown, and forward movement continued. By the middle of April, coming under the control of the 3rd U.S. Infantry Division in I Corps, 29th Brigade had moved up to the Imjin River and established a battalion position on the opposite bank beyond Line Kansas (near the 38th Parallel) without too much difficulty. Meanwhile, twenty-odd miles to the east, 27th Brigade, under the direct command of IX Corps, had advanced to Line Kansas and a mile or so beyond before being relieved by elements of 6th ROK Division and sent seven miles back to the Kapyong area to rest and refit. In neither brigade was there much inkling that a major defensive battle was in the offing.

The 27th Brigade, for one thing, except for 16 Field Regiment which was detached to support the 6th ROK Division, was no longer in the line but in corps reserve, while at the front itself reconnaissance patrols sent out by the ROKs revealed no enemy activity. Once out of the line the brigade was at once caught in the throes of a major reorganization, the original British battalions scheduled to exchange places with two other battalions of the Hong Kong garrison, the latter going in the near future along with 3RAR to form 28th Brigade while 2PPCLI was to join a new 25th Canadian Brigade. Indeed when the Chinese struck on 22 April the Argyll and Sutherland Highlanders were on their way to embark a day before the King's Own Scottish Borderers were due to arrive.[146]

As for 29th Brigade, though it was still in the front line, the enemy appeared to have vanished. A couple of nights after the Ulsters established themselves on the north bank of the Imjin an enemy company attacked and was repulsed by D Company, but this seemed to be an isolated incident; local patrolling north of the river in the following days produced little or no contact. The Chinese seemed to have disappeared, lulling men into what would turn out to be a false sense of security. As the adjutant of the Glosters explained, "there was no sign of the enemy," adding, "and this was in many ways a comfort."[147]

The brigade commander was less complacent, knowing that a Chinese offensive was in the offing. But like higher command he did not know when or where the enemy would attack, or indeed if, in the absence of the enemy, the advance in his sector would be resumed. Though his brigade covered a traditional invasion route, Brodie doubtless knew that the 3rd Division commander, Major General Robert H. "Shorty" Soule, believed that the enemy would most likely launch a thrust against the division slightly farther east so as to drive down Route 33, the Main Supply Route leading more directly to Uijongbu and thence to Seoul.[148] In the event that the Chinese in fact struck hard a bit farther west, the brigadier anticipated that he would be authorized to issue the code word "Foxhound" to his most exposed units, thereby allowing them to withdraw and conform to Line Kansas behind the Imjin as part of an orderly fighting retreat.[149] Yet with other Eighth Army formations in I Corps still advancing northward as part of Operation Dauntless, and in the absence of the enemy for miles in front, it remained unclear when, where, and to what extent 29th Brigade would be involved in a defensive battle rather than a renewed advance. The positioning and posture of brigade units was therefore somewhat ambiguous, neither poised for a general advance nor arrayed for a full-scale defensive battle.

The 29th Brigade was on the left flank of the divisional front, situated between the 1st ROK Division to the west and the 65th Infantry Regiment to the northeast. The battalion farthest forward, initially the Ulsters, occupied what became a comparatively well-fortified hill position, 196 meters high in the bend of the Imjin a mile or so north of where the river met a tributary, the Hantan. This position was connected with the positions of the rest of the brigade and the 65th by a couple of engineer-constructed vehicle and foot bridges over the Imjin and Hantan. More or less due south of the Hill 196 position, on the south side of the Imjin, lay the Northumberland positions. The four fusilier companies each occupied a hill feature over 200 meters in height, a distance of a mile or two between them, with battalion HQ located below the westernmost feature near the road designated as Route 11. Behind and in support lay the gun batteries of 45 Field Regiment – one battery per battalion[150] – and the tanks of C Squadron, 8th Hussars. About three miles farther south down Route 11, as the distant heights on either side grew to several hundred meters, Brigade HQ was established; and nearly two miles behind that the Belgians were resting in brigade reserve. Situated on the left flank, a mile or two south of the Imjin and separated from the Northumberlands by a distance of three or four miles and an imposing massif known as Kamak-san rising to 675 meters, were the Glosters. As with the 5th Fusiliers, the four infantry companies of the Glosters were spread out over the local terrain features (none more than 182 meters in height), each separated from one another by a mile or so of open ground and together supported by a troop of 4.2-inch mortars from 170 Battery.[151] The Glosters were covering a ford across the Imjin, known as Gloster Crossing, a mile or two to the north, and Route 57 (or 5Y, also known as Five Yankee) which ran south from it through the villages of Choksong and Solma-ri. Route 57, which was essentially just a track, eventually linked up with Route 11, a slightly more substantial track, a few miles south of Kamak-san.

The way in which 29th Brigade was deployed at the battalion and company level left much to be desired if the Chinese chose to launch a major assault across the Imjin along the brigade front. The battalions were miles apart, the three forwardmost separated from one another by either a river or a small mountain, and hence unable to offer each other immediate aid. Moreover, within the two forward battalions immediately south of the river, the Northumberlands and the Glosters, the infantry companies were themselves widely dispersed and not in a position to offer each other much fire support beyond mortar and medium machine-gun fire in the forward positions. The danger was particularly acute for the Glosters, essentially cut off from the rest of the brigade by the Kamak-san massif. As a U.S. combat historian who investigated the Imjin battle shortly after it took place later noted: “The rifle companies were located on separate hills . . . and were not mutually supporting, thus lending themselves to enemy attack separately and to the danger of being overrun separately."[152]

There was a reason why the battalions, if not the companies, were so dispersed across the brigade front – the sheer amount of territory they were collectively required to cover. The amount of front line that 29th Brigade was responsible for between the 1st ROK Division and the rest of 3rd Division was huge. Even after Brigadier Brodie had managed to persuade I Corps to extend the territory covered by the South Koreans eastward, his brigade was responsible for fourteen miles of front. Once again a British brigade was being asked to take on something really meant for a division-sized formation, and once again Brodie, perhaps thinking that there would be time to withdraw and consolidate if push came to shove, and eager to preserve the idea that British troops could collectively do what Americans or South Koreans had apparently not been capable of during the great bug-out, accepted the challenge. As an army circular on the campaign thus far had noted proudly the previous month, "defence of wide fronts against infiltration or heavy odds is nothing new to us."[153]

It was not at all certain to the men in the field, moreover, that 29th Brigade would be fighting a defensive battle along the Imjin at all. The Chinese had broken contact, and it seemed entirely possible to everyone, from war correspondents to battalion officers and ordinary soldiers, that the brigade as a whole would be at any moment ordered to advance north of the river. "On the Imjin we checked [stopped]," the second in command of the Glosters explained, "took up defensive positions and patrolled hard and prepared for the next move forward." As the chronicler of 45 Field Regiment put it: "We were still mentally in forward gear."[154]

This expectation would have serious consequences in relation to prepared positions. On the north side of the Imjin the Ulsters, with the companies in close contact with one another, made a serious effort to dig deep slit trenches and lay wire around what some dubbed "Fort Nixon" in honor of company commander Christopher Nixon, expecting as they did that the Chinese might try to pinch out this exposed, single-battalion bridgehead at some point. On the south side of the Imjin, however, officers and men tended to be much more complacent. "We asked about [building wire defenses] when we first occupied the position," remembered the CO of the Glosters, "but were told not to, as the advance north of the river was to be continued." And quite apart from the expectation that another northward movement would soon be in the offing, anyone thinking about a Chinese attack might take comfort from the fact that Imjin lay between them and the enemy. "The river itself was thought to be a good defensive barrier against possible assault by the enemy," a sergeant in the Glosters remembered. At a certain time of year this would have been true, but from the middle of the month after the spring rains had passed the water level began to drop, and as it turned out the Chinese knew of crossing points that the British were not watching. "We didn't really know where the fords were," Malcolm Cubiss, a Northumberlands platoon commander, conceded decades later. "We knew about one, we didn't know about the others." The presence of this apparent water barrier, though, in combination with the stone-laden, hard ground on the hills and the expectation of imminent movement, meant there was little effort expended on digging deep slit trenches or bunkers, and little or no wire or mines were laid in front of company positions. There were, to be sure, shortages of defensive stores. "It took eight days to get the first truck load of barbed wire," the Glosters' adjutant complained, "and the second did not reach the battalion until it had been in position for 17 days." But there was also no sense of urgency about obtaining them in light of the factors already mentioned. The end result, as a Gloster private recalled, was that by the time of the battle "nothing elaborate had been prepared in the way of defences, obstacles, minefields or wire."[155]

There were those in the brigade who still thought it likely the Chinese would attack in April, including Brodie himself. The brigadier asked for U.S. units from 3rd Division to be shifted to support his sector, but in light of other divisional commitments none were made available. Rightly suspicious of enemy intentions, Brodie insisted on vigorous local patrolling across the Imjin, and sent out large-scale, deep-penetration armor-plus-infantry sweeps in the third week of April.[156]

The Chinese, though, seemed to have vanished. Apart from occasional brushes with small enemy parties which immediately withdrew, there was no contact, even when sweeps penetrated many miles into no-man's-land. Only two days before the Imjin battle began, "Lowtherforce," consisting of Centurions led by Lieutenant-Colonel William

Lowther working in conjunction with two companies from the Glosters, had gone an estimated twelve miles northward beyond the Imjin without encountering anyone but the odd fleeing individual. "We never found a bloody Chinaman," a Gloster private recalled, "never found one."[157]

Field commanders dislike knowing virtually nothing about the location and strength of the enemy, and Brodie was no exception. "But they must be there!" he exclaimed after being told that the reconnaissance sweep of 20 April had failed to find the Chinese, nervously banging his tennis racquet handle against his thigh. The deliberate breaking of contact by the Chinese People's Volunteers was to him an ominous sign. Well out of artillery range, the enemy could be – and according to intelligence reports was – building up for a new offensive.[158]

Brodie, though, evidently still believed he would have time to marshal his forces when the enemy finally chose to strike southward. He may have thought that aerial reconnaissance and patrolling would reveal the presence of significant Chinese formations in advance of their arrival on the Imjin in force, and that enemy movement would be confined to the hours of darkness in order to avoid air strikes and observed artillery fire. The brigadier also seems to have assumed that any major offensive would be in any case heralded by tell-tale reconnaissance probes in order to give Chinese unit commanders a clear picture of the location and strength of British defenses. This, after all, was what had happened in earlier encounters. Unfortunately the enemy would behave very differently on the Imjin. "All previous Chinese offensives had started with strong probing patrols," a war correspondent working from brigade headquarters in the fourth week of April later explained, adding; "and there had been none of these."[159]

The belief that there would be time to make adjustments, indeed to put "Foxhound" into effect – that is, withdraw exposed forces – may explain why four days before the battle began Brodie ordered the Ulsters and the Belgians to exchange positions. On 20 April the Belgian battalion moved forward to relieve the Ulsters on the north side of the Imjin, the latter taking the place of the former as brigade reserve. The hill position the Belgians found themselves occupying was comparatively well fortified, but they themselves mustered only about half the strength of the battalion they were replacing. In light of what was shortly to come this has struck Belgian observers as an extremely odd move. The brigadier, however, seems to have thought that there would be enough advance warning to withdraw the Belgians across the Imjin before the main attack began. After all, the day after the Belgians moved in, two of their officers were allowed to reconnoiter no-man's-land in a U.S. light plane, and could find no signs of the enemy to a depth of fifteen miles.[160]

Meanwhile, the failure of long-range patrols to bump into the Chinese in any force that seems to have concerned Brodie only added to the complacency of many junior officers and men. As the chronicler of 45 Field Regiment noted, the fact that Lowtherforce returned unscathed "seemed to give the lie to intelligence warnings of an imminent offensive." Captain Mike Harvey later admitted that neither he nor his D Company commander in the Glosters, Major "Lakri" Wood, had "the remotest idea" that an enemy attack was imminent, while to men of other companies the fact that the Chinese had not been found in the sweep of 20 April signaled that there was no imminent danger of an assault. They were not alone. "At our level, the troops, nobody knew about an attack on the Imjin" recalled Armand Philips of Platoon B, Company C of the Belgian battalion. "Nobody was expecting the Chinese to attack," remembered a C Squadron trooper of the 8th Hussars. "Nobody had got *any impression at all* that the enemy was going to put this attack on," agreed a Hussar captain. The mood continued to be one of comparative relaxation, men sunning themselves on the reverse slopes of the scrub-covered hills their companies occupied and no attempt being made to improve defenses by, for example, enlisting the Korean porters to deepen slit trenches.[161]

In both brigades the spring weather added to the sense of peacefulness and ease, the temperature "not too hot, just nice and comfortable," as Gunner Eric Stowe of 45 Field Regiment reported to his sweetheart.[162] For practically the first time since they had landed in Korea, British and Commonwealth soldiers did not feel assaulted by the climate. After a good deal of rain the sun came out, trees and shrubs sprouted leaves, flowers bloomed, and grass grew. "The weather had warmed," a corporal in the Patricias recalled, "and I was looking forward to idle days. . . ."[163] 3RAR was enjoying hot baths, a beer ration, football, open-air cinema screenings, and the preparations to mark ANZAC day with a full-scale remembrance parade on 25 April to which representatives of the Turkish brigade as well as the New Zealanders were invited.[164] At the same time in the nominal front line some twenty miles to the west the infantrymen of 29th Brigade acted as if they too were on holiday. "People moved about in shirts and trousers and the cook sang in the sunshine as he peeled the potatoes," as a British war correspondent put it. "With the end of winter, half the horror of the war vanished, and for a few weeks Korea was a lovely land: its ancient poetic name, 'Chosin' – The Land of the Morning Calm – was no longer a wry joke but something delicately appropriate to the country's mood." Even those with no aesthetic sense for the place could appreciate the spring. With the temperature now quite balmy, Rifleman Henry O'Kane remembered, "we sun bathed in the hot sun outside our dugouts."[165]

As it happened, the long-range patrols on the eve of the offensive had missed a few tell-tale signs that something was afoot. The noise of the tanks and the fact that the infantry accompanying them made no effort to keep out of sight and took pot-shots at the local wildlife made it easy for the many Chinese already in no-man's-land to quietly withdraw or exercise their considerable powers of concealment. A feeling that one was being watched could be simply dismissed. Nevertheless there were still indicators that might have been picked up on but were not, such as freshly dug trenches and caches of rice and grain found by the men. Everyone came back, however, convinced that the enemy, as Lieutenant Sam Phillips of the Northumberlands put it, "just weren't there."[166]

Perhaps lulled by the fact that right up until the day of the attack American aerial reconnaissance reports arriving at brigade HQ indicated there were no Chinese within a dozen miles of the Imjin, Brodie himself contributed to the general sense of complacency within the brigade by continuing to allow officers and men to go on leave to Japan. This meant that when the Chinese attacked, the absentees would include a company commander from the Glosters, the CO of the Ulsters, and the brigade's senior operations officer, the brigade major. Meanwhile, no attempt was apparently made to beef up the formation's infantry-support firepower in the event of an attack by recalling the rest of 11 Light Anti-Aircraft Battery from positions around Seoul to augment the single troop of 40-mm Bofors guns present on the Imjin, nor – just as importantly – to prevent the American artillery liaison officer from departing the brigade. Subsequently there would be no U.S. heavy artillery support available on call. The Ulsters and Northumberlands, meanwhile, were preparing to exchange their positions, something that could have made a bad situation worse if the switch had been in progress when the Chinese attacked. As Major Guy Ward, then in command of the 25-pounder battery supporting the Glosters, recalled of the time, the atmosphere was "relaxed." With the advantage of hindsight he commented: "Too relaxed."[167]

All seemed quiet on the I Corps front on 21st April, local patrols as usual making no contact with the enemy. There was, however, one small encounter in the 29th Brigade sector after the moon rose. A three-man listening post consisting of Private G. N. Hunter and Drummer A. P. Eagles under the command of Corporal G. H. Cooke had been established overlooking the ford known as Gloster Crossing, in front of the battalion position. An hour or so before midnight Tony Eagles thought he saw something move on the other side of the Imjin. "So I said to Scouse [Hunter], who was from Liverpool, 'Scouse, I think there's someone over there.'" Hunter agreed, and Corporal Cooke reported the sighting to battalion HQ using the field telephone with which the listening party had been equipped. The adjutant, Captain Tony Farrar-Hockley, ordered illumination flares to be fired over the position by the mortars of 170 Battery operating in support of the Glosters. Fourteen Chinese were revealed moving toward the crossing on the opposite bank. After the flares had died, the party began to wade across the Imjin. This was reported to Farrar-Hockley, who ordered the listening patrol to stop them: "I don't want them crossing." The three soldiers opened up with their rifles, seeing several Chinese go down and the rest retreat. Though it would not become fully apparent for more than twenty-four hours, the first shots in the Battle of the Imjin had been fired.[168]

We saw the Chinese advance . . . they were so numerous!

THEODORE DROOGMANS,
Platoon B, Company C, Belgian Battalion, c. 10:30 PM, 22 April[1]

The bastards must be breeding over there!

LEN ALLEN,
7 Platoon, C Company, 1st Glosters, c. 11:30 PM, 22 April[2]

ONE

Imjin: The First Day

AS EIGHTH ARMY INTELLIGENCE HAD RIGHTLY PREDICTED, the Chinese People's Volunteers were preparing to launch a major offensive in the spring of 1951 under the overall command of Peng Te-huai. What was less clear was when, where, and in what strength the enemy would strike, and what he would seek to accomplish. As it happened the ultimate objective remained to drive U.N. forces from the peninsula and unite Korea under Kim Il-sung. The immediate aims of the Fifth Phase offensive included the recapture of Seoul and the destruction of no less than three U.S. divisions, two ROK divisions, the Turkish brigade, and both 27th Commonwealth Brigade and "the British 29th Brigade."[3]

To accomplish this Peng had amassed over 350,000 men serving in forty assault divisions divided between eleven armies organized into three corps or groups. As in the past the Chinese had little in the way of artillery support and no air cover, but each rifle company now had two Soviet-made medium machine-guns, three Soviet-made light machine-guns, and a 60-mm mortar. As for the individual Chinese soldier, the mixture of Japanese, American, and British weapons with which he had initially been equipped had largely given way by the start of the offensive – albeit with comparatively limited supplies of ammunition – to plenty of Russian rifles and the notorious burp gun.[4]

The first part of the Fifth Phase offensive would involve more or less simultaneous attacks all along the western half of the U.N. line. Toward 29th Brigade on Sunday, 22 April came the 187th, 188th, and 189th divisions of the 63rd Army and 198th Division from the 60th Army. This meant that upwards of 40,000 Chinese troops were advancing against a force that consisted of a little over 3,500 officers and men.

It was the sheer number and bravery of the enemy they faced that would remain uppermost in the minds of many British survivors. Carrying only light bandoliers of ammunition and rations in addition to their weapons, wearing rubber-soled canvas shoes rather than boots, dressed in sand-colored, rather shapeless quilted cotton uniforms, sporting soft caps on their heads (very occasionally supplemented by helmets captured from the Japanese), and often far from intimidating in terms of stature, Chinese soldiers were nevertheless a great deal more formidable than their adversaries expected. "They kept coming in waves, large numbers of them," Corporal Ronald Norley of the Glosters would later vividly recall, adding that "however intense the fire they just seemed to keep coming."[5] It was analogous, a number of participants explained, to facing a crowd streaming out of a soccer stadium or motion picture palace, the effect made worse by the shouts, whistles, and trumpets calls – the latter sounding like "something between a hunting horn and a French horn" according to one unwilling auditor[6] – used in lieu of radios to signal actions. Indeed, so willing were the masses of shouting and screaming Chinese infantry to keep up attacks in the face of mounting losses that would have caused an equivalent British assault to collapse that it was widely thought they were drunk or drugged.[7] Making a difficult situation worse was the fact that, in contrast to earlier engagements, the Chinese soldiers on the Imjin were quite well armed; one Gloster private estimated that half were equipped with automatic weapons, the rest with rifles, and everyone with four or more stick grenades.[8]

At dawn on 22nd April, though, few in 29th Brigade were aware of what was about to happen. As the sun rose the spring weather was cool but sunny, and soldiers went about their business much as usual. The Northumberlands were preparing to celebrate their patron saint, St. George, the following day, having already taken delivery of paper roses to adorn their headgear and prepared a feast, while the Ulsters were relaxing in reserve and looking forward to a film show that evening. This being a Sunday, morning church services were being organized in all four battalions. None of the chaplains involved can have known that for some who attended, this communion would be their viaticum, though Father Ryan with the Ulsters apparently took no chances. "Boys," a subaltern recalled him saying, "some of ye'll not see another day. So if you will all make a good Act of Contrition I'll give you General Absolution."[9]

Meanwhile at battalion and brigade headquarters there were signs of a major increase in enemy activity within no-man's-land. A local Glosters patrol north of the Imjin bumped into a Chinese force and by 6 AM was withdrawing in the face of the enemy. Three hours or so later a 1RNF patrol was also in contact a few miles north of the river. Lieutenant Sam Phillips, commanding 9 Platoon in Y Company of the 5th Fusiliers – a regiment which for reasons of heritage labeled its companies from the end rather than the beginning of the alphabet – was in command.

> On the morning of the 22nd it was my turn to go across the river. Early in the morning we went across on a couple of small, punt-like boats, and I took the platoon across. The only thing I noticed when we landed on the north bank of the river was that there appeared to be a lot of wires down to the river, telephone wires; and you know one just snipped them and thought no more about it. Then we moved up, and were about two miles north of the river. Coming to the edge of a village, when suddenly, on the hill in front of us, I saw a [Chinese] sentry running around, waking people up who were asleep (or I assumed were asleep). We had stumbled on what I thought were just a platoon of enemy; but it turned out to be more, and I wirelessed back and said "we have met enemy." We fired on them and I then called down fire from 45 Field Regiment. When that happened, I was then told to return back.[10]

By about noon reports were coming in that parties of twenty or more Chinese were moving toward Gloster Crossing. More contacts were relayed by Northumberland patrols in the afternoon, and reports were arriving from fleeing civilians, by 6 PM. Belgian patrols were also encountering enemy groups, and before nightfall the guns of 45 Field Regiment had started to engage multiple targets north of the river. It was the same elsewhere in 3rd Division and across the I Corps front, with reports coming in from American air reconnaissance flights of not only hundreds of men on the move but also towed guns. In the afternoon the news was relayed to brigade headquarters that the Turks had captured a Chinese survey party whose leader had revealed that an offensive was about to begin that night and that it should "be prepared for a general CCF offensive."[11]

The first reports of contact on Sunday did not cause much of a stir among the Glosters. "The news caused no alarm," remembered Padre Sam Davies of the post-service gathering of Gloster officers; "we received it carelessly." Others confirmed this mood of equanimity. "Oh, the Chinese are supposed to be on their way down," replied Major Pat Angier of A Company to a query from his RAMC corporal, "but there's nothing to worry about." As Private Lofty Large later wrote, "No one seemed to take this news as anything of note." This did not mean that the Glosters did not think the Chinese were coming. Major P. W. "Sam" Weller, in command of Support Company, recalled distinctly that once the reports came in, "we were all then alerted, and the whole battalion was then keyed up to expect an attack." The expectation, though, and hence the *sang-froid* among the officers, was based on the faulty premise that the enemy would not strike at first in any strength hill positions which were regarded, in Weller's words, as "fairly secure."[12]

At dinner with representatives of the press at brigade headquarters, Brodie appeared unruffled by the day's events. "Might be tonight," he casually answered a correspondent's query as to when the long-anticipated Chinese offensive was to start. "Your guess is as good as mine," he added when pressed by others. All the indications now were that the enemy was intent on an assault. The brigade commander, though, like those above and below him, was assuming that the offensive would begin with probing moves to ascertain the location and strength of U.N. defenses. Contacts had been made in no-man's-land, but aerial reconnaissance on the 22nd indicated that the enemy main body was still fifteen to twenty miles from the Imjin. This suggested to I Corps Headquarters that the main attack could not start until after sunset on the 23rd, because the Chinese would have to cover a lot of ground and lie up during the day on their way down to avoid air attack. The real battle, in short, was twenty-four hours away, and hence there would be plenty of time to make necessary adjustments to the dispositions of individual battalions.[13]

Unfortunately, the Chinese did not behave as expected. For one thing, units were able to move much faster on foot than anticipated, arriving in strength on the Imjin by nightfall. For another, in contrast to earlier observed behavior, they were neither preparing for probing attacks nor willing to lie up during daylight hours. Thanks to small reconnaissance parties that had largely gone unobserved by British patrols and observation posts, the enemy already knew exactly where and in what strength the units of 29th Brigade lay. They intended to achieve as much surprise as possible and, despite what it might cost, maintain their momentum by continuing to operate during the day as much as possible. The result, as Major T. V. Fisher-Hoch of 170 Independent Mortar Battery bluntly noted, was that reaction by brigade HQ to the strength and speed of the Chinese offensive "was slow, and we were left to meet it still well dispersed."[14]

That brigade HQ was not anticipating anything serious that night was reflected in the orders that Brodie issued in the evening. The brigadier put the Ulsters on notice that their mobile Battle Patrol might be needed along with an infantry company at some point, and ordered the Northumberlands to prepare a company-sized patrol meant to go north across the Imjin the next morning.[15]

The headquarters of forward battalions, meanwhile, prepared to meet what they thought would be probing moves in the darkness. At first this seemed to be the case. A listening post of the 5th Fusiliers overlooking the one known ford across the Imjin in the Northumberlands' sector reported at around 8:30 PM that parties of enemy soldiers were crossing. Defensive artillery fire was subsequently brought down on the area, and by 10 PM X Company on the battalion left flank was undergoing what appeared to be probing attacks.[16] Farther to the west, in the wake of enemy parties being observed approaching Gloster Crossing earlier in the day, Colonel Carne had put his battalion on fifty percent stand-to and in addition to sending out the nightly listening party had given orders for the setting up of an ambush party to meet what he thought would be an enemy attempt to cross the Imjin that night. Carne seems to have suspected that the enemy might be coming in force, but the intelligence he had been given indicated he could anticipate only small patrols. "I think the most we'd expected to cross was a company or two," Anthony Farrar-Hockley, the battalion adjutant, later admitted. Carne's orders to Lieutenant Guy "Guido" Temple, leading a sixteen-man fighting patrol (from 7 Platoon, C Company), were to surprise the enemy, capture a prisoner for interrogation purposes, and withdraw if there seemed to be more than a platoon of Chinese making use of Gloster Crossing.[17]

Temple himself had a sixth sense that there would be more of the enemy than expected, and made sure that his fighting patrol, delivered to riverbank slit trenches just to the right of Gloster Crossing by Oxford carrier, had three Brens with four thousand rounds of ammunition each plus six grenades per man and ample mortar rounds. At about 11:30 PM his men heard shouts and splashes from the other side of the Imjin. Temple put up a flare, which revealed forty to fifty Chinese starting to cross. The fighting patrol opened fire, and the Chinese withdrew. After a period of comparative silence, the lieutenant and his men heard more noise from the opposite bank – "they were very unquiet in their movements," Temple observed – and sent up another flare. "This time there were very, very many more people," he recalled, "like battalion strength." Defensive fire from the nearest artillery battery was called down through a radio link with Gloster battalion headquarters and from there to 45 Field Regiment HQ, and after some adjustments 25-pound shells starting exploding in the water of the crossing. "That put them off their stroke for a bit," Guido recalled, "and they appeared to go back and reassemble, and next they came forward in what I can only assume was the equivalent of brigade strength." More artillery defensive fire was called for, first in battery strength and then in "Mike Target" strength, involving all twenty-four guns of 45 Field Regiment. Huge amounts of rifle, mortar, and Bren gun ammunition were also expended, "so much so that the Bren gun tips were actually glowing a sort of dull pink in the night they were so hot." The Chinese, despite several hundred casualties sustained at the ford, were still coming and could be heard now on the south bank. The fighting patrol, meanwhile, was running very short of ammunition, and Temple asked for and got permission from Colonel Carne to withdraw under covering fire from the artillery to the main battalion positions.[18]

The departure of the fighting patrol from Gloster Crossing coincided with the unanticipated arrival of the listening party. Captain Mike Harvey, temporarily in command of D Company, had ordered twenty-two-year-old Second-Lieutenant David Holdsworth earlier in the evening to take four men from 12 Platoon – mostly made up of crotchety reservists a decade older than their officer – down to the Imjin west of Gloster Crossing where the river curved south, attach a field telephone to a previously laid wire, and report what he saw. They reached the Imjin where the wire was supposed to be, but could not locate it in the dark. Holdsworth decided to move northeast along the south bank of the river toward Gloster Crossing, where he knew there was another telephone wire along with Temple and his men. "Anyway," Holdsworth related, "me and my merry men started to wander along the riverbank." Suddenly they heard shells exploding in the direction of the crossing. "What the hell's going on, *sir*?" he was asked, and had to admit he did not know. After being discouraged by his men from using his whistle to alert the ambush patrol to their imminent arrival – it was urgently pointed out to him that the Chinese used whistles too – Holdsworth moved his party eastward along the south bank of the Imjin. "We marched on a bit," he later explained, "and suddenly we saw hundreds of people scurrying around the [south] bank of the river." At first Holdsworth thought these were Korean porters attached to the battalion, but it quickly became apparent that they were in fact Chinese soldiers. "It was like Wembley [Stadium]," Lance-Corporal Len Swatton remembered. "You couldn't miss, there were so many of them and they were so close. I looked down, and there was a face sticking up out of the river, right in front of me. He got an army boot in the face." Wisely deciding that discretion was the better part of valor, the officer and his four men very rapidly retraced their steps southwestward, and after dodging artillery bursts and Chinese troops attacking A Company, eventually made it back to D Company. As Holdsworth put it, "we were bloody lucky that none of us were killed."[19]

The enemy, meanwhile, had been active elsewhere along the brigade front. Other than, for a time, at Gloster Crossing, it was the advancing Chinese who mostly held the initiative.

Like "Fred" Carne at the other end of the brigade front, the commander of the Belgian battalion, Lieutenant-Colonel Albert Crahay, wondered if the signs of enemy movement during the day meant that a night attack was being prepared. In his exposed position north of the river he was "anxious not to be surprised," so a listening post of five men led by First Sergeant Médard Leiding had been set up in the afternoon on a small feature over a thousand yards out from Company C. By 8 PM Leiding was reporting by telephone the spotting of the odd enemy soldier, but within half an hour parties of about twenty or thirty Chinese were being observed, and just before the line was found and cut by the enemy a couple of hours later there were so many that Leiding's telephone operator was nervously exclaiming, "Now I can't even count them!"[20]

Defensive artillery fire from 45 Field Regiment was called in on the approaches to the Belgian positions, the bursting of 25-pounder shells adding to the cacophony of small-arms fire, shattering grenades, and exploding mortar bombs fired by the troop from 170 Battery attached to the Belgians. In the hours before and after midnight Company C came under repeated attack, the Belgian defenders aided by the barbed wire and mines in front of them but frustrated by a shortage of manpower and the fact that the slit trenches did not often connect with one another, making movement from one threatened sector to another quite hazardous. The Chinese were able to seize an unmanned bunker in the Company C area from which they directed accurate machine-gun fire on their opponents. Grenades and bazooka rounds proved ineffective against the bunker, and it was only after it was hit by an artillery shell that the enemy machine-gun was temporarily silenced. Meanwhile, amid the noise and flare-pierced darkness, with the Chinese apparently everywhere and firefights breaking out on all sides, isolated men sometimes took counsel of their fears. Roger Pauwels, a member of section one of Platoon B, Company C, admitted that after seeing several of his comrades wounded "I had the impression that all was collapsing around me."[21]

Though all three forward battalions were reporting firefights – the Chinese had also crossed the Imjin to the east of the Glosters beginning about half past eight in the evening and were attacking the platoons of X Company of the Northumberlands by 10 PM[22] – at around midnight Brodie was still operating on the assumption that these contacts were only the result of enemy probes. In the darkness the forward battalions knew they were coming under fire but had no way of knowing or reporting back to brigade how many troops were bypassing them using either the gaps of up to around a mile between most companies or the several miles of uncontested ground between the battalions and on the open brigade flanks. Brodie did, however, want to make sure that the Belgian line of retreat was clear when the eventual order to withdraw across the Imjin needed to be issued under the code word "Foxhound." This was why, after reports reached him that the Chinese were now south of the Imjin, the brigadier had decided at about 10:30 PM to commit his reserve formation, the Royal Ulster Rifles, to securing the bridge crossings across the Imjin and Hantan.[23]

Thus far the Ulsters, situated roughly five miles south of the Imjin, had been largely unaware that anything serious was happening. While the riflemen were enjoying an open-air film showing (*Tea for Two* with Doris Day and Gordon MacCrae), the officers were having a party in a tent to celebrate the announcement of various awards arising from the engagement in January. "Suddenly in walked the duty officer and said 'The Chinese have taken Ulster Crossing,'" remembered Second-Lieutenant Mervyn McCord, a platoon commander in B Company, "at which everyone threw things at him and said 'Stop being so stupid, go away, don't start trying to wreck a good party.'" It took some time to convince those present that the news was real. ("You've never seen a party sober up so quickly in your life.") The Chinese, indeed, were by the early hours of 23rd April infiltrating small parties as far south as they could manage. Rifleman Albert Tyas, also in B Company, recalled that the first indication he had that a battle had started was when the sounds of firing and the sight of firework-like arcs of tracer bullets coming from the north reached those watching *Tea for Two* in the open air. "Good God, what's happening?" he remembered thinking. Shortly thereafter the film was stopped and everyone was hurriedly ordered to take up positions.[24]

With Lieutenant-Colonel R. J. H. Carson on leave, the Ulsters were under the authority of the second-in-command, the tough and experienced Major Gerald Rickord. With the battalion so far from the Imjin and having to suddenly gird itself for battle, Rickord decided that the only way to quickly secure the bridges was to send forward the Battle Patrol in their Oxford carriers, accompanied by fourteen field engineers. The orders given to the Battle Patrol commander, Lieutenant Hedley Craig, were to dismount from the carriers on arrival at the Imjin so that the vehicles could return and be used by the rest of the battalion as transport, then to fight forward to the Belgians or withdraw if pressed heavily.[25]

When the Battle Patrol eventually arrived at the Imjin bridges around two in the morning there was initially no sign of the enemy. Craig stopped his column just south of the river and conferred briefly with his second-in-command:

> "Looks a bit fishy."
> "Yes."
> "Better push on a bit, though."
> "Yes."

The carriers rattled over the vehicle bridge and were then ambushed by the waiting Chinese. The night suddenly erupted in sound and light, Oxfords started going up in flames, radio contact with the battalion was lost, riflemen scrambled to get out, and any semblance of order rapidly disintegrated; "all is confusion," wrote Second-Lieutenant P. J. Kavanagh in a lightly fictionalized version of his experiences that night. Craig attempted to salvage something from the disaster by organizing a party of riflemen to cover the withdrawal over the bridge of the remnants of the Battle Patrol. Of the eight carriers and fifty-plus soldiers who had crossed the bridge, only a single Oxford, the wounded Kavanagh, and five wounded riflemen initially made it back. Craig, though he eventually escaped the clutches of the enemy with one or two others of the covering party, was so traumatized by the ambush that he eventually lost his mind.[26]

By the early hours of 23rd April it was starting to becoming clear that, rather than making isolated probing attacks, the Chinese were engaged in a full-scale offensive right across the brigade front. The Belgians, the Northumberlands, and the Glosters were all fending off serious assaults in the hours before dawn.

On Hill 196 north of the river, the three Belgian companies were being cut off from one another and from the battalion command post by enemy infiltration parties, and coming under periodic attack from a variety of directions. "Were they numerous?" Max De Kerpel, a soldier in Company C, asked rhetorically regarding the Chinese. "Yes, I would say hundreds, perhaps thousands. . . . Fire as much as possible and duck the head . . . in the end, they came from all sides." A few spontaneous withdrawals had taken place along the Company C perimeter, and ammunition was getting very scarce indeed. Colonel Crahay was understandably worried about in exactly whose hands were the all-important bridges as the night drew to a close.[27]

Three miles to the southwest, the Fusiliers were also finding themselves in difficulty on the south side of the river. Using a ford unknown to the British, the Chinese had infiltrated across the Imjin near X Company and were preparing to attack it from several directions. "They're coming," a corporal warned 6 Platoon, immediately adding, "they're here." After an initial brush between the two sides a call was made in broken

English for 6 Platoon to surrender, which was at first misinterpreted to mean the Chinese wanted to throw in the towel. Any confusion on either side about pacific intentions was quickly cleared up by the outbreak of a fierce firefight in front of 4 Platoon. By about 2 AM, in the wake of heavy mortaring and machine-gunning by the enemy, 4 Platoon was in trouble. Its commander, Malcolm Cubiss, encouraged his men to "hold your ground!" despite mounting losses, but returning to the platoon position after having a wound dressed found that only the dead remained: "The remnants of the platoon decided that they'd had enough and had buggered off, which surprised me." In retrospect he thought he could guess what had happened. "We had lost fourteen out of twenty-six [men] in three hours. Most people don't want to let their pals down – that is why you have slit trenches with two men and Bren trenches with three men. But once you start losing people, it changes the character. Chaps think, 'Christ, he's gone – I could be next.'" The spontaneous retreat of 4 Platoon exposed the flank of 5 Platoon and put the whole X Company hilltop position in jeopardy.[28]

"First we were winning," commented Fusilier Derek Kinne, "then we were losing." Learning what was happening by radio, Brodie at 2:15 AM gave permission for X Company to retreat and join up with Battalion HQ several miles to the east if necessary. Within half an hour it did become necessary, Lieutenant-Colonel Kingsley Foster giving the company commander, Major Reggie Pratt, the authority to withdraw at his discretion. These were not the only fusiliers under fire from infiltrating enemy parties. W Company on Hill 217 a mile to the east held up relatively well; though as the second-in-command, Captain Andrew Scott, later admitted, "it was a bit disconcerting to be attacked from four directions at once." More alarming was the state of Z Company a mile to the northeast. 11 Platoon, occupying the commanding heights of Hill 257, was caught totally by surprise when the Chinese scaled the heights and appeared on the company right flank at around 3 AM, it not having been realized that the Imjin was fordable just to the north. Fusilier Roy Rees remembered that a young mate of his was so alarmed by the sudden appearance of enemy parties among the slit trenches that he simply bolted. By 4:45 AM 11 Platoon had withdrawn or been pushed off the heights in some disarray; Rees recalled with some indignation that he had found himself on his own because "nobody had come round and told us we were pulling out." Colonel Foster had discovered about an hour earlier that his Battalion HQ, half a mile to the east of Z Company, was coming under sporadic enemy fire. This quickly necessitated its withdrawal southward into the protective ring offered by the leaguered Centurions of C Squadron, 8th Hussars.[29]

The 70 Field Battery of 45 Field Regiment was also threatened by the enemy overrunning Hill 257. While continuing to shoot in support of the Glosters, Lieutenant George Truell was forced to divert the fire of one of his 25-pounders, at a range of only 150 yards and virtually over open sights, in order to break up further enemy advances before they could overrun the gun lines. After about twenty minutes of point-blank fire, the danger eased; "firing stopped and the Chinese took themselves off," Truell later remembered.[30]

A further three miles in a southwesterly direction from the Northumberlands' position, the Glosters were also under pressure. The enemy advance over Gloster Crossing had been only temporarily checked by Lieutenant Temple and his men, and a mile upstream the Chinese were using a ford unknown to the battalion. Dug in atop a 485-foot feature known as Castle site (Hill 148), A Company, farthest forward, was the first to feel the full weight of the Chinese offensive shortly after midnight, followed by D Company on Hill 182 a mile to the southeast. Within a few hours B Company, a mile west of D Company, was also coming under attack. Fire from the field guns of 70 Battery, 45 Field Regiment, the mortars of C Troop, 170 Battery, and the battalion Vickers and Bren machine-guns, along with grenades and bullets took an enormously heavy toll on the attackers, but one bugle-led wave of brave men shooting burp guns and throwing stick grenades was always succeeded by another.[31]

Chinese numbers were staggering to the defenders, even in retrospect. "There were about a million Chinese there," exclaimed Walter Cleveland of 9 Platoon, D Company, with understandable exaggeration. "There were thousands," Nick Carter, a private in B Company, remembered a bit less wildly: "I've never seen so many soldiers in my life," he added. "There seemed to be hundreds of them," the commander of 11 Platoon, D Company, Second-Lieutenant Denys Whatmore, wrote rather more cautiously. "They kept coming," recalled Bill Clark of 3 Platoon, A Company. "We were more or less firing continuously during the night," recalled Ronald Norley, a section leader under Whatmore, but as John Grosvenor of 12 Platoon noted, "as fast as you was killing 'em there was more coming."[32]

Six or so hours into the battle, Brodie had ascertained that 29th Brigade was dealing with far more than probing attacks, and that important decisions would have to be made concerning movements and dispositions. Knowing that the bridges had not been secured but little more, Brodie was concerned that if the Fusiliers lost control of their sector south of the Imjin the enemy would nullify his efforts to prevent Route 11 south of the Imjin from falling into their hands. If the brigade was pushed back, then the Chinese might be able to thrust southeast, take Route 33, the MSR, and outflank the 65th Infantry. Brodie was also worried about the Glosters, partly because they covered the less important Route 57 and also because he was concerned that if his left flank was pushed in then the enemy would be in a position to exert further flanking pressure on the Fusiliers or turn right and outflank the 1st ROK Division. The fact that the Belgians were holding on north of the river helped delay the enemy, but the brigadier did not want to press for a general retirement or individual withdrawals until it was clear that the U.N. forces on either side of the brigade were safe from being flanked when 29th Brigade pulled back. So far he had been given no orders to retreat by I Corps or 3rd Division, which Brodie took to mean he should hold on and try to shore up his defenses. With both the Glosters and the Northumberlands under heavy pressure, Brodie had to reconsider what to do with the Ulsters. His first inclination was to split his reserve, with A and D companies being sent up Route 11 to support the Northumberlands and prepare to retake the bridges, and first B Company and then (briefly) C Company being taken into brigade hands in preparation for a forthcoming counterattack in support of the Glosters to the northwest.[33]

The first hints of dawn were welcomed by all, the common expectation being that the Chinese would stop and go to ground rather than leave themselves open to more accurate ground fire and, especially, rocket and napalm strikes from roving American fighter-bombers. Brodie also knew that in daylight the Centurion tanks of C Squadron, 8th

Hussars (leaguered behind the lines at night because their crews could not spot or hit targets at any distance in darkness as well as out of a desire to avoid the kind of nighttime ambush that had befallen Cooperforce in January) could move forward and add their main guns to the fire-support efforts of 45 Field Regiment and 170 Mortar Battery. From the perspective of brigade HQ a dangerous situation had not as yet become perilous, and it was anticipated that the morning, as in past engagements, would witness an improvement. Alas, as the commander of the Belgian battalion reflected later, "this time instead of helping us the light would scarcely bring us any relief."[34]

They'll give up at dawn. Mark my words, sir;
they'll go back across the river.

RSM JACK HOBBS,
in conversation with Padre Sam Davies,
1GLOS HQ, C. 6 AM, 23 April[1]

As I sit talking to Richard, I wonder if he realizes how gravely we are situated: a vast body of enemy pushing south; our flanks open; the road cut behind us.

CAPTAIN TONY FARRAR-HOCKLEY,
with Captain R. A. St. M. Reeve-Tucker,
1GLOS HQ, C. 3 AM, 24 April[2]

TWO

Imjin: The Second Day

THE COMING OF SPRING DAYLIGHT TO THE LAND OF THE Morning Calm on Monday, 23 April revealed just how serious the situation was becoming for 29th Brigade after a night of hard fighting. The Chinese, instead of slackening their assaults, seem to have redoubled their efforts to break resistance, and not without effect. The decisions made by those in command in the next few hours would help save one battalion but contribute to the destruction of another.[3]

On the western flank, the two forward Gloster companies were in serious danger. In particular A Company on Hill 148 had been steadily ground down during the previous night's fighting, often virtually hand-to-hand in nature as the Chinese kept pushing and machine-guns were knocked out. Platoons were being reduced to the strength of sections and officers were being felled one by one. At around six in the morning the enemy managed to take the summit of Castle Hill and installed themselves below it in a covered observation post that had been built to offer General Ridgway a view over the Imjin during his next tour of inspection. A couple of shots from a super bazooka drove them out for a time, but as with the Belgians and their troublesome bunker, within half an hour the Chinese were back and had set up a machine-gun that dominated the lower reaches of the position and threatened to force what was left of A Company to abandon it entirely.[4] Desperate times call for desperate measures, and Major Pat Angier – having ordered his platoon commanders to report to him in person as phone lines had been cut and the forward radio link proved unreliable[5] – detailed one of his remaining young subordinates, Lieutenant Philip Curtis, to take the remnants of two platoons and make a last-ditch effort to retake the top of Castle Hill.

> "You've got to shift 'em off it, Phil."
> "Right."[6]

The primary aim was to silence the machine-gun in the observation post; "our object," Sam Mercer, one of the participants in the counterattack explained, "was to go in there and winkle the enemy out." The chances of success were slim at best. 70 Field Battery of 45 Field Regiment fired in support, but the roof of the observation post protected the occupants from anything other than a direct hit; the USAF was occupied elsewhere, so there would be no air strikes; the bazooka had evidently run out of ammunition, meaning grenades would have to be thrown close in; and there was no real ground cover. Curtis nonetheless, revolver in hand, valiantly led a charge from the trenches lying two hundred yards below the summit. "He was the sort of person who was not content to lead from the back," Mercer remembered; "he was not content to chivvy you on from the rear; he was very much a leader." Soldiers were cut down one after another in seconds by bullets and grenades, and a bad situation was apparently made worse by Curtis and some of those he led mistaking a British trip flare for an enemy explosive device and scattering. Curtis was hit in his right arm and left side – one jaundiced observer said the buttock – but despite severe bleeding insisted that other casualties be seen to by the medical corporal and took it upon himself, pistol in one hand, grenade in the other, to make a final solo effort to silence the machine-gun under the covering fire of those who remained unwounded. Just as he was fatally cut down Curtis threw his grenade into the observation post with deadly effect. For this valiant effort he was posthumously awarded a Victoria Cross.[7]

This act of heroism, alas, counted for little in the wider scheme of things. With the officer having been killed, the counter-attack sputtered out. Indeed, even as Curtis was organizing his "winkle group," Pat Angier was on the radio to Battalion HQ – which Carne had prudently relocated to the top of Hill 235 held by C Company – making it clear that A Company was in a bad way. "I'm afraid we've lost Castle Site," he told the adjutant, Captain Tony Farrar-Hockley. "I am mounting a counterattack now but I want to know whether to expect to stay here indefinitely or not. If I am to stay on, I must be re-enforced as my numbers are getting very low." Farrar-Hockley passed the message on to the CO, who then spoke to Angier himself over the radio. Carne knew that both A and D companies could not resist the encroaching enemy indefinitely, even with the extra ammunition he was sending forward in Oxford carriers. Nevertheless he also did not want to withdraw his two forward companies in case this allowed the Chinese to outflank either units of the 1st ROK Division, presumed to be somewhere to the left of the battalion, or the Northumberlands, known to be several miles to the right. In any case his orders from brigade were to hold Route 57 between the hamlets of Choksong, which the two forward companies overlooked, and Solma-ri, behind C Company. The CO's response to Angier's situation report therefore consisted of a brief and direct order: "You will stay there at all costs until further notice." The commander of A Company had been told to fight on with his men until they were all dead or wounded, a fate which even the normally imperturbable Colonel Carne found difficult to contemplate; the adjutant noticed that after talking to Angier he was very pale and that his hand shook as he relit his trademark pipe.[8]

Battalion HQ kept Brigade HQ updated about the deteriorating situation by radio. As a brigade log notation at ten minutes to seven in the morning stated, "CO 1 GLOSTERS report that posn in front of A and D Coys serious. Did not give much hope of lasting much longer against 1000 enemy reported to in the area." Carne also wanted to know, "Could the people on the right [i.e. the Northumberlands or possibly the Ulsters] do anything to help"? If the brigade commander was in any doubt about the seriousness of the Glosters' position any uncertainty was removed when a light reconnaissance aircraft confirmed to Brodie that a thousand enemy troops were indeed swarming around A and D companies.[9]

Unfortunately, despite the query from Carne there was little that the brigadier thought he could do to aid the Glosters at this point, due to the deteriorating situation farther east. The Belgians and the Northumberlands were both in serious trouble.

North of the Imjin, all three Belgian companies along with the battalion HQ were being attacked. Company C, its ammunition almost exhausted and one of its platoons "practically *wiped out,*" according to a verbal report given to its commander, Paul Janssens, had been partially overrun. Having heard firing from the area of the bridges in the early hours but nothing more, Colonel Crahay was anxious to discover "in whose hands" the bridges now were. A reinforced platoon was dispatched with orders "to reconnoiter the bridges and free them" if necessary. At first there was no sign of the Chinese bar some battle detritus, but near the east bridge over the Hantan the platoon ran into an ambush and lost six men before it could be withdrawn over the Imjin using the west bridge. The enemy had effectively pinned the small Belgian battalion against the Hantan, and Crahay radioed Brigade HQ for help toward half past seven in the morning.[10]

On the south side of the Imjin, just to the southwest, the Northumberland position was also looking increasingly fragile. Y Company was now pretty much cut off to the north of the rest of the battalion in its forward position inside a bend in the river. And not everyone was behaving well under pressure, as a 1953 interrogation report on the views of a returned prisoner of war from 7 Platoon revealed.

> At dawn on 24 April 1951, his platoon position was heavily attacked. Without [his] knowledge, his section moved back, and he discovered that they were just clear of his position, so he continued to shower grenades upon the enemy to cover their move. He expected his section to cover his own exit, but they did not. [He] feels very strongly on this point, and is of the opinion that he was let down considerably by his section for not warning him, and failing to cover up his own withdrawal.[11]

Moreover, the Chinese now controlled the heights that 11 Platoon of Z Company had lost, which overlooked the valley through which any column aiming to rescue Y Company would have to pass.[12] An effort by the Fusiliers to retake the high ground with fire support from four Centurions initially showed some promise but collapsed when the troops, on reaching the summit, came under machine-gun fire from some disoriented artillerymen. "This tragic affair caused the valley to become untenable through the loss of the hills," the Hussars' regimental historian noted, "and also severely lowered the morale of the Fusiliers."[13]

The Northumberlands, in short, were in no position to assist the Glosters and indeed would need more help from the tanks of the 8th Hussars in extracting Y Company from its untenable salient. Only after this was accomplished could C Squadron support any further effort to retake the ground lost south of the bridges, and for the moment it was the Chinese who were pushing the British back, not the other way around. As for the brigade reserve, it was already becoming obvious that an Ulster company could not arrive in time to help the forward Gloster companies – the enormous Kamak-san massif would have to be circumnavigated first, which would easily eat up three or four hours – and that the rest of the Ulsters would be more productively employed moving directly north to shore up the weakening Northumberland defenses near Route 11. The process had already begun a few hours earlier when both A and D companies had occupied Hill 398 behind the Fusiliers. Not surprisingly, Brodie could not give Crahay any estimate as to when the tanks would arrive.[14]

With so many threats to deal with, Tom Brodie decided to report his situation to his immediate superior, Robert H. "Shorty" Soule, and ask for help. The commander of 3rd Division already had plenty to think about, the Chinese having struck heavily against the 65th U.S. Infantry Regiment and attached 10th (Philippine) Battalion Combat Team to the northeast of 29th Brigade covering the MSR. At this stage quite optimistic that the enemy – whose numbers and intent he seriously underestimated[15] – could be contained, Soule assured Brodie over the radio at around 7:30 AM Monday that the battalion would get air support and helicopter evacuation for the wounded, and committed two platoons of Sherman tanks and a rifle company to helping extricate the Belgians, and part of his divisional reserve – the first battalion of the 7th U.S. Regimental Combat Team (1/7th RCT) – to shoring up the Northumberlands.[16]

This was welcome news, but these reinforcements would take time to arrive and the future of the Glosters was still unresolved. Knowing that the Northumberlands would have to move back shortly and informed by Soule that the brigade left flank would not be exposed if he did so, Brodie, immediately after speaking to the divisional commander, contacted the Gloster command post and told Carne that it was now safe to withdraw A and D companies if necessary and consolidate the Glosters in the area of Solma-ri.[17]

Safety, though, was a relative thing. Pulling back A and D companies might no longer adversely affect the units on either side of the Glosters, but a withdrawal while in close contact with the enemy could be potentially disastrous. To retreat would mean discarding the limited cover of slit trenches and going down from hills 148 and 182 into the intervening valley with the enemy most likely in hot pursuit and now able to occupy the heights and set up machine-guns to sweep the low ground. Within the hour, however, Carne would have little choice but to order the withdrawal of both forward companies.

He had hoped that air strikes and artillery fire would allow the two companies to hold on for a time, but the USAF was occupied elsewhere along the front, while the gun batteries of 45 Field Regiment – though their commander, Lieutenant-Colonel Maris Young, desperately wanted to help the Glosters – could not concentrate exclusively on supporting them given the needs of the other battalions. Farrar-Hockley had also contacted the commander of C Squadron, 8th Hussars, to ask if a tank troop could not try and support the Glosters by driving northwest round Kamak-san. Captain Peter Ormrod, temporarily in command of C Squadron, "did not like this idea at all" since the tanks involved would have to advance several miles without infantry support into enemy-held territory in order to get to the forward Gloster companies. When he deployed the squadron reconnaissance troop of four vehicles to scout out a possible path, "they came under severe fire, and I then had to do quite a bit of fighting to get them out, to get them back." There was a deep ravine between the river and the massif ideal for an ambush, and Ormrod concluded that a northwesterly armored thrust would stand no chance of success.[18]

Meanwhile pressure from the Chinese on the two forward Gloster companies was unrelenting. Monday, 23 April was developing into a sunny and warm spring day, but not one that anyone in A or D companies could appreciate much.

On Hill 182 the perimeter held by D Company came under relentless assault. "And still the attacks came on," Second-Lieutenant Denys Whatmore, in charge of 11 Platoon, remembered. "We all fired our weapons – there were plenty of targets – until they were hot and uncomfortable to handle." Then his Sten ("that weapon had an infamous fault, in that occasionally it managed to feed two rounds into chamber at once, causing an explosion which left jammed in the barrel the split brass casing of the first round") stopped working and he seized a rifle. Phone lines were cut and radio contacts between company and platoon command posts were intermittent at best, which forced the acting company commander, Captain Mike Harvey, to sprint out to try and discover what was going on in person. "I ran down the ridge to 11 Platoon's HQ Foxhole," Harvey recalled, "to see an unruffled Denys Whatmore knocking down Chinese like snap targets on a range. I noticed that the sustained fire of the last hour had heated his rifle so that the packing grease seeped out of its woodwork."[19]

It soon became apparent, though, that 11 Platoon, which bore the brunt of the ongoing enemy attacks, was not only sustaining and inflicting casualties but also rapidly running out of ammunition. Having used up all his rifle and pistol rounds, Whatmore was reduced to firing a flare gun at the enemy while husbanding his single remaining grenade.

> I now had to decide what to do. 11 Platoon had been sited in that position to prevent the enemy capturing it and I was reluctant to leave. But to stay without ammunition was impossible; we had fought to pretty well the last round – to fight to the last man seemed pointless. The field telephone line had been cut long since so whatever decision had to be taken, it had to be mine and it had to be quick. I made the decision; we would go. I yelled at the top of my voice to the Sections, ordering them to retire as soon as they saw my last 80 [smoke] grenade burst. Then I threw the grenade to screen us from the nearest enemy, yelled "Go" and joined the rush towards 12 Platoon's position.

Thankfully, the Chinese did not immediately give chase, and the remnants of 11 Platoon, a mere thirteen men in all, were able to reach 12 Platoon, which had been giving covering fire. The retreat of 11 Platoon, however, made the position of 12 Platoon more precarious, and Harvey decided to withdraw what remained of all three of his platoons into a tighter perimeter on the slopes of Hill 182.[20]

Dangerous as the position of D Company was becoming, of the two forward Gloster companies it was A Company that was in greatest difficulty. Pat Angier had tried to reassure Tony Farrar-Hockley that the order from Carne to hold was not a death sentence for A Company – "Don't worry about us," he had said over the radio, "we'll be all right"[21] – but within fifteen minutes he had been killed. So too by that point had the other company officers, bar one wounded platoon commander. Only about half the men of the company remained, they were short of ammunition, and a number were suffering from battle exhaustion. “They get tearful and they get afraid of bangs or anything,” as RAMC Corporal Cyril Papworth, who was with the company at the time, later explained. “They’ve had enough and they can’t take any more. They’ve reached the limit.”[22]

With both his forward companies, as he later put it, “hard and closely pressed,” and with no outside help forthcoming, Carne decided sometime shortly after eight in the morning to cut his losses while he still could.[23] Orders were issued for D Company to give supporting fire from Hill 182 as the fifty-seven remaining men of A Company withdrew off Hill 148 and then follow A Company down the valley floor and regroup slightly north of the village of Solma-ri where battalion headquarters had once been located. Luckily for what remained of A Company, the Chinese seemed more interested in switching their full attention to D Company on the hill across the valley than in immediate pursuit. The wounded Second-Lieutenant Terry Waters, with a lot of help from the veteran CSM, Harry Gallagher (“he in a sense took control,” according to Private Sam Mercer), brought A Company off Hill 148 and down the valley on foot, the wounded riding on the single available Oxford carrier. Despite sporadic enemy mortar and machine-gun fire, no one was injured. Then it was the turn of D Company, which had lost men supporting A Company but which was not attacked at all after it moved off Hill 182 at about 8:30 AM. “The Chinese no longer seemed to be pressing us and when the time came to leave the company position,” Denys Whatmore recalled, “I was not aware of any pursuit or even of hostile fire directed against us.” Thanks to rounds from the heavy mortars of C Troop, 170 Battery commanded by Captain Frank Wisbey, and a limited prearranged barrage from all three gun batteries of 45 Field Regiment directed at their former positions, what remained of both A and D companies made it safely back to the old battalion HQ position. The Chinese, for now, did not pursue.[24]

As the survivors of A and D companies were served a well-earned meal by Corporal I. M. Watkins of the Catering Corps – the first since the battle began and, as it happened, the last until it was over – Colonel Carne redeployed B Company to Hill 314. C Company was already established on high ground ahead of the battalion command post just under two thousand yards to the west of Hill 314, and after their meal the men of A and D companies were sent up to join Support Company on Hill 235, what would soon be called Gloster Hill. The Korean porters showed their worth in carrying huge loads up the slopes, but as the soldiers discovered, the ground on Gloster Hill was hard and stony, making entrenching extremely difficult. The fact that both A and D companies had been forced to leave tools behind when they retreated only made the task of digging slit trenches much harder, and the resulting foxholes tended to be shallow and only partially protected by impromptu low ramparts made up of loose stones.[25]

The extent of overnight enemy infiltration between forward units of the brigade was becoming disconcertingly apparent. Though more than a mile behind the Northumberland positions, the gun crews of 45 Field Regiment suddenly found themselves under fire from dozens of Chinese who had appeared on an adjacent hill. Two troops of field engineers from 55 Field Squadron were pressed into service as infantrymen to drive the enemy off with supporting fire from the Bofors guns of A Troop, 11 Light Anti-Aircraft Battery. This counterattack was partly successful, but the appearance of Chinese behind the lines persuaded Maris Young that it was necessary to pull back his 25-pounders before they could be surrounded and overrun. In the afternoon the batteries, still under fire and sustaining casualties, leapfrogged one another southward in pairs in order to provide ongoing fire support, but the withdrawal seriously diminished the extent to which barrages could be provided anywhere along the brigade front.[26]

Meanwhile the enemy, using the high ground, was engaged in bypassing the main Gloster positions and moving down to cut off the battalion's line of retreat. One of the first signs that the Chinese were infiltrating behind the Glosters and down the Route 57 valley came when the anti-tank platoon of the Glosters, covering the northern entrance to the pass, started to come under sporadic sniper fire. This was silenced with a couple of 17-pounder rounds,[27] but shortly thereafter it became alarmingly evident that Forward Echelon, the battalion supply center more than five miles to the rear, had been overrun by the enemy.

The second-in-command, Major Digby Grist, was being driven back south in his jeep toward F Echelon in the wake of a visit to Carne that morning. "George [Bainbridge, the 2 i/c's driver/batman] and I were lost in our private thoughts as we traveled back down the track," Grist later wrote. Suddenly:

> "Christ!" muttered George. A machine gun had opened fire. We were on the last run down to the ford over the stream in front of F Echelon. The bullets were kicking up the gravel about our wheels. I felt a lurch and we ran unevenly. They had holed a tire.
>
> The fire was coming from our old position. The enemy must have captured it. I knew the weapon pit from which they were firing. I had sited it myself. I knew it was designed to catch anyone who tried to cross the ford. That's where we would cop it!
>
> "Keep driving whatever happens," I said fatuously.
>
> George grunted and bullets shattered the windscreen. I felt a sharp pain in my wrist. Now we were at the ford.
>
> I could see the machine gunner outlined against the sky thirty yards away. Above him stood another Chinese. That man saved our lives. Just as we entered the ford and were at our most vulnerable he struck the gunner on the head. Angry that we had not already been stopped, I suppose. The bullets passed harmlessly over our heads.
>
> We were through the ford and under the temporary cover of a bluff of land but we still had a long way to go and, miraculously, the jeep was still running on its shot-away tires.
>
> There was nothing I could do but watch and pray. To my right was an ambulance jeep which had crashed – a body still hung head-down over the side. To my left I saw officers and men whom I had lately commanded standing as prisoners. (Two years later when he was released from captivity, [Second-Lieutenant] Tony Preston told me he had the illusion that he was watching Toad of Toad Hall drive past.) And still they fired and still they missed anything vital. But the odds were lengthening in our favour, the range was increasing with every second that George could keep the vehicle on the move.
>
> The overtaxed wheels grated over a particularly vicious rock and we were flung in the air. I looked back to see my sleeping bag – an unusual thing with arms – flying through the air. Did I imagine a Chinese cheer? They had scored a hit at last. Face saved! The firing stopped and we rattled into Brigade headquarters.

The brigade commander thus learned very quickly that the Chinese had in effect surrounded the Glosters. Yet by this point, as Grist could perceive, "Brigadier Brodie had more troubles on his plate" to deal with.[28]

The Northumberlands remained under heavy pressure as the morning progressed. Y Company, in the forwardmost position, was more or less cut off inside a bend in the Imjin River and under attack. In accord with a plan developed by the battalion commander, Lieutenant-Colonel Kingsley Foster, by noon Major Robert Leith-Macgregor had made contact with a troop of tanks from the 8th Hussars sent forward to cover a fighting withdrawal by Y Company, initially with appalling results. "Unfortunately there was a misunderstanding, and I think what happened was that they [the tank commanders] thought that the people sitting on the top of the hill were Chinese and the people round the bottom of the hill were ourselves," Second-Lieutenant Sam Phillips in command of 9 Platoon remembered, "and they opened fire, and during the period of the evacuation, the other two platoon commanders and myself were hit." Lieutenant Tony Macnamara and Second-Lieutenant Ben Smith were both killed by exploding 20-lb. shells while Phillips received two Besa machine-gun bullets in one of his legs as he came down the hill; he was generously philosophical about this, later commenting, "these things happen." Once the identity of the Northumberlands had been confirmed, the withdrawal went comparatively smoothly, the survivors arriving at the battalion command post by 2 PM.[29] Morale, however, was still shaky, the company commander subsequently accusing some of his men of cowardice to their faces.[30]

An afternoon counterattack designed to retake the ground lost by Z Company on Hill 257 had a less satisfactory outcome. As the battalion war diarist recorded:

> 1245 hrs. 'Z' Coy counter attack begins on Hill 257. Tanks supporting by firing on right-hand side of ridge.
> 1300 hrs. 'Z' Coy report nearly at top of hill.
> 1301 hrs. 'Z' Coy report attacking force being in trouble from enemy grenades.
> 1310 hrs. 'Z' Coy report pl withdrawn having been thrown back by enemy on hill.
> 1320 hrs. 'Z' Coy ordered to withdraw to CP.

The high ground overlooking the Imjin bridges on the south bank of the river therefore remained in enemy hands.[31]

Presumably because both the telephone and radio links between battalion and brigade headquarters were down and he wanted to see the situation for himself, Tom Brodie arrived at the Northumberland command post in a Daimler Dingo scout car. His orders were to withdraw all four Fusilier companies southward, with Y and W companies to occupy features to the right of Route 11 in line with the Ulsters on Hill 398, and

X and Z companies to protect a relocated battalion command post down toward the valley floor. The process was not entirely without incident, as Chinese infiltrators continued to snipe. As the battalion command post was abandoned under fire, Brodie standing up in his scout car almost became a target. "He was wearing – I'll always remember it – one of those sheepskin coats that officers wear; very, very noticeable because it was a light color," recounted Sergeant David Sharp of the intelligence section. Advised by Sharp that the Chinese were close behind and that a booby trap left in the evacuated command post was about to blow up, "the brigadier told me to get the hell out of it," and drove off.[32]

Shortly after three in the afternoon the Fusilier companies and headquarters had all moved to their new locations. The CO, Kingsley Foster, was feeling the pressure after more than twenty-four hours without sleep trying to solve one crisis after another. "I noticed that he was not his usual cheerful self," Major Tony Younger, the senior Royal Engineers officer and a friend, wrote of visiting the newly established battalion HQ. "As I prepared to leave," Younger explained, "he asked me to follow him. He led me along the ridge and then said he must tell me something that he did not want his officers or men to hear. 'Tony,' he said, 'I have had a premonition that I am going to die on this hill. I feel that I must tell somebody, but not any of my own people.' He looked utterly depressed and miserable." Younger, though he himself had earlier experienced a strong sense that he would be killed in Korea, tried to dispel such sentiments by arguing that nobody could foretell the future. Foster though, remained "dejected" as Younger took his leave. Officers as well as men were feeling the strain of a fighting retreat.[33]

Whatever pressures the battalion commanders may have felt, those of the brigade commander were necessarily greater. Brodie had to concern himself with the fate of his entire command, and though there is some evidence to suggest that it took the brigadier longer than necessary to recognize the scale of enemy actions to the west of Kamak-san,[34] once he did, Brodie took what steps he could to help the Glosters. Since the commander of 3rd Division had promised air support, the brigadier – who knew a thing or two about air supply to friendly units behind enemy lines from his time leading a Chindit column in Burma in World War II – apparently arranged for a mass airdrop of supplies from USAF

C-119 Flying Boxcars based in Japan that was due to take place Tuesday morning.[35] Meanwhile, though, there was plenty to worry about on the east side of Kamak-san.

Several hours earlier I Corps had finally issued the order for a general withdrawal to Line Kansas based on instructions from Eighth Army commander James A. Van Fleet. On the right of 29th Brigade the 65th U.S. Infantry Regiment, well covered by air attacks on the Chinese, retreated southward without incident starting at 1:30 PM, and by 3:00 PM most of its units were across the Hantan tributary of the Imjin. The danger of the Chinese swinging southeastward across the Imjin to cut them off therefore evaporated, and with it the need to keep the Belgians in the hinge position in the curve of the Imjin where it met the Hantan. The "Foxhound" plan, however, was impossible to implement with the Chinese still controlling the two bridges over which the Belgians were supposed to retire without difficulty.[36]

Though many Chinese units were moving past the Belgians rather than trying to overrun them at this point, the Belgians had been cut off for more than ten hours and were still being attacked. If something was not done soon then attrition and shortages of ammunition would inevitably lead to the destruction of the three weakened rifle companies. With so many problems developing south of the Imjin, the response of Brigadier Brodie to the initial morning request by Colonel Crahay for help had consisted of a commitment to do something when it became possible at some later, indeterminate, point in time. Frustrated by the lack of action to save his comrades and desperate to help, the Belgian liaison officer at 29th Brigade HQ, Major Moreau de Melen, eventually decided to go over the head of the brigadier and appeal directly to 3rd Division HQ. General Soule agreed to detach four Sherman tanks from the 7th RCT north of the Hantan tributary and allow Major de Melen to conduct them westward to try to retake control of the bridges. The appearance of these tanks – armed not only with a 76-mm high-velocity gun but also coaxial and hull-mounted .30 caliber machine-guns and a swivel-mounted .50 caliber heavy machine-gun on the turret – drove the surprised enemy from the north bank of the Imjin in the vicinity of the two bridges, but the Chinese maintained control of the heights on the south bank and the bridge egress points.[37]

How to extract the Belgians had been the focus of a telephone conversation between the commanders of 3rd Division and 29th Brigade in the late morning. More aware of the magnitude of enemy success than General Soule, Brigadier Brodie was of the opinion that the best chance of survival for the Belgians was for them to abandon their vehicles and move on foot across country to try to link up with the U.S. forces – an infantry battalion from the 65th Infantry Regiment, a reconnaissance company, and the 64th Tank Battalion – to the east of the Imjin as it turned northward. The divisional commander, though, believed a counter-thrust could regain control of the bridgehead area long enough to open a southward route for both the Belgians and their vehicles. Subsequently, the divisional chief of staff, Colonel O. P. Newman, was dispatched in the afternoon to relay instructions to the commander of the 1/7th RCT, then part of the U.S. divisional reserve, to gather his forces. "Fred," Newman bluntly told Colonel F. C. Weyand, "we've got to get the Belgians out and you'll have to do it." The operations officer, Captain William F. Long, Jr., however, argued that a single battalion would not be able to establish and maintain a corridor given the nature of the terrain: "I would suggest that they come out across the Imjin River and work east to the 65th Infantry, covered by our attack." Brodie agreed – "It might work," he commented when pressed by Newman, going on to assert more robustly that "it might work very well" – and a new plan developed in which the 1/7th would move westward with support from fifteen tanks of the 8th Hussars to attack, among other features, Hill 257, originally held by Z Company, primarily to divert enemy attention away from the Belgians. An American liaison officer lifted by helicopter into the Belgian perimeter close to 6 PM informed Colonel Crahay that he should immediately prepare to break out.[38]

Even before they moved north from their start lines the assault companies of the 1/7th found themselves coming under enemy fire. Rather ad hoc planning and lack of accurate intelligence as to exactly where the Chinese were and in what strength quickly led to disorientation – the officer leading C Squadron was surprised to be asked by officers of the 1st battalion "in which direction the enemy were"[39] – and to a very unfortunate case of friendly fire. As a Centurion tank commander who witnessed the event wrote:

> Late in the afternoon, the NFs [Northumberland Fusiliers] were holding a hill [presumably part of 257 in the aftermath of the Fusiliers' failed counterattack] which overlooked a valley. The Chinese were trying to dislodge them, but without success. Then a column of American jeeps turned up from behind me. The Officer in charge of this column pulled up, blew a whistle, which caused the occupants of the jeeps to stop, dismount with browning machine guns on tripods and I was wondering what the hell was going on. Then some 12 machine guns opened up on the NFs on the hill. The NFs, thinking the Chinese had got behind them started down the hill. The Yanks, seeing men coming down the hill, took them for Chinese and carried on firing. I smartly traversed my gun on the column of Yanks and shouted down to the Officer in charge. "Get the hell out of here or I'll blast you out." My gun was trained on the column. The Officer blew his whistle. The firing ceased, they remounted their jeeps and swung round and left.[40]

The taking of lesser features had already exacted a toll in dead and wounded Americans, and from the perspective of British observers on Hill 398 to the south it looked as if the main assault by the 1/7th on Hill 257 did not succeed in wresting control from the enemy. These efforts, however, did keep the Chinese occupied while the Belgians made their move.[41]

The wounded having been evacuated by helicopter, a column of the Belgian battalion's vehicles was assembled under the command of Major Georges Vivario with orders to move at speed across the western bridge under covering fire from the four U.S. Sherman tanks. Under cover of a prearranged USAF air strike, the Belgian infantry companies would then withdraw east on foot over a ford near battalion HQ. It was the withdrawal of the vehicles that posed the greatest risk, as a single truck, ambulance, or jeep immobilized on the bridge would strand the remaining vehicles on the north bank of the Imjin. The enemy, however, responded quite weakly when the column drove over the bridge, those on board firing their weapons with wild abandon while the tanks tried to draw enemy fire. Riding in one of the trucks, the battalion doctor compared the experience to a rodeo. "The entire convoy charged along at top speed on this bridge," he later recounted, and "from each vehicle came a heavy fire from all who could fire towards the facing hill." Though four vehicles were hit and had to be abandoned, none was immobilized on the bridge, and casualties were minimal. "There was a God for the Belgians," the battalion MO explained; "we passed [over the bridge] without suffering a death." The infantry withdrawal was also successful, thick smoke from brush fires started by napalm bombs dropped in the preplanned air strike covering Crahay and his men as they moved eastward. Those on foot were heavily laden and had to negotiate the steep banks of the Imjin under sporadic enemy fire, all of which made the operation, in the words of one sergeant, "extremely risky." Chinese mortar rounds landing on the east side of the ford, however, happily fell wide of the mark. Moving eastward north of the Hantan, the Belgians successfully linked up with other elements of the U.S. 7th Infantry.[42]

The Belgian battalion was safe; and though the Chinese 187th and 189th divisions were firmly established on the hills immediately south of the Imjin, the regrouped Fusiliers on the heights to the left and the Ulsters a thousand yards to the right on Hill 398 a few miles below the river – though having come under periodic attack – were effectively blocking any direct enemy advance down Route 11.[43] As night fell, Brodie could afford to turn his attention once again to the surrounded Glosters. In the afternoon Soule had transferred control of the 10th (Philippine) BCT, consisting of three rifle companies armed with U.S. weapons, a battery of self-propelled artillery, and a reconnaissance company of Chaffee light tanks and armored cars, to Brodie as a reserve force now that all of 29th Brigade was fully engaged. Already having seen a lot of action thus far in the battle elsewhere on the 3rd Division front, 10th BCT had not arrived behind brigade headquarters until the late afternoon, and Brodie made a deliberate decision not to send it immediately forward to try to reinforce or relieve the Glosters. Though worried by the fact that the Glosters were isolated and an awful lot of Chinese had been seen moving on the undefended Kamak-san feature (Hill 675), the brigadier was probably right in thinking that the Filipino troops would be comprehensively ambushed if he sent them at night forward up the narrow Route 57 track that wound through a gorge toward Solma-ri.[44]

Darkness, however, did not discourage the Chinese from continuing their operations. Less exposed to accurate artillery fire and bombing, enemy troops continued to infiltrate and launch massed assaults on various companies across the brigade front.

The riflemen of A Company of the Ulsters on Hill 398, though their slit trenches were shallow due to the difficulty of digging into the stony soil a few hours earlier, had managed to build up some stone barriers in front and lay some wire, and twice in the early hours of Tuesday the 24th successfully fired everything they had at advancing Chinese (identified by booby-traps going off and subsequently located by flares sent up by the 2-inch mortars), including super bazookas and machine-guns; "our Bren gunners fired incessantly," Lieutenant Gordon Potts of 1 Platoon remembered.[45]

A thousand yards or so to the southwest on the other side of Route 11 the Northumberlands were in greater difficulty. Between 3 and 4 AM, Y Company was heavily attacked. All the platoon commanders had been wounded the previous day, and now the company second-in-command was added to the casualty list. Despite fire support from 4.2-inch mortars, the entire company was eventually forced to withdraw from its hill position. W Company was sent forward to try to restore the situation, but a patrol reported shortly after five in the morning that the Chinese were in full control of the hill W Company was supposed to occupy. W Company nevertheless protected the battalion left flank from further penetration during the hours of darkness.[46]

The Glosters had an even rougher night. Starting at around midnight successive attacks with machine-gun and mortar support were launched against B Company on Hill 314. "The next few hours were a hell of noise, screams, shouted orders, crackling machine gun bullets," Private Lofty Large later wrote, "then scrambling, panting [Chinese] men coming up the slope and spraying us with their sub-machine guns and falling in doll like heaps as we fired and fired and fired again." Private Nick Carter, who was subsequently wounded, remembered this fight in similar terms. "I was firing that Bren gun non-stop, for about an hour," he recalled. "They came at us in waves, and we were managing to hold 'em off." The Forward Observation Officer, Captain A. M. L. Newcome, called down fire from 45 Field Regiment to within fifty yards of the company perimeter. The enemy thus had no luck in breaking in to B Company positions, though at dawn there were only fifteen men left alive and unwounded. But a strong series of attacks against C Company (located on lower ground and covering the approaches to battalion headquarters) that began at about 3:30 AM met with greater success.[47]

Approaching to within two hundred yards of C Company before being spotted, the Chinese achieved a measure of surprise. "There's bloody hundreds of 'em!" David Green of 9 Platoon heard a man in 8 Platoon shout. A sharp firefight ensued, but with the Chinese in amongst the positions, first 8 Platoon and then 9 Platoon began to spontaneously retreat. "I was quite alone in my dugout," Green wrote, "seeing the blokes in the next one climbing out was all I needed to make me follow suit." The company commander, Major Paul Mitchell, tried to rally the men and get them into a kneeling firing line, but without much success. "Neither of us were too keen to obey that order to kneel," Green remembered of his and a mate's reactions. "So we didn't!"[48]

The men of Company HQ and 7 Platoon in C Company held their ground, but the enemy had infiltrated between B and C companies and the positions of the latter – and by extension battalion headquarters and the heavy mortars located in the valley to the rear – were becoming increasingly precarious. Mitchell decided to telephone battalion HQ to report his situation and ask for orders. "I'm afraid they've overrun my top position," he told the adjutant, "and they're reinforcing hard. They're simply pouring chaps in above us. Let me know what the Colonel wants me to do, will you?" Carne's response was immediate and unequivocal. "Pack the Headquarters up," he said to Farrar-Hockley, "and get everyone out of the valley up [on Hill 235] between D Company and the Anti-Tank Platoon position. I'm going to withdraw C Company in ten minutes; and I shall move B over to join us after first light." The vehicles and supplies in the valley had to be abandoned, men carrying what they could in the way of medicine, bandages, and ammunition to the top of Gloster Hill, where Support Company as well as A and D companies were already located. "It was a stiff climb," Padre Sam Davies wrote, "and tracer bullets began to whip across [from the abandoned C Company positions], their red witch-balls floating eerily." Adding to the troubles of the battalion commander was a breakdown in the rear-link radio connection with brigade headquarters. The signals problem was, fortunately, only temporary. An enemy noose, though, was clearly tightening around the Glosters. Carne had to think about how to support the now isolated B Company while Brodie and his superiors debated how to extract the entire battalion. Decisions made and actions taken in the upcoming hours of daylight on 24 April would be crucial in determining their collective fate.[49]

This is not the way to run a war, it is most ungentlemanly!

MAJOR, 45FR, re. Chinese infiltration tactics[1]

You couldn't sleep, there was so much noise going on, and you were on the move, and you were concerned with whether or not positions had to be adjusted, so very few people slept.

MAJOR PATRICK "SAM" WELLER,
OC Support Company, 1GLOS[2]

THREE

Imjin: The Third Day

AS DAWN CREPT IN FROM THE EAST ON TUESDAY MORNING, the most pressing problem along the brigade front was unquestionably the precarious position of the Glosters. Forced to abandon successive company hill positions, cut off for more than fifteen hours, losing comrades one after another, and running low on supplies, the surviving Glosters could not hold out forever against Chinese attacks.

The commanding officer, Lieutenant-Colonel J. P. Carne, had already decided that his battered and dwindling battalion would have to concentrate on a single feature, so as soon as there was enough daylight he ordered B Company to cross the valley and join the other companies on Hill 235. The order came none too soon, since the isolated B Company was almost at the end of its rope.

The men on Hill 314 under Major Denis Harding had endured more than half-a-dozen assaults by heavily armed Chinese. "Lofty" Large of 6 Platoon recalled how at one point amidst bursting mortar shells he heard an officer cry, "Stand fast the Glosters – remember the Back Badge!" a reference to the fore-and-aft cap badges of the Glosters commemorating their back-to-back action at the Battle of the Nile in 1801. Immediately an anonymous squaddie replied, "Fuck the Back Badge – I want out!" a remark much appreciated by others at the sharp end. "I was amazed to find myself laughing," Large related, "and heard the laughter of others through the clatter and roar of the battle." The pressure, however, was unrelenting. Large also remembered how the other man in his slit trench reacted some time later as they repelled yet another assault, when he, Large, was hit and blood sprayed everywhere:

> The other man looked around, relief on his blood-specked face, as he realized we had survived another rush. Then he saw the blood and said, "I'm hit." [*sic*] He stared in disbelief for a few seconds, then crawled into a poncho for a few seconds, and just shook. A few minutes later [Second-]Lieutenant [Arthur] Peal came over with more ammo, saw I was hit and asked where the other chap was. I looked at the poncho. How he knew I'll never know in that place of dead and half dead. He called the man's name, pulled back the bolt of his Sten gun, and said, "You have three seconds to get out of there – *one!*" The man came out like a startled rabbit, stared at Mr Peal, then at me for a few seconds. Mr Peal said, "You OK now?" The man nodded and resumed his firing position, then carried on as normal as if nothing had happened . . .

The man was, his trench companion added, "a damn good soldier too." Nevertheless time was running out for those on Hill 314.[3]

The breaking point occurred in the sector occupied by 4 Platoon. As the B Company commander, Major Denis Harding, later reported:

> By now the situation was very serious. Ammunition was virtually expended and many wounded were lying in the company area with little or no cover to protect them. After withdrawing for reorganization, a short pause ensued and the seventh and final [Chinese] attack was launched at 08.10 hours. Hordes of Chinese rushed up to the summit of the hill and charged through 4 Platoon's area. Sheer weight of numbers forced the platoon over the rear face of the hill . . .

"I lost six men and nearly everyone was wounded" noted the platoon commander, Lieutenant Geoffrey Costello, who did not escape injury either: "I was hit twice in the leg and once in the head."[4]

It was pretty much a case of every man for himself as the company disintegrated. Many of the enemy troops in the valley, intent on moving south toward the main front, simply ignored the small parties of Glosters making their way toward what would become known as Gloster Hill: "They weren't taking any notice of us at all," remembered Nick Carter. There were, however, also Chinese soldiers whose job it was to mop up enemy stragglers, and despite covering fire from Gloster Hill some men were either killed or captured before they could find a clear route, including Peal. Only some fifteen to twenty men, including Major Harding, were able to reach Hill 235.[5]

Even before Hill 314 was lost, Carne was contemplating the possibility of leading an attempt to strike southward with what remained of his fighting strength. Indeed he had broached the subject the previous day with the D Company commander. "Mike, we will probably soon have to break-out down the Solma-ri road south," the CO had explained, "in which case D Company [C Company having been considered not strong enough] will lead it." Unfortunately, the Eighth Army commander, Lieutenant General James A. Van Fleet, had made it clear to his subordinates that he was not keen to allow withdrawals in case orderly retreat turned into panicked flight, as had been the case when the Chinese first intervened in Korea. Thus when Carne put the case for a breakout to Brigade HQ by radio at 7 AM he was informed that Major General Robert H. "Shorty" Soule, commanding 3rd Division (to which 29th Brigade was currently attached), had vetoed the idea. In light of the recovery plan described below this decision was reversed two hours later, but by nine in the morning Carne no longer felt he should try to force his way south, especially as it would mean abandoning the growing number of non-walking wounded.[6]

In the meantime, fighting on the slopes of Hill 235 continued. Carne himself, equipped with a rifle and grenades, personally led two military policemen and a driver in defeating a small party of Chinese who had infiltrated the position. "What was that all about, sir?" the adjutant asked. "Oh, just shooing away some Chinese," the CO calmly replied as he relit his pipe. The *sang-froid* with which Carne presided over his dwindling command on Gloster Hill won a lot of admiration from those around him. Corporal Ronald Norley of 11 Platoon, D Company remembered that "he was an inspiration to everyone."[7]

For the Glosters to hold out even for a few more hours, however, was going to be well-nigh impossible unless something could be done about the supply situation. Radio batteries were running down, there were serious shortages of ammunition, and most of the men were hungry as well as thirsty. Unfortunately the Flying Boxcar airdrop previously arranged, of a kind that the next day would help 2PPCLI at Kapyong, had to be aborted. An American journalist produced an account of what happened, presumably after interviewing some of the participants:

> At dawn on the twenty-fourth, three Flying Boxcars were poised high over the Glosters' positions, waiting for the morning mist to lift so they could descend close enough to drop their cargo accurately. But when the mist rose, the pilots found the Glosters, and not a few Chinese, fighting literally inside a curtain of falling shells that the brigade's gunners and mortarmen were throwing around them. The planes couldn't dip down unless the shelling was halted, and the decision was up to the Glosters. The Glosters waved the hovering [*sic*] Boxcars away.[8]

As Sergeant Frank Cottam of A Company put it, when the transport planes "came over, we were too busy to take delivery of anything except Chinese," so the C-119s "had to go away again."[9]

A plan was therefore hatched to send down a party of men from Support Company, Battalion HQ, and the Korean porter company to raid the stores left behind on the valley floor when Carne had shifted his headquarters to the top of Gloster Hill the previous day. The Chinese had been unable to carry off much themselves since the abandoned position was covered by machine-guns set up on Hill 235, and under cover of a smoke screen laid down by mortars it was hoped that parties led by the aptly named Sergeant-Major F. G. "Muscles" Strong from the Army Physical Training Corps, Major Guy Ward of the Royal Artillery, and the Glosters' own Regimental Sergeant Major, Jack Hobbs, would be able to retrieve vitally needed material. The audacious plan worked, machine-gun fire and mortar bombs warding off the Chinese who tried to penetrate the smoke screen. Batteries, a little food and water, and a satisfyingly large amount of ammunition were retrieved. "I marveled at the strength of our South Korean porters," the adjutant, Captain Tony Farrar-Hockley, noted admiringly. "The wooden frames upon their backs – shaped like an 'A', and so called 'A-frames' – were heaped from waist to head with wooden boxes, crates, and jerricans."[10]

The extra supplies meant that men, in addition to reloading magazines, could grab a few mouthfuls of nourishment and try to rehydrate. "The food was shared out, it was very little," recalled Corporal Ronald Norley of D Company, "a can amongst four or five of you." There was also "a drop of water, which was the main thing," he added. Others were not much luckier. "We had a bit of [tinned] cake and a drop of water and that was it," RAMC Corporal Cyril Papworth, then working with A Company, remembered. The shortage of water was such that little could be spared to replace what had been used up in the cooling water-jackets of the Vickers machine-guns, necessitating a not terribly successful attempt to use urine as an emergency substitute coolant. Nevertheless the four-hundred-odd still unwounded Glosters could now hold on again, at least for the time being.[11]

For the most part the enemy ignored them. The Glosters, however, were still willing to engage the Chinese heading southward when they could. Private Sam Mercer, also of A Company, recalled someone saying, "Oh, look over there towards the village, Choksong." A platoon or so of Chinese on bicycles had been spotted peddling down the track that led past Hill 235. Cycling single-file, these soldiers seemed to be chatting and enjoying themselves, as Private David Green of C Company put it, "as if on a Sunday outing." At a range of about 3,000 yards a pair of surviving Vickers machine-gun crews and a Bren gunner opened up on this seemingly oblivious party. "The result was almost comical," another C Company man observing the scene, Robert Holles, later explained. "The company of cyclists piled up on the roadsides in a writhing chaos of flailing limbs entwined with wheels and handle-bars." This roused cheers from the watching Glosters, according to Green, "followed by gales of laughter as the Chinks spilled over one another in a huge pile-up!"

> One man stood up for a second or two in shock and then ran like a hare across the paddy, with bullets kicking up the earth around his ankles, just to help him on his way! The pile gradually got disentangled and figures could be seen scuttling like rabbits into the sparse cover on each side of the road. Whether any of them had been hit was of no importance; it had been a fine show of defiance and welcome light relief . . .

Such defiance, though, came at a price. As soon as the Chinese survivors had withdrawn, mortar bombs began to land on Gloster Hill and long-range machine-gun fire played across the slopes.[12]

In the meantime, back at 29th Brigade HQ, thoughts had been turning to the rescue of the Glosters. The two other British infantry battalions were already fully committed to the protection of Route 11 – the Ulsters on Hill 398 would be attacked more than a dozen times that morning while the Northumberlands were forced back – and the Belgians would not be ready to go back into the line until the afternoon.[13] Brigadier Tom Brodie did, however, have available the 10th (Philippine) Battalion Combat Team, along with four U.S.-built Chaffee light tanks and ten Centurions from C Squadron, 8th Hussars (the others being fully occupied in support of the Northumberlands). Not authorized to go forward themselves but understandably anxious to help, the two senior Gloster officers then present at brigade headquarters on the morning of 24 April, Major Digby Grist (second-in-command) and Major John Watkin-Williams (commanding A Echelon), decided to draw up a plan for the use of these uncommitted forces. In consultation with the acting brigade major, "we hatched a plot to re-open the route to the Gloucesters."[14]

Having already been urged by Soule at a predawn meeting at 3rd Division HQ to send the Filipinos to link up with the Glosters,[15] Brodie gave the plotters his blessing. The plan, put into play by 8 AM, involved three rifle companies and the light tanks from 10 BCT, reinforced by about half a squadron of Centurions and rounded-up rear-area Glosters mounted on carriers, moving northwest up Route 57, joining up with the Gloster main body.[16] Carne himself had grave doubts that this operation would work in light of the distance involved and the large number of enemy troops that had passed to the south of Gloster Hill.[17] Yet though four and a half miles and a narrow gorge separated the Filipino forming-up area from the beleaguered Glosters on Hill 235, the firepower of the relief column was not insubstantial, and at first things seemed to go well. By about 11 AM the task force had set off, the Filipino infantry deployed along the hill crests on either side of the track and the vehicles advancing at a walking pace so the foot-soldiers on the ridges to either side could keep up. No resistance was at first encountered. "It was very tedious," Captain J. C. Gorman of the 8th Hussars related. "There appeared to be no enemy in the area, and we were all very bored."[18]

At 12:40 PM Major Henry Huth – who had hurried back from leave to resume command of C Squadron's tanks once the battle had started – reported a successful advance of about a mile. "Our old position at F. Echelon was reached without difficulty," Grist later wrote; "the enemy had abandoned it." The Glosters' second-in-command was happy enough to discover that six of the battalion vehicles were still roadworthy and that a lot of gear could be salvaged. The scenes of battle lost, though, were troubling to those such as Gorman who had not fully taken in the implications of what had been happening to the Glosters.

> It was a shambles. Rifles and equipment lay scattered everywhere, among burnt out carriers and smoldering trucks. Dead Englishmen lolled behind shattered steering wheels, and rows of holes in the vehicles showed the line of enemy machine-gun fire. Short Chinese [burp-gun] cartridge cases littered the area. Dead men lay in profusion, sightless eyes staring up at the sky. It was definitely depressing. The thought occurred – "That dead man, but for the grace of God, is me." There was not a single enemy body. It is nerve racking to see only your own dead, for it gives the impression of disastrous defeat. Of course, the Reds had removed their own dead, as they always did.

It was also disconcerting to see evidence that features cleared by the Filipino infantry were being quietly reoccupied by the Chinese after they had moved on.[19]

By two in the afternoon another mile had been covered, and a badly wounded Gloster who had been hiding in a dry creek bed for over twenty-four hours was discovered and retrieved. The hill features on either side of the route, however, were becoming steeper, and the Filipino infantry began to close in to the track. Near the hamlet of Kwangsuwon the first serious resistance was encountered in the form of an enemy machine-gun nest. This was silenced by tank fire, and the advance continued, the column passing into a gorge only 200 yards wide overlooked on either side by lines of hills 100 feet high. The Filipino infantry were now advancing along the valley floor, not the hills on either side. In the lead were three Chaffees, each crowded with infantry with the hatches left open for better visibility. Suddenly, as the lead element turned past a bend in the track shortly after half past three in the afternoon, the Chinese sprang their ambush. The first enemy mortar bomb went straight into the lead Chaffee through the open driver's hatch while machine-gun fire was sprayed onto the hull, killing the dozen infantrymen clinging to it. The tank caught fire, swung left, and stalled across the track.[20]

To deal with this setback the officer in overall command, Lieutenant-Colonel Dionisio Ojeda, ordered Major Henry Huth to send a tank forward to push the disabled Chaffee off the road and continue the advance with the half-troop of Centurions in the lead. This proved problematic. The fiercely burning Chaffee had lurched in such a way that it was jammed up against a rock face and could neither be pushed nor pulled out of the way; meanwhile two Centurion crews tried to rescue the surviving Filipino crew members under mortar and machine-gun fire. The column could perhaps have made its way around the disabled tank, but Huth – who had crawled forward under the bellies of the vehicles in front of his to see what was going on[21] – was dubious about putting the Centurions in the lead. The gorge was becoming too narrow for the big tanks to navigate easily and elevate their guns for supporting fire, and if one was knocked out by a mine it would entirely block the route and be too heavy for any other vehicle in the column to pull away. Just as Huth was conveying his thoughts to Ojeda by radio, the rest of the column round the bend was ambushed by two Chinese battalions. As Gorman recalled:

> There was a rattle of fire . . . then the whole of the ridge, on either side of the road, blazed with rifle and machine-gun fire at less than a hundred yards. Men dropped into the [drainage] ditches, and a dozen sprawled dead or wounded on the track. Every gun we had opened up. . . . We had only fleeting glimpses of the Chinese, but they could pick out every single man we possessed. . . . The infantry ranks in the ditches thinned out rapidly, and men fell in dozens.

Brigade HQ was contacted by radio in order to report the situation and request further instructions. Gorman spoke for Ojeda (whose accent made his speech more or less incomprehensible to British ears over the airwaves) from a scout car while Huth contacted brigade on a separate tank frequency. "I got some fool signaler at brigade," Gorman remembered. "It seems hours before an officer came on."[22]

Meanwhile, perhaps sensing that greater force would be needed to shore up the left flank of 29th Brigade, General Soule had let it be known shortly after 3 PM that a further force, made up of two infantry battalions of the 65th Infantry, the bulk of the 64th Tank Battalion, and the 10th Field Artillery Battalion, was being assembled to fight its way through to Solma-ri. "How are the Glosters doing?" he had asked the brigadier at about four, wanting to get a sense of how urgent the situation was. Brodie replied: "A bit sticky; things are pretty sticky down there." An unfortunate misunderstanding developed as a result of this response. Unfamiliar with British understatement, Soule took this to mean that the Glosters were under pressure but not in dire straits; whereas Brodie, himself not taking into account the American tendency toward adjectival overstatement, had actually meant to convey that the position of the Glosters was quite serious. The result was that a renewed relief effort was postponed until dawn the next day and the Glosters were ordered to hold fast. It would take several hours for the second relief force to concentrate, and if the Glosters could hold out, then it made sense to fight forward and back in daylight rather than darkness. This was what Soule told his worried superiors – Frank W. Milburn (I Corps), James A. Van Fleet (Eighth Army), and Matthew B. Ridgway (U.N. Forces Commander-in-Chief) – when they paid a collective visit in mid-afternoon and asked why no immediate effort to extract the Glosters was being made. "Get the

Glosters out before withdrawing," Milburn warned Soule, "even if you have to counterattack!" The divisional commander's assessment was accepted, however, and the senior brass left without further intervention.[23]

It was left to Brodie to convey the bad news to Carne by radio. By mid-afternoon the Glosters had less than 400 fighting men left, were short of key weapons such as Bren guns, and were once again facing the prospect of shortages of radio batteries and bullet clips. ("Guy, you will stay here with your chaps unless you get orders from me to the contrary," Tony Farrar-Hockley had earlier instructed Lieutenant Temple of 7 Platoon, adding: "If your ammunition runs out, hurl bloody rocks at them."[24]) In these circumstances the CO of the Glosters was gravely forthright in his response: "I understand the position quite clearly. What I must make clear to you is that my command is no longer an effective fighting force. If it is required that we shall stay here, in spite of this, we shall continue to hold. But I wish to make known the nature of my position." The brigadier knew that he was asking of lot of the Glosters to continue to hold on Hill 235. According to the adjutant, who was listening, "I could tell by his voice that he did not like committing us to such a desperate task." Brodie indeed did not, publicly admitting later on that ordering Carne to stay put "was probably one of the worst moments in my life, certainly the worst in this campaign."[25]

An order was also issued at 4:15 PM to 10 BCT to stand its ground for the time being. Brodie, though, was soon made aware through Gorman's reports that the column was not just stalled but had been ambushed (the headquarters staff officer with whom Gorman was in contact sounded "somewhat staggered" when the scale of the fighting was relayed to him). Aware as well of just how desperate the Glosters' situation was becoming as a result of his conversation with Carne, Brodie phoned Colonel O. P. Newman, chief of staff at 3rd Division HQ, at about half past five, asking, in Newman's words, "for permission to withdraw the Philippine Battalion, which had made an attempt to reach the Gloster Position and to order the withdrawal of the Gloucester Battalion that night." General Soule quickly came in on the conversation. "I heard him direct Brig. Brodie to leave the Philippine and Gloucester Battalions in their present positions," the chief of staff recalled. "He stated that he was certain that the Gloucesters would suffer severe losses if they attempted to break out at night; that he was ordering an attack by two battalions of the 65th Infantry to relieve the pressure on the Gloucesters."[26]

Soule, however, said nothing about the half-troop of 8th Hussars Centurions; and while Brodie did not ignore the order to have the Glosters stand fast during the night, either by accident or by design the orders reaching Huth and Gorman from Brigade HQ five minutes later seemed to indicate that the Filipino troops as well as the Centurions were to withdraw. Only at 6:45 PM was 3rd Division informed that "Relief force of 10th BCT and T[an]ks have been ordered back because leading T[an]k became immobilized in a ravine blocking road completely about 2000 yds short of GLOS positions – further progress of 10th BCT was considered by Brigadier to be unwise. BCT being returned to [map reference] 2097, T[an]ks go back to Brig."[27] It was only after moving more than a mile in reverse gear down the defile that the tanks were able to find enough space to turn around.[28]

A second attempt to establish an overland route to the Glosters would have to wait until the next day, but at Brigade HQ thoughts had turned to making contact by air. A planned helicopter evacuation of the wounded from Hill 235 had to be abandoned because any landing zone would be in range of enemy fire (seeing the machine flying low over his hole before heading away, Private David Green "imagined myself clinging to its undercarriage and heading for freedom"[29]), but that still left open the possibility of airdrops. Thanks to the efforts of the second-in-command, Digby Grist, marooned at Brigade HQ, a second airlift involving Flying Boxcar transport aircraft stationed in Japan was organized for the following morning. But the Glosters might not last the night – "Need Batteries and am[munitio]n URGENTLY – also want food and water" read the record of a radio message received at 4:45 PM.[30] So, urged on by Major Watkin-Williams, two captains in the Royal Engineers asked for volunteers from headquarters to help drop supplies from L5 light spotter aircraft onto the Gloster positions. The planes would have to fly slowly in order to identify the target and at minimum height for the same reason and also because there were no airdrop parachutes available. A certain amount of bravery was thus required, but there was no shortage of volunteers. "I've never flown in an aircraft, let alone drop anything out of one," one soldier remarked, "but I'll have a go. At least I'll feel that I'm doing something." Five attempts were made to drop supplies from about thirty feet into the Gloster perimeter using two light planes, but because of the steepness of the terrain and lack of experience, all but one drop failed to reach the intended target. "Towards sunset, planes flew low over the ridge and attempted an air drop," Padre Sam Davies wrote. "It was disheartening to see the bundles missing our positions and falling inaccessibly on the lower slopes." The fact that most of the brightly colored aircraft recognition panels had apparently been left behind during the retreat up Hill 235 probably did not help. The single successful drop was due to the actions of a sapper who had once been an airdrop specialist with the RASC. Two boxes of mortar rounds were retrieved along with some small-arms ammunition and medical supplies.[31]

Luckily for the hard-pressed Glosters, the Chinese concentrated their attentions elsewhere during the afternoon and early evening of 24 April, and Colonel Carne was able to shrink his perimeter to accord with his diminished strength without serious molestation. As the sun set in a reddish glow and dusk arrived, men moved out of their positions and climbed toward the topmost ridge. Perhaps sensing that the colonel was doubtful that the Glosters could hold out much longer, a soldier from Support Company tried to reassure him, saying in a strong Gloucestershire accent: "We shall be all right, sir, 'twill be like the Rock of Gibraltar up there." Grouped around the highest point on Hill 235 were the remnants of A Company facing northwest, D Company facing south, B and C companies turned toward the southwest, with Support Company in reserve. The men dug in as best they could, though there were few tools with which to work. In many cases rock ramparts had to be built to make up for the shallowness of the holes being scraped from the hard and rocky soil. "Everyone worked with a driving sense of fear and necessity," the Padre remembered.[32]

During the hours of daylight the Chinese kept busy with more than squeezing the Glosters and making sure they remained cut off. On the other side of Kamak-san the enemy was pushing hard against the forces defending Route 11.

To the west of the track, the Northumberlands fought hard, especially in the evening, when Z Company was heavily attacked. The Chinese captured the heights overlooking 10 Platoon, but under orders from

Major John Winn the platoon commander, Second-Lieutenant Bill Sheppard, was able to mount a successful counterattack. The noise generated by the enemy "was incredible," Captain Andrew Scott of W Company recalled, "Chinese shouting and yelling and blowing their bugles." Though supported by the tank fire of the other half of C Squadron, 8th Hussars during the day, the Northumberlands were gradually pushed southward by evening.[33]

On the other side of the road, on Hill 398, the Ulsters, particularly A Company, had endured sixteen separate attacks. There was a bad moment in the later afternoon when the brush near A Company caught fire from white phosphorous smoke bombs and the men were forced to abandon their slit trenches to avoid being roasted. "Luckily it happened before dark," company commander Major Christopher Nixon recalled, "and we were able to reestablish ourselves before the main [night] attacks came in." The stockpile of rocket ammunition acquired by the company also came in handy, shots from super bazookas at a range of 100 yards helping halt an attack on a neighboring Ulster company: "The effect on the Chinkie morale was, to put it mildly, pretty devastating." The porter company, meanwhile, continued to carry supplies up Hill 398.[34]

Korean porters, though, could find themselves in trouble so near the fighting. British units were not contiguous, and through the somewhat aerated front line across Route 11 enemy snipers and small parties had managed to infiltrate themselves. This made any face of an Oriental cast seem like a potential enemy to Caucasian eyes. Trooper Denis Whybro, for instance, later explained that while operating in support of the Fusiliers on Tuesday the 24th he had suddenly seen a group of Koreans approaching from the north. A warning burst from the Besa machine-gun of his Centurion was fired, and the Koreans very sensibly sat down in a gesture of surrender. They turned out to be porters attached to 55 Field Squadron trying to escape after the enemy had overrun the village in which they had been billeted and started killing them. In all, fifty-nine survived the trek back to U.N. lines thanks to the levelheadedness of their leader, Oom. If he and they had run when the warning burst was fired, they would have been gunned down. Chinese infiltrators were suspected of having posed as South Koreans, and had already been mistaken as such at least once in the battle.[35]

Amidst all the shot and shell, there were occasional signs of confirmation that on the U.N. side the Imjin battle was indeed a very British affair. The habit of stiff-upper-lip understatement on the part of officers was one such indicator. Another was the stress placed on what might be termed keeping up appearances. Second-Lieutenant John Mole of the Ulsters, for example, recalled how on the morning of the 24th, Major John Shaw, then liaising with brigade, had come up to the battalion command post to talk with the acting CO. After chatting with Mole for a moment, Shaw looked him up and down and said: "'John, I don't believe you've shaved this morning.' I said 'no, I haven't had time really, and there's not much water here.' He gave me a very severe look and he said 'John, I can see no reason whatsoever why you can't shave. Officers set an example, you should jolly well shave.'" Mole did as he was told, but had the last laugh the following day when the pressures of battle meant that Shaw – who had the grace to smile at the situation when he glimpsed the clean-shaven Mole – could not find the time to wield a razor. This sort of thing, it should be noted, was not unique to the Ulsters. When Major John Winn met the second-in-command of the Northumberlands twenty or so hours later in the wake of a prolonged and bloody engagement fought at close quarters in which he had been wounded twice, the first mildly reproachful words out of the mouth of Major Miles Speer were "Good morning, John. You're looking extremely untidy."[36]

After nightfall the Chinese renewed their efforts on either side of Kamak-san. During the daylight hours of Monday and – especially – Tuesday, American fighter-bombers had made a series of rocket and napalm strikes on Chinese concentrations in front of 29th Brigade units that were of great help in weakening enemy assaults. Though on the night of 24/25 April attacks in darkness by medium bombers were added to the USAF repertoire, the damage inflicted was far more random than during the day. As before, the enemy used the hours of darkness both to infiltrate further and to close up unseen to British positions in preparation for new assaults. Achieving surprise was now rare, as aircraft randomly dropped illuminating flares and squaddies kept their eyes peeled and their ears cocked: "Coughs, rustling, even chatter alerted our defence as their soldiers crept forward to attack," Farrar-Hockley noted. Darkness, however, still cloaked some movements, and the Northumberlands, the

Ulsters, and especially the Glosters would find themselves fighting hard through much of the night.[37]

To the west of Route 11, it was Z Company of the Fusiliers under the command of Major John Winn on a ridgeline that saw the heaviest fighting. Starting at about nine o'clock at night the Chinese launched a series of attacks supported by mortars and machine-guns. The first to feel the full effect were Second-Lieutenant William Sheppard and the men of 10 Platoon, who fought at close quarters for hours to hold their ground and recapture any that was lost. Winn himself, accompanied by only two fusiliers and later a Bren gunner, undertook the ultimately successful defense of a key high point. By the time the Chinese drew back toward dawn, several men had been killed and twenty-eight others wounded, most of them seriously.[38]

To the east, on Hill 398, A Company of the Ulsters fended off attacks from 1:30 AM onward. At 3:00 AM an attack was launched against 11 Platoon of D Company that managed to penetrate the position. Close-quarters fighting involving small-arms and grenades went on until first light, when the Chinese withdrew. B Company, left four miles farther back down Route 11 on a saddle hill position near Hwangbang-ni, found itself coming under Chinese mortar and machine-gun fire from the southeast slope of Kamak-san, which the enemy now occupied, as a prelude to assault. According to Rifleman Albert Tyas of 4 Platoon, "we fired all night, we threw hand grenades all night, we had a right major attack on our positions." Casualties were high, but with mortar support B Company held its ground.[39]

Meanwhile the Chinese showed considerable interest in eliminating the Glosters, whose redoubt, though small, was miles inside the territory conquered in the past several days and overlooked an important route southward over which reinforcements would pass. If the Glosters were not overwhelmed on Hill 235 then accurate artillery fire could be directed onto Route 57 by radio along with harassing Vickers machine-gun bursts from the hill itself once daylight arrived. Two major nighttime attacks on Gloster Hill were therefore launched.

The first assault, which was principally directed at A and B Company positions, began shortly after 10 PM. "On the south-eastern end of the ridge, Denis's Company [Major Denis Harding, B Coy] and Frank's

Mortar Troop [Captain Frank Wisbey, C Troop, 170 Mortar Battery] were engaged by frequent assaults and a good deal of machine-gun fire that was uncomfortable in view of the shallowness of their trenches," the adjutant recorded. In the meantime A Company was fighting for a scrub-covered mound a little north of the peak of Hill 235. "Here," Farrar-Hockley continued, "[Captain] Donald [Allman] had forgotten that he was the Assistant Adjutant and was commanding seventeen men – in name, a platoon – who were hanging on by little more than the skin of their teeth."[40]

The second attack began several hours later. Denys Whatmore, commanding 11 Platoon, wrote of how on the D Company front "apart from a bit of probing which was fended off by small arms fire, they waited till well after midnight to launch their next major assault."

> Then, the bugles started again and massed Chinese infantry came up the spur at the north west end of Hill 235 in the way we were now used to, non-stop, in waves, firing their weapons and guided by the bugles. The depleted A, B and C Companies were very hard pressed to keep the enemy out and only part of D Company was located with a field of fire suitable to join in the action and provide some enfilade fire.

"The racket went on and on, gunfire and grenade explosions mixed with shouts," Whatmore related. Thanks in part to very accurate support fire from 45 Field Regiment, with shells landing only twenty-five to thirty yards from the slit trenches at the adjutant's insistence, the enemy was not able to break into the Glosters' perimeter.[41]

Despite their predicament, the Glosters, with nowhere to go, do not appear to have been particularly downhearted. Farrar-Hockley was struck by a snatch of overheard conversation between two signalers – "I don't care about your fancy London beers, Jack," one, hailing from Bristol, said to the other. "As far as I'm concerned, there's no beer in the world like George's Home Brewed" – that suggested that being cut off was not diverting soldiers from their primary trains of thought. The word had spread that a second relief effort was going to be made in the morning, and during the night the colonel and his adjutant, through contact with brigade headquarters, had been promised both substantial air strikes and a full-scale USAF airdrop of ammunition and other vital supplies. Fred Carne, though, still expected a lot of sharp fighting in the morning, perhaps hand-to-hand. "It seems to me," he told Farrar-Hockley as dawn approached, "that we [in the command post] are going to find a job for ourselves as riflemen before much longer."[42]

How to save the Glosters was very much on the minds of those at higher formation headquarters. General Soule had indicated to Brigadier Brodie in the afternoon of 24 April that a task force from the Puerto Rican 65th Infantry Regiment would launch a second relief attempt in the morning, and in the early hours of 25 April the 3rd Division commander had telephoned the regiment's CO, Colonel William W. Harris. The CO recalled, "he ordered me to go over to the [29th] brigade position and see if I could give the brigadier some help in extracting his Gloucester Battalion." He was not happy to hear this, as all his units were already engaged "and we were fighting for our lives." Soule insisted, however, and Harris prepared to make the forty-minute journey by jeep to 29th Brigade HQ.[43]

Four miles or so away as the crow flies, a meeting of unit commanders had been called for 4 AM at brigade headquarters to discuss operations for the coming day. Major Tony Younger, the chief engineer, and Major Henry Huth, the commander of the Centurions, had arrived on time, but there was no sign of the brigadier. Fifteen minutes after the meeting was due to start, the youthful-looking acting brigade major, Jim Dunning, came into the command post tent and apologetically explained that he was unable to rouse the brigadier because he had taken sleeping pills. Younger could understand why Brodie had done this:

> I know only too well how much strain we were under during this intense battle. I was finding it impossible to sleep at night, with a host of thoughts running through my mind – should I do this? – should I do that? This was the strain of battle, when one knows that the lives of the men one commands are at stake, and from which all commanders suffer. Tom Brodie, whose responsibilities greatly outweighed those that the rest of us carried, would have been under proportionately greater strain. Also he was a good deal older than his subordinate commanders [*sic*]. It is not surprising that he succumbed to the very human response to take sleeping pills to try to get some much-needed rest.

On the other hand only Brodie could make command decisions, and Younger told Dunning that the brigadier must be woken, "even if it meant pouring a bucket of water over him."[44]

It took another quarter of an hour for the brigadier to appear, time which Huth and Younger put to good use discussing what could be done to help the Northumberlands and the Ulsters after dawn. It was clear by now that the Chinese were infiltrating more and more men behind the positions the two battalions occupied on either side of Route 11 six miles to the north, the proof including the fact that Brigade HQ was itself coming under fire. When Colonel Harris and three staff officers arrived, they were disconcerted to find that rifle bullets were zipping through the tops of tents and that the whole area was under sporadic mortar fire, and amazed to see that their British counterparts seemed entirely indifferent to the risk of getting killed. Fearing that it would be not only the Glosters who would end up being cut off, Huth and Younger were therefore thinking in terms of a phased withdrawal of the two battalions covered by fire from the Centurions. There were no infantry to spare who might serve as a backstop except for the weakened Belgians, so Younger volunteered his sappers to hold a crucial saddle feature across the track about halfway to Hill 398.[45]

By the time the brigadier appeared in the command tent, Lieutenant General Milburn at I Corps HQ had decided that the withdrawal to Line Kansas was not going to be enough to prevent the enemy from breaking through and cutting off major parts of his command. To the left of 29th Brigade, the 1st ROK Division had been pushed back well below the Imjin, while to the right of 3rd Division the enemy was striking hard at 25th Division. The entire I Corps front was under pressure, with units inside and outside 29th Brigade threatened with piecemeal destruction. At 5 AM Milburn issued orders for a preplanned withdrawal from Line Kansas to Line Delta, several miles to the rear. "He was in a rather dazed state," Younger wrote of Brodie, "and talked about the Brigade withdrawing to new positions south of the Han river."[46]

Brodie agreed to Huth's plan to extract the two infantry battalions on the right of the brigade front. That still left open the question of whether or not anything could be done to save the Glosters. General Soule had earlier promised that a task force from the 65th Infantry would launch a second rescue effort in the morning. But by the early hours of 25 April the commander of 3rd Division was worried that the enemy troops pouring through the gaps in 29th Brigade's front were preparing to swing to the east and cut the MSR, Route 33, down which he was preparing to withdraw toward Uijongbu. Soule therefore whittled away at the strength of the rescue force, sending off two infantry battalions from the 65th as well as 10 BCT to counter any such outflanking attempt. A third battalion from the 65th was to be used to guard the lower reaches of Route 11 as the rest of 29th Brigade withdrew, which left precious little with which to try anything else. Milburn, however, had made it clear to Soule that some sort of rescue attempt should be mounted and, under orders from the 3rd Division commander, Colonel Harris was instructed to come up with a plan using only a battalion of medium tanks and a company of light tanks.[47]

As dawn approached Harris and Brodie discussed what to do, but both men knew that the die was already cast. It was agreed that a platoon of medium tanks should attempt to retrace the steps of 10 BCT up Route 57, but this was mere tokenism. "I believe it was the consensus that there was little I could do to help under the circumstances," Harris noted. If tanks had been unable to force their way forward with infantry support on the 24th, what chance was there that tanks without infantry support would succeed on the 25th? Knowing that the Glosters were doomed, Brodie blamed Soule for not allowing a withdrawal while there had still been time. According to Harris, he "said that he had been warning Shorty Soule for the previous thirty-six hours or so that if they [higher command] didn't authorize him to draw them back they [the Glosters] were going to be cut off." The withdrawal option had been ignored and now rescue was impossible. "The brigadier was furious," the colonel related, "and I didn't blame him."[48]

In the predawn darkness back on Gloster Hill one of the most well-known incidents in the entire Imjin battle was about to occur. Yet again, Chinese bugles sounded as a prelude to a massed charge of infantry. "It'll be a long time before I want to hear a cavalry trumpet playing, after this," the normally taciturn CO commented to the adjutant. Half-jokingly, Farrar-Hockley suggested that if the Glosters played their own bugles it would confuse the enemy. Carne took him seriously, and Farrar-Hockley ordered Drum-Major Philip Buss to sound every bugle call in his repertoire except Retreat. Having borrowed a bugle, Buss got out of his slit trench and stood to attention, delivering his famous battlefield recital of British and American calls, starting with Reveille and ending with Taps.[49]

Buss came close to being shot by a soldier who assumed that the bugle must be Chinese and that the enemy had to have infiltrated the British positions. "At about 0500 hours," wrote Denys Whatmore of D Company, "without warning a bugle blasted off immediately behind me, so close!" Private T. R. Bingham swung round too with finger on rifle trigger, ready to fire. Thankfully, he could not see Buss, who was in fact just over the ridgeline – Whatmore guessed that he "would immediately have shot the bugler had he been in sight." After a few seconds Whatmore recognized the calls and realized that the bugler could not be Chinese. The effect on other soldiers and the enemy was generally positive but limited. Though some men who had not slept for several days were irritated to hear Reveille being sounded and therefore made "a few ribald remarks and suggestions about what he might do with his bugle" according to Sergeant Frank Cottam of A Company, Padre Davies and others recalled that "there was a cheer from the hills." Corporal Ronald Norley with D Company thought that this act of defiance "cheered everyone up" and according to Major Weller of Support Company the bugle playing "was extremely heartening to everybody." As for the enemy, the Chinese seem to have been momentarily confused, but once Buss had ceased playing "they came just the same" according to Doctor Bob Hickey, albeit this time without trumpet directions.[50]

All in all, the fourth and final day of battle of the Imjin was shaping up to be a bad one for the Glosters. What was not yet apparent was that the finale on Wednesday, 25 April, would come near to shattering what remained of the other British infantry battalions too.

They're coming on all sides.

WARNING FROM RSM JACK HOBBS,
Gloster Hill, c. 6:00 AM, 25 April 1951[1]

Come on then, you bastards, and get your breakfast.

ANONYMOUS SOLDIER,
Gloster Hill, c. 6:00 AM, 25 April 1951[2]

FOUR

Imjin: The Final Day

AT FIRST LIGHT ON WEDNESDAY THERE WAS NO APPRECIABLE letup in Chinese pressure on either side of Kamak-san, with fighting going on around as well as to the rear of all three British infantry battalions as the night gave way to dawn. On what would turn out to be the concluding day of battle for the brigade, there would be alternating scenes of heroism, cowardice, tragedy, and farce.

Just after six in the morning, Brigadier Brodie contacted Colonel Carne by radio and made it clear that the relief column promised the day before effectively had been canceled. What remained of the relief force after other parts had been shifted elsewhere by General Soule, namely the tank platoon from the 65th Infantry, would go through the motions of trying to get through a couple of hours later, but as the regiment's commander, Colonel William H. Harris, admitted, "we all knew that that was sending too little too late." The fact that they were not going to be extracted after all was certainly very bad news for the Glosters. According to Carne, the brigadier "left it to me to decide whether to surrender on the spot, fight it out to the end or slip away." Not surprisingly the colonel favored the third option, but that would be impossible unless the enemy could first be driven back.[3]

The fact of the matter was that as dawn broke on 25 April, Gloster Hill was under heavy attack. "Very hard pressed," was how the battalion's situation was reported to brigade at 6:10 AM, followed ten minutes later by the terse message: "Surrounded. Impossible to withdraw." The fighting was in fact so fierce that the parachute drop of supplies and ammunition by twin-engine USAF C-119 Flying Boxcar aircraft arranged the previous day had to be canceled at a quarter to seven as no cleared area could be established on top of the ridge and because a drop would interfere with the attack runs of the even more desperately needed fighter-bombers.[4]

The CO, meanwhile, did his best to encourage his men through a personal display of sustained *sang-froid* under fire. "I shall never forget how on that last morning Colonel Carne strolled round our positions," a corporal with battalion HQ remembered, "cool, calm and collected, dropping words of encouragement here and there." Morale, according to a private in C Company, never faltered even as it became more and more obvious that there would be no happy ending.[5]

There was fighting everywhere atop Hill 235, with what remained of A Company being hit particularly hard. With all the officers dead or wounded, and a complement of only thirty fighting men, the company had been forced to retreat from its original position atop a high point. This loss might have had catastrophic consequences if it had not been for the actions of the battalion adjutant after he arrived on the scene to take command of the situation. Viewed in quieter times as something of a martinet by many of the other ranks, Captain Tony Farrar-Hockley inspired confidence in those around him as he moved from one slit trench to another, chatted with the occupants, gave orders, and displayed exemplary coolness under fire. "He was outstanding," a corporal later reflected. Farrar-Hockley was a veteran of the hill fighting in Italy in the latter stages of World War II and he knew that the permanent loss of any high ground on the top of Gloster Hill would spell disaster. After rapidly sizing up the situation and chatting jokily with the surviving soldiers, Farrar-Hockley announced his intentions. "Now then," he stated briskly, "who's going to win the VC? We're going back there, and that means all of you." With the adjutant in the lead, a company that was down to the strength of a platoon charged thirty yards uphill and, after some hand-to-hand fighting, was once more in command of the high ground. Another officer who was present at the time described Farrar-Hockley as the bravest man he had ever met.[6]

The Chinese, however, came again and again, and if they had been forced to rely on their own dwindling supply of arms and ammunition it is likely that the Glosters would have been completely overrun by around eight in the morning. Fortunately the 25-pounders of 45 Field Regiment and the F-80 Shooting Star fighter-bombers of the USAF were, as requested, able to offer vital support in breaking up massed assaults before they could start.

To ensure maximum effect, artillery fire was called in almost on top of company positions by a Forward Observation Officer, Captain Ronnie Washbrook of the Royal Artillery. The danger of friendly-fire casualties from shells falling short was great, but as Lance-Corporal R. F. Matthews of C Company noted, the gunners knew their business: "A solid mass of Chinese was surging toward the hill when the first salvo landed. It was superb gunnery. With pin-point precision, shells crashed down as near as thirty yards in front of us." The attack, as he put it, "dissolved abruptly." The results were similarly devastating near A Company. Farrar-Hockley was worried that the barrage might come too late. "They will have to get a move on with the shoot," he remembered thinking; "the Chinese are coming . . . At any minute they will rush forward from their cover." But just in the nick of time the shells arrived. "Ah! there is a whistling in the air. We all duck down into our trenches. The sky darkens; the whole ground is shaken with the noise of explosions. The Gunners are doing us proud. I lie on the bottom of my slit trench, covered with earth blown in from the bursting shells." After a minute or two contemplating an unconcerned beetle at the bottom of his hole, the adjutant heard the firing stop. "I kneel up to shake off the loose earth. What a wonderful view; not a Chinese in sight . . ."[7]

Around two hours after it had been requested, air support arrived – "at last," as Carne commented at the time – in the form of multiple strafing and bombing runs by flights of F-80 Shooting Stars beginning at about 8:30 AM and lasting for sixty minutes. Rockets, heavy machine-gun fire, and above all napalm created spectacular explosions around the hill and in the valley. The latter was a liquid fire weapon that revolted some soldiers, but the adjutant was certain that everybody that day on Gloster Hill was far more concerned with survival than ethics. Second-Lieutenant Holdsworth with D Company, as well as the Padre, thought that the air strikes "didn't seem to stop them very much," but in their aftermath the Chinese did draw off, needing time to reorganize and reinforce for another assault.[8]

"Things were really looking up!" the adjutant remembered himself thinking at this point. It was a bad omen, though, to see the promised Flying Boxcars turning away before they reached the river, and the ammunition situation was now critical. The men of A Company, for instance, had only three rounds for each rifle, seven hand grenades, half a magazine per Sten, and less than two full magazines for the remaining Brens. As the commander of D Company, Captain Mike Harvey, put it, "there was insufficient ammunition left [in the battalion] to meet another [assault] of the current intensity."[9]

Carne, meanwhile, had been getting more bad news over the single remaining, fast-fading, 62 Set radio link with brigade shortly before eight in the morning. In compliance with orders from I Corps and in order to avoid encirclement themselves, the other units of 29th Brigade were pulling back, including 45 Field Regiment. That meant that there would soon be no more artillery support for the Glosters and that the gap between the brigade and Gloster Hill would only expand with each passing hour. The best that Brodie could suggest was that Carne split his men into groups and have them make their way toward the forward elements of the 1st ROK Division to the southwest. Distraught at what he suspected was a death sentence, Brodie scrawled down his famous last message for transmission to the men on Hill 235: "NO ONE BUT GLOSTERS COULD HAVE DONE IT."[10]

At nine Carne called his company and other commanders together to inform them of what had happened and how he intended to proceed. "The news of the cessation of artillery support made me abandon plans for fighting our way out," the CO later explained; instead, individual parties would "attempt to slip away."[11] The adjutant, who had no clue as to what was to come due to the colonel's business-as-usual demeanor, was the first to hear and respond to the bad news. Each officer behaved with classic British Army stiff-upper-lip imperturbability:

CARNE "You know that armoured/infantry column that's coming from 3 Div to relieve us[?]"
FARRAR-HOCKLEY "Yes, sir."
CARNE "Well, it isn't coming."
FARRAR-HOCKLEY "Right, sir."

As the adjutant reflected several years later, there "did not seem to be much else to say." Once the group was assembled, Carne explained that no help could be expected and ordered that starting at 10 AM each company or group in turn should make its own way down Hill 235 and head southwest toward the 1st ROK Division. After a pause, Carne turned to the Medical Officer, Dr. Bob Hickey. "He said he was very sorry," Hickey recollected, "that he didn't think he could take the [non-walking] wounded." The MO paused a moment to let the implications sink in, then responded: "I said yes, I understood that perfectly well." Along with the Padre, Hickey felt duty-bound to stay with the stretcher cases and deliberately allow himself to fall into enemy hands. This was a brave thing to do, given the uncertainty as to how the enemy would behave toward prisoners. Hickey also insisted that while married medical orderlies could try and break away, the unmarried ones should stay behind too to assist the wounded. "British soldiers are very good, you know," he reflected admiringly several decades later; "they do what you tell them to." The MO and Padre both remembered later telling those unfortunates around them that it looked like they were soon all going to have a holiday in China. "Any questions?" Carne asked in conclusion. There were none, and the group dispersed at 9:30 AM.[12]

Just before 10 AM the first groups from A Company, to be followed by parties from other companies, began to scramble down Gloster Hill, unmolested by the enemy. Walking among those who stayed behind – the seriously wounded and "four or five able-bodied but very dazed Gloster men" who according to the Padre suddenly "stumbled into the aid post" – the medical sergeant, S. J. Brisland, thought that it would be a good idea to indicate to the Chinese where the aid post was and started to wave a Red Cross flag. Drum-Major Buss, who happened to see this and was among those who had not received word of the plan to abandon the hill, raised his rifle and shouted, "Put that bloody white flag down!" before the Padre interjected "The battalion's gone, drum-major. For heaven's sake run for it, man – it's your only hope." Buss stared for a moment, and then disappeared down the slope.[13]

The chances of a successful trek to U.N. lines were extremely slim. With I Corps in retreat, the distance to friendly forces by the most direct route had lengthened to over a dozen miles. If firefights developed, the Gloster parties would run out of ammunition almost at once. "We probably didn't have more than a dozen or so rounds between us," Frank Cottam remembered of his group from A Company. The Chinese, while no longer assaulting Hill 235, could observe its slopes from adjoining hills and had troops on every feature and in the valley. What was more, once off the hill men tended to bunch together, making them easier to spot. Under orders to capture rather than kill the enemy for propaganda purposes, Chinese troops simply corralled most parties by firing warning bursts of machine-gun fire from the hills. The experience of David Kaye of C Company was fairly typical. "I just followed everybody else, off the hill, and up this valley [moving southward], going towards our own lines, we hoped," he recalled. During this period "we were fired at overhead by machine-guns [located on higher ground], and various people, each time there was a burst of firing, threw up their hands and stopped where they were." Kaye and others kept going, but eventually gave up too once the Chinese came into the valley.[14]

Though very unwilling to throw in the towel, even Farrar-Hockley came to the conclusion that there was no choice. He found that once in the valley the group of soldiers who had attached themselves to him was attracting Chinese fire from the hills. "They fired behind us and in front, warning shots across our bows in effect from light machine-guns," the adjutant recalled. "They were plainly inviting us to stop. The rounds got nearer and nearer. . . ." Eventually, with the Chinese closing in, Farrar-Hockley was forced to conclude that there was no chance of avoiding a slaughter if the hint was not taken. "OK chaps," Bill Westwood remembered him saying, "that's as far as we can go." Rifle bolts and breech blocks were flung away and hands were raised over heads. "A very shameful moment, really," the adjutant later reflected.[15]

The sentiment was shared by the other captured Gloster officers. According to a summary of post-release debriefing reports there were some sharp exchanges among the officers after they had surrendered as to who had and had not pulled his weight during the battle. As for Colonel Carne, he was so angry at what had happened that he was not on speaking terms with some of his subordinates for some time after they all fell into Chinese hands.[16]

The only group that escaped this fate consisted of the remnants of D Company, soon joined by eleven Vickers machine-gunners, collectively led by Captain Mike Harvey. The commander of 11 Platoon, Lieutenant

Denys Whatmore, described in his memoirs the plan that Harvey had outlined to his subordinates after studying his map.

> He proposed to avoid the obvious shortest way out, that is, due South, where he thought it was probable that the enemy lay in strength. He would take the Company due north to start with, into ground from which the enemy were likely to have moved on. He would then go West along the lower, North facing slopes of the hills and then turn South towards friendly lines. It would be a long way round but, with luck, we should meet fewer Chinese that way.

Ammunition was scarce, but as Harvey noted, "I made sure that that the leading elements had at least a few rounds in their magazines to deal with any unexpected contact."[17]

At first all went well for the several officers and eighty-one men involved, the occasional surprised Chinese soldier encountered being dealt with without much difficulty. As they turned southward, Harvey and his men were identified as friendly troops by an American L5 light spotter plane. "We took out our [dark] blue berets from concealment in our pullovers and waved them," Harvey later wrote, "and I hand-signaled our intention to continue south down the valley." The L5 "waggled its wings, an acknowledgement and to us, an encouragement, and thereafter repeatedly over-flew us."[18]

Then, however, things started to go wrong. The valley narrowed into a canyon only a hundred yards wide, and suddenly the group started to come under machine-gun fire from multiple positions on the western heights. Men took what cover they could in stream beds and behind whatever earth or rock features they could find, sprinting on southward when the opportunity offered. Casualties mounted, and several men were captured when, contrary to orders, they tried to help wounded comrades. As a number of officers involved later put it, they had all become targets in a shooting gallery. Forty men were killed or captured. Shortly before noon the survivors turned a bend in the valley and saw a troop of American tanks about five hundred yards in front of them. Help seemed to be at hand, but unfortunately the tank crews, from the 73rd Heavy Tank Battalion, did not know that there was anyone but the enemy in front of them and opened fire with their machine-guns.[19]

Harvey tried to make it clear that they were not Chinese by putting his beret on a stick and waving it, only to see the beret shot away. As everyone took what cover they could, Second-Lieutenant David Holdsworth of 12 Platoon passed along his white handkerchief for Harvey to wave instead, while the L5 spotter plane made low passes over the tanks to try and indicate that something was wrong. The firing did eventually stop, either as the result of a hastily written note dropped with a streamer by the L5 pilot, because the commander of the 12th ROK Regiment accompanying the tanks recognizing rolled-up British shirtsleeves, or due to the brave actions of men such as Private Walter Cleveland and Lieutenant Denys Whatmore, who got close enough to wave and shout their identity. Four men, an NCO, and an officer had by then been wounded by friendly fire.[20]

Though a few individuals managed to evade capture or to immediately escape, the vast majority of the battalion, along with the attached Korean porter company, had either been killed or taken prisoner between 22 and 25 April. In all, 58 officers and men of the regiment had been killed in action and another 522 captured. Thanks to the Chinese desire to use U.N. prisoners for propaganda purposes, survivors outnumbered the dead (though 27 prisoners would die in Chinese or North Korean custody over the next two years). Nevertheless, the fact remained that in fighting terms the 1st Battalion, The Gloucestershire Regiment, had been destroyed between late Sunday night and early Wednesday afternoon.[21]

The Glosters were no longer part of the calculus of battle for either side. Brodie had guessed long before dawn broke that their fate was sealed. What he did not anticipate was how close to destruction some of his other fighting units would come on 25 April. This would turn out to be the last day of the Imjin battle, but it would rank among the toughest for many of those involved in what became a very bloody fighting retreat for the remainder of 29th Brigade.

Just how perilous the situation of the remaining forward battalions, the Northumberlands and the Ulsters, actually was in the hours around dawn on Wednesday morning was not entirely apparent at Brigade HQ, located about six miles south on Route 11 from their main positions. There had been signs that the Chinese were coming over and around Kamak-san from the northwest since Tuesday, and it was to prevent any cutting of the escape route by enemy forces skirting southeastward over the southern slopes of the massif that Brodie had ordered the Belgian battalion to take up a blocking position less than a mile to the west of

Brigade HQ that same day. At 5:30 AM on Wednesday, moreover, ten Centurions from C Squadron, 8th Hussars, were sent up Route 11 under the command of Captain Peter Ormrod accompanied by a troop of Royal Engineers acting in the infantry role to clear away any enemy soldiers who had infiltrated over Kamak-san and posed a threat to the safe withdrawal of the Ulsters and the Northumberlands. These moves, however, were predicated on Chinese infiltration being quite limited in scope. By this point the battle-weary Belgian battalion numbered less than one hundred fighting men, while the force designated to clear and keep open Route 11 behind the two forward infantry battalions, the Fusiliers and the Ulsters, was not strong enough to both sweep and then hold about five square miles of valley floor if the enemy came down from Kamak-san in large numbers.[22]

Though one tank threw its tracks and another got stuck in a paddy field in the process of moving up the valley, the Centurions, initially supported by the Bofors guns of 11 Light Anti-Aircraft Battery firing over open sights, were able with the help of the sappers of 1 Troop, 55 Field Squadron, Royal Engineers, to drive off the limited number of Chinese soldiers they encountered as they moved north up Route 11 in heavy mist, and to allow a column of three Oxford carriers to deliver ammunition to the Northumberlands. This was enough for Brodie to conclude that the withdrawal route was now clear, and to order the Northumberlands, followed by the Ulsters, to begin their withdrawal southward down the valley floor under the overall direction of the Fusilier CO, Lieutenant-Colonel Kingsley Foster.[23]

Among the Ulsters in particular there were doubts about this plan. The thick dawn mist had prevented the clearing force from seeing any Chinese except those immediately around them. At the sun burned off the mist, however, it became apparent that instead of a few dozen infiltrators there were hundreds of Chinese establishing themselves on the eastern slopes of Kamak-san overlooking Route 11. To those who remembered the chaotic running battle fought on the night of 3/4 January the idea of withdrawing down the valley floor with the enemy established in force on the western heights seemed distinctly ominous. Indeed, the man in command of the Rifles, Major Gerald Rickord, was dubious enough about going down the valley to send a message to HQ asking if he could lead his men out over the high ground to the east of the valley instead. Rickord was told to stick to the plan.[24]

Orders were orders, then, and at about ten in the morning the Northumberland companies began to move off the hills they had occupied one by one, a single platoon covering the others in each case. By eleven the whole Fusilier battalion was on the move southward passing through the Ulsters, who would themselves be marching south within an hour and a half. Many of the battalion vehicles, including the carriers, were sent on ahead.[25]

All seemed quiet at first, the companies having broken contact with the enemy and withdrawn off their hill positions without too much difficulty. An exception was the Ulster rearguard force, C Company. Some shells from a 45 Field Regiment barrage designed to prevent the Chinese from following too closely fell into the company positions just as the men had left the protection of their trenches, and several riflemen were killed or wounded. Otherwise the withdrawal began well. Colonel Foster, though, who had hoped to make a dash southward before the Chinese could react in force, grew increasingly agitated over the time it took for Rickord and his men to get moving – "I'm going to court-martial that bastard," he fumed – and not without reason.[26]

After about half an hour of marching down the valley sniper and machine-gun fire had begun to fall from the western slopes with growing intensity on both battalions. "We got about two miles down this road," Major Charles Mitchell of W Company explained in a letter to his parents, "when masses of fire burst upon us from all sides, a real ambush if you like." Men had to go to ground and move from one piece of cover to the next as best they could. Acting as rear guard, the soldiers of 8 Platoon, Y Company, found themselves irrevocably pinned down by Chinese machine-gun bullets. Casualties began to mount and command and control of the column started to break down as signalers were hit and radio sets were damaged or simply failed to operate effectively. "I saw for the first time men who I had a great regard for, good fighting men," recalled Corporal Thomas Cunningham-Booth, who worked at the RNF command post, "running like the clappers to get out, slinging their weapons, and generally behaving like a demoralized mob." The worst, though, was yet to come.[27]

The Chinese for several hours already had been attempting to establish a blocking force in the narrowest part of the valley, known as the saddle, a few miles to the south of the Ulster and Fusilier positions being abandoned. Fortunately this saddle position, by the village of Hwangbang-ni, had been occupied by B Company of the Rifles under the command of Major John Shaw for much of the battle, and with help from the tanks of C Squadron, 8th Hussars – several of which were ambushed and put out of action – and the sappers from 55 Field Squadron, the saddle was kept open. To the north and especially south, however, Chinese infantry were laying down heavy fire from the western heights and starting to pour into the valley. "When I looked back, through the gap in the bushes towards the paddy fields where I'd just run out of," Rifleman William Gibson – who had become separated from his comrades in A Company – recalled, "I could see it was just a mass of figures moving forward, just a mass, in waves, running forward, running forward. Chinese – there must have been tens of thousands of them [*sic*]."[28]

Unable to find out what was going on through the radio net, Tom Brodie drove northward from Brigade HQ up Route 11 to investigate. Near the saddle position he came across Kingsley Foster. Their encounter was recorded by a black sheep of the battalion, Fusilier Derek Kinne of 6 Platoon, X Company:

> I saw the Colonel standing by the side of the road watching the Brigadier's scout car come up from the south. The Brigadier was sitting on the top, dressed in his white sheepskin coat with his red [banded] hat on, looking as cool as if he was looking at an exercise.
>
> "My God, you're a target in that hat, sir," said the Colonel as he got down and walked over. The Brigadier smiled.
>
> "Where are the Chinese?" he said.
>
> "All around," said the Colonel, pointing. "And they're pushing along the hilltops as fast as they can."
>
> "I think I'll go a bit further down," said the Brigadier. "I want to see what's happening to the Rifles."

Kinne never expected to see Tom Brodie alive again, but it was in fact Kingsley Foster who, as the CO had unhappily predicted to Tony Younger, would die fighting in the Imjin battle, receiving a machine-gun burst in the head and chest at about one in the afternoon while driving a jeep southward along Route 11.[29]

In point of fact there was nowhere along the line of withdrawal where the Chinese had no presence. The gun crews of 45 Field Regiment, each battery leapfrogging southward, came under small-arms fire and at times shot their 25-pounders over open sights. BBC cameraman Ronnie Noble observed one of the batteries in action as the guns withdrew.

> GUNNER "Enemy infantry on the hill-tops to our left, sir!"
> BATTERY COMMANDER "Can they hit us?"
> GUNNER "No sir! They're only carrying small arms, sir!"
> A few minutes later:
> GUNNER "Getting rather close, sir!"
> BATTERY COMMANDER "Can they hit us yet?"
> GUNNER "Just about, sir!"
> BATTERY COMMANDER "Thank you! *Five rounds rapid fire!* . . . All right [as bullets sprayed the track], let's move back."[30]

Behind the gun lines, the vehicles of Brigade HQ, withdrawing several miles south of the infantry battalions and tanks, also came under small-arms fire, and their route had to be cleared by bursts from the single available troop of Bofors guns. Still, there was no doubt that the units in the rear – namely the Northumberland Fusiliers and the Ulster Rifles – were facing the largest numbers of infiltrating Chinese.[31]

By the afternoon the column of Fusiliers and Riflemen had fragmented into sometimes quite small groups led by officers, NCOs, and even other ranks around which parties of men had coalesced. With the overall column commander dead and radios out of action, it was these figures who had to decide how best to proceed in the face of Chinese fire from the west and, in places, from the north and south as well.

Some rose to the challenge while others did not. Major W. D. C. Holmes of the Royal Engineers vividly recalled the "incredible calm" of an RUR company commander who sacrificed his life while leading his men out. On the other hand, Corporal Thomas Cunningham-Booth was understandably upset after being ordered by the Fusiliers' transport officer, Captain J. W. Wilson, to have the section he found himself commanding dig in on a hillside facing the enemy in order to help cover the retreat. In his view the section should have been on the crest or the reverse slope, but what really offended Cunningham-Booth was Wilson saying, "you will stay here until you get my personal command to be relieved" and then pulling out without informing him, the end result being needless casualties. To be fair to Wilson, the every-man-for-himself atmosphere that developed during the retreat tended to make it hard to be sure that men would actually obey orders. Captain F. W. Chester of the Northumberlands, trying to lead to safety the machine-gun section of support company, had to use persuasion rather than threats to get Fusilier Thomas McMahon, a reservist, to abandon a soldier whose leg had just been blown off ("leave him, Tom, he's dead already anyway"); and when the captain dressed down another reservist, Corporal George Dunkley, after he threw away the Vickers tripod he had been assigned to carry, he received the disconcerting reply: "If you want the bloody thing, you go get it yourself!"[32]

Yet it remained true that some officers apparently gave poor orders and did not always put the interests of those serving under them before their own. The Ulsters' signals officer, Second-Lieutenant Mervyn McCord, remembered very clearly the moment when he and the adjutant, Captain Hugh Hamill, took shelter behind the same rock and how Hamill then ejected him. "There's only room for one here, you'd better go," the adjutant announced in an authoritative tone of voice, adding "I'm the senior officer." Whether the adjutant was thinking primarily of his own safety or – as one knowledgeable commentator has suggested – was in fact making sure the signals officer kept moving while selflessly remaining behind to cover him and others, Hamill was subsequently pinned down behind his one-man piece of cover by enemy fire.[33]

Other officers continued to lead effectively – "they were very good," Rifleman John Dyer conceded – even when their men started to lose their fighting spirit. In some places in the valley the dangers involved in moving from cover behind paddy bunds and rocks were such that a few "shaky" soldiers refused to budge while others simply cracked up. According to Lieutenant Gordon Potts of the Ulsters, still more or less in command of 1 Platoon, A Company, a little physical therapy worked wonders: "you give 'em a good kick" and they recovered. "I had one chap who started screaming," Potts added, "and I just got hold of him, gave him two or three good slaps on the face and told him to pull himself together and be British." This hands-on approach to restoring discipline was not unique to Potts. "I can remember one chap getting very frightened," McCord later explained, "and starting to run away." Aware that in a blind panic the man was likely to break cover and get himself killed, McCord warned him that "if you come past me again I'll biff you." The rifleman could not restrain himself, "so I did biff him over the head with the butt of my pistol." Recognizing what would have happened if he had not been shocked back into awareness of the perils of blindly running into the open, the man later thanked McCord for saving his life. A refusal to move, on the other hand, could in some cases be the result of rational calculation. Where there was no one to tell them to do otherwise, some men could and did play dead, hoping the Chinese would not bayonet or shoot inert bodies and that they themselves would be able to steal away once night had fallen.[34]

For those willing and able to go on moving southward, there seemed to be three alternatives. The first was to continue on foot down the valley; the second was to hitch a ride on one of the tanks; and the third was to try to climb the slopes on the east side of Route 11 and move southward along the ridgeline. All three options posed dangers, but as the day unfolded it became clear that some could be more hazardous than others.

Sticking on foot to the region of the track was in accordance with the original plan of withdrawal and, at least in theory, held out the possibility of reasserting command and control at the unit level. It also minimized the danger of men without maps or compasses becoming disoriented and losing their sense of direction. This was why, where possible, men from the Northumberlands were ordered to continue marching down Route 11. The low ground, though, especially the track path, had become something of a shooting gallery, with the Chinese laying down automatic fire from the heights and infiltrating in large numbers into the valley itself, setting ambushes and making it more and more difficult to reestablish order along the column of route. "There was carnage on the valley floor," Rifleman Albert Tyas remembered. As Captain Peter Ormrod (who commanded the tanks farthest forward in the valley) later observed, bodies of men from "the Northumberland Fusiliers insisted on going back down the main, principal road [Route 11], and I think a lot of them became casualties."[35]

An alternative to running from one point of cover to the next that could seem attractive to men desperate to get out of what had turned into a valley of death was to try to shelter behind or hitch a ride on one of the Centurions. Some experienced soldiers, though, knew this was a mistake. One of the RUR platoon sergeants warned Lieutenant Potts to avoid leading his riflemen near the tanks because the enemy tended to focus his attention on them. "Never be near a tank in battle," a more senior member of the Ulster Rifles, Major John Shaw – who, like Kingsley Foster, seems to have had an accurate premonition that he would die that day – cautioned Mervyn McCord; "keep away from them, because they draw fire." The second-lieutenant took these words to heart, but for others, with very little other transport available and an every-man-for-himself mentality prevailing, the allure of the fast-moving Centurions proved irresistible.[36]

Unfortunately, the tanks did indeed tend to attract Chinese attention. Where they could get close enough, enemy parties armed with pole charges and various other explosive devices swarmed the Centurions. Fire from the tanks killed a large number of the attackers; "we just mowed them down," as Ormrod bluntly put it. Yet the Chinese were persistent, the main gun and coaxial machine-gun could fire only in the direction in which the turret happened to be traversed at a particular moment, and there was no swivel-mount machine-gun on the turret top. The squadron commander himself, controlling a Centurion that had got stuck in a paddy ditch, suddenly found Chinese clambering onto his vehicle undeterred by fire from his pistol. He was saved by the commander of a nearby Centurion who radioed "get your head down; I'll blow these people off." Hosing down each other with coaxial machine-gun bursts (or even, on at least one occasion, cannon fire) caused enormous slaughter, as did simply driving over those in front. "But the Chinese were still running along beside the tanks," recalled Rifleman John Dyer, "throwing grenades onto the tanks, trying to disable them."[37]

It was understandable that the wounded should be placed aboard the Centurions, as there was apparently only one soon-to-be-disabled half-track ambulance in the valley. So many other men sought to grab on to the hull exteriors, however, that it became almost impossible for the crews inside to see through vision slits or traverse the turret without injuring someone; in some cases as many as thirty men were on a single tank. The crews, though, still had armor protection, whereas the dozens of men clinging to the hulls or turrets simply became a bunched-up target for Chinese troops already intent on knocking out the Centurions. "It was rather like hail hitting the tank," Lieutenant Peter Whitamore of the Ulsters remembered, "and people were being shot and people were falling off." One tank after another was ambushed or otherwise disabled – six were lost in all – and almost everyone who tried riding out with the 8th Hussars, whether ultimately successful or otherwise, was struck by enemy or friendly fire. "It was a wild, swaying, bouncing ride on the Centurion," wrote Rifleman Henry O'Kane. "It didn't last long – but I shall never forget it. The dust, the rattle of the tracks, the Besa machine gun, the screams of wounded men as we were repeatedly hit."[38]

The last option for withdrawal, pursued by parties from both battalions and likely by the Korean porters, was in fact the best. Going out by way of the high and in places wooded ground to the east of the valley involved a lot of physical exertion and was a slow means of movement, but made those involved much more elusive targets for the Chinese positioned on the western heights. Hence the decision by the second-in-command of W Company, Captain Andrew Scott, to lead two platoons up and along the eastern heights, and the answer given by a large group of riflemen when Captain Ormrod leaned out of his turret hatch and queried their intentions: "They said that they were not going down the valley behind us, but they would march off over the hills; which they did in single file." Taking this route was not without its hazards, however. When they were spotted from the opposite ridgeline, parties were fired at, and as elsewhere it was sometimes difficult to pass back through U.N. lines without incident. A group from the Ulsters' command post, coming down into the valley at a point where they thought it safe to do so, suddenly came under "friendly" machine-gun fire from tanks a thousand yards off. "I can distinctly remember [RSM] Alec [Patterson], who had a walking stick, waving his stick [and calling], 'For God's sake, we're English,'" said Sergeant Roy Utting. Eventually Patterson's shouts and gesticulations caused the tanks to stop firing.[39]

By the time the remnants of the two forward infantry battalions reached the blocking position established by American forces at the crossroads where Route 57 joined up with Route 11 southeast of Kamaksan in the latter part of the afternoon, the retreat had become, in the words of Lieutenant Gordon Potts of the Ulsters, "a rout, not a withdrawal." In the course of 25 April the Fusiliers alone had lost twenty-two killed and fifty-six wounded, more than in any other period of the battle, while by the end the Ulsters had discarded much of their equipment and mustered only fourteen officers and 260 men. Though they were exhausted, the survivors regrouped sufficiently to establish along with the Belgians – who had made their own fighting withdrawal accompanied by tanks, during which their colonel was wounded[40] – a blocking position at Tokchong four miles back. Despite protests from Brigadier Brodie, the divisional commander, General Soule, still intended to employ 29th Brigade in the front line as a rear guard. It was only after the British liaison officer at I Corps, Captain William Ellery, who happened to be from the 5th Fusiliers, appealed in person to the corps commander, General Milburn, that the men of the brigade, "depleted in strength and with their tactical situation somewhat tangled," as a later American post-mortem report put it, were relieved by the 15th RCT and pulled out of the line toward midnight on 25 April. This was just as well. Ammunition was in very short supply, with 45 Field Regiment having fired off over 11,500 shells, and 170 Mortar Battery around 12,000 bombs, in the course of the battle. Just as importantly, both officers and men were by now utterly spent. As Captain Jim Pearson, second-in-command of Z Company, put it inelegantly but accurately in a letter to his hospitalized company commander, Major John Winn, a couple of days later, "everybody was in no fit state to do anything." The Battle of the Imjin was over, the final parting shot probably fired by the coaxial machine-gun of the last Centurion to depart the battlefield, commanded by Major Henry Huth.[41]

Tom Brodie, commander of 29th Brigade at the Imjin, ten years on.

Courtesy National Portrait Gallery

Brigadier Brian Burke (in beret), commanding 27th Brigade at Kapyong, with Brigadier George Taylor of the new 28th Brigade, April 26, 1951.

Courtesy Australian War Memorial

Lieutenant-Colonel J. P. “Fred” Carne of the Glosters in a relaxed mood in the days prior to the Imjin battle.

Courtesy Soldiers of Gloucestershire Museum

Lieutenant-Colonel J. R. "Big Jim" Stone directs action from his 2PPCLI tactical HQ while eating cold beans, March 1951.

Courtesy Library and Archives Canada

Lieutenant-Colonel Bruce Ferguson strikes a pose, November 1950.

Courtesy Australian War Memorial

A Bren carrier belonging to 3RAR photographed October 1950.

Courtesy Australian War Memorial

Oxford carriers belonging to 29th Brigade, Uijongbu, 1951.

Courtesy Soldiers of Gloucestershire Museum

A Canadian M3 half-track in Korea a few months after the Kapyong battle. Note the. 50 caliber machine-gun.

Courtesy Library and Archives Canada

Gunners of 45 Field Regiment manhandling a 25-pounder gun into position.

Courtesy Imperial War Museum

A 2PPCLI Korean porter expresses his dismay at the noise created by 16 Field Regiment in action, April 16, 1951.

Courtesy Library and Archives Canada

A Centurion of 8RIH carries men of 1RNR back across the Imjin from a patrol into no-man's-land, April 17, 1951.

Courtesy Imperial War Museum

Padre Davies conducts Sunday Service for the Glosters, April 22, 1951.

Courtesy of Gloucestershire Museum

The knocked-out Chaffee that halted the column aiming to save the Glosters on April 24, 1951, here bulldozed away weeks later.

Courtesy Soldiers of Gloucestershire Museum

An M4A3E8 Sherman crew getting into position to support 3RAR above the Kapyong Valley, April 23, 1951.

Courtesy Australian War Memorial

The gravestone of Major General Robert H. "Shorty" Soule, dead from a heart attack precisely eight months after leading 3rd Infantry Division, to which 29th Brigade was attached during the Imjin battle.

Arlington National Cemetery

James A. Van Fleet (left) inspects soldiers of 3RAR after awarding the Kapyong Presidential Unit Citation. To his left is John W. O'Daniel, who succeeded Frank Milburn as I Corps commander.

Courtesy Australian War Memorial

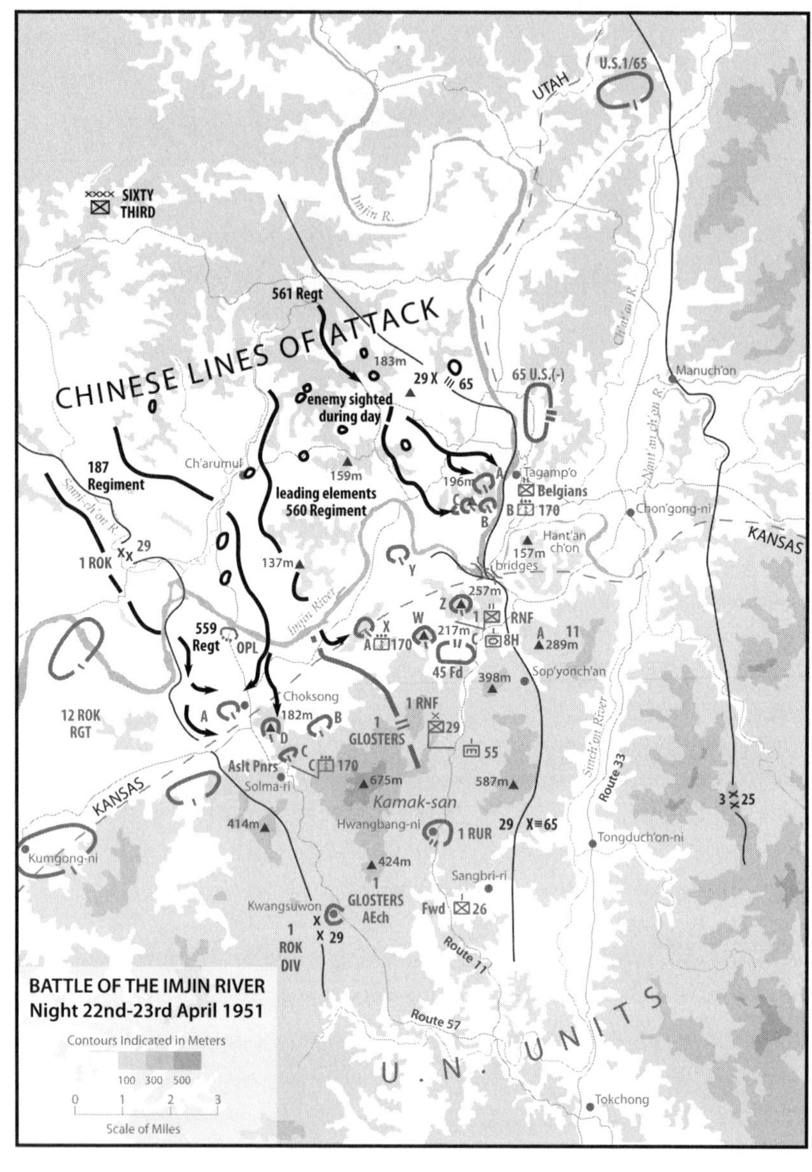

SIXTY THIRD
UTAH
U.S.1/65
Imjin R.
561 Regt
CHINESE LINES OF ATTACK
183m
29 X
65
65 U.S.(-)
enemy sighted during day
Ch'arumul
187 Regiment
159m
leading elements 560 Regiment
196m
A
Tagamp'o
Belgians
B
B 170
Manuch'on
Chon'gong-ni
KANSAS
Hant'an ch'on
157m
bridges
29
1 ROK
137m
Y
Imjin River
257m
Z
1 RNF
559 Regt
OPL
X
A 170
W
217m
C
8H
A 11
289m
45 Fd
398m
Sop'yonch'an
12 ROK RGT
A
Choksong
182m
B
1 RNF
29
1 GLOSTERS
D
55
C
C 170
Aslt Pnrs
Solma-ri
675m
587m
KANSAS
Kamak-san
414m
Hwangbang-ni
1 RUR
29
X=65
Kumgong-ni
Tongduch'on-ni
424m
3
25
Sangbri-ri
Kwangsuwon
1 GLOSTERS AEch
Fwd
26
1 ROK DIV
29
Route 11
Route 33
Route 57
U.N. UNITS
Tokchong
BATTLE OF THE IMJIN RIVER
Night 22nd-23rd April 1951
Contours Indicated in Meters
100 300 500
0 1 2 3
Scale of Miles

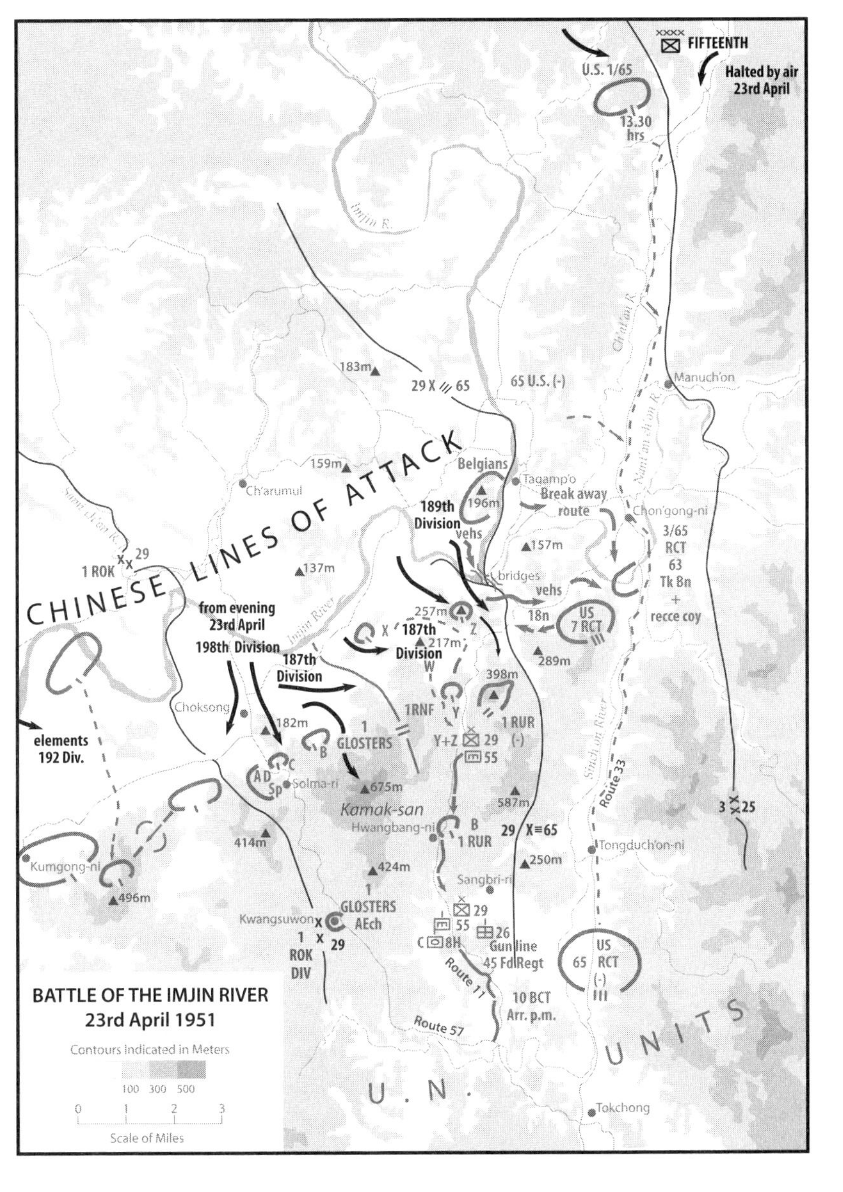
BATTLE OF THE IMJIN RIVER
23rd April 1951
Contours indicated in Meters
100 300 500
0 1 2 3
Scale of Miles
CHINESE LINES OF ATTACK
U.N. UNITS
FIFTEENTH
Halted by air 23rd April
U.S. 1/65
13.30 hrs
Imjin R.
183m
29 X 65
65 U.S. (-)
Manuch'on
159m
Belgians
Tagamp'o
Break away route
196m
189th Division
vehs
Ch'arumul
Chon'gong-ni
157m
3/65 RCT
63 Tk Bn
+
recce coy
1 ROK
29
137m
bridges
vehs
from evening 23rd April
198th Division
257m
18n
US 7 RCT
187th Division
217m
187th Division
289m
398m
Choksong
1RNF
1 RUR (-)
182m
1 GLOSTERS
Y+Z 29
55
elements 192 Div.
AD
Sp
Solma-ri
675m
Kamak-san
587m
Hwangbang-ni
B 1 RUR
29 X 65
414m
424m
250m
Tongduch'on-ni
Route 33
Sinch'on River
3 25
Kumgong-ni
496m
Sangbri-ri
1 GLOSTERS AEch
Kwangsuwon
1 ROK DIV
29
55
8H
26
Gun line
45 Fd Regt
US 65 RCT (-)
Route 11
10 BCT Arr. p.m.
Route 57
Tokchong

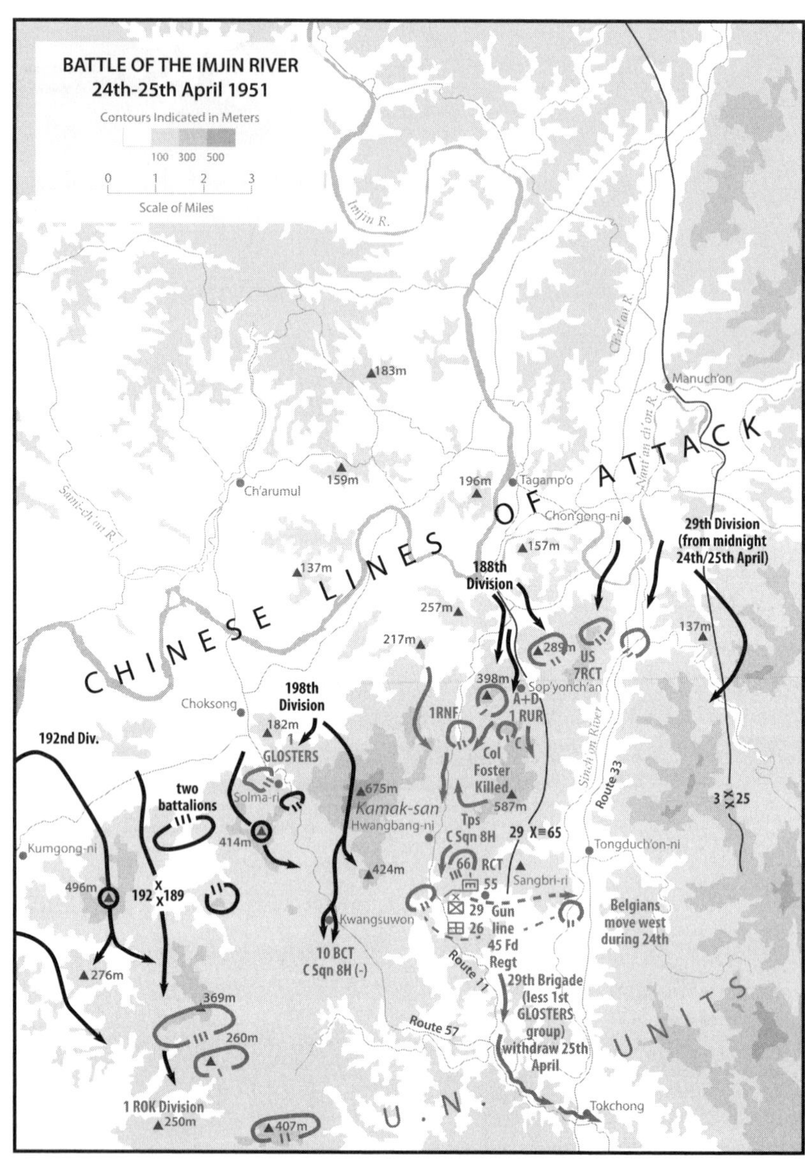
BATTLE OF THE IMJIN RIVER
24th-25th April 1951
Contours Indicated in Meters
100 300 500
0 1 2 3
Scale of Miles
Imjin R.
CHINESE LINES OF ATTACK
U.N. UNITS
29th Division (from midnight 24th/25th April)
188th Division
198th Division
192nd Div.
1 GLOSTERS
two battalions
1RNF
A+D 1 RUR
Col Foster Killed
US 7RCT
Tps C Sqn 8H
29 X≡65 RCT
10 BCT C Sqn 8H (-)
Gun line 45 Fd Regt
Belgians move west during 24th
29th Brigade (less 1st GLOSTERS group) withdraw 25th April
1 ROK Division
Kamak-san
Manuch'on
Tagamp'o
Ch'arumul
Chon'gong-ni
Sop'yonch'an
Choksong
Solma-ri
Hwangbang-ni
Kumgong-ni
Kwangsuwon
Sangbri-ri
Tongduch'on-ni
Tokchong
Route 33
Route 11
Route 57
Sinch'on River
Ch'at'an R.
Nant'an ch'on R.
Sami-ch'on R.
183m
159m
196m
157m
137m
257m
217m
289m
398m
182m
675m
587m
414m
424m
496m
276m
369m
260m
250m
407m
192 X X 189
3 XX 25
66
55
29
26

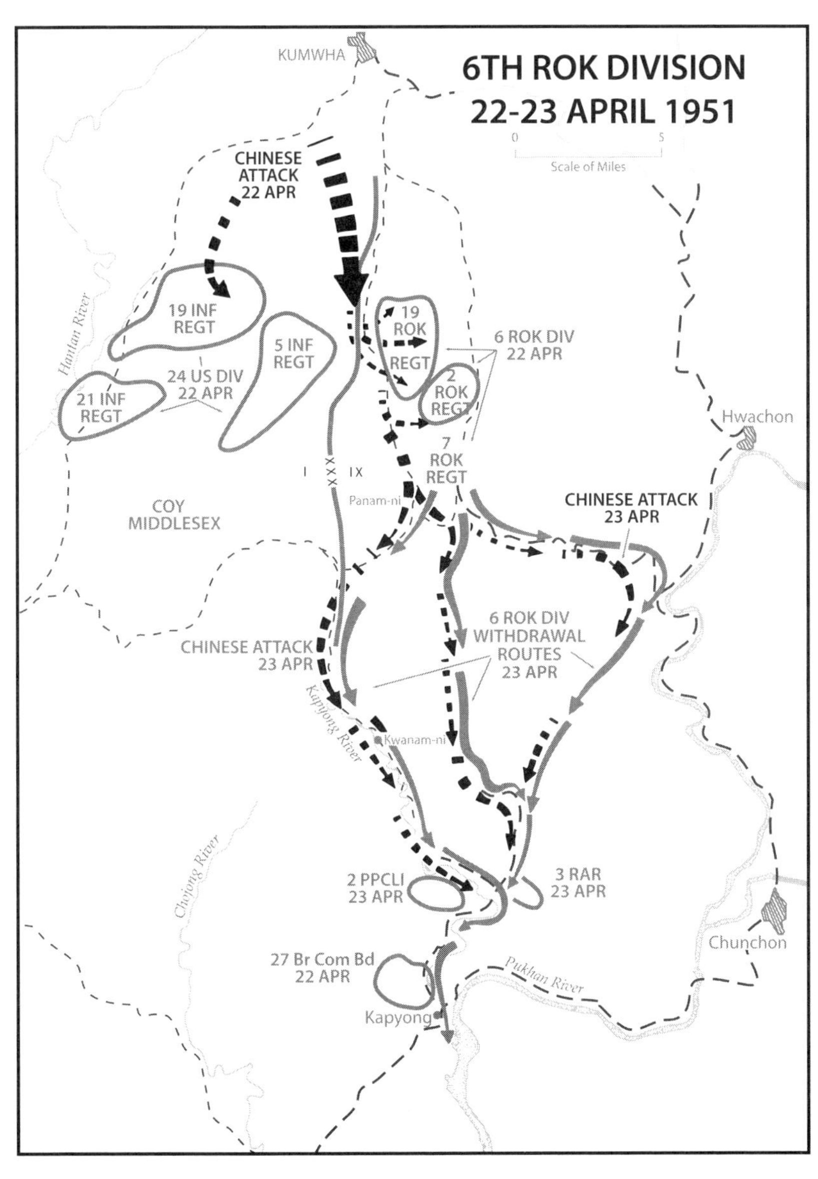
6TH ROK DIVISION
22-23 APRIL 1951
0
5
Scale of Miles
KUMWHA
CHINESE
ATTACK
22 APR
19 INF
REGT
5 INF
REGT
21 INF
REGT
24 US DIV
22 APR
Hantan River
19
ROK
REGT
2
ROK
REGT
6 ROK DIV
22 APR
7
ROK
REGT
I
XXX
IX
Panam-ni
Hwachon
CHINESE ATTACK
23 APR
COY
MIDDLESEX
6 ROK DIV
WITHDRAWAL
ROUTES
23 APR
CHINESE ATTACK
23 APR
Kapyong River
Kwanam-ni
Chojong River
2 PPCLI
23 APR
3 RAR
23 APR
Chunchon
27 Br Com Bd
22 APR
Pukhan River
Kapyong

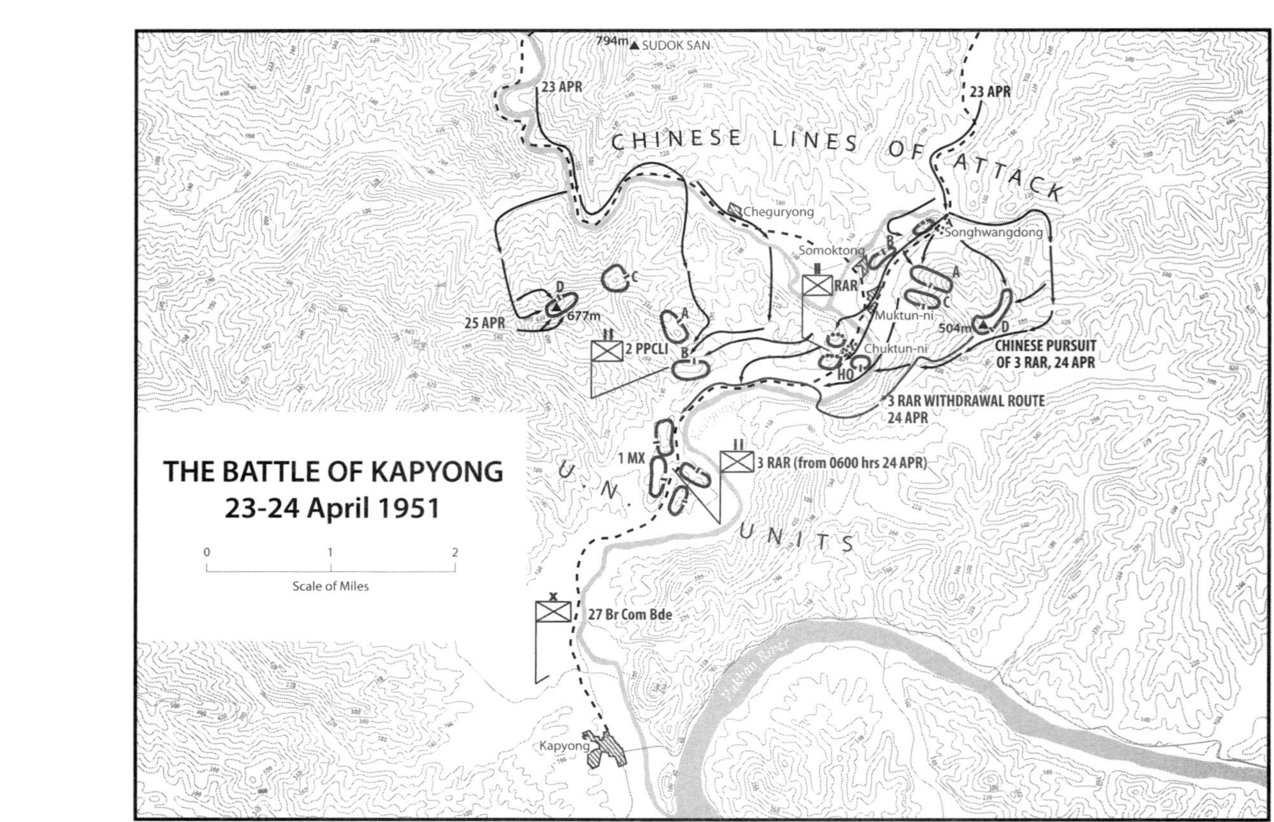
THE BATTLE OF KAPYONG
23-24 April 1951
0
1
2
Scale of Miles
794m SUDOK SAN
23 APR
23 APR
CHINESE LINES OF ATTACK
Cheguryong
Somoktong
Songhwangdong
RAR
Muktun-ni
Chuktun-ni
504m
677m
25 APR
2 PPCLI
HQ
CHINESE PURSUIT
OF 3 RAR, 24 APR
3 RAR WITHDRAWAL ROUTE
24 APR
1 MX
3 RAR (from 0600 hrs 24 APR)
U.N. UNITS
27 Br Com Bde
Kapyong

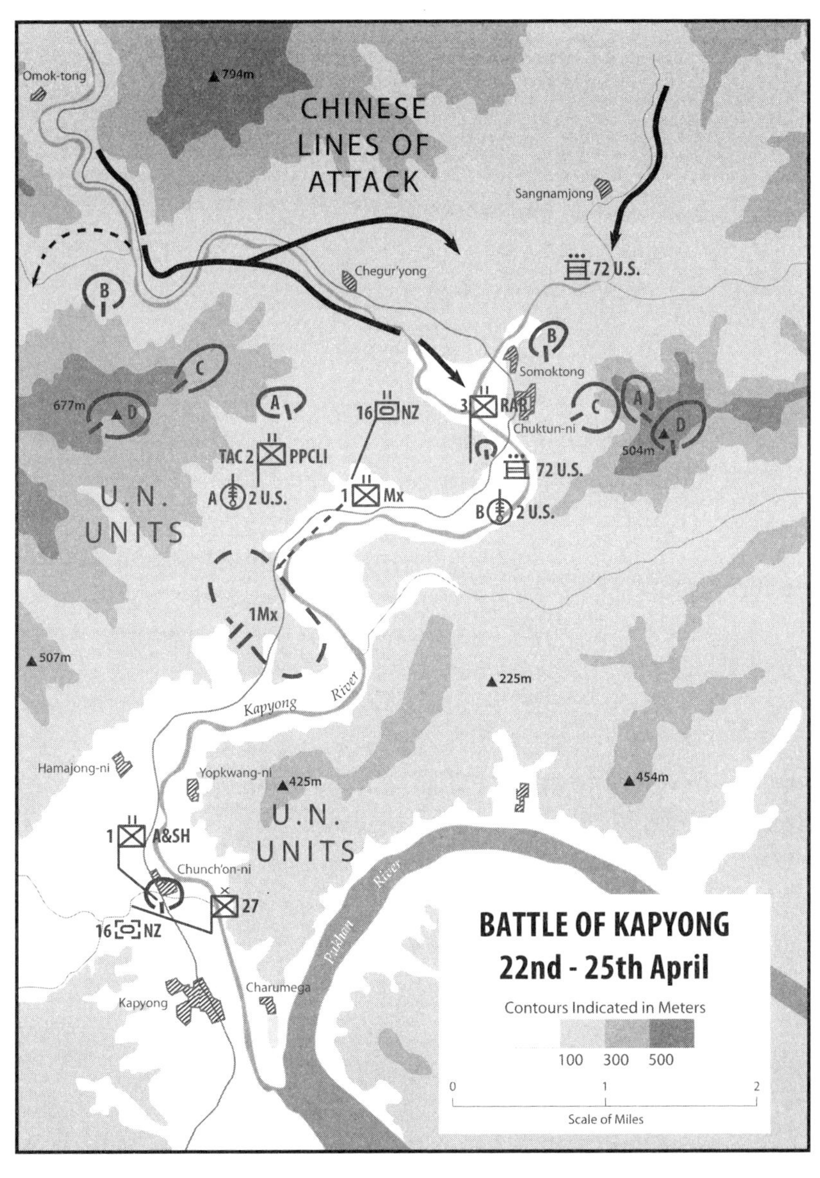
Omok-tong
794m
CHINESE
LINES OF
ATTACK
Sangnamjong
Chegur'yong
72 U.S.
B
B
Somoktong
C
3 RAR
C
A
677m
D
A
16 NZ
Chuktun-ni
D
504m
TAC 2 PPCLI
72 U.S.
U.N.
UNITS
A 2 U.S.
1 Mx
B 2 U.S.
1Mx
507m
225m
Kapyong River
Hamajong-ni
Yopkwang-ni
425m
454m
U.N.
UNITS
1 A&SH
Chunch'on-ni
27
16 NZ
Pukhan River
Charumega
Kapyong
BATTLE OF KAPYONG
22nd - 25th April
Contours Indicated in Meters
100 300 500
0 1 2
Scale of Miles

A bit of a sticky wicket is developing at the front, gather all Brigade officers and return [to Brigade HQ] at once.

Telephone instructions from 27BCB Duty Officer to 2PPCLI Liaison Officer during farewell party for departing 1A&SH, evening, 22 April 1951[1]

IX Corps ordered 6 ROK to hold this line [KANSAS]. It however became more obvious as time went on that the 6 ROK Div was incapable of holding any line.

16FR WAR DIARY, situation c. 3:30 AM, 23 April 1951[2]

FIVE

Kapyong: The First Day

ON SUNDAY, 22 APRIL 1951, MOST OF THE MEN OF 27TH Brigade were if anything even less concerned about the prospect of battle than their counterparts in 29th Brigade. After all, when they had departed the front line a few days earlier for a couple of weeks of well-deserved rest and reorganization in IX Corps reserve, the Chinese were still withdrawing. Arrayed by unit north of the village of Kapyong in relatively idyllic surroundings variously dubbed "Sherwood Forest" and "Happy Valley" – located at this point over twenty-two miles behind the front – soldiers for the first time in weeks had the opportunity to properly bathe, play soccer, watch films, drink their beer ration, and generally put themselves at ease. "Life was very relaxing and pleasant," Bruce Ferguson, the CO of the Australians (3RAR) recalled. "The weather was warm," Mike Czuboka of the 2PPCLI mortar platoon remembered, also noting how he and his fellow Canadians "appreciated getting periods of uninterrupted and peaceful sleep" along with hot meals for the first time in weeks.[3]

Aside from the occasional parade and guard mounting, the only duties revolved around prearranged changes in formation and command structure. In the following days and weeks the two British infantry battalions were due to exchange places with fresh battalions from Hong Kong, 27th British Commonwealth Brigade giving way to 28th Commonwealth Brigade. The first steps were already under way over the weekend, the Argylls departing for Pusan in preparation for the arrival of the 1st Battalion, King's Own Scottish Borderers the following

Monday. Brigadier Brian Burke was already making arrangements for the handing over of command to Brigadier George Taylor, while within the remaining units the opportunity was taken to send officers and men on R&R to Tokyo, including a pair of company commanders – one from 2PPCLI, the other from 3RAR – and a battery commander from 16 Field Regiment. Lieutenant-Colonel Jim Stone, commanding officer of the Patricias, had only just returned after a mild bout of smallpox. As a 3RAR company commander later reflected, "we believed it was impossible that we could be committed to operations."[4]

Though as content as the next man that weekend, a few of those who would find themselves fighting for their lives over the next few days recalled obvious signs that the three South Korean regiments that had relieved 27th Brigade in the line between 16 and 19 April might not be up to the task if the Chinese suddenly turned around and attacked. In marked contrast to the veteran 1st ROK Division on the left flank of 29th Brigade, the 6th ROK Division twenty-plus miles to the north of 27th Brigade was hastily raised, undertrained, inexperienced, and poorly led. Barry Reed, a Middlesex subaltern, remembered thinking at the time that the Korean soldiers taking over his positions "weren't terribly well organized." Young conscripts in some cases did not know how to fix bayonets or indeed load their rifles, while junior officers were observed caring more about their personal comfort than the security of unit positions. "I reckon we'll be back into it soon," a Digger was overheard to remark. "Somehow I don't reckon we can depend on these blokes."[5]

The Chinese, as it happened, had their sights set on the destruction of both the relievers and the relieved. At the time the Commonwealth troops were going into reserve, Peng Te-haui was summarizing for his army group commanders the main objectives of the Fifth Phase offensive due to start within a few days, objectives for which the elimination of both the 6th ROK Division and 27th Brigade were a necessary prelude. Concerning the South Koreans, the Chinese operational directive read:

> The main task of the Fortieth Army [attached to the 8th Army Group] will be to wipe out the 6th Puppet [ROK] Division and open up a critical breach so as to sever the links between the American forces on the eastern and western fronts; once they have succeeded in doing this, the main force will penetrate directly to Mu-dong-ni and Kap'yong and cut the Ch'unch'on road.

While the 40th Army was to strike the left half of the 6th ROK Division, the 20th Army was assigned to the right half. Concerning the Commonwealth brigade, the relevant passage from the operational directive was as follows:

> The three armies of 9 Army Group will first concentrate an absolute superiority of troop strength and fire power, and quickly wipe out the British 27th Brigade, while using part of their strength to pin down the American 24th Division, and sever the links between the British 27th Brigade and the American 24th Division; once they have succeeded in doing this . . . attacking from the south east to north west, they can wipe out the American 24th and 25th Divisions.[6]

That the Chinese were preparing an offensive was well known within the U.N. command, not least because by the middle of April 1951 enemy radio propaganda had been warning of the imminent recapture of Seoul.[7] Exactly where and in what strength the enemy would strike, however, remained unclear.[8]

On 21 April, the 6th ROK Division was still moving forward. The next afternoon, as motorized patrols were ranging three miles ahead of the division main body without incident, artillery observation aircraft from IX Corps began to spot large numbers of the enemy moving southward. Once he had been alerted in the latter part of the afternoon to this development, the divisional commander, Brigadier General Chang Do-yong, ordered his two leading regiments, the 19th on the left and the 2nd on the right, to halt and close up around mutually supporting defensive positions on high ground, and brought up his reserve regiment, the 7th, in direct support of the 2nd.[9]

In theory, the 6th ROK Division now held a strong defensive position anchored on tactically significant heights between the 1st Marine Division (IX Corps) on the right and the 24th Division (I Corps) on the left. The infantry battalions could call for support from the 105-mm guns of the 27th ROK Field Artillery Battalion and the 25-pounders of 16 Field Regiment – the New Zealanders not having gone into reserve with the rest of 27th Brigade the previous week – as well as the U.S. 4.2-inch mortars of C Company, 2nd Chemical Mortar Battalion. The IX Corps commander, Major General William M. Hoge, also sent forward the self-propelled 155-mm guns of the 92nd Armored Field Artillery Battalion, plus the 105-mm howitzers of the 987th Armored Field Artillery

Battalion and 2nd Rocket Field Artillery Battery to positions from which they could support the South Koreans.[10]

In practice, as dusk approached, a disaster was in the making. Even at the divisional headquarters, where map boards showed all to be well, General Chang had been worried enough about the morale of the 2nd Regiment – against whom it was thought the main blow would fall – to try to bolster fighting spirits by ignoring the advice of his senior U.S. liaison officer about maintaining a contingency reserve and placing the 7th Regiment behind the 2nd. This move, however, could do little to alleviate the problems that were developing on the ground hours before the enemy made contact. What was not known at headquarters was that preparation of forward defensive positions was slow and ineffective, that the men were increasingly scared, and that their mostly apathetic and incompetent officers and NCOs were unable to bring order from chaos.[11]

Thus an hour after dark elements of the Chinese 179th Regiment (60th Division, 20th Army) and elements of the 120th Division (40th Army) were able to pass easily through the gaps and around the open flanks that had not been dealt with, striking without warning first at the left-flank battalion of the 2nd Regiment and then getting behind the rest of both the 2nd Regiment and the 19th Regiment. "Someone's pushed the panic button up here," Captain Floyd C. Hines, the 92nd Armored Field Artillery Battalion liaison officer with one of the regiments, radioed back. Terrified of being surrounded, the South Koreans of the two forward regiments "broke and ran," all and sundry abandoning their weapons and equipment and streaming southward. They were soon joined by the men of the 7th Regiment and the 27th Field Artillery Battalion – which abandoned its vehicles and guns on contact – in what had become a disorganized, headlong flight for safety. As the corps commander bluntly put it a week later, all elements of the 6th ROK Division had during the night of 22–23 April "fled in disorder without offering the slightest resistance, abandoning weapons and equipment and permitting friendly supporting elements to be overrun."[12]

The reference to the overrunning of American supporting units was a slight exaggeration, but it was a near-run thing. As the other U.S. artillery units struggled to link up with the 92nd Armored Field Artillery

Battalion to the east during the hours of darkness they had to endure both sporadic enemy fire and roads jammed with fleeing ROK troops and their vehicles. The end result was that the 987th Armored Field Artillery Battalion had to abandon half its equipment while Company C, 2nd Chemical Mortar Battalion and 2nd Rocket Field Artillery Battery lost every tube and gun.[13]

The 16 Field Regiment was luckier, though it was at times in serious jeopardy. Left in support of the 6th ROK Division near the village of Panam-ni when 27th Brigade had gone into reserve, it had reverted to brigade control at 7:30 PM on the 22nd and been ordered to return to the brigade area north of Kapyong. Since the brigade was in reserve and the front as yet inactive, the CO, Lieutenant-Colonel John Moodie, decided to postpone the relocation of his batteries until the following morning. 162 Battery, after all, was fully occupied in its own farewell party – a traditional Maori feast – for invited Argylls. As the battalion's chronicler intimated, the Chinese were the last thing on anyone's mind:

> The *plat du jour* was a whole bullock [requisitioned from a Korean farmer[14]] cooked on red-hot stones in a hollow in the ground. This was covered over and water was then poured into it through a small hole in the top. The effect of the steam rising from the heated stones produced the most delicious dish which was one of the gastronomic memories of the war. And after the meal, the New Zealanders gave traditional songs and war dances until it was time to go home.[15]

It was only later in the evening that news of something seriously going wrong at the front reached the CO. Major David Wilson, a company commander in the Argylls who had evidentially lingered after the party had ended, remembered how "panic stations set in" and thinking to himself "'What the hell?' – we were used to foul-ups by now, but this seemed to be on another plane altogether."[16] A telephone call from IX Corps artillery HQ indicated that the Chinese had attacked in strength and that the 6th ROK Division was retreating, and Moodie was strongly advised to start the withdrawal to the Kapyong area scheduled for the following morning. Contact was made with the tactical headquarters of the 6th ROK Division to try to confirm the seriousness of the situation. There was clearly a good deal of confusion, but Moodie was left with the impression that the ROK division was now in the process of regrouping. He therefore decided to stick to the original plan for a daylight withdrawal, and the gunners who had been stood-to when the first reports of trouble had come in were allowed to go back to sleep.[17]

Within an hour or two, however, South Korean soldiers steadily began to filter back through the regimental position. The intelligence officer, Second-Lieutenant H. K. Griffiths, was roused from slumber and sent off to find out what was happening at the headquarters of the 19th ROK Regiment. Making his way there in a scout car with an interpreter, Griffith found only confusion and disorganization. Radioing this information to Moodie, he was ordered back to 16 Field Regiment HQ. At 2:30 AM on Monday the 23rd, the gunners were once more woken up, and shortly after 3 AM put on immediate notice to decamp.[18] By this time more and more ROK soldiers were passing through the gun lines, and as Gordon Menzies (162 Battery) observed, these thoroughly demoralized Koreans were not inclined to rally:

> There was no sign of officers or any NCO willing to take command and we could not communicate with them except by signs. They made gestures with their fingers pointing to their rifles which did not make sense to us but they eventually conveyed that they had no ammunition. It was a capital offence for them to discard their rifles but they had cleverly decided that they could not be asked to fight with no ammunition. We had no ammunition for their American rifles and there was no sign of any Korean command to handle these surplus soldiers. So our hopes of some infantry protection vanished as fast [as] they vanished down the road when we let them go.[19]

Even those few ROK officers who tried to halt the flight by firing their weapons over or even into groups of fleeing men were unsuccessful in stemming the tide, and by 4 AM, with small-arms fire observed 1,200 yards in front of the forward battery, it was clearly time to go. Taking everything with them, the batteries found their progress impeded by the masses of ROK troops clogging the road paralleling the longitudinal Kapyong River. At first there was some sympathy for the plight of youths who were clearly terrified and in some cases crying with fear. A growing sense that this mass of humanity was imperiling the safety of the guns by slowing and sometimes halting vehicular movement, however, caused empathy to turn into concern. "They were trying to clamber on our trucks," Corporal Tom Frazer related, "but [our officers] told us 'don't let anyone on the trucks, we don't know who the hell they are, they could be infiltrators' . . . quite frightening." Boots and rifle butts were used to try and loosen the dozens of youngsters trying to climb aboard, and some of those who fell off may have been run over by the following truck. By 8 AM 16 Field Regiment had reestablished itself near the village of Naechon, about four miles north of Kapyong.[20]

Though the 1st Marine Division to the right and the 24th Infantry Division on the left were soon under attack as well, it was only the 6th ROK Division that disintegrated. A gap several miles wide had opened up overnight in the IX Corps line as a result of the rout of the 6th ROK Division. "The Chinese were pouring through mile after mile without opposition," as Eighth Army commander James A. Van Fleet recalled.[21] As yet, however, the full magnitude of what had happened was not apparent at corps HQ due to breakdowns in communication. Through the night the more patriotic ROK officers, up to and including the mortified divisional commander, had been desperately trying to stem the headlong flight to the rear. Toward dawn a motley force of about 2,500 men had been assembled about ten miles south of the original positions.[22] At this point the retreat had outstripped the enemy advance, and once communication had been restored between divisional and corps headquarters, the twenty-eight-year-old Chang – whom Hoge later dismissed as "no good"[23] – seems to have allowed his corps commander to believe around dawn that there was a chance that the 6th ROK Division could pull itself together and advance three miles north to establish a defense along Line Kansas (roughly the 38th Parallel).[24]

Having monitored the progress of the New Zealanders through the night, 27th Brigade HQ was already in a state of alert when Brigadier Burke awoke at 7 AM and heard over the Armed Forces Radio network that the expected enemy offensive had begun. Studying his maps, the brigadier at once guessed that the Chinese would – as they had in their last offensive – come down the Kapyong Valley. He therefore ordered that a reconnaissance party be assembled and sent north to reconnoiter possible defensive positions.[25] This was prescient; at 8:30 AM a message arrived from IX Corps ordering Burke to establish locations for a possible blocking position northeast of the village of Kapyong. General Hoge, it seemed, was not completely convinced that the South Korean troops could be relied upon to hold Line Kansas, given that it was becoming increasingly clear that "the situation had collapsed beyond control" the previous night. It later emerged that well over 2,000 rifles, 168 machine-guns, 66 bazookas, 42 mortars, and 87 trucks had been abandoned by the South Koreans. Hoge thus wanted to prepare to "form a line in rear of 6ROK Division" as insurance.[26]

As the sun rose in the east it became obvious that Monday, 23 April was going to be another sunny, fine, clear day, the temperatures by the afternoon reaching what felt like 80° Fahrenheit.[27] What was less clear was what the men of 27th Brigade would be facing in the course of the coming hours, though as an officer in the Argylls put it, there were "disquieting signs" after Reveille was sounded that something was up. "Firstly," he noticed, "the Middlesex had not run up their Union Jack and Regimental flag outside their camp; and secondly, there was a certain ominous activity round Battalion Headquarters, and the sight of company commanders hurrying to and fro boded ill."[28] Much would now depend on the behavior of the Chinese People's Volunteers and of what remained of the 6th ROK Division in the coming hours.

We were in a rest area; and then they broke through, and they just pulled us off rest, shoved us back up, and said "here, hold this," you know, that was our position.

2PPCLI VETERAN, 1976[1]

You're sitting there, you're listening to all these noises of rifle fire, grenades going off, artillery shells going off, the whistle blasts, the bugles, the screams . . . it's the noise, it's like, it's like a symphony of war . . .

3RAR VETERAN, 2000[2]

SIX

Kapyong: The Second Day

HAVING BEEN ALERTED BY IX CORPS TO THE POSSIBILITY that his brigade might have to assume a blocking position, Brigadier Brian Burke had to decide how best to deploy his units. Topographically the most secure defensive position appeared to be just over three and a half miles north of Kapyong, where three major features dominated the valley floor through which the Kapyong River sinuously curved its way southward and down which any enemy was likely to come. On the western side the irregular high ground peaked at Hill 677 opposite, the hulking form of Sudok-san (Hill 794) to the north, and Hill 504 to the east. With a frontage of almost four and a half miles to defend, a mere three infantry battalions were not going to be able to form a continuous line, but if they each held one of the three main hill features they could collectively still dominate the valley floor. This was likely what was running through the brigadier's mind when he called an O [Operations] Group of his unit commanders around 9 AM. If the call to arms came, the Middlesex would occupy Hill 794, the Patricias Hill 677, and the Australians Hill 504.[3]

By the time the battalion commanders were ready to return to their units, however, the possible deployments as imagined by Burke had to be modified. Still hoping that elements of the 6th ROK Division could rally and push up to Line Kansas – Brigadier General Chang Do-yong had indicated that this could be achieved by the late afternoon – the corps commander, William M. Hoge, ordered Burke to send 16 Field Regiment forward again in support of the South Koreans.[4] Having seen firsthand the state of the 6th ROK Division, Lieutenant-Colonel John Moodie and his second-in-command, Major R. J. H. Webb, were deeply concerned about the safety of their men, and after returning to their regiment decided to ask for both a written order and an infantry battalion from within the brigade to protect them. As yet the brigadier seems to have thought, in light of what he had heard from corps HQ, that there was still a good chance the rest of 27th Brigade would not in fact be required to move forward, or, if it were, still might not have to fight a major engagement. The Kiwi gunners, on the other hand, would be in the forefront with the ROKs, and he could see that they might need more protection than the unreliable South Koreans could offer. Burke therefore agreed to divert the Middlesex to act as "a bodyguard" for 16 Field Regiment: "Just to make sure we can get you back if there is an emergency," as he put it to Moodie.[5]

There were already some indications that the South Koreans were still moving rearward rather than rallying. "From the air," a New Zealand officer attached to the IX Corps air observation flight noted, "it was a scene of chaos and retreat." It did not take long for those on the ground to notice that all was not well. "I guess it was the morning of 23 April that someone came shouting around for everybody to get the hell up," a Patricia remembered. "We looked out the [tent] window and all we could see were South Korean troops flying past us along with those monstrous American vehicles they were supplied with. We didn't know what the hell had happened."[6] That something was seriously wrong was becoming more and more evident. "Rumors had been sweeping through camp all morning that things were going bad at the front," recalled a Digger, "These rumors were backed by civilians hurrying past the camp heading south."[7]

As yet, however, lack of information from higher formation headquarters meant that the battalion reconnoitering operations in relation to hills 504 and 677, which began before noon on brigade orders, were merely a precautionary measure, the active front supposedly still being at least six to seven miles to the north of these features. "It was a beautiful, warm day with clear, blue skies," the 3RAR Intelligence Officer (IO) remembered. "War seemed a long way off."[8]

He was not the only Australian officer to feel relaxed. "I lay stretched out on the grass enjoying a carefree doze," admitted the A Company commander, Major Ben O'Dowd. His nap was curtailed in the early afternoon when news arrived that Lieutenant-Colonel Bruce Ferguson – who, accompanied by his IO, Lieutenant "Alf" Argent, had gone forward to survey the vicinity of the hamlet of Chuktan-ni, and then returned for a leisurely lunch – wanted his company commanders to join him and go forward for an O Group. "Our task," wrote O'Dowd of the orders Ferguson gave, "was to reconnoiter the Hill 504 area and the approaches to it for a possible blocking force position should it become required later on." Once this task was completed, "we could return to the battalion area and get on with our relaxation."[9]

At 2:15 PM – at which time Ferguson was still briefing his officers in the valley to the west of Hill 504, and the Canadian reconnaissance party led by Lieutenant-Colonel Jim Stone likely had corrected an earlier navigation error and was moving toward the northern approaches to Hill 677[10] – General Hoge arrived at 27th Brigade HQ and personally passed on the news that reconnaissance would give way to physical occupation of the Kapyong Valley blocking positions.[11]

Recognizing that what had started out as a mere reconnaissance for future reference was evolving into an actual deployment with the growing chance of contact with the enemy sooner or later, Brigadier Burke was starting to worry that his forces were too dispersed if there was a real likelihood of meeting the Chinese head-on in force. Still sporting a rose in his cap in honor of St. George's Day, he reminded Hoge that neither the Argylls nor the Borderers were immediately available, as the former, about to set sail for Hong Kong, were handing over much of their equipment to the latter, just arriving from the colony. One or the other could be brought forward within a day or so in an emergency, but for the time being 27th Brigade had only two infantry battalions – 2PPCLI and 3RAR – to work with, as the Middlesex already had been committed to moving forward with 16 Field Regiment in support of the 6th ROK Division. The corps commander seems to have agreed that, if push came to shove and the two battalions were to hold Hill 677 and Hill 504, they would need more support, and he attached – though apparently without ceding clear command authority – two companies of the 2nd Chemical Mortar Battalion, two companies of the 74th Engineer Combat Battalion, and most of a company of M4A3E8 Sherman tanks from the 72nd Tank Battalion.[12]

By mid-afternoon, when news of the change of plan had reached battalion headquarters, there had been further signs that a deployment which Ferguson was still talking of in terms of a precaution "in the event of an enemy break through further north"[13] was more and more likely to result in a full-scale fight for 27th Brigade.

Lieutenant Ron Middleton, then 2PPCLI duty officer at brigade HQ, later recalled that about this time an agitated U.S. Army lieutenant colonel had appeared at the door of the command vehicle. He turned out to be the commander of the engineers who had positioned themselves about a mile to the rear of the positions soon to be occupied by 2PPCLI and 3RAR, and stated dramatically that the front had broken and that he wanted to know where he and his men should go. The brigade major, J. D. Stewart, laconically explained that he did not have the authority to give orders to U.S. engineers, but he presumed that if they had to decamp at all they ought to go south. The American officer terminated the exchange by exclaiming, "I'm hauling ass outta here!"[14]

This was just as the bulk of 16 Field Regiment, accompanied by the Middlesex, had begun to move forward toward the hamlet of Kwanam-ni, roughly two and a half miles south of the gun positions vacated the previous night. As they advanced up the road over the next few hours the infantrymen and artillerymen were impeded by refugees and stragglers moving in the opposite direction, among them ROK headquarters personnel and U.S. advisors. Remembered Corporal Nick Hutley of C Company, 1st Middlesex:

> My company marches up the road, and I felt a little peeved then, cos we're marching up the road and all these Koreans from the 6th ROK, Republic of Korea troops, they're all pouring back; they've left their arms up there and everything, you know, cos they had no rifles or anything. All in trucks just pouring down the road south. And here's the poor old bloody British Tommy who's got to go up there.[15]

Meanwhile as the afternoon wore on the commanders of 3RAR and 2PPCLI were being forced to decide how their limited forces should in practice rather than just in theory be deployed on Hill 504 and Hill 677 respectively. As elsewhere, the high ground was rocky and largely covered in brush and scrub. Both features, particularly 677, had a variety of sharp ridges, spurs, and gullies. Steep slopes were of course helpful to the defense, but the jagged topography meant that once deployed, companies or even platoons would have both a limited field of vision and a circumscribed ability to offer mutually supporting fire, while the Chinese could make use of gullies and other dead ground to approach unseen.[16]

On the right, Colonel Ferguson was constrained in his planning by the fact that, under pressure from IX Corps headquarters – which wanted a solid presence on the valley floor in order to set an example and to steady any fleeing ROK troops – Burke ordered him to set up his HQ astride the road to the southwest of Hill 504.[17] Another constraint was that, because the shift from a theoretical to an actual deployment had caught him unawares and as CO he felt he needed to get back and organize the Australian battalion for its move forward, Ferguson in his own words had "no opportunity for personal reconnaissance" of the high ground.[18]

Before going back to collect his men the Australian CO roughed out a deployment, very much aware that he had what he estimated to be only half the troops necessary to use Hill 504 – as ordered – to adequately protect the northeastern approaches to the hamlet of Chuktun-ni near where a tributary emptied into the Kapyong River. Battalion headquarters would be located by the road southwest of Hill 504, loosely protected by the machine-guns, anti-tank weapons, and mortars of Support Company. On Hill 504 itself, one and a quarter miles to the northwest, the infantry companies would of necessity each be located in separate areas. D Company was to occupy the summit while A Company took up position on a ridgeline spur extending to the northwest and C Company – acting as reserve force – placed itself on a rear spur. Farthest forward and lowest topographically, B Company would occupy a smallish hill that overlooked the road and a ford northeast of Chuktun-ni. It was, however, left very much up to the company commanders to reconnoiter the ground and decide how best to deploy their platoons. In support of 3RAR were fifteen Sherman tanks under the command of Lieutenant Kenneth W. Koch. These were distributed by platoon, respectively to guard a road north of B Company, to provide direct support for B Company on high ground, and to protect the battalion headquarters area.[19]

On the left, Jim Stone eventually led his reconnaissance party – which included not only the IO but also company commanders and various officers in charge of signals and supporting arms – to the north side of Hill 677. "I kept thinking that if I was the one trying to take the hill [the CO having undertaken plenty of such tasks with the Loyal Edmonton Regiment in Italy some seven years earlier[20]], I would move in such and such direction, and so on." In essence Stone was placing himself in the enemy's shoes and deciding how to respond. "I then decided which way the attack would come and deployed the battalion accordingly."[21] D Company would occupy the top of Hill 677, with B, C, and A companies occupying lower, separate islands of defense in an arc running from north (B) to west (C). As the CO put it to his officers in an O Group at six in the evening after the company commanders had been given a chance to look over the ground and the party had returned to the Kapyong area half an hour before, "Because of the topography and the extent of the battalion area to be defended, Patricias' companies cannot be deployed in the classical manner to be mutually supportive of one another."[22]

In the earlier part of the afternoon, when Stone and Ferguson had first received word that 2PPCLI and 3RAR were to move up and deploy, the thinking higher up the chain of command was still based on the premise that a reorganized 6th ROK Division would by then have advanced to Line Kansas, that the Middlesex and most of 16 Field Regiment thus would be able to concentrate on defending Hill 794, and that the units farther back on hills 504 and 677 would "settle in for a quiet night" since even if the Chinese pushed the South Koreans back it would take them many hours to advance this far south. These assumptions – which may help explain why the Australian move up to Hill 504 was apparently conducted in a rather leisurely manner[23] – were soon to be tested to destruction.[24]

By 4:30 PM the Kiwi gunners had reached Kwanam-ni, a mile or so northeast of Sudok-san, and Moodie, accompanied by Webb, went off to divisional HQ to find out how the 6th ROK Division was faring. The answer was not well, though it was difficult to know for sure what was happening at the front – due to breakdowns in communication – beyond the fact that its regiments definitely had not moved forward to Line Kansas. At the time Stone was briefing his officers for the move to Hill 677, word arrived at divisional headquarters that the 7th ROK Regiment had been hit from the right and was withdrawing in the face of what turned out to be the newly committed 118th CPV Division (40th Army, 13th Army Group). Going forward to the regimental headquarters to investigate what was happening, the 16 Field Regiment IO, Lieutenant Kelley Griffiths, found a dire situation. The Chinese were in among ROK positions everywhere, and soldiers were fleeing even in the face of ROK military police using their weapons liberally.[25]

A Middlesex private recalled how by the time the battalion arrived around 6 PM to support the gunners, ROK troops "were already streaming past us to the south, led by jeep-borne staff officers in a mass 'bug-out.' Behind them came streams of struggling soldiers, all falling over one another in their haste to escape." One group of about fifty men passed through aboard a bus that they had somehow acquired, talking wildly of being overrun from all sides. "By nightfall the road was completely blocked with a surging mass of troops," Julian Tunstall noted, "all but with one intent – to put as many miles as possible between themselves and the Chinese."[26]

The total collapse under way put both the Kiwi gunners and the Middlesex infantry in grave peril, and Burke, alerted to the situation over the radio by Moodie, authorized a withdrawal that started at 7 PM when the Middlesex companies were ordered off the hills they had occupied and into the artillery vehicles. The 25-pounders continued to fire blind for over an hour as ROK troops – some in good order, others not – passed southward, the ranges steadily diminishing. By about nine at night the last battery troop had limbered up to go, carrying the regiment's Korean porters with it, by which time the South Korean retreat had obviously turned into another rout. Civilian refugees, along with sobbing young soldiers (who had to be beaten off when they tried to clamber aboard already overloaded vehicles), slowed the Kiwi retirement to a crawl, and eventually those who refused to move out of the way were simply run over. By 10:30 PM most of the gunners and infantry had reached the positions at Naechon (in the Kapyong Valley southeast of Hill 677) from which they had started out earlier in the day, and efforts were made to get the guns back into action.[27]

As the Australians moved toward Hill 504 in the late afternoon, they too could see that something had gone badly wrong. "We trucked up the road and after several miles started to pass masses of South Korean soldiers heading in the opposite direction to us," recalled Joe Vezgoff of 7 Platoon. According to the commander of A Company, "they were streaming down the road, they were shouting, some didn't have weapons, they were obviously in a panic, in terror of the Chinese."[28]

Between about 5:30 and 8:00 PM four companies of 3RAR climbed up and deployed across Hill 504.[29] The official line from IX Corps, passed down to the troops, was still that "there was not a Chinaman within 10 miles of our position and we probably wouldn't see one till the next afternoon at the earliest."[30] In light of what had been observed coming down the valley, though, the Diggers did what they could to improvise defenses before darkness engulfed them. This was not easy, however, with so much rock, brush, and thin topsoil to contend with. But since conventional slit trenches were nearly impossible to dig, walls were the only option; "the hard, rocky ridgeline caused us to build 'sangers,'" a lance-corporal in C Company reported, "an above ground shelter built of rocks." No wire or mines had been brought forward.[31]

Owing to the late return of the reconnaissance party, the Patricias did not set off by vehicle toward Hill 677 until seven in the evening.[32] As the battalion prepared to move out, many officers appear to have had a sense that serious fighting was in the offing, practically swamping the quartermaster with requests for extra ammunition.[33] For many of the men, on the other hand, it was still not clear that they were heading into a fight. "See, the people above knew what was going on," one 2PPCLI driver reflected, "and they didn't funnel it down to the little people to the effect that you're going out, and somebody's – for real – going to be shooting at you."[34]

Initially, therefore, the mood among the men was quite carefree.[35] Then the Canadians began to see ROKs fleeing the Chinese advance. One soldier recalled:

> The first part of the journey was by truck. I was sitting right in the back. There was just a stream of Koreans heading south and we were heading north. I began to think to myself, "Lord Jesus, I am over here supposed to be helping these people and they're running one way while I am going another." These guys were coming out as if they were piling out of a bank building. It was like those guys going down the road. It went on for hours and it wasn't that encouraging.[36]

Growing apprehension was often mixed with anger toward those who by bugging out were forcing the Canadians back into harm's way. "I shudder in disbelief at seeing our allies running hell-bent away from the advancing enemy," remembered Corporal Rollie LaPointe of C Company; "they are a disorganized rabble! Leaving us to face their enemy, to fight for their bloody country!" The sight, he admitted, made him increasingly fearful as to what the immediate future might hold.[37]

At the village of Tungmudae on the southwestern corner of Hill 677 the infantry debouched from their trucks and started to toil their way up the steep slopes. "We walked our asses off up there," one soldier remembered.[38] Lieutenant Brian Munro of A Company found it "difficult to restrain" his men from shooting at retreating ROKs in the valley as they climbed upward.[39] By 11 PM the PPCLI companies were in position, with the exception of elements of Support Company which, owing to the steepness of the single track leading up the hill from the south and the breakdown of a half-track, were not in place until four the next morning when Stone located his HQ on the rear slope overlooking Tungmudae.[40]

The threat of a night attack suggested a policy of rapid entrenchment. "I can remember on the evening of the 23rd," related Wayne Mitchell, "the Company Commander, Major [Vince] Lilley, had come up to our forward position which was 6 Platoon Baker Company and he says, 'we're here on our own so get over there and dig in deeply, we don't have much time.'"[41] Some soldiers remained unconvinced, leaving entrenching until about dawn when firing broke out across the valley. "I remember not digging our trench too deep that night," one veteran related; "we went maybe two feet." Only near dawn when the sounds of war were heard did he and his buddy decide "that we'd better dig that trench a little deeper."[42] The trouble was that the hard, scrub-covered slopes made creating slit trenches problematic, as did the darkness. "We could only dig down three or four feet because of the rocky ground," remembered Corporal Ken Campbell of D Company.[43] In many other cases men could get only to a depth of about two feet or less.[44] "It was very difficult to dig there," recalled Lieutenant Brian Munro of 2 Platoon. "We never really got properly dug in. The slits were shallow."[45] There was, however, enough loose rock and gravel to build a little protection at ground level. "As was often the case," a corporal in A Company explained, "we couldn't dig very deep in the rock, so we piled the rocky soil into parapets."[46] There was no wire to be had, but trip flares and booby-trap grenades would eventually be laid out in front of various positions the next day.[47]

Luckily, aside from a few brief encounters with probing Chinese patrols and parties of retreating ROKs, the Canadians on Hill 677 were left in peace overnight. Not so the Australians on Hill 504 to the east across the valley, who were soon – as the Canadians would see and hear – battling for their lives under a full moon.[48]

As the light slowly began to fade, a stream of ROK soldiers, which soon became a veritable flood of frightened men, passed southward through the gap between B Company in its forward position near Chuktun-ni and the other 3RAR companies grouped atop Hill 504. "Soldiers were no longer walking to the rear but jogging along and displaying all [the] signs of panic," wrote Major Darcy Laughlin of B Company. By about nine in the evening white-clad civilians were observed mixed in with the military refugees. To Major Ben O'Dowd commanding A Company this, though "a pitiful sight," was also an ominous development: "From past experience we knew that, come dusk [c. 9:15 PM], the Chinese would mix in with the refugees, and ROK soldiers for that matter, and use them as cover to infiltrate to our rear."[49]

How likely this was is open to debate, for while Caucasian troops may not have been able to distinguish between Koreans and Chinese, the former could spot the latter, in which case their most likely reaction would be to scatter off the tracks.[50] The commander of B Company declined to post a filtering party on the track below covered by the Vickers guns when O'Dowd called him up, and when O'Dowd requested of the CO for a second time permission to open fire in order to halt movement on the track, Ferguson accused him of panicking unnecessarily.[51]

Whether or not there were Chinese mixed in with the refugees, it quickly became apparent that elements of the 354th Regiment of the CPV 118th Division, mostly undetected, had managed to infiltrate from the northeast down into the Kapyong Valley along the western face of Hill 504 and toward 3RAR Battalion HQ. About 9:30 PM that Monday night encounter firefights broke out in several locations.[52]

Farthest forward of the U.S. units supporting 27th Brigade was the 4th Platoon of Company A, 72nd Tank Battalion. Deployed to cover the northeastern track approaches to Chuktun-ni, but not in radio contact with the Australians and with no infantry support from the fleeing ROKs, its five Sherman tanks were on their own. An enemy patrol of about two dozen men managed to infiltrate the platoon area but was easily mown down by machine-gun fire. About half an hour to an hour later, however, the Chinese were back in company strength.[53] Now that the light had completely faded, the tank commanders found that, owing to the absence of proper night vision equipment, even under the full moon they could not see what was going on with turret hatches closed. They were therefore forced to operate with their turret hatches open, which quickly led to several fatal and non-fatal wounds to the head. The subsequent shutting of the hatches allowed the Chinese to close in and do all they could to disable the Shermans, including firing a captured bazooka at close range. No damage was done, but just before being mortally wounded the platoon commander decided to pull his tanks back. With no one in command the withdrawal was, as the gunner in one Sherman delicately put it, "somewhat out of control." Reviewing its actions later on, the company commander was blunter. "Disorganized," wrote Lieutenant Kenneth W. Koch, "the platoon began to withdraw in flight."[54]

The 1st Platoon was located about 6,000 yards farther back, its tanks camouflaged and positioned on the left flank of Hill 504 in support of B Company. In command was First Lieutenant Wilfred D. Millar, who had heard over his radio that 4th Platoon was under attack but little else. Alerting his crews to prepare for action, Millar went down on foot onto the valley floor road to try to get a sense of what was happening. There he met Lieutenant Jim Young, the second-in-command of B Company, 3RAR, also engaged in a personal reconnaissance. Suddenly the 4th Platoon tanks appeared. Millar signaled for them to halt, which, though their crews were "excited and nervous" and talking of the enemy "coming in great numbers," they did.[55]

Millar had the wounded loaded onto two of the Shermans and sent them rearward. Still on foot, he ordered the remaining three tanks to turn around and follow him up the road. Jim Young, meanwhile, had been conversing with one of the tank commanders, and in return for a promise to see to the evacuation of the wounded had persuaded him to turn his tank around and move forward with Young on foot acting as a guide. Seeing one of the three Shermans turning northward, and assuming – incorrectly, as it happened – that the other two were about to follow suit, Millar started forward on foot as well. Suddenly he spotted two columns of figures less than a hundred yards ahead on either side of the road. Unsure if they were Chinese or ROKs, Young shouted out "come here" in Korean. The sight of stick grenades having made it clear that these were enemy troops, both Millar and Young dove off the road to avoid those that were thrown at them and the single Sherman sharply reversed away at speed down the road. Both officers managed to dodge the Chinese and eventually join up with their units, but the tanks of 4th Platoon did not stop until they reached the 3RAR HQ area and were flagged down by Lieutenant Koch with 2nd Platoon.[56]

At about the time the first enemy patrol bumped into the tanks of the 4th Platoon, Chinese parties were probing between the positions held by B and A companies, 3RAR.[57] Initial probing attacks launched against elements of both companies were easily beaten off, but it was obvious that, in order to properly secure the route southward down the Kapyong Valley, the Chinese would have to take on 3RAR in force. Between ten and eleven at night the Chinese focused their attention on A Company in general, and 1 Platoon – on the lower-left flank of the company – in particular, launching successive massed infantry assaults.[58]

Bugles and whistles heralded the forming up of troops below and their approximate location, which prompted O'Dowd to call for artillery support to help break up the enemy before they could close in. He was horrified to discover this was not possible. Second-Lieutenant Dennis Fielden, the rather inexperienced New Zealand FOO dispatched to the company earlier in the day, told him that, since 16 Field Regiment had occupied its current position after dark, the guns had not been surveyed in and that therefore – even if he could contact the regiment, which he could not because the terrain was interfering with his radio and there was no landline established – he could not relay target information.[59] Telling Fielden to get out of his sight, O'Dowd then turned to the American FOO sent up by B Company, 2nd Chemical Mortar Battalion. He too could offer no help, since it seemed that the mortar company, coming into direct contact with the enemy, had abandoned most of its tubes and vehicles located down the valley and disappeared into the hills to the east. That left the battalion's own 3-inch mortars, but as the Mortar Platoon was itself under attack by this point, they could offer no support either. The fight would therefore be "soldier against soldier in the dark at very close range."[60]

The attacks on A Company quickly developed a pattern. Once the Chinese had formed up and bugles and whistle blasts had ceased, the enemy advanced en masse but quite quietly on soft-soled canvas shoes, their arrival in front of the trenches heralded by a shower of grenades – some men seemed to be armed with nothing but a good supply of these, picking up other weapons from fallen comrades as they went – preceding a general rush forward. Supported only by Vickers and Bren gun fire, the Diggers, their commander said, in addition to their Owen guns and grenades "had to employ every bit of rapid fire they could, with those murderous, stupid bloody single-shot rifles we had." Illuminating parachute flares fired by the 2-inch mortars of 3 Platoon proved to be more of a hindrance than a help, as they destroyed night vision and could not be kept in the air indefinitely. O'Dowd therefore ordered them stopped, which left men straining to see an enemy who might only appear at a range of five and a half yards or less.[61]

Successive waves were beaten off after about fifteen or twenty minutes and the wounded sent back in the intervals, but each assault took a toll, particularly among the more exposed men of 1 Platoon, who by midnight had endured three major attacks. "The bugles would start again," the acting CSM related, "and 1 Platoon would cop it again."[62] By midnight all three Bren gunners had been killed or wounded and only thirteen men, some wounded, remained out of the original thirty. Around one o'clock in the morning the platoon commander, Lieutenant Fred Gardiner, took the opportunity afforded by a pause between assaults while the enemy regrouped to dash up to Company HQ and report on his situation. O'Dowd ordered him to bring the remnants of 1 Platoon farther up the feature and deploy them between 2 and 3 Platoons. Immediately thereafter Company HQ and the Vickers section – which had lost its sergeant – regrouped around 3 Platoon.[63]

The Chinese advanced and occupied the position vacated by 1 Platoon and probed the rest of the A Company perimeter down to about 4:30 AM – 3 Platoon enduring at one point a particularly ferocious forty-five-minute attack ("we just never thought it was going to finish," one private recalled[64]) – and vigilance had to be maintained to prevent the enemy from exploiting a gap between 2 Platoon and 3 Platoon. At about 2:30 AM a Chinese officer or NCO, having identified the weak spot, climbed a scrub pine and began blasting on his whistle to summon assistance. "For Christ's sake, get that bastard," O'Dowd shouted out to anyone within firing range. This particular individual was quickly silenced,[65] but two hours later ten or so well-armed Chinese soldiers, including one with a light machine-gun, arrived at the same spot and, as O'Dowd put it, "proceeded to make life very uncomfortable by directing fire into us."[66] Thankfully the machine-gunner, who loosed off what sounded like over two dozen magazines, fired rather high, but he and his companions were well hidden in a gulley and making movement very difficult. Toward dawn a handful of men armed with Owen guns and sent down from 2 Platoon to make contact with Company HQ accidentally reached a point where they could see the enemy party and at once charged in and killed six at the cost of one fatally wounded private.[67]

By this point the enemy's attention had widened to include B Company for about the last six hours. On their own but arrayed for all-round defense on a long, relatively low-lying feature (roughly 100–150 meters in height) near the northwest base of Hill 504 and supported by the Shermans of 1st Platoon, Major Darcy Laughlin and his men had been witnesses earlier on to the retreat of the 4th Platoon Sherman tanks with the Chinese in hot pursuit. Laughlin had called for artillery and mortar fire into the now open track between B Company and A Company through which the enemy was pouring, but with – initially at least – no more success than O'Dowd.[68] In the hour before midnight, having discerned signs that the enemy was massing for an assault, Laughlin prudently withdrew an isolated outpost on a high point back into the main company positions. Close to one in the morning 4 Platoon was attacked, but with the help of concentrated fire from a Vickers machine-gun section and bombs from 2-inch mortars the Diggers were able to force the Chinese to withdraw within the space of forty-five minutes. For some hours the enemy confined himself to infiltrating past B Company down into the Kapyong Valley.[69]

Then, at 3:30 AM, 6 Platoon was attacked fiercely by a force of about sixty Chinese while ten others attempted to engage 5 Platoon. "The enemy made a determined thrust and succeeded in penetrating our perimeter," Laughlin later reported. A section position in the 6 Platoon sector was overrun and the enemy broke into the company area, something that might have caused the collapse of the entire position, but thanks to support from the well-camouflaged Shermans of 1st Platoon, 6 Platoon was able to regroup and recapture the lost ground. A final major assault came at a quarter to five in the morning and involved anywhere between fifty and seventy Chinese soldiers. "This attack was launched from the right flank," the company commander added, and was evidently meant to split the company by driving into the Company HQ position. This too was driven off through a combination of tank and small-arms fire, the enemy never getting beyond the edge of the perimeter.[70]

Compared to A and B companies – each overlooking as they did one side of the gap through which the enemy would have to pass from the northeast in order to move southward down the Kapyong Valley – C and D Companies had only sporadic and limited contact with the enemy that night.[71] The men in these companies had no idea how their fellow Diggers were faring. According to a member of 9 Platoon, "we had no information at all" on how things were going; "nothing came down my way when I was in my platoon."[72] The fighting, though, was uncomfortably close and audible, which made him uneasy. Particularly worrying for those with an aural sense of direction was the fact that many of the sounds of war were coming from the valley floor where 3RAR Battalion Headquarters was located, slightly to the southwest.[73]

When the HQ position astride the road had first been established in the afternoon, its location had not appeared problematic. It was there to help stiffen the resolve of 6th ROK Division, whose own headquarters was ahead of it and the regiments of which were supposed to be fighting hard. Several U.S. units were also deploying in the Kapyong Valley behind the ROK division: two companies of engineers, most of a tank company, and a mortar battalion. Moreover, toward midnight the 25-pounders of 16 Field Regiment and the 105-mm howitzers of the U.S. 213th Field Artillery Battalion had moved in behind. 3RAR HQ, as well as being located far below and a mile or so away from the four infantry companies on Hill 504, was therefore not arrayed for battle. Its various components, including the Regimental Aid Post, as well as the sub-units of Support Company, were spread out over a square kilometer of ground and were mostly not dug in beyond what the MO described as occasional "shallow weapon pits."[74]

In the course of Monday night it became rapidly apparent that Ferguson and his headquarters were in a precarious position. After dark those in the valley encountered first a trickle and then a stream of South Korean soldiers in headlong retreat, shedding equipment, abandoning vehicles, fleeing the sound of isolated shots behind them. The ROK divisional HQ, it later emerged, had decamped without informing 3RAR. The enemy was indeed very close behind the retreating Koreans, as Temporary Sergeant Fred From, acting commander of the anti-tank platoon, soon discovered. ROK soldiers were trotting down the road, with South Korean officers "running down there with their pistols in hand trying to stop this flow of people going past." Fred From left his position and went up the road a few dozen yards to try to find out what the situation was, but those he tried to interrogate simply pushed past and he suddenly became aware that the men coming down were now dressed in light khaki rather than army green.[75]

Starting at around 10 PM it became clear that the Chinese were not only coming down in front of 3RAR HQ but had infiltrated behind it and established a road block. Bullets started flying and men were hit, wounded, or killed as fighting flared up around and indeed inside the HQ area. There was a good deal of noise and confusion, with sub-units ranging from the anti-tank gunners to the military police having to defend positions as best they could. By midnight Lieutenant Koch was issuing orders to the American crews of 2nd Platoon to "fire in all directions, to cover each other, and to prevent enemy soldiers getting on the tanks."[76]

Colonel Ferguson was largely in the dark, both literally and figuratively. Though he was able to reach some of his subordinates by telephone – "What's happening down there?" he queried Fred From after the initial exchanges of fire, adding "don't let anybody panic"[77] – of those up on Hill 504 only the commander of B Company could be contacted.[78] Tanks and other vehicles had cut the wires across the road and elsewhere, while radio communication proved extremely problematic.[79] The mass of Hill 504 between his HQ and the forward infantry companies certainly played a role in this, as, perhaps, did unfamiliarity with recently received 31-type sets. According to the signals sergeant, "some of the senior people who should have known better didn't really understand them."[80]

About an hour after midnight Ferguson decided that, in order to let Brigadier Burke know in detail what was happening to 3RAR – at least insofar as he could work it out from what he himself was witnessing and the limited intelligence he could glean from others – he would have to go back to the position occupied by the Middlesex battalion HQ about two miles farther down the valley; it likely seemed from the amount of firing going on in his vicinity that his current position was in danger of being overrun. Leaving at about 1:15 AM in a jeep, the colonel took the rear-link 19 Set with him, depriving those who remained in the HQ position of any chance of directly communicating with brigade (the brigade war diary notes that communication with 3RAR was lost). Ferguson, though he did not take his signalman along, had presumably planned to use the 19 Set farther back. Unfortunately it failed to work, and he was forced to use the 1MX rear-link radio to converse with Burke at 1:40 AM.[81]

By this point the brigadier was getting reports of contacts with Chinese infiltrators from other parts of the valley floor. With the enemy apparently in the vicinity of the gun lines, 16 Field Regiment along with the American 213th Field Artillery Battalion began withdrawing from the vicinity of Naechon southward toward the village of Chunch'on-ni near brigade headquarters shortly after two in the morning. 163 Battery continued to do what it could to support the Australians for another forty-five minutes, one of its troops holding on until dawn in support of 3RAR until its ammunition was exhausted.[82]

In fact the situation in the early morning hours on the valley floor may not have been as bad as it first seemed, since the initial contacts with the Chinese did not quickly develop into large-scale attacks. Once the Shermans of 4th Platoon had rallied, moreover, there was enough tank support to allow for the breaking of the Chinese roadblock to the rear.[83]

Ferguson, however, who seems to have been on the move much of the time, remained worried that 3RAR battalion headquarters was in danger of being overwhelmed. He was not alone in this, the commander of the tanks later asserting that the HQ had in fact been overrun by a force of about 300 Chinese during "a fierce battle" in the hours after midnight. Shortly after four, Ferguson requested that brigade send reinforcements to help shore up the position.[84]

Within twenty minutes D Company of the Middlesex was on its way up the main track, soon coming under mortar fire and having to double forward and use the paddy bunds on one side as protection against splinters.[85] The infantry company was met 200 yards south of the headquarters by Ferguson and directed to deploy on high ground to the west that overlooked the position. D Company raced up in the face of tracer fire around 5 AM to take the ridge, but as soon as it got up there, came under attack from Chinese troops located on higher ground about seventy-five yards away. A nasty grenade, light machine-gun, and rifle firefight developed, the Middlesex unable to match a Chinese light mortar because the single 2-inch mortar brought along broke after the first bomb was launched. A sergeant in addition to his grenades used a super bazooka as an anti-personnel weapon to great effect, but the Chinese, firing a captured U.S. recoilless rifle, wounded five men at once in one section of 10 Platoon and caused momentary panic until the men were rallied by Second-Lieutenant Barry Reed (who was later awarded an MC for his efforts). The enemy also began to work their way round the left flank in an effort to cut the road behind 3RAR headquarters. Throughout this action the company commander, Major Clinton Nolda, had been very much on his own, as his 31 Set appeared to be dead. Suddenly, however, the radio came back to life, and Nolda was able to report on his increasingly precarious situation to the battalion CO. Hearing that D Company was being cut off and facing superior numbers, Lieutenant-Colonel C. H. Nicholson gave orders for Nolda to withdraw his men. Thanks to a wide detour the company was able to extricate itself with minimal casualties and join up with the rest of the Middlesex roughly seven hours later.[86]

The withdrawal, however, further exposed the Australian headquarters area. Though the enemy refrained from shooting when ambulances with Red Crosses prominently displayed were being loaded with wounded for transport rearward, the Regimental Aid Post (RAP) across the road from HQ had been under sporadic fire all night. The enemy not only proved chivalrous but also apparently had a sense of humor, one Chinese sniper around dawn tying his shirt to his rifle and waving the signal for "washout" after Fred From of the anti-tank platoon tried and failed three times to hit him.[87] Nevertheless, sporadic firing from all directions, coupled with the way in which radio failures left individual sub-units in the dark and without artillery support, contributed to a feeling that the Chinese had the upper hand. "Although we had little information in the R.A.P. area about what was going on," Chaplain A. W. A. Laing remembered, "it was quite obvious that a serious situation was rapidly developing."[88]

By about 4 AM, as the Chinese intensified their fire, Ferguson had concluded that the time had come to go:

> Just before dawn I decided that the position of my headquarters would not enable it to regain control of the battle and that I should withdraw to the higher ground occupied by the Middlesex Regiment. Hopefully, with better communications there, I could regain control and thus provide the full weight of supporting fire, including aircraft and artillery support, both of which were vital if the forward companies were to receive the relief they so urgently needed.[89]

This, though, would leave the forward Australian companies cut off more than two miles behind enemy lines. It therefore appeared to Ferguson that it would be best to start thinking about ordering B Company, still on its own, to cross over and join up with C and D companies on the main part of Hill 504, "thus forming," in the words of Major Darcy Laughlin, "a complete perimeter on the high ground."[90]

As dawn approached 27th Brigade was in an ambiguous but potentially perilous position. On the one hand, 2PPCLI held Hill 677 on the left flank, while in the center Brigade HQ, 16 Field Regiment, and the Middlesex had moved back in good order to positions guarding the southern end of the Kapyong Valley. Brigadier Burke also had 1KOSB in reserve. On the other hand, the main fighting strength of 3RAR had been cut off, leaving it vulnerable to assault and possible destruction as casualties mounted and ammunition ran out. As for the Australian headquarters and its supporting units, their withdrawal down the valley might turn into a catastrophe if it turned out the Chinese had infiltrated enough men to once more cut the road behind. If both these eventualities occurred, then 27th Brigade would lose approximately one-quarter of its fighting strength and half of its most experienced infantrymen. Much would depend on what the Chinese chose to do once full daylight arrived and with it the threat of air attacks and increased danger from U.N. artillery units.

For the guns, now like an orchestra, their targets they engage,
With a symphony of anger, a cacophony of rage.

MAURICE GASSON, 16 FR, 2003[1]

There's dirt, there's dust, there's people hollering, there's people dying on both sides, you can hear them. It was terrifying . . .

DON HIBBS, 2PPCLI, 1999[2]

SEVEN

Kapyong: The Third Day

AS DAYLIGHT CREPT ACROSS THE KAPYONG VALLEY ON Tuesday, the 24th of April, the Chinese found themselves exposed. Without the protection offered by darkness, infantry on the move could be seen at more than a few yards' distance, which in turn opened up decent fields of fire for those Australians in range. There was no compunction about taking immediate and full advantage of this turn of events; as Major Ben O'Dowd of A Company 3RAR later explained, with those enemy soldiers caught in the open "the Diggers were having the time of their lives potting them all off all over the place." Now that they could easily be seen, groups of Chinese forming up for assaults could also be broken up by artillery bursts.[3]

From their ridge positions just to the northeast the men of B Company played their part. "By this time it was dawn," Major Darcy Laughlin recorded, "and in the growing light the enemy could be clearly seen in the valley between B coy across to A and C coys. This position was quite open and the area between [B and A plus C] coys was an excellent killing ground. This area was now subjected to intensive fire from t[an]ks and all other available weapons." Those caught in the withering crossfire from machine-guns began to withdraw northeastward.[4]

Just how deadly the area between B Company and Hill 504 was became clear when Laughlin sent out a clearing patrol at 6 AM under CSM Eric Bradley during a pause in the firing. Along with the many dead and wounded it was revealed that there were between fifty and sixty healthy Chinese soldiers who had gone to ground in the paddy fields. Most seemed to be happy to surrender when ordered to stand up in pidgin Chinese, but one threw a grenade. This was met with instant retaliation: Owen gunfire mowed down over thirty surrendering men before Bradley gave the ceasefire order. Forty-odd terrified and entirely docile prisoners were taken and distributed among the B Company platoons.[5]

The enemy, though, was not about to give up on achieving a key objective. If the Australians continued to hold Hill 504, then southwest movement would be hindered by directed enemy fire. To drive them all off, the Chinese would have to take the summit; once this position had been taken then all the lower-elevation defenses would become exposed, and as O'Dowd put it, "would fall like apples on the end of a branch."[6] This in turn put D Company, 3RAR, squarely in the enemy's sights in the hours after dawn.

From 7 AM onward assaults were mounted from the north every half-hour or so, with 12 Platoon taking the brunt of the action. As the company commander, Captain Norm Gravener, later noted, a pattern quickly developed:

> The attacks on this pos[itio]n were always launched in depth on a narrow frontage of 4–5 men and each series of attacks were supported by Pl[atoon-] size f[or]m[atio]n assisted by mor[tar] and grenade attacks in the initial stages. 12 Pl[atoon] met these attacks with LMG [Bren] SA [rifle] fire and 36 mm [*sic*] grenades in the final stages of the enemy as[sau]lt. The enemy suffered h[eav]y cas[ualties] in each of the 6 attacks launched thus far and estimated enemy Pl[atoon] destroyed. Our cas[ualties] at this stage were very light.[7]

In the aftermath of ranging shots arranged through Gravener's 31 Set, shells from 16 Field Regiment made life even more difficult for the attackers.[8]

Meanwhile the withdrawal of the headquarters troops down the valley toward the Middlesex position had got under way starting before 6 AM. Conducted on a rather ad hoc basis, amid ongoing communication difficulties and under sporadic enemy fire, the movement nevertheless resulted in relatively few Australian casualties, thanks in part to fire support from the tanks of Company A, 72nd Tank Battalion which also carried out many of the wounded.[9]

At some point shortly before 8 AM the CO, Lieutenant-Colonel Bruce Ferguson, who had narrowly escaped death when a mortar round exploded by his jeep during the withdrawal, ordered B Company to join up with the other companies on Hill 504.[10] Supported by a pair of 1st Platoon tanks and a smoke screen laid by 16 Field Regiment, one platoon after another moved off in good order with its quota of prisoners, B Company having accounted for around 200 dead and 40 captured Chinese at the cost of one wounded Australian.[11]

The relocation of B Company went smoothly, but not everyone was happy that the original position was being abandoned. It had not been on the verge of being overrun, and had allowed very effective enfilade fire to be directed at Chinese approaching Chuktun-ni down the valley from the northeast. Moreover, as the rather shocked commander of A Company observed, the enemy would quickly move in to the vacated high-ground positions, allowing the Chinese in turn to pour fire onto the western flank of Hill 504. Deciding that Colonel Ferguson, now many miles to the rear, did not grasp the implications of the B Company move, Major O'Dowd called up the CO on the radio and urged that the order be reversed. Ferguson – who may have been suffering from a concussion due to his earlier close encounter with a mortar bomb explosion[12] – temporized, asking for a situation report and implying that as senior company commander O'Dowd knew best, but not formally handing over tactical command of Hill 504 or authorizing O'Dowd to send Laughlin and his men back the way they had come.[13]

Major O'Dowd, it turned out, was not the only officer who wanted B Company to retrace its steps. With South Korean and a few U.S. units streaming southward toward Kapyong, Major General William M. Hoge was under the impression that a "great big hole" had opened up that needed plugging. Mindful of the warning he had received the previous day from Brigadier Brian Burke that the Commonwealth Brigade had not been expecting to be thrown back into action and worried that 3RAR had "gone off" since its headquarters had retired before dawn, the IX Corps commander decided to commit his main reserve formation. As he later explained, "I got hold of the 5th Cavalry [RCT] and threw them in there."[14]

The 5th Cavalry – which included not only several infantry battalions but also the 61st Field Artillery Battalion and A Company of the 70th Tank Battalion[15] – would move up the Kapyong Valley and occupy Hill 794, the key position once allocated to the Middlesex but never held.

This would be made more difficult, however, if the Chinese continued to occupy the high ground near Chuktun-ni that B Company had just vacated. Burke therefore ordered Ferguson to send the company back and retake the abandoned feature. "Orders were received at 0930 hrs 24 Apr to the effect that as further t[roo]ps were expected to reinforce our position as soon as possible the ground that B coy had withdrawn from would be secured again if possible," Major Laughlin later noted.[16]

Hoping that the Chinese had not sent in that many troops, since few had so far been observed on the old position, Laughlin ordered Lieutenant Ken McGregor, commanding 5 Platoon, which had barely reached C Company, to turn around and go back at once: "I want you to go back straight away." McGregor, like Laughlin a veteran of the fighting in the Southwest Pacific, was not happy to hear this – "How expensive do you want this to be?" he asked rhetorically – but acted on the shared assumption that with enough speed his platoon could deal with what were thought to be limited numbers of Chinese.[17]

The first task was to secure a knoll on the valley floor known as the honeycomb which lay between Hill 504 and the old B Company position. Though there were plenty of trenches and bunkers on this little feature, no fire had come from it when B Company had moved across to Hill 504 earlier that morning. Therefore when movement was observed in the honeycomb, McGregor assumed the knoll was occupied by only a few enemy stragglers. At about 10:30 AM he therefore lined up number five section to assault the feature and drive them off. "We believed that the [forward] trench was occupied by eight to 10 Chinese," Private Stan Connelly recalled. "When we got within 20 yards of it, it was occupied by a great deal more than 10." It was too late to do anything other than charge forward. Eight men were cut down and the remainder forced to take what cover they could and return fire, McGregor himself lying stunned and bleeding after receiving a bullet to the jaw. The rest of the platoon swung round and came up in support, but they faced over eighty enemy soldiers. Miraculously everyone in this otherwise ill-starred section, including the nine wounded men, made it to safety. It was clear, though, that B Company was not going to have an easy time getting back to its original positions.[18]

Laughlin called up 4 Platoon under Lieutenant Len "Monty" Montgomerie to renew the assault on the honeycomb with 5 Platoon in support. At 11:45 AM, just as the attack was about to go in, further reinforcement arrived in the form of several Sherman tanks. This time, though the enemy responded with a fusillade of grenades along with rifle and light machine-gun fire, the Diggers succeeded in charging into the first trench at the point of the bayonet and then engaged in a fierce effort, using grenades and Owen guns, to clear the Chinese from their other positions on the honeycomb. After forty-five minutes of tough, aggressive, and mostly hand-to-hand combat, over eighty enemy soldiers had been killed and the honeycomb and another knoll secured at the cost of three Australians killed and two wounded. Lieutenant Montgomerie won an MC, and one of his section commanders, Corporal D. B. Davy, the MM, for the leadership and personal courage they displayed in this hard-fought but successful action. The old B Company position, though, had still to be assaulted.[19]

Bruce Ferguson, meanwhile, had decided that he needed to get a better sense of what was happening on and around Hill 504, and shortly before noon, accompanied by his intelligence officer, Lieutenant Alf Argent, and the MO, Captain Don Beard, hitched a ride aboard Lieutenant Wilfred Millar's tank, which, with others, was ferrying forward ammunition and supplies to the beleaguered Australian rifle companies and evacuating their wounded. The fact that Hill 504 was well behind enemy lines was underlined by the fact that on the journey northward, as Don Beard remembered it, "all the time we were being fired upon."[20]

On arrival at Chuktun-ni the tanks moved into a reentrant between C and A companies and off- and on-loading began. The CO struck an impressive figure in the eyes of Lieutenant Millar. "Colonel Ferguson was calm, acted like he was in total command of the situation," showing "great concern for his wounded and his encircled men and no apparent regard for his own personal safety." Heedless of enemy fire, he walked about in the open, talking to his men "as if it was just a practice drill back in Australia."[21] Of necessity the stretcher cases and their volunteer American attendants would have to be carried away on the Sherman hulls. Happily, the Chinese, while constantly firing at the tanks on the way up the valley, refrained from firing when they twice made the return journey with wounded aboard. "They let us through," Don Beard reflected in a television interview fifty years later, "for which, you know, I'll always be grateful."[22]

The care and safety of the wounded, though, was of necessity not the primary concern of the CO as he called an impromptu O Group of his company commanders.

What Ferguson needed to know from Ben O'Dowd, as senior officer on the spot, was whether Hill 504 could be held overnight until the cavalry arrived. "This put me in a rather invidious position," O'Dowd later complained:

> It was obviously an extremely important decision, one on which rested the next move of the Brigade and a Cavalry Regiment, and he was waiting for an answer. Many things went through my mind. The battered A Company would have to go into reserve and the untouched C Company brought forward. The forward positions would have to be thickened up with support from the Pioneer and Anti-Tank company platoons [now back with the Middlesex]. There was a mass of artillery available now, which could be employed to tremendous advantage. Also, if the Cavalry Regiment was able to blast its way on to Sudok San [Hill 794], the enemy would have plenty to occupy his mind.

O'Dowd decided in favor of holding on, but warned Ferguson that if B Company could not take and hold its former position and the cavalry did not come forward in a timely manner, then "an attempt had to be made to extract the rifle companies." Ferguson then drove off aboard a tank to observe how B Company was getting along.[23]

Laughlin's men had won the fight for the knolls but, unknown to O'Dowd, their primary task remained unfulfilled. "It was now evident that B Coy's former position was occupied by the enemy," the company commander later reported, "and that a major attack would have to be launched to reoccupy it."[24] O'Dowd also admitted later that he underestimated the pressure being exerted by the Chinese on Hill 504 itself. C Company was not in fact "untouched," with lots of sniping going on and both the company HQ and 8 Platoon coming under attack in the course of the morning.[25] A Company was also in difficulty because enemy machine-gun fire made it nearly impossible to retrieve the ammunition and other supplies delivered by the tanks below the position. At considerable risk Sergeant George Harris and two privates ran down and grabbed what they could, only to discover that though .303 in caliber, what they had recovered in belts was meant for Vickers guns and was liable to jam in the breeches of Lee Enfields and Bren guns.[26]

Nevertheless, most Chinese activity remained focused on D Company, against which a new series of assaults were launched between 11:30 AM and 1:30 PM. Despite "grand work" by 16 Field Regiment, the Chinese kept coming. "The main feature of this action from an enemy point of view," Norm Gravener recorded, "was the rapidity with which each series of enemy attacks was prepared and launched" in spite of U.N. air and artillery efforts, "practiced drill" overcoming the disruption caused by bursting shells and bombs. Chinese mortaring was "quite effective," light machine-guns were well placed to offer supporting crossfire, and attackers always seemed to have grenades to throw during infantry assaults. O'Dowd admitted that when he made his affirmative reply to Ferguson about holding out he did not realize that the fighting in front of D Company was in fact escalating rather than diminishing in intensity.[27]

The 12 Platoon, under the command of Lieutenant Johnny Ward and farthest forward on a wooded knoll, once more bore the brunt, with the left-forward section, led by Corporal Bill Rowlinson, invariably getting hit first. In the course of six hours this section was attacked heavily a dozen times, but despite the loss of six men to wounds, Rowlinson, himself hit in the leg, heroically led the remaining men and replacements sent forward by Ward throughout the fight, for which he was later awarded the DCM. "Corporal Rowlinson although wounded," the citation read in part, "displayed leadership of a very high order and outstanding courage by holding the section together during the continuous attacks on his section position and thereby securing the company position vital to the successful conduct of the battalion defense." It was estimated that his section had seen off around 150 attackers and definitely killed twenty-five of them.[28]

Unfortunately it was not only the Chinese that members of the company had to worry about. Those atop Hill 504 not directly engaged with the enemy during the morning had periodically noticed a spotter aircraft accompanied by three USMC Corsair fighter-bombers in the vicinity. At some point in the first half of the afternoon, despite prominently displayed "friendly" fluorescent identification panels, the spotter plane loosed a target marker into the forward position held by 10 Platoon – 12 Platoon having pulled back – and a Corsair rolled in and dropped a napalm bomb. Frantic radio signaling from American tanks and Australian radio men caused a second Corsair to peel away, but two men were killed and several others horribly injured. The Chinese took advantage of the confusion to attack 11 Platoon, but without success.[29]

"Every man on that hill knew fear," reflected Private John Hawkins of 12 Platoon many years later, adding: "I never thought I was going to make it out alive."[30] For a few, the strain of pitched battle proved too much. Don Beard recalled that during the withdrawal of battalion HQ during the night his driver broke down in terror.[31] Rather more seriously, a Bren gunner in 11 Platoon left the slit trench he was occupying with Private K. R. Gwyther, promising to return but never doing so. This man did not let anyone know that Gwyther – knocked out by a mortar burst – was missing when the company withdrew later in the day, so that when Gwyther woke up he found himself alone among the Chinese and had to surrender.[32] Most of the Australians present at Kapyong nevertheless overcame or held their fears at bay. "We were not going to retreat," Sergeant Ray Parry remembered forty years later of the handful of men he led while successfully defending an isolated but important knoll in the original B Company position around 4 AM on Monday: "We were going to stay there and engage the Chinese and, if they overran us, well then we were finished."[33]

It was the danger of this eventuality for those on Hill 504 that prompted Brigadier Burke to intervene once more at about noon on Tuesday. Having confirmed that owing to congested roads the 5th Cavalry would not arrive before nightfall, Burke contacted Ferguson once he had returned to the Middlesex area and ordered him to withdraw from Hill 504.[34]

Ferguson, having decided that he was not in a position to lead a breakout himself, contacted O'Dowd and told him "that the cavalry regiment would not be coming through, and I had authority to withdraw the rifle companies."[35] The news did not come entirely as a surprise to O'Dowd, who was getting a better sense of the strain certain companies were under and had just had an unsettling radio exchange with the

1st USMC Division on the right flank of the brigade. As one observer recalled:

> During the previous night all our radios had been damaged, but after a few hours frantic work they managed to get one going. Major O'Dowd then directed the radio operator to contact *anyone*. The American 1st Marine Division answered but [when] their operator refused to believe who our operator was speaking for, Major O'Dowd took the phone and demanded to speak to the commanding officer. The General in charge of the Division came on the phone and told O'Dowd we [3RAR] didn't exist as we had been wiped out the night before [presumably a reference to reports of 3RAR HQ being overrun[36]]. Major O'Dowd said "I've got news for you, we are still here and we are staying here." O'Dowd then asked for assistance. The General replied that he couldn't help, as his Division was about to do a Strategic withdrawal. O'Dowd blew his cool and said that if they withdrew we could be out flanked. The General then agreed to keep his Division in place as long as we stayed. Major O'Dowd put down the phone, turned to the Company [A] and said in a loud voice "Cop on to this. The mighty 1st American Marine Division has agreed to stay as long as we do."[37]

As it was clear that a general withdrawal was in the air, O'Dowd had already begun to think about how best to break out and make a successful fighting retreat. "I had to decide the route, the timing and the method," O'Dowd remembered. "From my point of view there were two ways out: one was to fight straight back down the road the way we had come the night before; the other way was to get in behind Don [D] Company and beat our way down the long ridge line that led to where the Middlesex were, some two miles away."[38]

Going down into the valley presented the greatest hazard, since it was clear that the Chinese had infiltrated quite some way down and would have ample time to prepare to meet the Australians as they climbed down the left flank of Hill 504. That meant taking the ridgeline running southwest. O'Dowd planned to start moving in the latter part of the afternoon; daylight would make it easier to engage beyond close quarters any Chinese who attempted to block or follow up the move and bring down observed artillery fire, while the onset of darkness would aid the last company in making a clean break. The first step would be to neutralize the Chinese who occupied the old B Company position and could most easily see what was going on atop Hill 504 through concentrated smoke and high-explosive artillery fire; the second stage involved sending B Company ahead to clear the ridge; the third step would mean moving A and C companies behind D Company in preparation for their own move; the penultimate move, once the other companies were in motion, involved extracting D Company; and the final stage would witness the companies leapfrogging their way down the ridge toward the checkpoint manned by men from Support Company under Captain Jack Gerke that Ferguson had agreed to set up at a ford near the lower end of the ridge.[39]

It was a good plan, but there were plenty of things that could turn a fighting withdrawal into something far less orderly and potentially quite bloody, as elements of 29th Brigade would discover the following day farther west. Things got off to a shaky start in the late afternoon when the promised smoke and high-explosive shelling of the old B Company position failed to materialize. O'Dowd waited with mounting impatience for something to happen, eventually calling the CO to find out what had gone wrong. After the CO had contacted 16 Field Regiment it emerged that because the wind had shifted the guns would have to re-register their targets before laying down a barrage. With B Company and its POW contingent already on the move, O'Dowd decided not to wait, and ordered C Company to take up position behind D Company. By the time this move was nearing completion a couple of Shermans had trundled up the road and started blasting the old B Company position with their 76-mm guns. "I had not been informed that they would come to our assistance," O'Dowd later wrote, "but could not have been more grateful for such timely intervention." Shortly thereafter the Kiwi gunners finally opened up as well, "with a tremendous thump."[40]

There was a further delay due to the fact that D Company, the last to move, was too heavily engaged to withdraw immediately. Eventually, though, the Chinese drew back. "I led it back and located it behind A Company," O'Dowd later wrote, "then withdrew C Company and sited it behind D Company, and in this way we rolled back, always one company in a blocking position and one in movement." Once D Company had vacated its overnight position 16 Field Regiment was informed and made up for the earlier delay with a very impressive barrage on the former positions – aided by the big 155-mm self-propelled howitzers of 213 Armored Field Artillery Battalion and a battery of even bigger 8-inch howitzers as well as 105-mm field pieces from 61st Field Artillery Battalion, making up a total force of 64 guns – that deterred the Chinese and allowed the rifle companies to make a clean break.[41]

B Company reached the checkpoint at the ford shortly after dark without having had to break through any enemy blocking force, and the withdrawal as a whole proved to be a success. It was not, however, without incident. O'Dowd, who moved back and forth along the column as the companies leapfrogged one another, experienced a nasty shock at one point in the darkness:

> I was horrified to find myself in the midst of a group of armed Chinese soldiers but very relieved to identify them as prisoners assisting the stretcher-bearers. I stopped the first escort to come my way and rather brusquely demanded to know why prisoners were bearing arms. The soldier responded immediately with the curt reply, "Well, you don't expect the bloody wounded to carry them, do you?" While I was digesting this piece of logic, the group disappeared into the gloom.[42]

Another anxious moment occurred later that night when B, C, and D companies had all safely crossed the ford and only A Company remained to be accounted for. Over the radio O'Dowd learned from his second-in-command Captain Bob Murdoch that the company was coming under fire. O'Dowd stressed to him that he had to break contact and make a break for the river; "otherwise you will get shot up getting across this ford in the moonlight." Eventually Lieutenant Lou Brumfield and 2 Platoon appeared down the escape route, but it quickly became apparent that the rest of A Company was no longer behind them. Machine-gun fire from across the valley made O'Dowd worry that the Canadians were firing on the missing Australians, but over the radio Ferguson confirmed that their targets were Chinese. The remaining three platoons suddenly appeared, moving south down the riverbank rather than the designated path from the east. It emerged that Murdoch had got lost, and, realizing his error, had made for the river and made a sharp left turn. The pursuing Chinese assumed the Australians had crossed the river, and had plunged into the water, thereby attracting the attention of 2PPCLI. By 11 PM everyone had passed within the Middlesex perimeter.[43]

The Australians were now safe. "The Chinese were quite happy to just stay on 504," Corporal Len Opie of 11 Platoon recalled; "there was no follow up."[44] But having driven away the enemy from the east side of the Kapyong Valley, the Chinese People's Volunteers could now turn their full attention to the Canadians dug in on Hill 677 on the west side.

That 2PPCLI would become a target had been evident for some time. In the first six hours of Tuesday, 24 April, the Canadians had not only seen and heard the signs of fierce battle across the valley but had also continued to encounter fleeing ROK troops. As one Canadian remembered, "they came back through our position, and they were coming in bunches, they were scared to death, they just dropped everything and ran."[45] In B Company, on the northwest flank of Hill 677, there was a strong sense that these military refugees "were pretty well infiltrated with Chinese soldiers,"[46] and when it was possible to see into the valley orders were issued to open fire. Shortly after, the company received a new set of orders, following which they not only ceased fire but also pulled back.[47]

By first light it was clear that, in addition to attacking Hill 504, the Chinese had infiltrated down the Kapyong Valley, thereby presenting a threat to the right flank of the Hill 677 position and cutting off the Canadians' road link to the rear. At about 6 AM Lieutenant-Colonel Jim Stone decided that he would have to reposition B Company, moving it southeast across Hill 677 to a point where it could protect the right flank and rear of the 2PPCLI position. Within ninety minutes the company was on the move and within three or four hours the men had arrived. In the meantime Stone had also ordered up as much ammunition as he could and prepared his HQ for a battle that the Patricias would have to fight while essentially surrounded by the enemy.[48]

As B Company once more tried to dig in through the afternoon, this time above the village of Neachon, enemy soldiers carrying pine branches could be seen in the valley below. This puzzled some Canadian observers – "they'd go right down the middle of the road carrying this stupid tree"[49] – but a FOO from 16 Field Regiment with C Company noted that every time a plane flew over they would freeze and try to become invisible to passing aerial spotters.[50]

The sheer number of Chinese determinedly trotting down beside and around Hill 677 made it even more obvious that, as another Patricia later commented, "we were in for a good fight before the night was out." He added: "I think I was scared shitless looking at them."[51] As another soldier put it, “Well, I was really scared; everybody was; anybody who says they were not scared, they’re lying.” But this Patricia also noted that he and his friends “would’ve never turned and run.”[52]

One way of coping with the strain of waiting was to seize the initiative. One officer took his batman’s rifle and, at extreme range, felled a “white-clad figure at a cross-roads,” much to his satisfaction and “the amazement of all ranks.”[53] A private admitted that “we’d take a shot at ’em [in the valley] every once in a while to keep ’em on their toes.”[54] And when 6 Platoon came under small-arms fire from a knoll below them, the B Company commander, Major Vince Lilley, led down a bayonet charge. The Chinese had gone by the time the Patricias arrived, and, rather unfortunately, Sherman tanks operating in support of 3RAR assumed they were Chinese and opened fire, slightly injuring Private Wayne Mitchell.[55]

Aware that 2PPCLI was next on the Chinese target list, Brigadier Burke decided to address the men of the battalion through a loudspeaker attached to an American cargo plane.[56] According to one version:

> He states that he knows the Patricias will do their duty [and] that we will fight and be a credit to our Regiment. Rather than a harsh order, it is delivered as a confident expectation, extended between trusted friends. It is a warmly reassuring and inspiring gesture; the troops are impressed that their Brigadier, responsible for so many decisions, would take time to personally address them.[57]

According to another version, soldiers reacted negatively to a call for stiff-upper-lip courage from a senior British officer who was both literally and figuratively far above the battle; “it is highly unlikely that Burke’s fly-by did much to steel the nerves of the men on the ground, and his well-meaning words of encouragement probably only served to reinforce their apprehension about the coming battle.”[58]

As night drew on the Chinese began to gather below B Company. At 9:30 PM Major Lilley reported that he was coming under machine-gun and mortar fire and 400-odd enemy troops were assembling below his lowest position, occupied by 6 Platoon, and called for mortar and artillery support.[59] Within half an hour 6 Platoon was heavily engaged. “They were on top of us before we knew it,” Sergeant Roy Ulmer explained to a war correspondent after the battle. “They’re quiet as mice with those rubber shoes of theirs and then there’s a whistle. They get up with a shout about [ten] feet from our positions and they come in. The first wave throws its grenades, fires it weapons and goes to ground. It is followed by a second wave which does the same, and then a third comes up."[60] Large numbers of the attackers were cut down, and the first attack failed, but as Ulmer and others observed, the Chinese "just keep coming."[61] They enemy was not always well armed. "I got at one guy with a big satchel of grenades and no rifle," recalled Del Reaume, adding that a fair number of the Chinese did not have firearms. "Some had rifles or burp guns and others just had grenades."[62] But they were brave and there were a lot of them. Within the hour Lieutenant Harold Ross had to report to Company HQ that his position had been partially overrun, and Lilley decided that the platoon would have to pull back to the main B Company position. By around midnight and in the wake of three successive attacks several men had been killed or sustained wounds from everything from grenade blasts to bayonet thrusts in confused close-quarter fighting.[63]

B Company, though, was not the only enemy target in the hours before midnight. The Chinese had infiltrated farther south, and by 11 PM were also moving in to attack the battalion headquarters area. The first word of this attack led officers at IX Corps to assume the Canadians were now done for.[64] In fact they were about to inflict a devastating reverse on the Chinese. Warned by Lilley that the enemy was heading his way – "there are about three hundred Chinamen moving up the valley toward your entrant, towards battalion headquarters"[65] – Lieutenant-Colonel Jim Stone decided to use the considerable firepower at his immediate disposal to break up the impending assault. As he later wrote:

> The mortar platoon, located with HQ [but in a reentrant between the headquarters and B Company], was mounted for traveling on twelve half-tracks. Each vehicle was equipped with one .50 and one .30 caliber machine gun. Ammunition belts for these guns were loaded with one tracer bullet to four ball, or ordinary bullets. Fire was held until the Chinese had broken through the trees about two hundred meters away. Twenty-four machine guns cut loose together. Only those who have experienced being under the fire of a heavy concentration of tracer bullets can appreciate the terror induced by this volume of fire. With the crack of the machine guns and the 81 mm mortars firing at their shortest range, the enemy never had a chance.[66]

Inside twelve minutes the Chinese attack had completely disintegrated.[67] Having disposed of one threat, and able to see some distance in the bright moonlight, the machine-gunners then turned their attention to over a hundred Chinese who could be seen fording the Kapyong River several hundred yards away. The result once more was entirely one-sided.[68]

In the hours after midnight B Company continued to be attacked, a sense of the fierceness of what was at times very much a hand-to-hand engagement made evident by the fact that Bren-gunner Private Wayne Mitchell – who was awarded a DCM for his actions – was wounded twice but felt he could not afford to stop moving and firing while the battle raged.[69] Yet without the element of surprise and in the context of set-piece attacks the enemy's vast numerical advantage melted away. "The Chinese telegraphed the direction and timing of their attacks by using medium machine-gun tracer ammunition for direction," Lilley reported, "and by sounding bugles as signals to form up on their start lines to begin the assault." This was a godsend for the defenders, the men being able to predict in which direction to roll their grenades downhill or fire their bazookas and the officers and NCOs having the time "to bring down accurate artillery, mortar, and machine-gun fire."[70] At around 1 AM on Wednesday the 25th, by which time the moon had risen enough to significantly extend vision range, "a fourth assault party was detected forming up in the valley about 500 yards to our front," Lilley recalled. "The enemy was dispersed by quick and accurate mortar fire."[71]

In retrospect, though, it seemed clear that these attacks on the rear-right flank of the battalion were at least in part diversionary, designed to distract attention from an impending assault on the front-left flank.[72] About an hour after midnight, movement was heard to the left of D Company, and thirty minutes later the acting company commander, Captain Wally Mills, called battalion HQ requesting artillery and mortar fire. By 2 AM it was clear that several hundred Chinese were approaching 10 Platoon to the west accompanied by a large amount of supporting mortar and machine-gun fire.[73]

The 10 Platoon, led by Lieutenant Mike Levy, took the brunt of the initial attack on three sides. Medium machine-gun fire from 12 Platoon initially held off the enemy, but the Chinese pressed on. Within the hour the Vickers gunners had been killed – possibly by friendly fire[74] – 10 Platoon cut off, and 12 Platoon, overrun, forced to retreat back to the company HQ area.[75] The acting company commander, with no clear idea of what was happening at the platoon level and perhaps a little overwhelmed by his first crisis of command in battle, at first wanted to pull back the entire company. This did not go down well with the more experienced Levy, who knew that no contingency plans had been made for a fighting withdrawal and guessed that such an unplanned move with the enemy in close contact would invite disaster. He requested more specific instructions, at which point Mills thought to check with Stone concerning withdrawing D Company. The CO was adamantly opposed, recognizing that this would open up the other companies on lower ground to downward enemy fire and essentially mean the loss of Hill 677. "Big Jim" was determined to fight it out, his signals officer recalling the CO sitting by the radio set with a rifle across his knees and growling "let the bastards come!" while almost shaking with anticipation. "Mills wanted to pull out," Stone recalled; "I told him to stay there, that nobody could pull out!"[76]

If the troops were going to hold out, though, they would need support. Cut off as it was, the battalion was running short of food, water, emergency medical supplies, and most importantly, mortar and small-arms ammunition. Stone therefore requested through brigade that an air drop be made.[77] This, however, would take hours to arrange, and in the meantime parts of D Company seemed on the verge of being overrun. To try to redeploy elements of either of the two companies that had not yet been attacked was not really an option, since even in moonlight the chances of platoons losing their way or engaging in fratricide were high, and Stone had from the start operated on the assumption that each company had to stay in the comparative safety of its island of all-round defense. The only alternative – as the officer in the forefront of the action well understood – was heavy shelling.[78]

Confident that his men could survive if they kept low enough down, Levy called up Company HQ asking several times for massed artillery fire to be brought down on the vacated 12 Platoon location as well as on the 10 Platoon position. These requests were passed on by Mills to Battalion HQ, where after some initial consternation they were acted on; indeed, upgraded from "mike" targets (the twenty-four 25-pounders of 16 Field Regiment) to "uncle" targets (16 Field Regiment plus the forty heavier U.S. weapons now also under brigade control).[79] Requests from other quarters for support were peremptorily dismissed. "I called for DF fire," one supplicant recalled, "and was told to get off the [expletive deleted] air. D Company was being overrun."[80] In one forty-minute period the New Zealanders alone fired 2,300 rounds; 16 Field Regiment expending 10,000 shells in total through the night.[81] Corporal Ken Campbell, a section leader, recalled the effect of concentrated barrage fire:

> Our slit trenches were within hollering distance; when we got the word, we all crouched down in the trench. The artillery dropped a ten minute barrage on top of us. It stopped that attack, but the Chinese came at us again. They were about to overrun us, when another ten minute barrage came in. Later, we were hard pressed and called in a third ten minute barrage. We were convinced the artillery would kill us all, but there were no direct hits on any of the slit trenches. The Chinese, caught out in the open, were stopped cold.[82]

Adding to the enemy's problems was the surprise intervention of two platoons of Shermans from Company A, 72nd Tank Battalion, further disrupting the infantry assaults.[83] This did not mean that no enemy soldiers got close enough to pose a danger, as Campbell himself discovered when he received three burp gun rounds in the shoulder after he incautiously leaned out of his slit trench to try to use his Thompson submachine-gun against a Chinese soldier who had taken cover. "It felt like I had been hit by a plank," he recalled. "It knocked me face down on the parapet of the trench." He was shot twice more, but survived.[84] By about 8 AM the enemy had finally had enough and withdrew, allowing 12 Platoon to reestablish its old position. The situation, as the brigade war diarist recorded, was now "under control."[85]

The Patricias, somewhat to their surprise, had survived the night; "come daybreak we were still there," a soldier in the mortar platoon remembered.[86] Yet 2PPCLI was still cut off, and D and B companies were running low on ammunition and there was a shortage of food and water everywhere. "As stand-to began that morning," a corporal in A Company recalled, "it didn't take much knowledge of the big picture from where I sat to guess that the battalion's situation looked precarious."[87] As before, much would depend that Wednesday on what the Chinese decided to do next.

What are those blinking white lights sparkling on the ground?

LIEUTENANT ROD MIDDLETON, 2PPCLI, to U.S. helicopter pilot above Hill 677, 8:00 AM, re. Chinese anti-aircraft fire[1]

It was the most beautiful sight I can ever remember seeing.

UNIDENTIFIED SOLDIER, 2PPCLI, re. 10:30 AM supply drop[2]

EIGHT

Kapyong: The Final Day

IF THE 118TH CPV DIVISION RENEWED ITS VIGOROUS ATTACKS on Hill 677 in the hours after dawn, then the chances of survival for the Patricias would be lower than they had been after midnight. "By that time our Mortar Platoon was almost completely out of mortar bombs," Private Mike Czuboka remembered. "The rifle companies were also down to a few rounds of ammunition. Our food and water was almost gone."[3] Some of the badly wounded, to be sure, could now be evacuated by two American helicopters, but ground fire from the Chinese as the machines flew in was a reminder that the enemy still surrounded the battalion and could close in again.[4] After a night of sometimes quite vicious hand-to-hand fighting one or two soldiers found they were unable to switch off their bloodlust. Decades later PPCLI veterans could claim that they had felt no hatred for the enemy, but early Wednesday morning after the fighting had died down two Patricias, discovering a pair of wounded Chinese forward of their position, first rummaged through their possessions and then deliberately picked them up and threw them to their deaths down a steep slope.[5] Other soldiers maintained a remarkable *sang-froid* in the face of imminent danger. "I responded to the desperate situation as soldiers are wont to do when they can't do anything about it," Corporal John Bishop of 2 Platoon later wrote. "I got my head down and fell into a comfortable doze."[6] But there was no doubt in the mind of the CO, Lieutenant-Colonel Jim Stone, that if the enemy kept pushing, "in all probability the 2 PPCLI would have been annihilated."[7] Or as an unidentified Patricia reflected a quarter century later, "what happened to the Gloucesters could easily have happened to us."[8] That it did not was due to the actions of both friends and enemies.

The situation of those atop Hill 677 improved considerably after 10:30 AM when the airdrop of supplies Stone had requested six hours earlier occurred. A flight of C-119 Flying Boxcars from Japan roared in low overhead and unloaded multiple parachute-retarded pallets on which food, water, and ammunition were stored. Luckily nobody below was hit—the pallets came down "really fast" recalled Harry Welsh, who was only three feet from where one bounced on impact[9]—and only four landed too far outside the perimeter to be retrieved. The small-arms ammunition delivered was all .30 or .50 caliber and the mortar bombs all 81-mm in size, but as the vehicles and weapons of the mortar platoon were American—as were the carbines and submachine-guns many men had unofficially acquired—this was still, as a member of the platoon put it, a "big help" to the battalion. "A minor miracle" had taken place, one of his buddies argued more feelingly. U.S. grenades presented no problems, and enough .303 ammunition was redistributed to keep the exhausted rifle companies going. Bishop, rudely awoken from his catnap by the cargo planes thundering in, immediately saw that "the battalion would be able to hold on."[10]

What the enemy was up to was initially not entirely clear. Lieutenant Peter McKenzie, the 2PPCLI Intelligence Officer who had suggested the air drop to Stone, worried that the Chinese were pausing only long enough to mass enough forces for a really big push.[11] Yet at about 9 AM, a platoon from C Company was able to retrieve one of the Vickers guns belonging to D Company that had been brought over the night before against minimal opposition.[12] Throughout the morning the men of C and D companies, particularly those in 10 Platoon, came under occasional grenade and rifle fire, and while some jeeps ran the gauntlet and successfully evacuated more wounded through the enemy cordon to the south the effort was not without cost in the form of further casualties.[13] But neither in the northwest nor anywhere else around Hill 677 did a Chinese assault develop.[14]

No soldier likes to be in a state of ignorance concerning the enemy, and even before the air drop a certain amount of patrolling was taking place. Unfortunately, and without enemy intervention, the first patrol sent out by B Company suffered a tragedy. Before the Chinese attack began on Tuesday night, the Pioneer Platoon had laid grenade booby traps to help protect the company's position. Shortly after 8 AM a platoon sergeant leading the patrol moved away from the safe path and into a booby-trapped area. A soldier tripped a grenade in a tin with the pin removed and it went off, killing him and seriously wounding another man. Guessing what had happened, Sergeant Red Pennel and Lance-Corporal Smiley Douglas of the Pioneer Platoon raced to the scene, only to witness another booby trap being tripped. Yelling to the rest of the patrol to lie down, Douglas dove in to try to throw the grenade in the seconds before the detonator worked, but the grenade exploded and blew off his hand.[15]

This incident was doubly tragic, as patrols later in the day revealed that the enemy was apparently withdrawing. "If there are Chinese in the area they must be asleep," a member of a D Company patrol remembered thinking.[16] By 2 PM it appeared from B Company reports that the road route to the rear was open, and Stone seized the opportunity to order up further supplies "in anticipation," as the battalion war diarist put it, "of continued Chinese attack."[17]

That the enemy had not vanished became clear in the afternoon. Late on Wednesday morning the 5th Cavalry RCT had moved up in preparation for a counter-thrust up the Kapyong Valley. At 1 PM the Americans moved forward on a two-battalion front.[18] At first things seemed to be going well. "They attacked a low hill across a rice paddy in extended lines," Dan Johnson recalled of what he saw from atop the feature held by the Patricias. "One line dropped and gave covering fire to the line that followed behind," he added. "'Fire and Movement.' I have never seen it demonstrated better. Hundreds of enemy soldiers erupted from the crest of the hill and began to retreat; the Americans followed."[19] After a mile or so, however, the advance was observed to be running into trouble. Sergeant Mike Melnechuk of C Company recalled watching mortar bombs bursting among them as they advanced in open order, the GIs hitting the dirt but then moving forward in what he could see was "a hard-fought battle." The assistance of two tank platoons helped, but they eventually ran out of ammunition and had to withdraw. As the 3RAR war diarist noted, due to "determined resistance," the two battalions "were unable to capture their objectives" by the end of the afternoon.[20]

The Chinese, however, though clearly able to fight an effective delaying action in daylight, were evidently no longer prepared to launch big night attacks. "By last light the situation on the Bde front was quiet," the brigade war diarist recorded, "and reports of enemy [activity] had ceased."[21] This was just as well, given that the stalling of the 5th Cavalry RCT battalions left them in a highly vulnerable tactical position.[22] The intention, as relayed to Colonel Stone in the early evening, was for elements from the 5th Cavalry to climb up at some point on Thursday to relieve 2PPCLI. On Hill 677 the night was uneventful, though the Patricias remained vigilant. "We still didn't know if they'd be back to test our resolve again," Bishop commented.[23]

At brigade headquarters, meanwhile, the situation now appeared stable enough to proceed with the planned change of command. In a special order of the day Brigadier Brian Burke formally announced the move and, in the words of the 2PPCLI war diarist, "commended the traditions of 27 Brigade and of those units of the Commonwealth Forces remaining with 28 Brigade in Korea."[24] With the Argylls having departed on Tuesday and the King's Own Scottish Borderers now operational, 27th British Commonwealth Brigade officially gave way to 28th Commonwealth Brigade at midnight on Wednesday, Burke handing over command to Brigadier George "Fluff" Taylor. In a mark of his respect for the Australians, Burke had given his brigade flag to Lieutenant-Colonel Bruce Ferguson earlier in the day.[25]

Anxious to make sure that all was well, the IX Corps and Eighth Army commanders flew in to visit Taylor around noon.[26] They seemed to have been satisfied, but in fact the relief effort on Thursday did not go entirely as planned, the Chinese once more proving that they could be tenacious in defense even if they were no longer capable of attacking in this sector. Despite artillery support there was heavy to moderate resistance to the renewed advance, and by last light none of the initial objectives had been reached. Nevertheless, late in the day 2PPCLI was finally reached by the 1st Battalion of the 5th Cavalry Regiment, a sergeant informing Lieutenant Mike Levy that in the course of the day his platoon had lost an officer and half its men.[27] "Our descent down Hill 677 was full of tension," Mike Czuboka later wrote. "We did not know if the Chinese were still present."[28] Happily they were not. "When we went out, nobody fired," another Canadian soldier recalled. "There was no firing at all as we left."[29]

At the base of the hill the men climbed aboard trucks and were driven to a village, and then on Friday transported farther south as 28th Brigade became a rear guard covering the withdrawal of a badly hit RCT of the U.S. 24th Division.[30] After bumping slowly down the road for thirteen miles in the lead vehicle through the early evening, Lieutenant Brian Munro of 2 Platoon suddenly saw, in the inky shadows ahead of the darkened trucks, a couple of figures, one of whom was motioning the column to stop. Munro ordered the driver to halt but, carbine in hand, was prepared to fight if the figures turned out to be part of a Chinese ambush. "I say, who are you?" a very clipped English voice asked. "Patricias," Munro replied to an officer who turned out to be George Taylor, the commander of the newly created 28th Brigade, accompanied by a British redcap armed with a Sten gun. "Brigadier here!" The reason Taylor had stopped the column was that while they were on the move it had been impossible to contact them by radio and the Patricias were needed to form a new defensive position. "Would you mind climbing that hill over there and digging in?" the brigadier asked. "We will sort it all out in the morning." Taylor then went down the halted column, sending the various companies onto the surrounding features. "As we dismounted and headed into the nearby hills, I had the impression of general confusion," wrote John Bishop. "Companies and platoons were sited hurriedly in the dark, and we hastily started to dig." It had begun to rain.[31]

Retreating and digging in under rotten weather conditions was dispiriting for the rest of the brigade as well, the absence of hard news about the state of affairs not improving morale at all. Yet the U.S.-led withdrawal was—comparatively at least[32]—executed in an orderly manner, and it gradually became clear that by the time the brigade had moved twenty miles south of Kapyong the Chinese were not pursuing with any vigor. As a Middlesex soldier put it, "they did not disturb us." Consequently the entire Commonwealth Brigade was sent back into IX Corps reserve at Yangpyong on 28 April.[33]

I hope I never, never have to fight a battle like that again.

LIEUTENANT-COLONEL J. P. "FRED" CARNE, 1GLOS, 1953[1]

When you achieve your objectives and you suffer very few casualties then you've fought a very fine battle and you've achieved a very great victory.

LIEUTENANT-COLONEL (RETD.) J. R. "BIG JIM" STONE, 2PPCLI, 1973[2]

Epilogue

TOM BRODIE, THE COMMANDER OF 29TH BRIGADE, WAS visibly distraught as he watched his torn and bloodied men stumble back to safety.[3] In a letter to his parents written on 26 April, a bandaged Lieutenant Malcolm Cubiss of X Company reported that four-fifths of the Glosters, half the Fusiliers, and half the Rifles had been lost during the Imjin battle, an estimate that reflected the widespread sense that casualties had been very high indeed.[4] Thankfully the initial tallies were a little off, as small numbers of stragglers from all three battalions made their way back to U.N. lines over the next few days. The final casualty figures, though, were shocking enough. The Belgians had gotten off comparatively lightly, with twelve of their number killed, six taken prisoner, and thirty wounded. The Ulsters had lost ten officers and 180 men killed, wounded, or captured; while the Northumberlands and attached personnel had suffered 32 killed, 96 wounded, and 38 officers and men captured. As for the unfortunate Glosters and those artillerymen and others with them, 63 had been killed, 106 wounded, and – because they had effectively run out of ammunition and were deep behind enemy lines – 610 captured in varying degrees of poor health. 29th Brigade as a whole had lost 1,091 men, about a quarter of its strength.[5]

Not surprisingly, in view of these figures, there was no shortage of behind-the-scenes finger-pointing in the aftermath of the Imjin battle, particularly with reference to the fate of the Glosters. Within the U.N. forces command structure there was a good deal of embarrassment and a consequent search for scapegoats.

As already noted, Tom Brodie thought the primary blame lay with the divisional commander, Major General Robert H. Soule, for ordering the Glosters to stand their ground despite repeated warnings from Brigade HQ about the deteriorating situation. Brodie did not, however, make his views public, confining himself by way of explanation to stressing that it was "a case of the Brigade being in the stickiest place" in the divisional line. Moreover, unlike some senior officers, the brigade commander knew that ultimately he was responsible for the fate of those under his command. When questioned by an American combat historian six months later, Brodie accepted half the blame for the destruction of the battalion on the grounds that he had not managed to effectively convey the seriousness of the battalion's predicament to division HQ in time to allow for a successful extraction. Some of his subordinates agreed. Major Charles Mitchell of the Fusiliers was happy to see the brigade later being integrated into a new Commonwealth Division under the command of Major-General James "Gentleman Jim" Cassels, "a first class chap who can really handle Americans!" As he added in a letter to his mother, dated June 3rd, "Tom Brodie I often felt didn't stand up to them enough – not really surprising as he was usually junior in rank – American Generals sometimes have a funny idea of what can and what cannot be done."[6]

As commander-in-chief of U.N. operations in Korea, General Matthew B. Ridgway tended to suspect that the blame for the loss of the Glosters went higher than just brigade or divisional headquarters. "I cannot but feel a certain disquiet that down through the channel of command," he wrote the Eighth Army commander on 9 May, "the full responsibility for realizing the danger to which this unit was exposed, then for extricating it when that danger became grave, was not recognized nor implemented."

> There are times, as I'm sure your experience in battle will bear out, when it is not sufficient to accept the judgment of a subordinate commander that a threatened unit can care for itself, or that a threat situation can be handled locally. The responsibility in each case goes straight up the command chain, through regiment, Div., Corps, to Army. Each commander should search his soul and by personal verification, satisfy himself that adequate action has been taken. It may be that such was the case with the Gloucesters. I have the feeling that it was not; that neither the Div., or Corps Commanders [Robert H. Soule of 3rd Division and Frank W. Milburn of I Corps] was fully aware by direct personal presence, as near the critical spot as he could have gotten, of what the actual situation was.

If that had in fact been the case, Ridgway added, "I feel sure that instant vigorous action would have been taken to extricate the unit."[7]

To paraphrase a famous saying, while victory has a hundred fathers, defeat is an orphan, and those fingered by Ridgway from bottom to top proved keen to avoid taking any major responsibility for what had happened. The commander of one of the largest U.S. units involved in the affair, Lieutenant Colonel William W. Harris of the 65th RCT, though privately accepting that Brodie had every right to blame Soule, doubtless spoke for others in the U.S. chain of command when he explained that "I did not intend to become the fall guy, come what may."[8] Lieutenant General James A. Van Fleet therefore refused to accept the implied criticism made by Ridgway of his leadership and that of his corps and division commanders. Though emphasizing to Milburn and the other corps commanders that care should be taken to prevent allied units from being cut off – "Don't use *any* U.N. forces that way" he had stressed with reference to what had happened to the Glosters in an afternoon meeting on 30 April[9] – the Eighth Army commander disputed Ridgway's analysis in a reply sent to Tokyo on 11 May. Having reviewed the situation, Van Fleet informed Ridgway that the primary blame lay with the British, and more specifically with Colonel J. P. Carne, who in the course of the battle "did not indicate the seriousness of his position and the need for either additional help or withdrawal."[10]

Up to a point Ridgway accepted this evaluation, which was shared by other U.S. officers. Writing many years later, he remembered that those who knew Carne had stressed "his exceptional coolness under pressure and his dislike for asking for help until every resource at his disposal had been exhausted." But in the aftermath of the battle he was not willing to assign all the blame to a single battalion commander. "With Carne's well-known characteristics of understating his own problems and not seeking help except as a last resort," he explained to the new I Corps commander, Major General John W. O'Daniel, "it should have been clear to higher commanders that his situation was much worse than his early reports indicated, and that earlier major efforts to break through to him should have been made."[11]

One of the things that many among the British and Americans involved in the Imjin battle did agree on was that the crisis with the Glosters had arisen because the brigade's flank had been exposed to enemy infiltration through the withdrawal of the South Korean division on the left of the line. As Ridgway later put it, "the enemy drove the ROK 1st Division south of the Kansas Line in a sudden surge, leaving exposed the left flank of the British 29th Brigade," thus allowing the Glosters to be encircled. This was also the explanation conveyed to London in an official post-mortem report drawn up by Lieutenant-General Sir Horace Robertson, the Australian officer in command of British Commonwealth forces in Japan, albeit using more qualified language, and it proved to be one that more junior officers eagerly grasped. "We always suffer from our allies the Koreans who run away and let the Chinese in behind us," wrote Major Charles Mitchell, the commander of W Company, in a letter to his mother from the hospital in May. This was also the consensus view among surviving Rifles officers, as newly arrived Lieutenant Edmund Ions discovered. "During the next few weeks I heard about the April battle," he later remembered, "and how the British Brigade had been quickly surrounded because the South Korean Division on the flank had 'bugged out' almost immediately."[12]

This blame game, though, was mostly played in private. The public posture concerning what had happened on the Imjin was to avoid the assigning of any responsibility and emphasize the bravery and achievements of those units involved, especially the Glosters. The Americans did not wish it to appear as if U.S. formations had abandoned a small allied force to its fate, while the British did not wish to undermine what limited influence they still possessed on the conduct of operations in Korea.[13]

Within twenty-four hours of the brigade being withdrawn from operations a representative of the Reuters press agency was reporting from 29th Brigade HQ that its "refusal to give ground" had "saved the United Nations flank" and broken "the onrush of at least one Chinese army corps." As for the Glosters, they had fought gallantly against overwhelming odds. Efforts by a column of Centurions to relieve them had failed due to enemy action, but a breakout had occurred on the last day in which – so the report suggested – the majority of the men had linked up with advancing British tanks. "Senior American officers described the British stand as 'an object lesson in the way troops should fight.'" The next day, 27 April, the British United Press service was reporting from

U.N. headquarters in Tokyo that until they had fought their way out of encirclement men of the 29th Brigade had borne the brunt of an attack by a grand total of 24,000 Chinese soldiers. "By blocking the Chinese drive southward for three days," the report continued, "they are believed to have set back the Communist time-table by 48 hours."[14]

Similar reports were filed by other Tokyo correspondents stressing, as Denis Warner put it in a piece published on the front page of the *Daily Telegraph,* that the "British stand upset the Chinese timetable" and that while losses among the Glosters "are officially described as very heavy," there was still a fair chance that "a good many" would successfully make their way to U.N. lines. The casualty figures from the battle released by the War Office on the evening of the 1st of May, running into the hundreds, therefore came as something of a shock, especially with reference to the Glosters. The *Express* military reporter, Robert Jessel, wrote a front-page story in which he wondered how it was that the Glosters came to be isolated, speculating that perhaps orders had been misunderstood and wondering if the brigade commander was responsible. The answer, Jessel admitted, "might never be known," but in pointing out that there was "no automatic court of inquiry after a loss of this kind" he seemed to be suggesting that there ought to be an official investigation.[15]

This was not, however, something that the authorities were at all keen to undertake. The British government was just as anxious as Ridgway and Van Fleet to avoid seeing what happened to the Glosters interpreted as a case of British troops left to their fate due to American orders. Cleared with the Prime Minister's Office, the speech given by the Minister of Defence to the House of Commons on 2 May to explain what had occurred was clearly calculated to reinforce the idea that what had happened on the Imjin was a necessary and heroic sacrifice.[16]

After he rose to address the House, Emanuel Shinwell first explained the context of the battle and then emphasized that "the 29th Brigade faced the full flood of the Chinese advance south of the Imjin River." Though all the details were not yet available, it was clear that "all the troops concerned . . . greatly distinguished themselves." The heavy losses incurred were not in vain. "This magnificent action played a vital part in the operations in the west," the Minister asserted, "since an enemy penetration at this point would have jeopardized the safety of the whole line." Shinwell then gave a summary of the part played by the Glosters in the Imjin battle, stressing that repeated efforts had been made to relieve them once they were isolated, hinting that some might still be wandering free, and concluding that while it "may be some little time before full details of this remarkable action" became known, "it is already clear that it will rank as one of the most glorious in which this famous regiment has taken part."[17]

MPs did not query this presentation of events, and neither did the leader writers of the national press. The *Telegraph,* for example, opined the following day that "the story is one to arouse the nation's pride and gratitude," adding that "the Gloucestershire Regiment in particular has fought an heroic engagement." Shinwell was clearly right to make the case that the Imjin engagement would "rank as one of the most glorious" in the regiment's illustrious history. *The Times* was equally impressed, its own leader stressing that while the Glosters deserved honorable mention for their achievements on the Imjin so too did the Northumberland Fusiliers and Ulster Rifles. "The account given by Mr. Shinwell yesterday of the British part in the United Nations' action must make everybody in these islands proud," the *Guardian* stated. The Glosters in particular deserved acclaim; "they held a position whose loss would have jeopardized the corps responsible for that sector of the Imjin River front," and thanks to their dogged tenacity other units had been able to make a successful withdrawal. The popular press was equally supportive, the *Daily Herald,* for instance, quoting facts and opinions voiced by Shinwell verbatim on the front page.[18]

In public, if not always in private, the U.S. authorities continued to praise the actions of the British on the Imjin. In the first week of May, General Milburn sent a congratulatory letter to Brigadier Brodie that was quickly made public. "I want to commend you and your officers and men for gallantry in action while defending the Imjin river line during the last days of April against the assault of greatly superior forces," the I Corps commander explained. "Subject to exceedingly heavy pressure, you did not falter, and met his attacks with fighting will and courage beyond his belief as is attested by the hundreds of enemy dead in close proximity to your positions." General Van Fleet in person presented a Presidential Unit Citation to the 1st Battalion, The Gloucestershire Regiment and 170 Mortar Battery, Royal Artillery, in front of the assembled troops of 29th Brigade and a host of press representatives – one "could hardly see him for the bloomin' photographers" an Ulsterman reported in a letter home[19] – during the afternoon of 8 May. "I have come to be in good company," the Eighth Army commander announced to the assembled throng, "and to pay tribute to the wonderful British Commonwealth forces. I wanted to get better acquainted with and pay tribute and give honor to your gallant stand."[20]

The two units, the actual document read, "are cited for exceptionally outstanding performance of duty and heroism in action," and after outlining the course of the battle the citation concluded that the units "displayed such gallantry, determination, and esprit de corps in accomplishing their mission under extremely difficult and hazardous conditions as to set them above other units participating in the same battle." All in all the men's "sustained brilliance in battle, their resoluteness, and extraordinary heroism" were such as to "reflect unsurpassed credit on those courageous soldiers and their homeland."[21]

Not surprisingly the Presidential Unit Citation was approvingly reported in the British press under headlines such as "Gloucesters Given U.S. Honour" (*Daily Herald*) and "Gloucesters Win Highest U.S. Military Honour" (*Daily Telegraph*). When film of the event was shown in British newsreels, audiences cheered.[22]

The fact that the Americans were publicly and effusively praising the British contribution to the Battle of the Imjin River seems to have subsumed any questions about how the casualty list came to be so long and why the Glosters had been left to their own devices. In the 16 May issue of *The Times* it was reported at some length that the previous day's *Washington Post* had printed a leading article titled "heroism in Korea" praising the actions of the Glosters. Less than a week later *The Times* proudly noted under the heading "Tribute to Gloucesters" that the *New York Times Magazine* had published a piece on the contribution of U.N. contingents to the fighting in Korea in which the Last Stand of the Glosters was specifically praised. Fourteen days after that, a story from the Washington correspondent of *The Times* headed "Gallantry of the Gloucesters" appeared, in which remarks made by the U.S. Secretary of State, Dean Rusk, before a Senate committee about the Glosters were enthusiastically reproduced. Their actions were "very gallant" and "held up the entire advance of the Chinese in the western sector." The fight was "one of the great stories in military history." The correspondent also reported praise from the *New York Herald Tribune*, the *New York Times*, and the *New Yorker* magazine.[23]

It was the article in the *New Yorker*, published on 26 May, which drew the most attention on the other side of the Atlantic. Written by the magazine's correspondent in Korea, E. J. Kahn, Jr., the piece was a lengthy and detailed narrative account of the part played by 29th Brigade in the Battle of the Imjin in which it was asserted that "the steadfast resistance of the British to this massive assault was very likely the most influential single factor in the dashing of the Communists' probable hope of celebrating May Day in the capital city of the Republic of Korea." Emphasizing in detail the heroism of the Glosters and implying that no other outcome was possible, the piece was so uncritically positive that the Central Office of Information in London sought and obtained permission to reprint it as a special pamphlet bearing the title *The Gloucesters: An Account of the Epic Stand of the First Battalion, The Gloucestershire Regiment, in Korea.*[24]

As spring gave way to summer in 1951 tributes to the Glosters continued to be reported, appearing everywhere from Australia to Canada as well as more from the United States. There was even one from President Harry S. Truman. Read out on 3 July by the U.S. Ambassador to the Court of St. James, W. S. Gifford, at a meeting of the English Speaking Union, the presidential message concluded: "The spirit which engendered this supreme sacrifice on the part of all but a handful of the 1st Battalion of The Gloucestershire Regiment, typifies our mutual determination that all who love freedom shall be protected and defended from aggression."[25]

The subjects of all this praise who were not either dead or in enemy hands were sometimes at first far from convinced that what came to be presented as a tragic but necessary sacrifice was anything other than a comprehensively awful experience. "We wanted to forget," Lieutenant-Colonel Digby Grist, the new CO of the Glosters wrote a year later. "Particularly the Reservists wanted to forget; so many of their mates had been left behind – and, remember, we did not know what we know now, that so many had survived [as prisoners]." When BBC cameraman Ronnie Noble visited the brigade in the immediate aftermath of the battle after it had retired to the Kimpo area, a tired and angry Gloster private told him to "Fuck off with the fucking camera!" which, for the only time in his career, he did. "They'd taken so much that the very sight of the camera might have made them temporarily insane," he later wrote. The situation was similar among the Ulsters, Major Gerald Rickord cautioning the cameraman with the words "please don't upset them. They've had quite a time!" Noble agreed after observing the dazed men sitting about in small groups. "It was as though they had seen the horrors of a lifetime in those three days," he observed. This was not just his own impression; a survivor from D Company of the Glosters noted how men after arriving at Yongdongpo "stood about in small groups in the hastily improvised cookhouse, discussing their experiences, their nerves still too taut for sleep, and their eyes unnaturally bright from fatigue and disbelief." The Ulsters were at first no happier to see Noble than the Glosters had been. "Oi'll smash yer fucking camera!" one of them threatened when it was pointed in his direction.[26]

There was a good deal of dejection and bafflement at the outcome of the battle. "I had the feeling that this should never happen," Sergeant Frank Cottam of the Glosters remembered, noting ruefully in the moments after he surrendered that despite the best efforts of all concerned "we'd been cut off, carved up and captured" by an enemy whom they had previously despised. As one among them admitted much later, captured officers tended to assume a burden of guilt for having failed to stop the enemy assault at the Imjin, an attitude widely shared by those with commissions who remained free.[27]

Among those who had avoided death or capture there were some who simply broke down once the adrenalin had ceased pumping. Denis Prout of the Fusiliers remembered how he "cried my eyes out" once it was all over. Officers too felt the strain. "It was very traumatic to see people, who have served you well and been really good soldiers, just die instantly," Captain Mike Harvey of the Glosters remembered much later. "One moment they are full of life and personality, the next instant they are just nothing. It is very difficult to deal with that." Second-Lieutenant Denys Whatmore thought "we were all in a fragile state" by the time Harvey and his group reached friendly lines. A platoon commander from

A Company of the Rifles was so traumatized by his experiences that he had to be replaced, and at least one wounded Gloster eventually deserted rather than face the prospect of going back into the line. "We were pretty demoralized," Lieutenant Gordon Potts, another officer from the Ulsters, later admitted.[28]

Luckily sleep, food, and some leave tended to work wonders with the majority, who according to many observers recovered quickly from the ordeal . . . though survivors might still have nightmares. Having been wounded in the battle and subsequently discharged, ex-subaltern P. J. Kavanagh must have thought he had put the war behind him when later that year he began studying for a degree in English at Merton College, Oxford. "On Guy Fawkes night [5 November] I went to sleep to the sound of fireworks and dreamt that Chinamen were climbing into my room from Merton street carrying machine guns, and I had to warn the porter at the lodge," he later wrote. "I woke up in the quadrangle on my way to see him."[29]

Those who remained in Korea might superficially recover quite fully yet feel the effects of post-combat stress even in the comparatively quiet period that followed the Imjin fight. Major Tony Younger, in command of 55 Field Squadron, Royal Engineers, noticed how both he and some of his key officers began to show the unhealthy symptoms of what he later identified as "battle fatigue."[30] Other ranks, meanwhile, including World War II veterans, occasionally broke down under fire, and were perhaps less willing to obey orders which went against their interests than in the past. It is worth noting that within two months of the Imjin battle six soldiers – two from each battalion – would be court-martialed for desertion and that a small-scale mutiny occurred within a section from the Fusiliers.[31]

The military authorities certainly did not want to leave either soldiers or the public with the impression that the brigade in general and the Glosters in particular had been so badly mauled that the men were no longer fit to fight. Once the brigade had been taken out of the line and placed in corps reserve and then moved to a quiet sector on the Kimpo peninsula west of Seoul, everything was done to bring units back up to operational strength as fast as possible. What one Fusilier company commander described as "a host of reinforcements" was immediately transported to Korea courtesy of the Royal Australian Air Force from the Commonwealth forces base at Kure in Japan, along with large amounts of communication and other equipment borrowed from American sources to replace what had been lost on the Imjin. "Reinforcements in men and material were flown in a continuous stream for at least three days from Iwakuni to airfields in Korea," an officer from the Northamptons suddenly posted to the Glosters remembered. To replace the large number of company officers killed, captured, or wounded, volunteers were recruited from various home units and, despite the expense, airlifted rather than shipped by sea out to the Far East.[32]

It was the Glosters, of course, who had suffered the highest number of casualties and who required the greatest number of reinforcements. Keen to make sure that the battalion not be considered so heavily damaged as to be broken up – there was a rumor that the remnants might be shipped to garrison duty in the Falklands – the then acting CO took matters into his own hands. Even with all those members of the regiment who had not taken part in the battle accounted for, the battalion barely exceeded 200 officers and men, so Digby Grist sent transport down to Kimpo airfield, those aboard equipped with the following instructions: "If any new arrival looks lost, pop him into a Gloucester truck and drive him to a good hot meal. After that it will be the easiest thing in the world to badge him 'Gloucester.'" Brigade HQ, if they knew about such unorthodox recruiting methods, did not interfere. Within three days the battalion Grist commanded could field three rifle companies, a skeletal Support Company, and a complete HQ Company. A signal was proudly sent: "We are operational again."[33]

Participants in the concurrent Kapyong battle were necessarily cast into shadow by the spotlight directed at the Imjin battle and the Glosters. In the days after the fight there was, to be sure, front-page coverage in the press in Australia and Canada. The third battalion of the Royal Australian Regiment, an editorial in the *Sydney Morning Herald* commented, "has once again won itself battle honours far out of proportion to its size," while a report on the front page of the Melbourne *Age* asserted that "Australian infantry and New Zealand artillerymen grimly upheld the Anzac traditions." Similar sentiments were expressed in the pages of Canadian newspapers. "It was known that the Princess Patricias would prove worthy of Canada," an editorial in the Toronto *Telegram* argued, "and recent dispatches which tell of their heroic stand against waves of attacking Chinese, show that they are making a name for themselves among the men of the United Nations, and that they are soldiers of whom Canada may be proud."[34] There was, however, comparatively little coverage of Kapyong in the British press, and it was symptomatic of the relative profile of the two battles that a famous cartoon immortalizing the heroic qualities of the Glosters actually first appeared in a Toronto paper.[35]

It is also notable that the U.S. military authorities did not announce unit citations for the Kapyong battle until seven weeks after the Glosters and 170 Mortar Battery had been valorized. In the third week of June 1951, General Van Fleet stated that 3RAR and 2PPCLI, along with A Company, 72nd Tank Battalion, would each receive a Presidential Unit Citation for their actions. All three units "displayed such gallantry, determination and *esprit de corps* in accomplishing their mission under extremely difficult and hazardous conditions as to set them apart from other units participating in the campaign."[36] There was, not surprisingly, good coverage of this award back home, but in contrast to the unit citation given to the Glosters, no mention of the award to the Patricias and Diggers appeared in the British or American press.[37]

On the other hand the battalions that had fought at Kapyong had not been as badly knocked about as those involved in the Imjin battle. 3RAR, to be sure, had suffered 31 killed, three captured, and 58 wounded; but though desperately tired and glad to find their part in the battle over, the Diggers were not downhearted.[38] As for 2PPCLI, it had sustained only ten dead and 23 wounded. As Lieutenant-Colonel Jim Stone later commented, "Canadian casualties had been light"; indeed, he was arguing within a few weeks that the withdrawal had been unnecessary.[39] Among the rank-and-file Patricias, there was initially little sense of having done anything that much out of the ordinary, even after the awarding of the Presidential Unit Citation. "I don't think most of us felt that Kapyong was the high point of our service in Korea," one veteran reflected; "I don't think that we at our level realized the significance of it."[40] Only decades later did it become commonplace for those who had fought at Kapyong to state that they had saved Seoul.[41]

Neither brigade was needed to fight again during the final, climactic days of the ultimately successful U.N. effort to stop the Chinese thrusts. By the end of April 1951 the enemy advance had ground to a halt and Chinese units were once again breaking contact and retreating northward. The enemy offensive was renewed in the east in mid-May, but again, after some southward movement and extremely bloody fighting, failed to achieve any decisive results. The initiative now lay once again with the Eighth Army, which began a general advance to regain the ground lost during the Fifth Phase offensive. By the end of May, therefore, 29th Brigade found itself once more on the line of the Imjin. By this time the Middlesex had departed for Hong Kong and 2PPCLI had transferred to the newly arrived 25th Canadian Infantry Brigade.

Thankfully the Chinese had not contested the reoccupation of the old Imjin line. "When the battalion moved up again it was just a clean move up to the Imjin itself," recalled Corporal Norman Sweetlove of the Ulsters. "The Gloucesters and the Northumberlands were there also. We were static there and we sent patrols periodically over the river . . . but, as far as fighting was concerned, there was no more fighting, only patrols going out." Still, it was a grim business cleaning up the battlefield, especially with reference to the identification of the decomposing corpses of fallen comrades.[42]

Even without such visual reminders, though, there was now a strong sense within 29th Brigade that the Chinese needed to be treated with extreme caution. No longer were the enemy dismissed as an ignorant peasant militia. "We were told to expect a well-trained, clever, cunning opponent who was used to the terrain," Keith Taylor, a replacement subaltern assigned to the Northumberlands, recalled, "and not to underestimate them."[43] The enemy was evidently once again in retreat, but survivors of the previous month's fighting were determined to ensure that history did not repeat itself. In the future, no matter how distant the enemy might appear, defensive preparations by infantry units of the brigade would never be pro forma. As Captain Andrew Scott of the Fusiliers noted, once the brigade was back on the Imjin the men "set about digging, wiring, laying mines against any future attacks or incursions by the Chinese hordes." Lieutenant Sam Phillips, another Fusiliers officer, confirmed that this was now standard policy; "whenever we stopped, we immediately dug as deep and as fast as we could, put out wire, put out mines."[44] When the author Eric Linklater toured the Imjin in the summer he found that the "rifle companies lived on hill tops which they had carved into redoubts and encircled with barbed wire," adding that "from a distance the thick entanglements that closed the narrow valleys between the hills shone like fields of bluebells."[45] Fire support was also increased; Keith Taylor noted that after the battle "it was realised that everything had to be beefed up – and it was."[46]

Battle reports from Centurion crews made it clear to the War Office that "there is an urgent operational requirement to fit a machine gun to the commander's cupola." Arrangements were made to manufacture a hundred special mountings and send them "as soon as possible" to Korea.[47] Prior to the arrival of the official fix, officers of the 8th Hussars sought to make up for the lack of a swing-mount machine-gun on the Centurion by trading whisky rations for .300 Browning machine-guns which could be placed on ad hoc turret roof mountings.[48]

It was telling that infantry officers increasingly sought to supplement or replace their personal firepower by trading for U.S. semi-automatic carbines. By the time Lieutenant Ions arrived as a replacement officer destined for the Ulsters, most junior officers had acquired them. As he explained, this was:

> a much more useful weapon than the officer's pistol with which we were supposed to attack enemy bunkers. The American carbine could fire automatically, had a slightly smaller bore [.300] than the British .303 rifle, and above all was lighter, handier, and almost as accurate. Ammunition was easy to come by, and there seemed to be plenty of it with any battalion in the line.[49]

Since U.S. units were officially dry, the beer and spirits issued to British troops could easily be exchanged for semi-automatics. When Major Dare Wilson arrived some months later to take over command of Z Company from Major John Winn, the new second-in-command of the Northumberlands stressed to Wilson that the Chinese could advance very quickly indeed, and that an ample supply of grenades should be kept at hand. Wilson decided eight per soldier would be enough; some of his men thought ten would be better. Photographs and testimony suggest that steel helmets were now commonly worn anywhere near the front line.[50]

The sector occupied by 29th Brigade remained relatively quiet through the summer, with plans being laid to replace each of the veteran battalions in turn with fresh units during the autumn. The front, however, began to move northward once more in the late summer and autumn, culminating for the Commonwealth Division in early October with Operation Commando. Though it was thought prudent not to involve the Glosters, the Fusiliers and the Rifles were temporarily attached to the 28th Commonwealth and 25th Canadian brigades, respectively, to reinforce the Australian, British, and Canadian infantry battalions detailed to take various tactically important hills and ridgelines. The Diggers once again did very well, but going into another full-scale battle was rough on the men of 1RUR and 1RNF who knew that they were due to leave Korea within a couple of weeks. Happily for the Ulsters, their part in Operation Commando turned out to involve almost no fighting. The Northumberlands, however, were not so lucky in their efforts to secure Hill 217. Thanks to strong enemy defenses the fighting on 217 was very fierce, and casualties among the Fusiliers numbered over a hundred. "It has been a nightmare," one subaltern wrote feelingly in a letter home.[51]

That, however, was it for the infantry battalions that had fought at the Imjin and Kapyong. In the second week of October the Ulster Rifles were relieved by the Royal Norfolks, in the third week the Northumberlands were replaced by the Leicesters, and in early November the Glosters gave way to the Welch Regiment. 2PPCLI was also relieved by 1PPCLI toward the end of the year, and while 3RAR remained, most of the veterans were rotated back to Australia and replaced by new men. It did not escape notice among the British soldiers concerned that while the Rifles, Fusiliers, Argylls, and Middlesex were sent by troopship to Hong Kong to complete their overseas tours, the Glosters – still very much in the public eye – went directly home to England.[52]

So too did Brigadier Tom Brodie, turning over command of 29th Brigade after almost a year in Korea to Brigadier A. H. G. Ricketts. This move was, it should be stressed, not because of any doubts in the War Office about his conduct of operations during the Imjin battle. Lack of confidence would lead to the premature withdrawal of Brigadier George Taylor from command of 28th Brigade in the aftermath of Operation Commando (he had replaced the competent Brian Burke, the latter posted after leading 27th Brigade in its final weeks to command 99th Gurkha Brigade on operational service in Malaya). On the other hand the career of Tom Brodie, an officer several months after the battle still "highly respected by staff and men," as an American observer noted, continued to prosper through the mid-1950s, culminating in promotion to major-general and service as GOC 1st Division, Middle East Land Forces, prior to retirement.[53]

With different commanders and different units rotating through every twelve months or so, 28th and 29th brigades continued to operate as part of the Commonwealth Division until after an armistice was signed and the fighting ended in the summer of 1953. The war fought by the successor battalions was a relatively static one. Though there occasionally would be significant efforts by both sides to retake tactically important ground in Korea, the front had essentially congealed into a series of opposing and increasingly well-fortified trench lines and bunkers located on hills stretching across the peninsula from just below the 38th Parallel on the west coast to well above it on the east coast. With notable exceptions, the final two years of the conflict were a matter of artillery duels and nighttime infantry patrols into no-man's-land. There were of course casualties, but these were spread out in time compared to the Imjin, a three-day battle which accounted for roughly a combined quarter of those officers and men of the British Army killed, missing, captured, and wounded in the course of the entire Korean War.[54] In comparison, less then ten percent of the Australian fatalities and under two percent of the Canadians killed in the conflict occurred at Kapyong.[55]

Meanwhile the version of the Battle of the Imjin River in which the "Glorious Glosters" had made a necessary and selfless sacrifice continued to be propagated for the rest of the war. Heroism, rather than accountability, would continue to be the dominant theme.

The Glosters received a hero's welcome when they arrived by troopship at Southampton on 20 December 1951, with relatives waiting to meet them on the quay, the Colonel of the regiment, Lieutenant-General Sir Edward Wetherall, coming aboard the *Empire Fowey* to greet the men, a civic reception and inspection put on the following day, and special arrangements made to make sure men were safely home on leave for Christmas. "The magnitude of the welcome was utterly bewildering," Lieutenant-Colonel Digby Grist recalled, adding that everyone was "stunned" by the enthusiasm of the dockside crowds.[56]

Messages of congratulation were conveyed from a variety of senior military and other figures, including Ridgway and the CIGS, Field-Marshal Sir William Slim. "I am extremely proud to have had the 1st Battalion, The Gloucestershire Regiment as a unit in the United Nations Command," Ridgway concluded his quite lengthy message, "and I personally commend it for its brilliant record." The missive from Slim was brief but to the point: "On behalf of all ranks of the British Army I welcome you home and congratulate you on the honours you have added to the glorious traditions of your famous regiment. The Army is justly proud of you. Well done." The king also sent a message welcoming the Glosters home.[57]

The first anniversary of the Battle of the Imjin was marked both at the front and at home. General Ridgway himself took the opportunity to thank the Glosters once more in a radio address:

> When our thoughts go back to the darkest and gravest days of this historic United Nations venture, to the enemy's spring offensive of 1951, the Gloster battle of last April stands forth in bold outline. It was an unforgettable action, executed in the best traditions of sheer doggedness and personal courage. The blackened hills and rocks of Gloster valley are silent these days, many miles behind our lines. They look very different from the green fields and hedges of the county to which this far away place in Korea is forever linked. Yet that lonely dark valley will be eternally illuminated by the memory of how the Glosters stood and fought there, against the human wave from the north. There is no need for me to recount the detailed story of that battle. It is well known in Gloucestershire, in England, indeed everywhere in the free world. The memory of it is more than just one additional battle honor added to the history of a famous regiment. The bravery of the Glosters has demonstrated, to a world plagued with conflicts and tension with which we live today, the power of collective security; a power recruited in farms, in villages, and an ancient cathedral city.[58]

The commander of the Commonwealth Division, Jim Cassels, attempted to be both briefer and more inclusive in his own message celebrating those who "played their part in breaking up one of the great offensives" of the war thus far. "I do not propose to single out any individual unit," he explained. "Each fought magnificently and in the best traditions of the British and Commonwealth forces." In England, though, the focus was still very much on the Glosters. Members of the regiment were given a special civic luncheon, presented with new colors, and sent marching past cheering crowds. Though still a prisoner of war, Colonel Carne was presented *in absentia* with the honorary freedom of the City of Gloucester.[59]

Meanwhile the military authorities were engaged in the production of an official booklet that they had sponsored on the British part in the war thus far. *Our Men in Korea,* written by Eric Linklater and published in the spring of 1952, dwelt at some length of the Battle of the Imjin. No fingers were pointed, of course, though the importance of what had been achieved was stressed: "Brigadier Brodie's stubborn fighters had spoiled the Chinese plan, and for three vital days had held the road to the south." Kapyong was also mentioned, but much more briefly.[60]

The second anniversary of the Imjin battle went mostly unremarked in the press, but when the war ended and prisoners were exchanged in the summer of 1953 much of the focus was on the returning Glosters, particularly Colonel Carne. Honored and feted on his return to the U.K. in October, he was at once awarded the VC for his valorous actions during the Imjin battle. "Lieutenant-Colonel Carne showed powers of leadership which can seldom have been surpassed in the history of our Army," the latter part of the VC citation read. "He inspired his officers and men to fight beyond the normal limits of human endurance, in spite of overwhelming odds and ever-increasing casualties, shortages of ammunition and water." The following month Carne was also presented with the U.S. Distinguished Service Cross, the highest military decoration that the U.S. government could award to a foreigner.[61]

The end of the fighting and the return of the last prisoners in 1953 did not mean that the Battle of the Imjin immediately became yesterday's news. In the mid-1950s a number of those who had fought and been captured there wrote and saw published to considerable acclaim their memoirs of rigorous captivity in Chinese hands, prefaced by accounts of their part in the battle.[62] The first postwar history of the Commonwealth forces in action also came out in Britain the year after the armistice was signed, predictably with twice the space devoted to the Imjin fighting as compared to events at Kapyong, though this was offset at least in part a couple of years later when the latter engagement took pride of place in a booklet issued by the Canadian Army.[63]

As the decades rolled by, to be sure, Korea would become for most people "the forgotten war," much to the chagrin of veterans.[64] Yet as noted at the start of this book, on those sporadic occasions when the Korean War generated newspaper articles and mass-market books, the

Battle of the Imjin and the "Glorious Glosters" continued to dominate the collective consciousness in Britain while the stand at Kapyong of the Patricias and 3RAR took center stage in Canada and Australia. An unparalleled feat of arms (that depending on the origin of the commentator concerned had either occurred at the Imjin or at Kapyong) had kept the South Korean capital out of enemy hands.[65]

In point of fact the defeat of the huge Chinese Fifth Phase offensive and the saving of Seoul was a collective U.N. effort that involved hard fighting by many units large and small, above all those of the United States, and which reached a crescendo in the days after the Imjin and Kapyong fights ended. The figure of 10,000–11,000 casualties inflicted on the enemy widely cited in reference to 29th Brigade – in marked contrast to more cautious reckonings of about 1,000 Chinese killed at Kapyong[66] – was in fact an allied estimate for the entire 3rd Division, of which the brigade was only a part.[67] It was an estimate, furthermore, based on a certain amount of guesswork by the authorities, as the Chinese often tended to carry away their dead precisely in order to make it difficult to judge their losses.[68] A more realistic approximation, which journalist Andrew Salmon arrived at a few years ago through correlating and making extrapolations from the body counts of the units involved, lowered the number of enemy casualties generated by 29th Brigade to between six and seven thousand.[69]

The patriotic portrayal of the Imjin as a particularly glorious and significant moment in the history of British arms, while something of a patriotic myth, had a significant impact on the future of the infantry units concerned, especially the Glosters. The battalion's place of honor in official and popular accounts of the action meant that the regiment's amalgamation as a result of successive rounds of army consolidation was deferred for more than half a century. The Royal Northumberland Fusiliers and Royal Ulster Rifles, unlike the 8th King's Royal Irish Hussars, escaped the first round of amalgamation in the latter 1950s, but were both merged with other regiments in 1968. The Gloucestershire Regiment, on the other hand, was only subsumed into a new infantry unit more than fifty years after the return of the 1st Battalion from Korea.[70]

Even if the Glosters garnered a disproportionate share of the limelight, all the British and Commonwealth units involved unquestionably fought hard on the Imjin and at Kapyong. However, the reality of what happened between 22 and 25 April 1951 is rather more complicated than the established legend suggests. Courage was on occasion matched by fear, mistakes were made, and above all an entire battalion was destroyed when it might have been saved. In the established narrative of events the loss of the Glosters has been portrayed as a more or less unavoidable and ultimately necessary sacrifice. Yet nobody at the time had actually intended to offer up the Glosters for destruction in the name of stopping the Chinese, and both British and American commanders were united after the battle in wanting to preclude such an outcome in the future. In order to avoid public embarrassment and inter-allied friction at the time, and later because the popular story constructed during the war had become the authorized and accepted version of events, those who spoke or wrote about the battle in public afterward tended to stress narrative over analysis, especially in relation to assigning responsibility for the fate of the Glosters. Moreover, in making the case for the necessity of what had occurred during the battle, both in relation to the Glosters and to the other units involved, some of those who sang the praises of 29th Brigade second- or thirdhand ended up presenting its stand as the decisive element in the defeat of the Chinese offensive. Now that we know about as much about what actually happened from the Western perspective as we are ever likely to, the Battle of the Imjin River, when shorn of accumulated exaggeration and mythmaking, appears as a "severe setback" for 29th Brigade, highlighting the extent to which 27th Brigade in the Battle of Kapyong, though its performance was far from flawless, emerged from what the War Office classified as separate but concurrent engagements comparatively unscathed.[71]

Having chronicled each fight in detail, it is time to compare and contrast the situations the two brigades found themselves in, and consequently speculate as to how events could have unfolded differently. After all, as Big Jim Stone himself reflected afterwards, there was nothing inevitable about the Patricias at Kapyong escaping the fate of the Glosters on the Imjin on 24/25 April 1951.[72]

It was a cock-up. The whole Imjin battle was a cock-up.

JOHN MOLE, former 1RUR officer, 2002[1]

Kapyong was not a great battle as battles go; yet it was a good battle, well-planned and well-fought.

JIM STONE, former 2PPCLI CO, 1988[2]

When Tom [Brodie] told Corps [*sic*] that his position was "a bit sticky" they simply did not grasp that in British Army parlance, that meant "critical."

Unidentified former 29 Bde HQ officer, c. 1986[3]

Conclusion

THE FIRST COMMENT, THE OPINION OF SOMEONE WHO LED A platoon during the Imjin fight, is an overstatement, though it serves as a useful corrective to those who have ignored the more uncomfortable aspects of the engagement fought by 29th Brigade along the Imjin. The second opinion, from the man who led the Patricias at Kapyong as part of 27th Brigade, while also something of an exaggeration in terms of what it implies about coherence of knowledge and decision making, accurately reflects the common view that while things had gone wrong for 29th Brigade they had gone right for 27th Brigade in their simultaneous responses to the opening of the Fifth Phase offensive.

As with virtually all battles the reality was in fact rather more complicated. The conduct of individual officers and men in both brigades between 22 and 25 April was by and large exemplary. Yet as we have seen, the generally high level of professionalism and indeed heroism on display was at times punctuated by instances of confusion, fear, and even – though very rarely – cowardice. In both engagements, moreover, from corps level on down to battalion headquarters, ignorance had produced some potentially or actually disastrous command decisions. On the Imjin various misunderstandings concerning what the Chinese were planning and above all were achieving in the first days of the offensive resulted in decisions that left several units dangerously isolated. Meanwhile lack of knowledge about the enemy, and also the state of allied forces, placed various elements of 27th Brigade in unnecessarily risky and sometimes untenable situations at Kapyong. There was, in short, a good deal of command confusion in both locations.

Nevertheless, casualties were proportionately much heavier in 29th Brigade than in 27th Brigade, and while more than one battalion in each engagement found itself surrounded at certain junctures, only the Glosters on the Imjin were effectively wiped out as a fighting force. Despite successful attempts to divert attention through concentration on an epic last-stand narrative, the fact remains that the number of soldiers killed, captured, and wounded from each brigade was greater by a factor of roughly ten on the Imjin compared to Kapyong.[4] What was it that made the losses in one battle so much worse than in the other?

Some of the explanations put forward both at the time and subsequently for the course of events in each engagement, it must be stressed, reveal themselves under scrutiny to be either partially erroneous or completely fallacious. In particular, drawing contrasts between the fighting spirits of various units yields little of substantive value beyond knowledge of prejudices.

The role of the much-despised ROKs is a case in point. It was understandable that Commonwealth troops should have looked askance at the behavior of Republic of Korea soldiers at Kapyong. After all, if the 6th ROK Division had not collapsed in the way that it did, 27th Brigade would not have been called out of reserve with practically no notice and forced to deploy so hastily as to leave little time for proper defensive preparations. On the other hand, it ought to be borne in mind that by their very presence in the front line the South Korean soldiers forced the CPV to overcome resistance, weak though it undoubtedly was, and travel on foot several miles before confronting the Commonwealth Brigade, their designated target, on un-reconnoitered ground. Thus, while on the Imjin the Chinese achieved surprise and had already identified the precise locations of 29th Brigade units, the withdrawal of 27th Brigade a few days before the Kapyong battle and subsequent redeployment as a stopgap force meant the enemy lost time, at least a few men, and a certain amount of energy pushing back the ROK regiments and then discovering exactly where and how the Commonwealth battalions had deployed farther south.[5]

Moreover, while the poor performance of the 6th ROK Division in front undoubtedly set in motion the involvement of Commonwealth troops at Kapyong, the widely held belief among U.N. soldiers that the retreat of the ROK division on the left flank of 29th Brigade had left the Glosters in the lurch during the Imjin battle was quite incorrect.[6] The 1st ROK Division occupying the positions to the west of 29th Brigade was by April 1951, in marked contrast to the 6th ROK Division north of 27th Brigade, a seasoned formation. Though pushed very hard by the Chinese, it retreated only slowly and in good order. The fact that the Chinese were able to move around the left flank of the brigade to the west of the Glosters had to do with the fact that there was an undefended gap of three and a half miles between the Glosters and the nearest ROK regiment, "so it wasn't very difficult to infiltrate," as the adjutant of the Glosters, Tony Farrar-Hockley, conceded.[7]

There is also no substance to the charge that Commonwealth troops fought more enthusiastically than British troops in the twin battles of Kapyong and the Imjin. As the fighting revealed, in both engagements there were men who were scared and a handful who were outright cowards. On the whole, however, both British and Commonwealth troops fought doggedly and to the best of their ability, and as the dispersal of various medals awarded for bravery illustrates, there were instances of unadulterated heroism in every battalion involved. Complaints that "it looked as if the Middlesex weren't very good soldiers" and that "there was no esprit at all" among them were unfounded given how hard D Company had fought at Kapyong, while British units on the Imjin clearly did not have "a morale problem."[8]

Both battles, of course, involved the defense of hill positions. But to some degree at least the frontage and ground that each brigade found itself defending favored one over the other. 29th Brigade was assigned a frontage more than twice that which 27th Brigade found itself defending, and that meant the battalions of the latter could be deployed in more concentrated fashion than those of the former. Along the Imjin the unoccupied Hill 675 cut the Glosters off from the rest of the brigade, while at Kapyong the height and steepness of the slopes of Hill 677 held by the Canadians put attackers at a distinct disadvantage.[9]

Some soldiers in each battle, faced with large numbers of charging Chinese, yearned for greater firepower than that afforded by standard-issue British personal and support weapons. Lieutenant John Pearson of 11 Platoon, 2PPCLI, for instance, wished that his men had "short-range rapid-fire weapons, such as the U.S. Carbine, the reliable Australian Owen Gun, or the Chinese Burp Gun, all of which would have been useful in nighttime close combat."[10] Yet while it is worth noting that both encounters spurred on the collective and individual search for greater firepower – the number of medium machine-guns allocated to each battalion in 28th Brigade, for instance, was officially raised in the summer of 1951 from six to nine, while the unofficial hunt for American personal weapons continued[11] – by and large arms and equipment were similar in each brigade. This means differences in weight of fire brought about by, for example, possession by the Australians of a more reliable submachine-gun than the one used by everyone else, likely had only a limited impact on the course of the battles. There were, however, a couple of significant differences that had a discernibly adverse or positive effect on the fighting on the Imjin and at Kapyong and are therefore worth mentioning.

Overall, the Shermans of 72nd Tank Company did better at Kapyong than did the Centurions of 8th RIH on the Imjin. The British tank was significantly larger and heavier, which caused maneuvering problems both during the attempt to rescue the Glosters and the withdrawal of the Ulsters and Northumberlands. Though lighter both in terms of armor and main gun, the Sherman mounted two medium machine-guns and one heavy machine-gun as against the single coaxial medium machine-gun on the Centurion. This explains why Company A was able to provide much-needed fire support to 3RAR during the Kapyong battle overnight as well as during the day, while C Squadron had to withdraw when darkness fell and thus could not offer anywhere near the same degree of supporting firepower to the British battalions on the Imjin. It also helps account for the fact that no Shermans were lost at Kapyong while a total of four Centurions were disabled on the last day of the Imjin battle.[12]

If at Kapyong the machine-gun fire of the Shermans ranks as an important factor in the survival of 3RAR, other vehicle-mounted U.S. weapons were equally significant in helping 2PPCLI repel the enemy the following night. Unlike the other infantry battalions in either engagement, the Canadians possessed American armored half-tracks on which were mounted the superior 81-mm mortar plus one medium and one heavy machine-gun. This provided a concentration of protected firepower that, as we have seen, made certain that Chinese attacks on the southeast flank of Hill 677 never stood a chance.[13]

Of equal significance to the Patricias was the weight of artillery fire that could be brought to bear. 45 Field Regiment, RA, exerted itself to the maximum during the Imjin battle, but was supporting several infantry units at once, which often meant the fire of only a single battery per battalion. Meanwhile, because the Chinese attacks were sequential against individual battalions rather than simultaneous against several, 16 Field Regiment, RNZA, once it had reorganized, could bring all of its batteries to bear in support of the Australian withdrawal and the Canadian defenses. Furthermore, and even more importantly, while no heavy artillery was available to 29th Brigade, batteries of 155-mm and 8-inch guns and howitzers were placed under the control of 27th Brigade by IX Corps on 24 April. Of the six infantry battalions heavily engaged in the Imjin and Kapyong battles, the Patricias suffered the fewest casualties. Extra firepower, and possibly better communications, undoubtedly played a part in this.[14]

None of these terrain and firepower advantages, though, would have ensured victory at Kapyong if the Commonwealth battalions had been less well deployed, had been poorly led, and if the Chinese had been in a position to press as hard as they were doing along the Imjin.

The 27th Brigade, as noted, had little time in which to prepare to repel the enemy. Moreover, as a result of ignorance concerning the state of the 6th ROK Division and enemy strength, some poor orders were issued through corps, brigade, and battalion headquarters which in turn placed in unnecessary peril elements of Commonwealth units such as B Company and the HQ of 3RAR. Nevertheless the decisions made at all levels were, on the whole, mostly sound. The defensive plan that Brigadier Brian Burke devised – to deploy three battalions forward to command the key features overlooking the northern entrance of the Kapyong valley, hills 794, 677, and 504, keeping a fourth in reserve – was sound, and though orders from Major General William M. Hoge to support the South Koreans meant that this deployment could not be properly carried out, the corps commander made up for this by providing American tank, artillery, and finally infantry support in a timely fashion and did not interfere when Burke decided to withdraw 3RAR from Hill 504 and the next day 2PPCLI from Hill 677. As a senior Australian military historian commented approvingly, at Kapyong "Burke was largely allowed to fight his own battle."[15]

Within the two forward infantry battalions, the veteran infantry leader Major Ben O'Dowd and the equally experienced Lieutenant-Colonel Jim Stone, respectively, made sure that the Australian and Canadian companies were well deployed to defend hills 504 and 677. Lieutenant-Colonel Bruce Ferguson, the officer technically in command of 3RAR, made several mistakes in the course of the battle, but wisely left it to the senior officer on the spot, O'Dowd, to organize the withdrawal of the 3RAR infantry companies rather than trying to micromanage without a clear idea of what was happening on the ground. The various veteran company commanders arrayed and directed their platoons competently, the one partial exception being made up for by the actions of an experienced junior officer.[16]

Those in command at Kapyong, in short, acted like professionals, trying hard to generate maximum difficulties for the enemy without engaging in needless sacrifice. Burke himself knew as a British officer that he would have a lot of explaining to do if either the first Canadian or Australian battalion in Korea was allowed to be cut off and destroyed.[17]

In retrospect, though, the likelihood of another Gloster-style disaster was not as great as it seemed. While both 3RAR and 2PPCLI found themselves more or less cut off at certain points, Brian Burke – in marked contrast to his counterpart Tom Brodie on the Imjin – retained significant reserves that were close enough to the forward battalions to be used as a rescue force if necessary. Brodie had to commit his reserve battalion, 1RUR, almost at once to shore up his defense line, but Burke never had to use the newly arrived 1KOSB or indeed fully commit 1MX in the latter stages of the fight.

This was due in part of course to a narrow frontage and the greater availability of American reinforcement units. But it also had to do with the Chinese. The attack over the Imjin was part of the main enemy thrust, and involved three CPV divisions. The move toward Kapyong, on the other hand, mostly involved a single enemy division. As noted, the soldiers of the latter, though victorious over the South Koreans, were not fresh when they reached the Commonwealth Brigade, and had already expended much of their mortar ammunition by the time the Patricias were attacked. The absence of further advance once the brigade had withdrawn indicated that the Chinese attack at Kapyong was a limited thrust. As the South Korean official history put it, though 27th Brigade had put on "an admirable performance in battle," it had faced what in effect was "an auxiliary attack of the enemy's April offensive."[18]

The situation facing those responsible for 29th Brigade along the Imjin was therefore more dangerous than for their 27th Brigade counterparts at Kapyong. Given enemy numbers and intentions, the fighting was always going to be both more intense and more prolonged on the Imjin than at Kapyong. Yet as a pioneering academic historian of the Commonwealth armies in the Korean War shrewdly observed a quarter century ago, the relative success of 27th Brigade at Kapyong as against 29th Brigade on the Imjin "revolved less around the size of the forces or intensity of the combat than around the command decisions when the forces met the enemy." In other words, there was nothing inevitable about the much higher casualties incurred, nor about the destruction of the Glosters; what was ordered and when, before and during the Imjin engagement, truly mattered.[19]

The question of whom to hold accountable tended, both at the time and subsequently, to divide along national lines. The Belgians blamed the British for leaving them exposed; the British blamed the Americans for preventing the Glosters from retreating while there was still time; and the Americans blamed the British for being both too optimistic and overly cautious concerning the Glosters.[20] All these assertions contain a certain amount of truth, and indeed they are not by any means mutually exclusive. What happened on the Imjin was to a great extent the result of inexperience, ignorance, and miscommunication at multiple levels of command. No one was entirely blameless, but there were mitigating circumstances in most instances.

It was perhaps inevitable that Lieutenant-Colonel J. P. Carne, as commanding officer of the infantry battalion which fared worst in the battle, should come under scrutiny. According to one angry ex-29th Brigade staff officer, the disaster was "the fault of a man who was still living in the 1914–18 era," reacting to, rather than anticipating events.[21] It was rightly pointed out by an American observer that he had positioned his companies on widely separated hills, unable to directly support one another.[22] Fred Carne was also notoriously taciturn, which American observers took to mean a reluctance to inform brigade of just how serious the Glosters' position was becoming. Furthermore, it seems possible that his disdain for the Chinese led him to underestimate what they could achieve, thereby limiting defensive preparations by the battalion and slowing his response to the scale and success of the assaults on his forward companies. Though it might only have delayed rather than averted the ultimate outcome, keeping up pressure for a Flying Boxcar air drop of supplies – of the kind which helped save 2PPCLI at Kapyong on Wednesday[23] but had to be aborted above the Glosters twice, once on Tuesday and again the following morning – would have allowed his battalion to fight on. "If we had had water and ammunition," one survivor has asserted, "we would still be up there now!"[24]

On the other hand Carne, like all the other battalion commanders, had been expecting probing attacks before any major assault and thus plenty of time to shift positions as necessary. Once the massive scale of the enemy attack became evident, "Fred," like the other lieutenant-colonels, did his best to consolidate, but was more isolated geographically and thus did not enjoy the benefits of support from adjoining units. As to the American assertion that Carne did not inform higher command of the precariousness of his situation, this was simply not true. Though keeping a stiff upper lip and not voicing his concerns in the flamboyant fashion common among U.S. Army officers, Carne nevertheless did not mislead Brodie – an officer of the same generation who shared the common British Army habit of understatement – about what was going on. Brodie knew perfectly well what was happening to the Glosters, which was why he was so distressed by 24/25 April.

As he manfully acknowledged, Tom Brodie bore his share of responsibility for what had happened during the battle. There was also probably some truth to the American suspicion that he was reluctant to withdraw his units until specifically ordered to do so even when 29th Brigade was coming under very heavy pressure. It may also have been the case that he did not press the efforts to rescue the Glosters on 24/25 April as hard or competently as the divisional commander ordered or expected. In the weeks prior to the Chinese attack, moreover, the brigadier had made a series of errors. He had allowed some of the brigade's heavy firepower, in the form of Centurion tanks and Bofors guns, to remain far in the rear. More importantly, he had not recognized how isolated the Glosters were on the west side of Kamak-san on his left flank, and how difficult it would be to either reinforce or withdraw them in the event the Chinese came in force. His reconnaissance sweeps prior to the battle had been poorly conceived, he had not pressed his battalion commanders to identify all the fording points over the Imjin or make serious defensive preparations behind it, had not canceled anyone's leave, and he had initially placed his weakest battalion in the most exposed position. On the last day of the battle, furthermore, still groggy from the effects of sleeping pills, Brodie had acquiesced in a withdrawal plan for the Ulsters and Northumberlands that ignored the lessons of the January engagement.

Tom Brodie, though, was by no means entirely to blame for what happened. It was his American superiors who thought that British units could handle the huge frontage they assigned to 29th Brigade, and he was led to believe that there would be an early withdrawal if the enemy came in strength. As for the 8th Hussars, it seems to have been higher authority, not the brigadier, that had issued the order to keep only one Centurion squadron north of the Han river, and it might be argued in any event that given the terrain restraints on big tank movement south of the Imjin the amount of added firepower and mobility the other squadrons would have brought to the battle might have been less than anticipated and offset by added congestion. It is worth noting in this context that though defensive firepower within infantry battalions was beefed up within the new Commonwealth Division in the wake of the Imjin battle, each of its three component brigades continued to be supported by only a single tank squadron. Like everyone else, moreover, Brodie expected any offensive to begin with limited probing attacks that companies positioned on hilltops could fend off. The brigadier certainly knew that the Chinese were planning an offensive, and was far less complacent about the future than many of the junior officers and men serving under him; hence his efforts, frustratingly ineffective as they were, to glean enemy intentions through a series of infantry-armor sweeps in the days prior to the attack. Once the battle started Brodie had tried hard not to expose the flanks of adjoining allied units, had wanted to withdraw earlier than he was allowed to by higher authority, had done his best to convey to division the seriousness of the Glosters' position – albeit using language liable to be misinterpreted by a superior versed in a very different military culture[25] – and arguably displayed a better grasp than his superiors of the near impossibility of rescuing the Glosters by 24/25 April.

The officer in charge of the 3rd Infantry Division, to which 29th Brigade was then attached, Major General Robert H. "Shorty" Soule, bore a fair amount of responsibility for the way in which the Battle of the Imjin developed, taking a more hands-on approach with Brodie than did Hoge with Burke.[26] The latter was allowed to withdraw first the Australians and then the Canadians before they could be overwhelmed. Soule, on the other hand, pushed Brodie hard to continue fighting as far forward as possible despite a request to pull back, and did not commit enough forces to stand a reasonable chance of rescuing the Glosters in the final phases of the battle. It should be kept in mind, though, that Soule did not have the background to understand the implications of British phrases such as "a bit sticky." Furthermore, he had to make sure that American units farther north on the right flank of 29th Brigade were not left exposed, helped successfully extricate the Belgians, possessed only limited reserves to meet multiple developing threats to the MSR (hence the whittling away of American forces committed to the reinforcement or rescue of the Glosters), and was himself under orders from higher authority not to withdraw precipitously.

The man in command of I Corps, of which 3rd Division was a part, Lieutenant General Frank W. Milburn, as well as his superior, Eighth Army commander Lieutenant General James A. Van Fleet, and the overall U.N. commander, Lieutenant General Matthew B. Ridgway, bore some command responsibility as well. Like most American commanders they tended to think of British Commonwealth units in terms of a shield, willing and able to stand their ground come what may while others withdrew, which perhaps made them less willing than they otherwise might have been to push Soule harder to prevent the destruction of the Glosters during their visit to his headquarters on 24 April. Van Fleet, indeed, was more rigid in his thinking than his predecessor concerning how best to contain the Chinese offensive – emphasizing that no withdrawals should take place without specific orders[27] – and in private made it clear to Ridgway after the battle that he thought that the Glosters had contributed more to victory by standing their ground to the point of destruction ("the finest flowering of courage in [the] whole war," as he later described their last stand privately to a U.S. combat historian[28]) than they would have if they had retreated.[29] In their collective defense, though, it should be borne in mind that as commanders at corps level and above, these three generals would not normally have been expected to meddle in the affairs of a single battalion four to six levels down the chain of command, and that they each had many other crises to handle at the time.

A thread that connected everyone involved in terms of responsibility for how the Battle of the Imjin unfolded concerns common misapprehensions relating to the enemy. It was widely known from Tokyo headquarters on down that the Chinese were planning an offensive. Yet as the former commander of the 1st ROK Division correctly asserted in his memoirs, the enemy advance across the Imjin had caught 29th Brigade "by surprise"[30] – a phrase never used in Anglo-American accounts. Brodie knew that at some point the Chinese were coming and sensed that his brigade would likely be attacked, but though the strategic information being provided to his HQ through Soule was sound, the tactical intelligence available to him in the lead-up to the battle was extremely limited and in certain respects simply wrong. The brigadier had done his best to discern the strength and intentions of the enemy forces in front of his brigade by mounting a series of deep-penetration infantry-armor sweeps into the void created by the earlier Chinese withdrawal. Nothing in the way of useful intelligence was achieved from these sweeps, however, which reinforced a dangerous sense of complacency already prevalent within the brigade.

From the army commander on down to the private soldier it was simply not appreciated how well camouflaged the enemy was, a skill allowing Chinese parties not only to keep themselves largely hidden from aerial and ground reconnaissance – evading the latter in front of 29th Brigade was made easier by the noise generated by large numbers of relaxed infantry walking along on hobnailed boots accompanied by tanks with roaring engines and squealing tracks – but also to infiltrate unseen at night and then map company positions. It was also not understood how far and how fast Chinese soldiers could move in darkness when advancing to contact en masse, nor, because enemy positions had already been ascertained, that the Chinese attackers could dispense with probing attacks. To be sure, some of what the enemy did during the Fifth Phase offensive on the Imjin ran counter to previous U.N. forces' experience and probably could not have been anticipated – notably attacking in force straight off the march and continuing to attack in daylight instead of going to ground to avoid air strikes. The fact remained, however, that Chinese numbers and capabilities were seriously underestimated, causing among other things 29th Brigade to be caught wrong-footed and, in light of orders from division, unable to respond quickly enough to save the Glosters. By the time reinforcement or rescue was attempted through the intervention of U.S. higher formation commanders, not enough forces either were or could be committed.

In short, there was no single decision or individual commander to hold responsible for what went wrong. In some respects those who fought at Kapyong were simply luckier than their counterparts on the Imjin, notably with regard to the fact that enemy aims were more limited and Chinese forces therefore not as strong. Kapyong was a success for the 27th British Commonwealth Brigade, insofar as the enemy was unable to exploit the unexpected collapse of the 6th ROK Division. With U.S. support its units had plugged the gap long enough to allow for an orderly corps withdrawal without leaving flanks exposed. For 29th British Independent Infantry Brigade Group the Imjin fight was at best a qualified success as a feat of arms, and at worst – especially with respect to the fate of the Glosters – a mitigated failure. Assumptions and choices were made weeks before the fighting began which would have a profound impact on the fighting, and once the battle was joined some of the decisions made by those in positions of authority made things worse rather than better.

The nature, outcome, and importance of the actions along the Imjin and above Kapyong came to be distorted by those seeking to burnish the military reputation of a particular country. Yet while neither battle may have been the Thermopylae of the Korean War that various advocates claimed,[31] all the British and Commonwealth units involved played a part in defeating the Fifth Phase offensive and ultimately forcing the enemy to settle for something other than total victory. Worst affected, of course, were the Glosters, but like the other British and Commonwealth battalions in action in the third week of April 1951, they had done their duty. "I always remember the way they took it," Tom Brodie explained with reference to reception of the order that the Glosters should hold on come what may, using words that could equally apply to the battalions of either brigade; "without a word, without a query, and just in the way that you would expect an infantry battalion of the line to take it."[32] His words can serve as a fitting epitaph for the few thousand ordinary men – English, Irish, Australian, Canadian, New Zealander, American, and South Korean (about whom we still know too little) alike – who suddenly found themselves caught up in two hard-fought engagements that would stand out long after Korea became the forgotten war.

Notes

PREFACE

1. Peter de la Billière, *Looking for Trouble* (London: HarperCollins, 1994), 67; see also, e.g., Andrew Salmon, *To the Last Round* (London: Aurum, 2009), xiii. The Imjin and the Last Stand of the Glosters were, as journalist Russell Spurr had once put it, "the story everybody knows" in Britain (*Daily Express,* 2 September 1953, p. 2).

2. "Out in the Cold: Australia's Involvement in the Korean War: Kapyong – 23–24 April 1951," www.awm.gov.au/exhibitions/korea/operations/kapyong/ (accessed 27 August 2009); see also, e.g., Brad Manera, "Kapyong Captured," *Wartime* 34 (2006): 33; George Odgers, *Remembering Korea* (Sydney: Lansdowne, 2000), 91.

3. Peter Worthington, *Looking for Trouble* (Toronto: Key Porter, 1984), 28.

4. The weight given to the Imjin or Kapyong is also reflected in the way in which they are highlighted on government or museum websites. On the Imjin see, e.g., www.nationalarchives.gov.uk/battles/korea/battle.htm (accessed 13 August 2007). On Kapyong see, e.g., www.forces.gc.ca/news-nouvelles-eng.asp?id=95 (accessed 10 July 2012); www.lermuseum.org/ler/mh/1945topresent/kapyong.html (accessed 25 September 2009); www.australiansatwar.gov.au/ko_akh.html (accessed 7 October 2009); cas.awm.gov.au/art/ART93183 (accessed 25 September 2009). On the prominence given to the Imjin battle in popular histories published in Britain see, e.g., Tim Carew, *Korea* (London: Cassell, 1967); Max Hastings, *The Korean War* (London: Michael Joseph, 1987); Bryan Perrett, *Last Stand!* (London: Arms and Armour, 1991); Andrew Marr, *A History of Modern Britain* (London: Macmillan, 2007), 102–103. Similar weight is given to Kapyong in many Australian and Canadian histories. See, e.g., Jack Gallaway, *The Last Call of the Bugle* (St. Lucia: University of Queensland Press, 1994); Victor Suthren, ed., *The Oxford Book of Canadian Military Anecdotes* (Toronto: Oxford University Press, 1989); David J. Bercuson, *Blood on the Hills* (Toronto: University of Toronto Press, 1990); see also Dan Bjarnason, *Triumph at Kapyong* (Toronto: Dundurn, 2011), 16.

5. 1RNF, for example, had an establishment of 38 officers and 945 other ranks at the time of the Korean War (see Anthony Perrins, ed., *'A Pretty Rough Do Altogether'* [Alnwick: Fusiliers Museum of Northumberland, 2004], xvii), but infantry battalions in Korea rarely exceeded 750 men in the field (see Salmon, *Last Round,* 24) and in April 1951, as we shall see, leave would mean even fewer soldiers were available to fight.

6. Salmon, *Last Round,* xiv; see also, e.g., the opening lines of the TV documentary *Forgotten Heroes,* produced by Alastair Lawrence (London: BBC, 2001).

7. E. D. Harding, *The Imjin Roll* (Gloucester: Southgate, 1981), 95; Special Army Order No. 65, June 1951, 1, WO 32/14247, TNA.

8. Ministry of National Defense, *The History of the United Nations Forces in the Korean War II* (Seoul: Ministry of National Defense, 1973), 623. On the British origins of this account see Michael Hickey, *The Korean War* (Woodstock, N.Y.: Overlook, 2000), 382. See also, regarding the accepted importance of the battle, e.g., Eric Linklater, *Our Men in Korea* (London: HMSO, 1952), 61; Noel Monks, *Eyewitness* (London: Muller, 1955), 320; C. N. Barclay, *The First Commonwealth Division in Korea* (Aldershot: Gale and Polden, 1954), 67; Basil Peacock, *The Royal Northumberland Fusiliers (The 5th Regiment of Foot)* (London: Leo Cooper, 1970), 105; Bryan Perrett, "The Chinese Counterattack," in *The Korean War,* ed. David Rees (London: Orbis, 1984), 83; *Forgotten Heroes,* BBC.

9. See, e.g., David Scott Daniell, *Cap of Honour* (London: Harrap, 1951), 329; Denis Warner, *Out of the Gun* (London: Hutchinson, 1956), 121; Carew, *Korea,* 88; Perrett, *Last Stand,* 213; Christopher Newbould and Christine Beresford, *The Glosters* (Stroud: Sutton, 1992), 126–27; Marr, *Modern Britain,* 103; *Forgotten Heroes,* BBC.

10. Pierre Berton, *Marching as to War* (Toronto: Doubleday, 2001), 558; Jeffrey Grey, *A Military History of Australia* (Melbourne: Cambridge University Press, 1999), 205. On the Kapyong presidential unit citations see WO 32/14250, TNA; Michael G. McKeown, *Kapyong Remembered* (Ottawa: M. G. McKeown, 1976), 41.

11. *Kapyong,* produced by John Lewis (North Fitzroy, Vic.: Arcimedia, 2011); Dan Bjarnason, CBC *The National* magazine, 27 July 1999, www.archives.cbc.ca/war_conflict/korean_war/clips/684 (accessed August 27, 2009); www.australiansatwar.gov/au/throughmyeyes/ko_akh.html (accessed 7 October 2009); see also, e.g., Gallaway, *Last Call,* 270; Bjarnason, *Triumph,* 16; John Melady, *Korea* (Toronto: Macmillan, 1983), 78; Berton, *Marching,* 501. On Australians conceding a role to 2PPCLI in the victory at Kapyong see, e.g., Ben O'Dowd, S02659, AWM. On Canadians conceding a contributory role to 3RAR see, e.g., www.army.forces.gov.ca/2PPCLI/RH-Kapyong.asp (accessed 25 September 2009).

12. Compare, e.g., Anthony Farrar-Hockley, *The British Part in the Korean War: Volume II* (London: HMSO, 1995), 111–50; Billy C. Mossman, *United States Army in the Korean War: Ebb and Flow, November 1950–July 1951* (Washington, D.C.: Center of Military History U.S. Army, 1990), 383–97; Robert O'Neill, *Australia in the Korean War, 1950–53: Volume II* (Canberra: AWM/AGPS, 1985), 131–60; Herbert Fairlie Wood, *Strange Battleground* (Ottawa: Queen's Printer, 1966), 72–79.

13. Peter Firkins, *The Australians in Nine Wars* (London: Hale, 1972), 419.

14. A. Hutley, 18205/4, IWMDS.

15. Peter Worthington, "The Not So 'Glorious Gloucesters,'" *Toronto Sun,* 7 May 2000, p. 4 (for an alternative explanation see Granatstein in Bjarnason, *Triumph,* 19); Robert Hepenstall, *Find the Dragon* (Edmonton: Four Winds, 1995), 103.

16. Jeffrey Grey, *The Commonwealth Armies and the Korean War* (Manchester: Manchester University Press, 1988), 82.

17. Ibid., 85.

18. See Salmon, *Last Round,* passim.

19. Bjarnason, *Triumph,* goes into considerable detail concerning the Canadian battle, but not that of the Australians or indeed any of the other participants.

PROLOGUE

1. René Cutforth, *Korean Reporter* (London: Allan Wingate, 1952), 107.

2. Ibid., 61.

3. See Farrar-Hockley, *The British Part, Vol. I,* chapter 1; O'Neill, *Australia in the Korean War, Vol. I,* chapters 2–6; Ian McGibbon, *New Zealand and the Korean War, Volume I* (Auckland: Oxford University Press, 1992), chapters 8–9, 11; Bercuson, *Blood on the Hills,* 26–34.

4. On the British Army between 1945 and 1950 see Anthony Farrar-Hockley, "The Post-War Army 1945–1963," in *The Oxford Illustrated History of the British Army,* ed. David Chandler and Ian Beckett (Oxford: Oxford University Press, 1994), 329–32.

5. See McGibbon, *New Zealand and the Korean War: Volume II* (1996), 9–60; Wood, *Strange Battleground,* chapters 2–3; O'Neill, *Australia, Vol. II,* chapter 1.

6. 29Bde History, p. 1, WO 308/42, TNA.

7. For an overview of 27Bde in Korea see B. A. Coad, "The Land Campaign in Korea," *The Journal of the Royal United Services Institution* 97 (1952): 1–11. An additional U.K. contribution came in the form of a special volunteer unit of Royal Marines which was raised in August 1950 and operated with the U.S. Navy and USMC in coastal operations along the eastern coast of North Korea starting in October 1950. See Fred Hayhurst, *Green Berets in Korea* (Cambridge: Vanguard, 2001); Peter Thomas, *41 Independent Commando Royal Marines: Korea – 1950 to 1952* (Portsmouth, U.K.: Royal Marines Historical Society, 1990).

8. McGibbon, *New Zealand, Vol. II,* 158; see also, e.g., Ben O'Dowd, *In Valiant Company* (St. Lucia: University of Queensland Press, 2000), 119.

9. See Andrew Salmon, *Scorched Earth, Black Snow* (London: Aurum, 2011), 45–46, 49–50; Salmon, *Last Round,* 26–31.

10. See J. M. Cowper, *The King's Own: Volume III, 1914–1950* (Aldershot, U.K.: Gale and Polden, 1957), 468.

11. Brodie commanded 14Bde in the second Chindit campaign.

12. On Carne see H. Moyse-Bartlett, *The King's African Rifles* (Aldershot: Gale and Polden, 1956), 621ff. On Foster see obituary, *St. George's Gazette* 69 (1951): 90. On Nicholson see Farrar-Hockley, *British Part, Vol. II,* 94 note. On Rickord see Salmon, *Last Round,* 103; and www.royalulsterrifles.com (accessed 10 July 2012).

13. See Salmon, *Last Round,* 32–33; Peter Ormrod, 09863/1, IWMDS (on Henry Huth).

14. McGibbon, *New Zealand, Vol. II,* 59.

15. See Hub Gray with Grania Litwin, *Beyond the Danger Close* (Calgary: Bunker to Bunker, 2003), 251; Shawn R. G. Brown, "The Loyal Edmonton Regiment at War, 1939–1945" (MA thesis, Wilfrid Laurier University, 1984), 143ff.

16. Ferguson, Ian Bruce (1917–1988), www.adb.anu.edu/biography/ferguson-ian-bruce-12484 (accessed 10 July 2012).

17. On Commonwealth company commanders being combat veterans see, with reference to 3RAR, Salmon, *Scorched Earth,* 152–53. An important exception, as it turned out, was Wally Mills of 2PPCLI, an acting company commander in April 1951, whose only combat experience had been on the day he was captured at Dieppe. See Gray, *Danger Close,* xvi.

18. Ibid., 76.

19. Douglas Johnson-Charlton, 15256/6, IWMDS; John Mole, 23221/3, IWMDS; Cutforth, *Korean Reporter,* 61; Ellery Anderson, *Banner Over Pusan* (London: Evans, 1960), 41. See also Carew, *Korea,* 138, 157; Norman "Taff" Davies, *Red Winds from the North* (Knebworth: Able, 1999), 77–78; Digby Grist, *Remembered With Advantage* (Gloucester: The Gloucestershire Regiment, 1976), 31; Edmund Ions, *A Call to Arms* (Newton Abbot: David and

Charles, 1972), 169; Lofty Large, *One Man's War in Korea* (London: Kimber, 1988), 42; Michael Newcombe, *Guns and the Morning Calm* (Newcastle: Minden, 1999), 10, 159; Ronnie Noble, *Shoot First!* (London: Harrap, 1955), 175; Richard Bryson and Blane Coulcher, *The West Yorkshire Gunners* (Tiverton: 45 Field Regiment, 1991), 20; Salmon, *Last Round,* 38.

20. Edward Beckerley, 10982/3, IWMDS; Preston-Bell in Salmon, *Last Round,* 33; Douglas Patchett, 16759/1, IWMDS; see also, e.g., Monks, *Eyewitness,* 322; Graham Thomas and Ronald Hutchinson, *Turn by the Window* (London: Cassell, 1959), 21. On the gentry manners of Phillips see Tisdall in Hastings, *Korean War,* 94.

21. Letter to Man, 4 April 1951, 2001-07-1187-46-19, NAM.

22. John Briton [pseud. for T. Ashley Cunningham-Booth], *Shapes of War* (Leamington Spa: Korvet, 1999), "One Man's Apostasy," n.d.

23. A. E. Younger, *Blowing Our Bridges* (Barnsley: Pen and Sword, 2004), 13.

24. Frank "Nick" Carter, 18262/1, IWMDS; see also, e.g., Sebastian Mercer, 1989-05-1-1, NAM; Albert Hawkins, 26353/1, IWMDS; Henry Ponsford, 18456/1, IWMDS. On the backgrounds and personalities of some of the leading figures in the fighting units of 29th Brigade see Salmon, *Last Round,* 26–36.

25. Gray, *Danger Close,* 3; Johnson in Hepenstall, *Find the Dragon,* 36. On Stone as a tough disciplinarian see also Melnechuck and Munro in ibid., 38, 53, 62.

26. John R. Bishop with G. W. Stephen Brodsky, *The King's Bishop* (Duncan, B.C.: Mossy Knoll, 2000), 79–80. On this incident see also Munro in Hepenstall, *Find the Dragon,* 262; James Riley Stone, SC407_SJR_198, UVic.

27. Len Opie ("hated his guts"), S02654, AWM; John Church ("hard man"), S02299, AWM; Don Beard ("drove mercilessly"), S02687, AWM. Ferguson took command of 3RAR in early November 1950. Salmon, *Scorched Earth,* 268.

28. Don Beard ("absolutely devoted"), S02687, AWM; Phil Bennett ("almost as if"), S02656, AWM; see also, though, David Butler, S02777, AWM; D. M. Butler et al., *The Fight Leaders* (Loftus, N.S.W.: Australian Military History Publications, 2002), 112, 154–55.

29. Len Opie, S02654, AWM; Gray, *Danger Close,* 3; see M. Servos and B. O'Dowd on Ferguson in *Kapyong,* produced by John Lewis (North Fitzroy, Vic.: Arcimedia, 2011). Another officer with a reputation among the other ranks for being tough but extremely professional was Anthony Farrar-Hockley, the 1GLOS adjutant. See Salmon, *Last Round,* 27; Henry Ponsford, 18456/1, IWMDS.

30. Tom Muggleton, S02652, AWM; see also Jack Gallaway, S02651, AWM; Phil Bennett, S02656, AWM.

31. On "Cinderella Brigade" see Reginald Thompson, *Cry Korea* (London: Macdonald, 1951), 229. On "Rolls Royce Brigade" see Kenneth Trevor, 09784/2, IWMDS.

32. 78 Coy RASC and 11 Infantry Workshop REME did their best to keep 27Bde's own vehicles on the road, but it was an uphill struggle and attrition took its toll. See: Report on Operations of 27BIB/BCB in Korea, 29 August 1950–31 March 1951, Appendix A, Transport, WO 308/45, TNA; John Dutton, *The Forgotten Punch in the Army's Fist* (Arborfield: kenandglen.com, 2004), 41; D. J. Sutton, ed., *The Story of the Royal Army Service Corps and Royal Corps of Transport, 1945–1982* (London: Leo Cooper, 1983), 216–17. During the period of advance and retreat in 1950–51, U.S. transport was essential.

33. Foulds in Hepenstall, *Find the Dragon,* 167.

34. On the M3 half-track, equipped with swivel-mounted .30 and .50 caliber

machine-guns, see Steven J. Zaloga and Peter Sarson, *M3 Infantry Half-Track, 1940–73* (Oxford: Osprey, 1995). On the usefulness of the fourteen M3s in 2PPCLI see Notes on Talk given by Lt.-Col. J. R. Stone, 5 June 1951, p. 3, File 681.011 (D3), DHH.

35. See Eric Linklater, *A Year in Space* (London: Macmillan, 1953), 61; Thompson, *Cry Korea*, 266; G. I. Malcolm, *The Argylls in Korea* (Edinburgh: Thomas Nelson, 1952), 66.

36. See David Wilson, *The Sum of Things* (Staplehurst: Spellmount, 2001), 165, 181–82; Pat Quinn, "A Rude Awakening," www.britains-smallwars.com/korea/pq.htm (accessed 7 May 2006).

37. See Julian Tunstall, *I Fought in Korea* (London: Lawrence and Wishart, 1953), 34; Tom Muggleton, S02652, AWM; Report on Operations of 27BCB, Appendix A, 9, WO 308/45, TNA.

38. See, e.g., D. F. Barrett, Korean War Diary, 29 November 1950, p. 63, 2000-08-55-4, NAM. Though some U.S. Army units and even headquarters did undoubtedly panic, it should be kept in mind that American policy called for breaking off with the enemy when retreating, rather than remaining in contact. Not knowing this, British and Commonwealth troops reacted with a mixture of puzzlement and contempt. See, e.g., CO 8RIH to DRAC, n.d. [c. 31 December 1950], sheet 2, WO 281/1142, TNA; Ben O'Dowd, S02659, AWM; Hugh Hamill, *The Royal Ulster Rifles in Korea* (Belfast: Mullan, 1953), 19, 22; Hawkins in Tom Hickman, *The Call-Up* (London: Headline, 2004), 98; D. E. Whatmore, *One Road to Imjin* (Cheltenham: Dew Line, 1997), 48. The ROK Army, which at this stage in the war mostly had little in the way of training and was poorly led (see Il-Song Park, "The Dragon From the Stream: The ROK Army in transition and the Korean War, 1950–1953" [PhD diss., Ohio State University, 2002], chapter 3), also developed a "bug out" reputation. See, e.g., Thomas Cunningham-Booth, 19913/2, IWMDS; Ben O'Dowd, S02659, AWM; Monks, *Eyewitness*, 318.

39. There were, for example, shortages of four-wheel-drive vehicles (see Cutforth, *Korean Reporter*, 15) and problems with the World War II–vintage "rebuilds" provided to 29Bde (see 29Bde History, p. 1, WO 308/42, TNA; Dutton, *Forgotten Punch*, 14).

40. See David Smurthwaite, *Project Korea* (London: NAM, 1988), 11, 18–19; H. B. Eaton, *Something Extra* (Durham: Pentland, 1993), 23. On the Centurion III see Simon Dunstan, *Centurion Universal Tank* (Oxford: Osprey, 2003), 11–20.

41. Lt. J. C. Butler, encl. 189A, WO 231/89, TNA; Olivia Fitzroy, *Men of Valour* (Liverpool: Tinling, 1961), 275. On the revolver as the official personal weapon of Centurion crews – only the driver possessing a submachine-gun – see, e.g., Kenneth Black, 18022/2, IWMDS. On the big and heavy Centurion not really being suited for Korean terrain see also, e.g., IWMDS; Doug Bone, 30635/6, IWMDS; Richard Napier, *From Horses to Chieftains* (Bognor Regis: Woodfield, 2002), 264; Eighth Army Command Report for January 1951, Book VII – Armor Section report, narrative dated 14 February 1951, p. 1, Box 1149, RG 407, NARA; Cutforth, *Korean Reporter*, 91. On Centurion crews learning to adapt see, e.g., William Bye, 20375/1, IWMDS.

42. Notes on lecture given by Brig T. Brodie, 9 Nov. 1951, p. 1, 681.011, DHH; see also, e.g., Lt. R. W. W. Smith, encl. 98A, Maj. C. J. Nixon, encl. 61A, WO 231/89, TNA; Jim Jacobs, "Korea Remembered," 67, IWMDD. Bren carriers also turned out to be too small to carry the support equipment for 8RIH and had to be replaced by the more spacious and mechanically reliable M3 half-track. See Doug Bone, 30635/7, IWMDS. On the carrier's history

see David Fletcher and Tony Bryan, *Universal Carrier 1936–48* (Oxford: Osprey, 2005).

43. Notes on lecture given by Brig. T. Brodie, 9 Nov. 1951, p. 1, 681.011 (D3), DHH.

44. On the vulnerability of British tracked vehicles lacking swing-mount machine-guns to close-in assault see, e.g., Frank Brodie, 19047/4, IWMDS; Mervyn McCord, 21563/4–5, IWMDS. On the Ulsters ditching their anti-tank guns and using their Oxfords to transport a special battle patrol see, e.g., Hamill, *Ulster Rifles,* 16; Henry O'Kane, *O'Kane's Korea* (Kenilworth: Henry O'Kane, 1988), 28. The Glosters also used Oxfords for patrolling. See Grist, *Remembered,* 18. On some members of the 1RUR battle patrol acquiring Browning machine-guns to mount on their Oxford carriers see Mervyn McCord, 20292/2, IWMDS. There is no mention of such machine-guns on Oxfords in the account of another member of the 1RUR battle patrol (see P. J. Kavanagh, *The Perfect Stranger* [Saint Paul, Minn.: Graywolf, 1988], 96ff.). On 1RNF Oxfords being equipped with Bren or Vickers guns see John Martin, *K Force* (Leamington Spa: Korvet, 1999), 39.

45. On the relative lightness of the 25-pounder shell, which became obvious during the Second World War, see David French, *Raising Churchill's Army* (Oxford: Oxford University Press, 2000), 90. For details on the gun itself see Chris Henry and Mike Fuller, *The 25-pounder Field Gun* (Oxford: Osprey, 2002).

46. Such heavy U.S. supporting fire would be available at Kapyong (see Bercuson, *Blood on the Hills,* 105–106) but not at the Imjin (see Barry Taylor, "Open Road Barred," *Military History* 7 [1991]: 50).

47. Tom Muggleton, S02652, AWM. On a 17-pounder being used to kill a sniper on the Imjin, see Salmon, *Last Round,* 179.

48. On the splitting of 11LAA see Farrar-Hockley, *British Part, Vol. II,* 118, footnote; see also, e.g., Letter of 11 April 1951, J. J. Potter Papers, IWMDD. On the Bofors being used in support of ground forces see, e.g., Hamill, *Ulster Rifles,* 48.

49. On 29Bde and bazookas see, e.g., Gordon Potts, 23213/7, 9, IWMDS; George Connolly, 18271/1, IWMDS; Frank Cottam, 21729/4, IWMDS; David Kaye, 17468/1, IWMDS; M. G. Harvey, *The War in Korea* (Eggleston: Raby, 2002), 17.

50. Younger in Adrian Walker, *A Barren Place* (London: Leo Cooper, 1994), 39; see, e.g., George Lang, S03786, AWM. On use of the 2-inch mortar for flares see, e.g., Brent Byron Watson, "From Calgary to Kap'yong" (MA thesis, University of Victoria, 1993), 57–59.

51. App. A to HQS 3201-151/25 (Trg 5), Gen. Trg. 25CIB, Vol. 1, British Information from Korea, p. 5, 111.41 (D22), DHH; see Farrar-Hockley, "Post-War Army," 338, 342; Bercuson, *Blood on the Hills,* 70. On six 3-inch mortars per battalion being insufficient see Keith Taylor, 1989-05-277-1, NAM.

52. Brent Byron Watson, *Far Eastern Tour* (Montreal: McGill-Queen's University Press, 2002), 44.

53. Jim Jacobs, "Korea Remembered," 34, IWMDD; see notes on lecture given by Brig. T. Brodie, 9 Nov. 1951, p. 1, 681.011(D3), DHH.

54. On the 36 Grenade see Watson, *Far Eastern Tour,* 42–43. It was appreciated (see Farrar-Hockley, "Post-War Army," 338), though not all batches manufactured in the Second World War had been properly maintained (see Melnechuck in Hepenstall, *Find the Dragon,* 52).

55. On the Vickers see, e.g., Dennis Matthews, 12729/2, IWMDS; Byron Murphy, 15338/1, IWMDS. On the need for more of them see Keith Taylor, 1989-05-277-1, NAM.

56. Gerald Gowing, www.veterans.gc.ca (accessed 10 July 2010); John Kelanchey, 19386/2, IWMDS; see also, e.g., David Green, *Captured at the Imjin River* (Barnsley: Leo Cooper, 2003), 26; Large, *One Man's War,* 46; Graham Dixon, Stuart Reitsma, www.veterans.gc.ca (accessed 10 July 2012). On the relatively slow Bren rate of fire see French, *Churchill's Army,* 87.

57. Walter Adams in Walker, *Barren Place,* 22; William Westwood, 19871/1, IWMDS; Roy Utting, 17568/2, IWMDS; Green, *Captured,* 70; see also Graham Dixon, www.veterans.gc.ca (accessed 31 July 2009); Hepenstall, *Find the Dragon,* 166. On the Sten jamming in action see, e.g., Whatmore, *One Road,* 72; see also Watson, *Far Eastern Tour,* 41; Dutton, *Forgotten Punch,* 162; Mike Czuboka in Bjarnason, *Triumph,* 59. The Sten was also disliked because, as the weapon of the platoon commander, it drew its bearer to the attention of enemy snipers. See Bishop, *King's Bishop,* 39. Those who defended the Sten did so in terms of its having a better rate of fire than semi-automatic or bolt-action rifles and revolvers (see Martin, *K Force,* 164; Ronald Norley, 15539/2, IWMDS; George Richards, 09859/1, IWMDS) and as good a range and reliability record as any comparable weapon in Korea (see Watson, "Calgary to Kap'yong," 65–66).

58. The burp gun – the Russian PPSh 41 or the Chinese copy, the Type 60 – got its name from the sound it made when fired, the result of its high rate of fire.

59. Campbell in Hepenstall, *Find the Dragon,* 51; see also Bjarnason, *Triumph,* 56. On Sten and Owen gun rounds not penetrating Chinese quilted jackets see, respectively, John Kelanchey, 19386/2, IWMDS, and Snow Dicker, "My Korean Adventure," *Wartime* 9 (2000): 28.

60. The British and Canadians were equipped with the Mark IV and short pig-sticker bayonet, the Australians the Mark III and 18-inch "sword" bayonet. On the bayonets see Salmon, *Scorched Earth,* 211.

61. Sebastian Mercer, 1989-05-1-1, NAM. On the reliability of the Lee-Enfield in the field in Korea see, e.g., John Kelanchy, 19386/1, IWMDS; notes on talk given by Lt.-Col. J. R. Stone, 5 June 1951, p. 7, 681.011(D3), DHH; see also Watson, "Calgary to Kap'yong," 62–64.

62. Large, *One Man's War,* 46; see also, e.g., Frank Carter, 18262/4, IWMDS; Richardson and Guthrie in Hepenstall, *Find the Dragon,* 166, 257. Though see also David Holdsworth, 15428/3, IWMDS; Salmon, *Last Round,* 194, 181, first footnote, which suggest that follow-up waves of attackers could be less well armed than Large remembered.

63. Frank Carter, 18262/4, IWMDS; see also, e.g., Pte. T. Pink, L/Cpl J. W. Riches, Pte. J. Neath, AI9/K/BRIT/392–394, A2151, KB1073/11G Part 6, NAA; Maj. C. J. Nixon, encl. 61A, WO 231/89, TNA; Adams in Walker, *Barren Place,* 22; Green, *Captured,* 105; Salmon, *Last Round,* 181; Hibbs in Bjarnason, *Triumph,* 60.

64. Sebastian Mercer, 1989-05-1-1, NAM; see also, e.g., Cote in Vincent R. Courtenay, *Patricias in Korea* (Windsor, Ont.: North American Heritage, 1999), 206. American infantrymen had the M1 Garand and M1 Carbine, both gas-operated semi-automatic weapons.

65. Green, *Captured,* p. 70; Ions, *Call to Arms,* 177; Notes on talk given by Lt.-Col. J. R. Stone, 5 June 1951, p. 7, 681.011(D3), DHH; see also, e.g., Maj. W. A. Wood, encl. 142A, WO 231/89, TNA. On the risk of M1s jamming if not kept scrupulously clean see Watson, *Far Eastern Tour,* 39–40.

66. Phil Bennett, S02656, AWM; see Watson, "Calgary to Kap'yong," 67, n. 52.

67. Ibid., 67.

68. Eric Hill, 12673/3, IWMDS.

69. Large, *One Man's War,* 45. On discarding helmets see, e.g., Tom Muggleton,

S02652, AWM; John Kelanchey, 19386/2, IWMDS; Knowles in Maurice Pears and Fred Kirkland, comps., *Korea Remembered* (Georges Heights, N.S.W.: Doctrine Wing, Combined Arms Training and Development Centre, 1998), 23; Kingsford in Walker, *Barren Place,* 4.

70. W. Oldale in Arthur W. Wilson, ed., *Korean Vignettes* (Portland, Oreg.: Artwork, 1996), 321; Younger, *Blowing Bridges,* 168; Temple in Salmon, *Last Round,* 100; see also, e.g., William Gibson, 16850/1, IWMDS; Czuboka in Bjarnason, *Triumph,* 57. On wearing a helmet being seen as a sign of extreme fear see Phil Bennett, S02656, AWM. On using helmets to hold water see John Hawkins in James Durney, *The Far Side of the World* (Naas: Leinster Leader, 2005), 110. On discarding helmets because of lack of enemy artillery see, e.g., Gray, *Danger Close,* 85. On discarding because of weight see, e.g., John Kelanchey, 19386/2, IWMDS. On carrying helmets but not wearing them, even in battle, see, e.g., John Mole, 23221/2, IWMDS.

71. Bob Walding in Walker, *Barren Place,* 95. On the study indicating that helmets would not have helped see Watson, "Calgary to Kap'yong," 70.

72. Maj. C. E. B. Walwyn, encl. 29A, WO 231/89, TNA; see also, e.g., Capt. H. J. Bergin, encl. 67A, WO 231/89, TNA; Peter Maxwell, *Home and Abroad* (Cronulla: P. Maxwell, 2005), 35. On the battery problem see, e.g., Arthur Hutley, 18205/4, IWMDS; Report on the Operations of 27BCB, 29 Aug. 1950–31 Mar 1951, App. A, p. 16, WO 291/188, TNA. On problems with the radios see also Col. Man, "Signal Lessons from Korea," chapter 10, p. 19, para 122, 2001-07-47-29, NAM. On 2PPCLI being forced to adopt the walkie-talkie because of battery problems see Gray, *Danger Close,* 109.

73. Bishop, *King's Bishop,* 63; Eric Hill, 12673/3, IWMDS; Survey of the communications of 27BCB, 8 Jan. 1951, p. 4, WO 291/1886, TNA; see, e.g., Lt. H. Atkinson, encl. 154A, WO 231/89, TNA; Temple in Salmon, *Last Round,* 205. On the 88 and 31 Sets see Louis Meulstee, *Wireless for the Warrior* (Broadstone: G. C. Arnold, 1995).

74. Gordon Potts, 23213/7, IWMDS; Large, *One Man's War,* 47. See also, e.g., Lt. J. Nicholson, encl. 206A, WO 231/89, TNA; Anthony Perrins, 19387/2, IWMDS, contradicting the official opinion that RNF sets worked perfectly (see CO report on the "Happy Valley" battle in Perrins, *'Pretty Rough,'* 55).

75. Notes on talk given by Lt.-Col. J. R. Stone, 5 June 1951, p. 6, 681.011(D3), DHH. There were, however, still some problems with radio communication within 2PPCLI at Kapyong (see Gray, *Danger Close,* 108–109) and the CO himself admitted that overall radio communication "was never good in Korea" (James Stone in *Duty First* 1 [1992]: 37). On the superiority of the SCR 300 see Bercuson, *Blood on the Hills,* 71. Even if sets operated as advertised there might be a tendency to underestimate the enemy and forsake R/T security procedure in order to communicate more easily. There are indications that the Chinese were indeed listening in to brigade-net traffic and thereby easily learning things that should have remained on the U.N. side of the lines. See, e.g., Jack Gallaway, S02651, AWM; Dan Raschen, *Send Port and Pyjamas!* (London: Buckland, 1987), 179. On the Chinese intercepting messages to good effect see Sung Chin-Yu in *Korea: The Unknown War,* produced by Michael Dorner (London/Boston: Thames Television / WGBH, 1988).

76. See, e.g., Hepenstall, *Find the Dragon,* 103.

77. Wilson, *Sum of Things,* 167; R. W. Thompson, *An Echo of Trumpets* (London: Allen and Unwin, 1964), 220; A. M. Man, The National Service Soldier in Korea, n.d., p. 1, 2001-1187-46-11, NAM.

78. On some 1MX national servicemen

not being psychologically prepared to fight for Korea see Tunstall, *I Fought*, 9–10; Hastings, *Korean War*, 103. On well-settled U.K. reservists or regulars not being particularly happy to be sent as replacements to 1MX in Korea see, e.g., John Shipster, *Mist on the Rice Fields* (Barnsley: Leo Cooper, 2000), 157; Bert Bartlett, http://www.thekoreanwar.co.uk/html/bert_bartlett.html (accessed 7 May 2006).

79. P. K. Kemp, *The Middlesex Regiment (Duke of Cambridge's Own), 1919–1952* (Aldershot: Gale and Polden, 1956), 349; R. C. B. Anderson, *History of the Argyll and Sutherland Highlanders* (Edinburgh: Constable, 1956), 187–88; Shipster, *Mist*, 129; Andrew Wilkie Brown, *A Memoir* (Aberdeen, U.K.: A. W. Brown, 2001), 124.

80. See Man to Hastings, 24 Nov. 1987, A. N. Man Papers, IWMDD; A. N. Man, The National Service Soldier in Korea, n/d, p. 1, 2001-1187-46-11, NAM.

81. Alan Whicker, *Within Whicker's World* (London: Elm Tree, 1982), 62; see also, e.g., Thompson, *Echo of Trumpets*, 215–16; Brown, *Memoir*, 120.

82. Tom Muggleton, S02652, AWM; see also, e.g., Jack Gallaway, S02651, AWM; R. Saunders in Harry Gordon, *The Embarrassing Australian* (Melbourne: Lansdowne, 1962), 150. It was true that 1MX was later blamed by a U.S. combat historian for supposedly not doing its part to rescue the U.S. 2nd Division from the debacle at Kunu-ri Pass in November 1950 (Roy E. Appleman, *Disaster in Korea* [College Station: Texas A&M University Press, 1989], 246), and that there were some in 3RAR who became prejudiced against 1MX national service types because of the unit's failure to take a particular feature that the Australians subsequently had to take in their stead in the second week of April 1951 (Ben O'Dowd, S02659, AWM; Phil Bennett, S02656, AWM). There is, however, no real evidence for the former charge (see, e.g., Salmon, *Scorched Earth*, 299, note) while in the later case the Australians took an indirect approach, moving so fast that the Chinese panicked and fled rather than slogging it out as they had with 1MX and thereby leaving the Diggers with the impression that resistance to the 1MX attacks, which among other things had suffered from some bad luck (see Farrar-Hockley, *British Part, Vol. II*, 94), had been lighter than in fact was the case (Patrick Knowles, 19388/1, IWMDS; Gallaway, *Last Call*, 236–37; O'Dowd, *Valiant Company*, 147–48).

83. Hepenstall, *Find the Dragon*, 103.

84. John Shaw, 20299/1, IWMDS; see also, e.g., Hastings, *Korean War*, 92; Salmon, *Last Round*, 39; Mervyn McCord in *Forgotten Heroes*, produced by Alastair Lawrence (London: BBC, 2001).

85. See, e.g., William Clark, 18459/1, IWMDS; Dennis Matthews, 12729/1, IWMDS; Ronald Wells's narrative, p. 4, IWMDD. True volunteers from other units – or indeed from among national servicemen already in the brigade who only had to go if they signed on as regulars – put their names down for reasons that ranged from a desire to see action (e.g., Kavanagh, *Perfect Stranger*, 78) and exotic lands (e.g., Hawkins in Hickman, *Call-Up*, 75–76), especially among young officers, to a wish to escape personal problems in their home units (e.g., William Bye, 20375/1, IWMDS).

86. Perrins, *'Pretty Rough,'* 7; 29Bde History, p. 1, WO308/42, TNA. The percentage of reservists varied between units. See, e.g., D. B. A. Grist, "The Korean Campaign as a Soldier Sees It," *The Back Badge* 14, no. 12 (1952): 43; John Smith, 18525/1, IWMDS; Perrins, *'Pretty Rough,'* 6; *Daily Telegraph*, 30 April 1951, p. 4.

87. The standard commitment was seven years with the colors and five in the reserves. 'A' men were those who had served mostly recently, 'B' those who had served earlier, and 'Z' those who had

served through the Second World War. 'C' men were those national servicemen over nineteen years of age who volunteered for Korea. 'K' stood for those who volunteered to rejoin the army or transfer from other units for the Korean War. Farrar-Hockley, *British Part, Vol. I,* 116.

88. See, e.g., Edmund Bruford-Davies, 22347/3, IWMDS; Andrew Scott, 16855/1, IWMDS; Kavanagh, *Perfect Stranger,* 79; John Mason, *Diplomatic Dispatches* (Canberra: National Library of Australia, 1998), 60; Thomas Cushing, *Soldier for Hire* (London: Calder, 1962), 275–76; Bryson and Coulcher, *Yorkshire Gunners,* 21; Hastings, *Korean War,* 93; Salmon, *Last Round,* 29.

89. James "Sam" Forward, 16078/1, IWMDS; see also, e.g., Gray in Walker, *Barren Place,* 72; Walter Cleveland, 17348/3, IWMDS; Eric Ellis, 23351/1, IWMDS; Alfred Gilder, 20057/1, IWMDS; David Holdsworth, 15428/1, IWMDS; Thomas McMahon, 18819/3, IWMDS; Lawrence Moreton, 19051/2, IWMDS; Cyril Papworth, 16618/1, IWMDS; Kenneth Trevor, 09784/1, IWMDS; F. Moxam, para. 13, AI9/K/BRIT/290, KB1073/11G Part 5, A2151, NAA; Denis Whybro in *Forgotten Heroes,* BBC.

90. Younger, *Blowing Bridges,* 126. For an example of someone being let off on compassionate grounds see John Smith, 18525/1, IWMDS. Among those released on medical grounds were men found to have artificial limbs. See Sebastian Mercer, 1989-05-1-1, NAM; Frank Carter memoir, p. 5, IWMDD; Younger, *Blowing Bridges,* 124–25.

91. Former POWs, for instance, might be judged fit for Korea: see, e.g., Green, *Captured,* 19; Sebastian Mercer, 1989-05-1-1, NAM. Serious bullet or shrapnel wounds dating from World War II were also not counted as a reason to demobilize reservists called up for 29th Brigade as long as they had healed sufficiently. See Len Swatton (Glosters) in *Soldier,* 26 March 1997, p. 18.

92. Kenneth Trevor, 09784/1, IWMDS; see also, e.g., "Notes from the 1st Batt. The Royal Ulster Rifles (83rd and 86th)," *North Irish Brigade Chronicle* 1, no. 4 (1952): 21 [also available in TS form as WO 308/46, f. 2, TNA].

93. Frank Carter memoir, p. 5, IWMDD; see also, e.g., Jack Arnall, 09972/1, IWMDS; Edward Beckerley, 10982/2, IWMDS; Sebastian Mercer, 1989-05-1-1, NAM; Thomas Cunningham-Booth, 19913/2, IWMDS; Davies, *Red Winds,* 17–18. The word "Bolshie" to describe the mood was used both by a recalled reservist in 8RIH (Denis Whybro, 20008/10, IWMDS) and a young subaltern in 1RNF (M. N. S. McCord, 1991-05-1-1, NAM).

94. John Mole, 23221/1, IWMDS; see also, e.g., Samuel Phillips, 17688/1, IWMDS, regarding the same problem in the Fusiliers. On indiscipline bordering on mutiny see, e.g., Hastings, *Korean War,* 93; William Tyler, *L/Cpl Bill Tyler's Letters from Korea* (London: Labour Publishing Society, 1951), 4; Thomas Cunningham-Booth, 19913/2, IWMDS; Frank Carter memoir, p. 5, IWMDD.

95. Frank Cottam, 21729/3, IWMDS.

96. Wear in Salmon, *Last Round,* 29.

97. Cutforth, *Korean Reporter,* 176. On the term "Old Man's Brigade" see ibid.; on "Grandfathers' Brigade" see James Forward, 16078/1, IWMDS.

98. See, e.g., O'Kane, *O'Kane's Korea,* 28, 52–3; Hickey, *Korean War,* 145; Peter Ormrod, 09863/1, IWMDS.

99. Frank Brodie, 19047/3, IWMDS; Jack Arnall, 09972/1, IWMDS; see also, e.g., Albert Hawkins, 26253/1, IWMDS; Green, *Captured,* 17.

100. Walter Cleveland, 17348/1, IWMDS; see also, e.g., Whatmore, *One Road,* 35; Jack Arnall, 09972/1, IWMDS.

101. See, e.g., Edward Beckerley, 10982/2, IWMDS; Green, *Captured,* 33,

34; *James Cameron in Korea*, T 3891 R3 C1, BLSA.

102. Mansergh to Harding, 2 February 1951, Report by Lt. Gen. Sir R. Mansergh on his visit to Korea, February–March 1951, p. 1, WO 216/836, TNA. On occasion, to be sure, fleeting cross-cultural contact could be made; see Green, *Captured*, 32–33. On horror at and sympathy among recalled reservists for Korean refugees on the move in winter see, e.g., John Dyer, 18474/1, IWMDS; Thomas McMahon, 18819/4, IWMDS.

103. David Holdsworth, 15428/1, IWMDS.

104. See David Kaye, 17468/1, IWMDS; see also Peter Ormrod, 09863/1, IWMDS; Gordon Potts, 23213/7, IWMDS.

105. Courts-Martial, Korea, 1950–1953, WO 93/59, TNA. At least one recalled older reservist was an incorrigible, though admiringly tolerated, troublemaker. See Cushing, *Soldier for Hire*, 275ff.; O'Kane, *O'Kane's Korea*, 50.

106. Cutforth, *Korean Reporter*, 53; see also, e.g., Fred From, S02649, AWM; Sebastian Mercer, 1989-05-1-1, NAM; Gordon, *Embarrassing Australian*, 146; Bishop, *King's Bishop*, 20; Worthington, *Looking for Trouble*, 40. For (rare) instances of anticommunist motivation see Linklater, *Year in Space*, 63–65; O'Dowd, *Valiant Company*, 31; McGibbon, *New Zealand, Vol. II*, 42; Patrick Weller, 12664/1, IWMDS; Ted Barris, *Deadlock in Korea* (Toronto: Macmillan 1999), 20.

107. On lack of knowledge of Korea see, e.g., Coad, "Land Campaign," 1; McGibbon, *New Zealand, Vol. II*, 42; Davies, *Red Winds*, 10; Green, *Captured*, 17; Edgar Green, 2, http://www.thekoreanwar.co.uk/html/interview.html (accessed 7 May 2006); Grist, *Remembered*, 7; Jack Arnall, 09972/1, IWMDS; Robin Bruford-Davies, 1989-05-163-1, NAM; William Bye, 20375/1, IWMDS; John Grosvenor, 16337/1, IWMDS; Sebastian Mercer, 1989-05-1-1, NAM; John Mole, 23221/1, IWMDS; John Shaw, 20299/1, IWMDS.

108. Pierre Berton, *My Times* (Toronto: Doubleday, 1995), 71; see Stone in Bjarnason, *Triumph*, 41. On somewhat ineffective efforts to explain to the troops why they were going to fight in Korea – often conducted by officers who knew little themselves – see, e.g., Jack Arnall, 09972/1, IWMDS; Robin Bruford-Davies, 1989-05-163-1, NAM; Edward Beckerley, 10982/3, IWMDS; John Grosvenor, 16337/1, IWMDS; Guy Temple, 15557/1, IWMDS; Newcombe, *Guns and the Morning Calm*, 1–2; Tunstall, *I Fought*, 18; Tyler, *Letters from Korea*, 9.

109. Len Opie, S02654, AWM; Alfred Holdham, 12311/3, IWMDS; Martin, *K Force*, 2; Gordon, *Embarrassing Australian*, 145–46; see D. Bruce Sealy and Peter Van De Vyere, *Thomas George Prince* (Winnipeg: Pegius, 1981), 29; see also, e.g., Dicker in Pears and Kirkland, *Korea Remembered*, 243; O'Kane, *O'Kane's Korea*, 12; Melnechuck in Hepenstall, *Find the Dragon*, 13; Barris, *Deadlock*, 22; *Five Nights*, broadcast 22 April 1976, CBC Radio, http://archives.cbc.ca/war_conflict/korean_war/clips/782/ (accessed 27 August 2009).

110. Bishop, *King's Bishop*, 20; see, e.g., *Five Nights*, CBC Radio. On a desire to escape dead-end manual labor in forestry, mines, and on farms see, e.g., McKeown, *Kapyong Remembered*, 1; Gerald Gowing, Suart Reitsma, www.veterans.gc.ca (accessed 31 July 2009); Cook in Hepenstall, *Find the Dragon*, 69. On having missed World War II as a motive see, e.g., McKeown, *Kapyong Remembered*, 1; Barris, *Deadlock*, 19, 40; Hibbs and Czuboka in Bjarnason, *Triumph*, 42–43. Younger men could also be fleeing from women. "I joined the army because I was mad at my girlfriend!" a private in 2PPCLI exclaimed ("Blood on the Hills," *In Korea: With*

Norm Christie, produced by Paul Kilback and Peter Williamson [Toronto: Breakthrough Films and Television, 2006]).

111. David Horner, *Duty First* (North Sydney, N.S.W.: Allen and Unwin, 1990), 382; Len Opie, S02654, AWM; see also Stan Bombell, S03787, AWM; McGibbon, *New Zealand, Vol. II,* 42; Patrick Knowles, 19388/1, IWMDS; Ronald Stewart, S03813, AWM. On the range of motives among the Australians see Richard Trembath, "'But to this day I still ask myself, why did I serve in Korea?': The Formation of K Force," in *The Korean War, 1950–53,* ed. Peter Dennis and Jeffrey Grey (Canberra: Army History Unit, Department of Defence, 2000), 104–35.

112. Gray, *Danger Close,* 16; Tom Muggleton, S02652, AWM; see also, e.g., *Five Nights,* CBC Radio; Watson, *Far Eastern Tour,* chapter 3.

113. David Butler, S02777, AWM; see, e.g., Len Opie, S02654, AWM; Knowles and Pears in Pears and Kirkland, *Korea Remembered,* 24, 81; Hepenstall, *Find the Dragon,* 22. On lying about prior experience – which seems to have affected the 3RAR signals platoon – see Jack Gallaway, S02651, AWM.

114. Bishop, *King's Bishop,* 24; see also Hepenstall, *Find the Dragon,* 65, 268; Watson, "Calgary to Kap'yong," 24. On the PPCLI murder case involving Koreans see Chris Madsen, *Another Kind of Justice* (Vancouver: UBC Press, 1999), 109–10; Munro in Hepenstall, *Find the Dragon,* 264–65. On the chaotic raising of the Special Force see Bercuson, *Blood on the Hills,* 41 ff.; Wood, *Strange Battleground,* 27–28. On the drinking problem in 2PPCLI see also, e.g., Gray, *Danger Close,* 14–15.

115. Ben O'Dowd, S02659, AWM; Stuart Reitsma, www.veterans.gc.ca (accessed 10 July 2012); see also O'Dowd, *Valiant Company,* 31; Gallaway, *Last Call,* 131. On the percentage of veterans in 16FR see McGibbon, *New Zealand, Vol. II,* 45. For the percentage in 2PPCLI see Watson, "Calgary to Kap'yong," 31.

116. Patrick Weller, 1664/2, IWMDS; see also, e.g., Frank Carter, 18262/1, IWMDS; Robert O. Holles, *Now Thrive the Armourers* (London: Harrap, 1952), 41.

117. Thomas Cunningham-Booth, 19913/2, IWMDS; see also, e.g., Tyas in Walker, *Barren Place,* 28.

118. James R. Stone and Jacques Castonguay, *Korea 1951* (Ottawa: CWM, 1988), 14; see, e.g., Patrick Knowles (3RAR), 19388/1, IWMDS; Cushing, *Soldier for Hire,* 275–76 (1RUR); Bishop, *King's Bishop,* 59, 63–65 (2PPCLI); see also Hepenstall, *Find the Dragon,* 53. In the depths of winter there were also a few cases of self-inflicted wounds in both 2PPCLI (see Bishop, *King's Bishop,* 96–97; Hepenstall, *Find the Dragon,* 81) and 3RAR (Don Beard, S02687, AWM; Phil Bennett, S02656, AWM). Some of the older Ulsters, to be sure, were said to be able to better endure conditions than some of the younger regulars. See "Notes from the 1st Batt.," 21; but see O'Kane, *O'Kane's Korea,* 52–53.

119. Cutforth, *Korean Reporter,* 53–54; see also, e.g., Edmund Bruford-Davis, 22347/3, IWMDS; George Connolly, 18271/1, IWMDS; Thomas Cunningham-Booth, 19913/2, IWMDS; Samuel Phillips, 17688/1, IWMDS; Grist, *Remembered,* 43; Farrar-Hockley, *British Part, Vol. I,* 118; Newcombe, *Morning Calm,* 4; Younger, *Blowing Bridges,* 127.

120. See, e.g., David Butler, S02777, AWM; Tom Muggleton, S02652, AWM; Jim Newall, S03789, AWM; Ben O'Dowd, S02659, AWM; Ronald Stewart, S03813, AWM.

121. Cyril Papworth, 16618/1, IWMDS; see also, e.g., Eric Hill, 12673/3, IWMDS; Green, *Captured,* 86; Grist, *Remembered,* 31; Large, *One Man's War,* 42. On 1GLOS as "the gloomies" – owing to relative si-

lence rather than mood – see Cutforth, *Korean Reporter,* 48; Linklater, *Year in Space,* 106.

122. 1MX, according to one former company commander, was not fully trained for war when 27Bde sailed for Korea (Hastings, *Korean War,* 102), a claim that was vigorously disputed by other 1MX officers (see Man to Hastings, 24 November 1987, A. N. Man Papers, IWMDD; Shipster, *Mist,* 157–59). On the mad dash to get 27Bde ready see Farrar-Hockley, *British Part, Vol. I,* 128–29. 3RAR, getting ready at top speed in Japan (see A. Argent, "A Battalion Prepares for War," B. A. Coad Papers, IWMDD; O'Dowd, *Valiant Company,* 2–6), also had weaknesses when it departed for Korea (see, e.g., Olwyn Green, *The Name's Still Charlie* [St. Lucia: University of Queensland Press, 1993], 251). The Canadians had longer to prepare but also more to do, since rather than expand existing battalions the decision had been taken in Ottawa to create Special Force battalions more or less from the ground up. Suffice it to say that when 2PPCLI arrived in Korea in mid-December 1950, Colonel Stone insisted on more than a month of additional fieldwork before his men were committed to battle. As he put it, "the necessary time was granted to train this motley mob as a fighting machine." Stone and Castonguay, *Korea 1951,* 13; see Bercuson, *Blood on the Hills,* 69ff. In 29Bde much had been achieved in the way of individual and unit training, but not enough to make the brigade an entirely coherent fighting force. As the brigade chronicler admitted, "neither the group as a whole nor the units themselves had really settled down as a fighting formation at the date of sailing." 29Bde History, p. 2, WO 308/42, TNA; see Farrar-Hockley, *British Part, Vol. I,* 119.

123. On the operations of 27BCB see 27Bde Report on Operations, 29 August 1950 – 31 March 1951, WO 308/45, TNA; 27Bde WD, Sep. 1950 – Mar. 1951, WO 281/710, TNA. See also the war diaries of 1A&SH (WO 281/1166, TNA), 3RAR (85/4/20–27, AWM), and 2PPCLI (vols. 18317–18318, RG 24-C-3, NLAC). On the operations of 29Bde see 29Bde History, pp. 2–4, WO 308/42, TNA. See also the war diaries of 1GLOS (WO 281/1244, TNA), 1RNF (WO 281/1160, TNA), and 1RUR (WO 281/1165, TNA).

124. See Martin, *K Force,* 9–10; O'Kane, *O'Kane's Korea,* 17. "The British Army is used to this type of enemy on the Indian Frontier and Burma," a widely circulated report claimed, "as a study of the Waziristan Campaign 1919–20 or any of the many other books on these campaigns will show." Korea Notes No. 1: Reactions to the first part of Korean campaign prior to the Inchon landings, paragraph 45, WO 291/2428, TNA. This paper was sent out to Commonwealth forces. See Sitreps and Notes on Fighting in Korea, June 50/Sep. 51, Appendix A to HQS 3201–151/25 (Trg 5a), 17 Sep. 51, 314.009 (D464), DHH. Comparing the tribesmen of the Raj frontiers with the Soviet-trained and -armed forces of North Korea was, to say the least, rather misleading.

125. Gordon Potts, 23213/8, IWMDS; Younger, *Blowing Bridges,* 147. By contrast Tony Farrar-Hockley, adjutant of 1GLOS at the time, remembered – albeit fifty years on – being uneasy at the sheer scale of Chinese intervention. Anthony Farrar-Hockley in *Forgotten Heroes,* BBC.

126. Malcolm, *Argylls,* 14.

127. Shipster, *Mist,* 132; Phil Bennett, S02656, AWM. On the fights in early November see 27Bde Report on Operations, 29 August 1950–31 March 1951, Part IV, pp. 2–4, WO 308/45, TNA.

128. Thomas Cunningham-Booth, 19913/3, IWMDS; see Perrins, *'Pretty Rough,'* 49–55.

129. M. N. S. McCord, 1991-05-1-1, NAM. On the Ulsters' battle in January 1951 see Farrar-Hockley, *British Part, Vol. I,* 385–92.

130. See, e.g., Richard Gale in *Journal of the Royal United Services Institution* 97 (1952): 14; Sitreps and Notes on Fighting in Korea, June 50/Sep. 51, Appendix A to HQS 3201–151/25 (Trg 5a), 17 Sep. 51, p. 7, 314.009 (D464), DHH.

131. Report by Lt.-Col. J. R. Stone on activities of 2PPCLI in Korea, 18/23 December 1950, p. 2, 145.2 P7013 (D6), DHH. Brodie was likely making these points on the basis of a smallish attack at Sibyon-ni by North Korean soldiers on the Northumberlands at the end of November 1950. See Salmon, *Last Round,* 51–52. On other 2PPCLI officers developing a healthy respect for the enemy in their first encounters see, e.g., Middleton and Munro in Hepenstall, *Find the Dragon,* 75, 81. Brodie from quite early on in Korea recognized the importance of operating in the hills and not becoming road-bound. See Hamill, *Ulster Rifles,* 38.

132. See CO 8RIH to DRAC, n/d [c. 31 December 1950], WO 281/1142, TNA.

133. Command Report, 3d Infantry Division, April 1951, p. 1, Box 2898, RG 407, NARA; see Napier, *Horses to Chieftains,* 269, 271; Roland Winn, *Korean Campaign Supplement to "The Crossbelts," 1950/1, Journal of the VIII King's Royal Irish Hussars* (Luneberg: Hoppe, 1952), 6, 8.

134. "Blood on the Hills," Breakthrough Films and Television.

135. Sebastian Mercer, 1989-5-1-1, NAM. See Farrar-Hockley, *British Part, Vol. II,* 50–51; 1GLOS WD, 16 February 1951, WO 281/1244, TNA; 29Bde History, p. 3, WO 308/42, TNA; Frank Carter memoir, pp. 18–19, IWMDD; Green, *Captured,* 81–85; Grist, *Remembered,* 36; Harvey, *War in Korea,* 70–71; Anthony Eagles, 12783/2, IWMDS; Byron Murphy, 15338/3, IWMDS; Ronald Norley, 15539/2, IWMDS; Guy Temple, 15557/1, IWMDS; see also Salmon, *Last Round,* 104–107.

136. Henry Ponsford, 18456/1, IWMDS [Carne comment]; see Gordon Potts, 23213/8, IWMDS; Younger, *Blowing Bridges,* 147.

137. See Roy E. Appleman, *Ridgway Duels for Korea* (College Station: Texas A&M University Press, 1990), 471. Douglas Johnson-Charlton, 15256/6, IWMDS.

138. Frank Cottam, 21729/4, IWMDS; Hamill, *Ulster Rifles,* 33; Mervyn McCord, 20292/2, IWMDS. On the Chinese seeming to lack arms see, e.g., Fitzsimmons in Richard Doherty, *The Sons of Ulster* (Belfast: Appletree, 1992), 153; Monks, *Eyewitness,* 318; Len Opie, S02654, AWM.

139. On contempt for "the Gooks," see, e.g., Sebastian Mercer, 1989-05-1-1, NAM; Anderson, *Banner,* 44; Tunstall, *I Fought,* 110, passim.; Watson, *Far Eastern Tour,* chapter 3.

140. M. N. S. McCord, 1991-05-1-1, NAM; see also, e.g., Tunstall, *I Fought,* 106; Wilson, *Sum of Things,* 184.

141. Bishop, *King's Bishop,* 156; Henry Ponsford, 18456/2, IWMDS; see also Malcolm, *Argylls,* 79. On the work of the Korean porters being appreciated and the men well liked see, e.g., M. J. P. M. Corbally, *The Royal Ulster Rifles, 1793–1957* (Glasgow: Paramount, 1960), 176; Watson, *Far Eastern Tour,* 65; Holles, *Now Thrive,* 142–43; O'Kane, *O'Kane's Korea,* 57; Linklater, *Year in Space,* 99; Kenneth Black, 18022/4, IWMDS; J. R. M. French, 1996-05-27-1, NAM; Denis Whybro, 20008/15, IWMDS; Pat Angier in *The Back Badge* 3, no. 10 (1951): 145. On porters getting lost and not liking to be near the firing line see *Quis Separabit* 19, no. 2 (1951): 75. There might also have been a suspicion – an entirely false one in light of ROK press-gang tactics (see. e.g., Anderson, *Banner,* 25) – that some of the younger porters were evading military service, with consequent resentment (see Whatmore, *One Road,* 92). The hardships they endured might be taken for granted (see Tunstall, *I Fought,* 106). On units unofficially adopting stray civil-

ians, especially children, see, e.g., Y. K. Choi, S03806, AWM; John Dyer, 18474/3, IWMDS; Cyril Papworth, 16618/1, IWMDS; Cutforth, *Korean Reporter,* 122–28; Holles, *Now Thrive,* 108; Tunstall, *I Fought,* 121.

142. Younger, *Blowing Bridges,* 186. For the "toughest" comment, see Grist, *Remembered,* 52. For the "wild-looking" comment, see Kavanagh, *Perfect Stranger,* 109. For the mortaring incident see John Mole, 23221/4, IWMDS. On the British view of the Belgians see also O'Kane, *O'Kane's Korea,* 57–58; Mervyn McCord, 21563/6, IWMDS.

143. Petra Gunst et al., *Une Saison en Corée* (Brussels: Racine, 1999), 146–47.

144. See Tedder in Frederick Aandahl, ed., *Foreign Relations of the United States 1951, Volume VII, Part 1* (Washington, D.C.: USGPO, 1983), 339.

145. See Appleman, *Ridgway Duels,* 412, 434, 440–49; Paul F. Braim, *The Will to Win* (Annapolis, Md.: Naval Institute Press, 2001), 246. On aerial reconnaissance see USAF Historical Division, Air University, *United States Air Force Operations in the Korean Conflict, 1 November 1950–30 June 1952* (Washington, D.C.: Department of the Air Force, 1955), 59.

146. See 1KOSB WD, 19–24 April 1951, WO 281/478, TNA; 1A&SH WD, 19–24 April 1951, WO 281/1166, TNA. On being in reserve and reorganizing and thus not expecting – or being briefed on – serious defensive action in 27Bde see, e.g., Ben O'Dowd, S02659, AWM; Tom Muggleton, S02652, AWM. On 6ROK patrols showing no sign of the enemy see Wood, *Strange Battleground,* 73. Part of the problem was enemy use of smoke screens to mask movement from aerial observers. IX Corps Command Report, Book 1, April 1951, pp. 22–23, Box 1797, RG 407, NARA.

147. Anthony Farrar-Hockley in David Scott Daniell, *Cap of Honour* (London: White Lion, 1975), 343. Farrar-Hockley was relieved because he knew the breadth of the brigade front. Ordinary soldiers, though, were just happy that they could live in comparative peace and quiet. See, e.g., R. S. Gill letter 62, 11 April 1951, IWMDD; O'Kane, *O'Kane's Korea,* 57. On establishing a foothold beyond the Imjin, see A. E. Younger, "Episodes from Korea," *Royal Engineers Journal* 65, no. 4 (1951): 338–43; R. S. Gill letter 60, 10 April 1951, IWMDD. On the isolated night attack on D Company on the north side of the Imjin see RUR Narrative No. 3, 27 Mar.–26 April 1951, p. 4, WO 308/46, TNA.

148. Mossman, *Ebb and Flow,* 386; Appleman, *Ridgway Duels,* 458, 465. Within 29Bde it was also thought that the enemy, if he came, might strike farther east. See Green, *Captured,* 95–96. On the growing evidence of an enemy buildup in front of 3rd Division see Command Report, 3d Infantry Division, April 1951, pp. 3–4, Box 2898, RG 407, NARA.

149. See Farrar-Hockley, *British Part, Vol. II,* 113.

150. 70 Field Battery supported the Glosters, 116 Field Battery the Fusiliers, and 176 Field Battery the Rifles.

151. The four 4.2-in. mortars of A Troop supported the Fusiliers, B Troop the Ulsters, and C Troop the Glosters.

152. Appleman, *Ridgway Duels,* 471.

153. On the brigade frontage see Farrar-Hockley, *British Part, Vol. II,* 89–90.

154. 45FR narrative, p. 67, WO 308/44, TNA; Digby Grist, "The Korean Campaign as a Soldier Sees It," *The Back Badge* 4, no. 12 (1952): 44; see also, e.g., Davies, *Red Winds,* 88, 89; Green, *Captured,* 96; Holles, *Now Thrive,* 140; Linklater, *Our Men,* 55; Whatmore, *One Road,* 57. The expectation that the advance would continue was shared by the special British military representative at Ridgway's headquarters in Tokyo, Air Vice-Marshal Cecil Bouchier (see Bouchier to MoD, 21 April 1951, DEFE 11/211, TNA).

155. Green, *Captured,* 96; Anthony Farrar-Hockley in Daniell, *Cap of Honour* (1975), 344; Cubiss in Salmon, *Last Round,* 117; Holles, *Now Thrive,* 141; Carne to Joslen, 24 July 1957 [see also Maj. B. J. Eastwood statement], CAB 157/23, TNA. On the river as a barrier see also Gordon Potts, 23213/6, IWMDS. On the water level dropping see Farrar-Hockley, *British Part, Vol. II,* 112. On shortages of defensive stores see also Harding, *Imjin Roll,* 10. On the hard digging conditions and shallow defenses see Whatmore, *One Road,* 57; Gordon Potts, 23213/8, IWMDS; David Holdsworth, 15428/1, IWMDS. On the better defenses prepared by the Ulsters north of the river see, e.g., John Dyer, 18474/2, IWMDS; George Hobson, 16853/1, IWMDS; John Mole, 23221/4, IWMDS. The only mines laid by the Glosters were on the south side of the Imjin at Gloster Crossing in response to a patrol contact north of the river on 22 April. Carne to Joslen, 24 July 1957, CAB 157/23, TNA.

156. On the deep sweeps with tanks see 8RIH WD, 14–20 April 1951, WO 281/1142, TNA; Fitzroy, *Men of Valour,* 273–75. On local patrolling see, e.g., 1RUR WD, 12–18 April 1951, WO 281/1165, TNA. On Brodie asking for more men see Cutforth, *Korean Reporter,* 182. For officers and men who suspected the Chinese *would* come at them on the Imjin see, e.g., 5 April 1951 letter in Mason, *Diplomatic Dispatches,* 70; Stowe to West, 19 Apr. 1951, E. S. Stowe Papers, IWMDD; Guy Temple, 1557/1, IWMDS.

157. Henry Ponsford, 18456/2, IWMDS; see 29Bde History, p. 5, WO 308/42, TNA; see also, e.g., Frank Carter, 18262/3, IWMDS; George Hobson, 16853/1, IWMDS; Sebastian Mercer, 1989-05-1-1, NAM; John Mole, 23221/4, IWMDS; Douglas Patchett, 16759/1, IWMDS.

158. Grist, *Remembered,* 41; see Farrar-Hockley, *British Part, Vol. II,* 93; see also Cutforth, *Korean Reporter,* 184.

159. Cutforth, *Korean Reporter,* 183; see also *St. George's Gazette,* 31 May 1951, p. 105.

160. On the light plane reconnaissance see J. Dargent, "Notes sur le combat de nuit: l'infiltration," *Bulletin Militaire* 65 (1953): 324. On expectations that a withdrawal to Line Kansas would take place when enemy probing began see, e.g., 1RUR Narrative No. 3, p. 5, WO 308/46, TNA. On retrospective analytical surprise that Brodie allowed the Belgians to replace the Ulsters north of the Imjin see Gunst, Philips, and Vehaegen, *Saison,* 146–47.

161. Peter Ormrod, 09863/2, IWMDS; Denis Whybro, 09863/2, IWMDS; Armand Philips in Gunst, Philips, and Vehaegen, *Saison,* 147; Harvey, *Korean War,* 97; 45FR narrative, p. 68, WO 308/44, TNA; see Noble, *Shoot First,* 182; Large, *One Man's War,* 41; Derek Kinne, *The Wooden Boxes* (London: Muller, 1955), 15; Salmon, *Last Round,* 116–17.

162. Stowe to West, 10 Apr. 1951, E. S. Stowe Papers, IWMDD.

163. Bishop, *King's Bishop,* 118.

164. Odgers, *Remembering Korea,* 82.

165. O'Kane, *O'Kane's Korea,* 57; Cutforth, *Korean Reporter,* 177–78; see also S. Mercer, http://www.youtube.com/watch?v=RzOrI2MU-A0 (accessed 27 August 2009); Holles, *Now Thrive,* 141–42; Frank Carter, 18262/3, IWMDS. A dissenting note had been struck by a Catholic reservist in the Glosters who refused point-blank to go back into the line in March when the brigade had finished its turn in reserve. "He said that he'd had a vision that the regiment would be cut off and massacred," one of the soldiers guarding him while he awaited court-martial remembered. Anthony Eagles, 12783/2, IWMDS.

166. Samuel Philips, 17688/2, IWMDS. On freshly dug trenches, etc., see Sebastian Mercer, 12605/4, IWMDS; David Sharp, 17929/3, IWMDS. On missing the significance of food caches see William

Westwood, 19871/1, IWMDS. On shooting at wildlife see Cyril Papworth, 16618/2, IWMDS. On a feeling of being watched see Peter Ormrod, 09863/2, IWMDS. The Chinese were in fact very good at concealing themselves when they wanted to. See, e.g., Maj. R. Leith-Macgregor, p. 2, encl. 102A, WO 231/89, TNA; Younger, "Episodes from Korea," 344; Napier, *Horses to Chieftains,* 272. According to Kenneth Trevor, the brigade major, a solitary prisoner was taken during the 20th April sweep who reputedly remarked: "I'm surprised you attacked us, I thought we were going to attack you." This was not taken to mean that Trevor should postpone his plans to go on leave. Kenneth Trevor, 09784/2, IWMDS.

167. Ward in Hastings, *Korean War,* 251, 253; see also S. Mercer in *Korea: The Unknown War,* Thames Television/WGBH. On the imminent rotation of the Ulsters and Northumberlands see, e.g., CSM Sean Fitzsimmons in Doherty, *Sons of Ulster,* 156. On the withdrawal of the U.S. artillery liaison officer and the consequences see Barry Taylor, "Open Road Barred," 50. On the brigade major, Kenneth Trevor, being on leave see Kenneth Trevor, 09784/2, IWMDS. On the difficulties this created see Peter Ormrod, 09863/2, IWMDS. On the CO of the Ulsters going on leave because he thought this was a quiet period see *North Irish Brigade Chronicle* 1, no. 4 (1952): 28. On "Lakri" Wood of D Coy, 1GLOS being on leave see Holles, *Now Thrive,* 148. On aerial reconnaissance reports suggesting the Chinese were far off see 29Bde History, App. G, pp. 1–2, WO 308/42, TNA.

168. Anthony Eagles, 17283/3, IWMDS; see Farrar-Hockley, *British Part, Vol. II,* 112–13; Harding, *Imjin Roll,* 11. On things being quiet on 21 April along the I Corps front see Robertson to Slim, 17 May 1951, Impressions of the British Commonwealth Part in the CCF Offensive on 22–26 April 1951 as seen by Lieutenant-General Sir H. C. H. Robertson, p. 1, WO 216/345, TNA.

1. IMJIN: THE FIRST DAY

1. Droogmans in Gunst, Philips, and Vehaegen, *Saison,* 168.

2. Allen in Carew, *Korea,* 185.

3. Farrar-Hockley, *British Part, Vol. II,* 109. On the objectives of the Fifth Phase offensive see also Shu Guang Zhang, *Mao's Military Romanticism* (Lawrence, Kans.: University Press of Kansas, 1995), 146–48.

4. Farrar-Hockley, *British Part, Vol. II,* chapter 8; Gordon L. Rottman, *Korean Order of Battle* (Westport, Conn.: Praeger, 2002), 174–75. On the limitations of Chinese artillery support in the first year of the war see Kevin Mahony, *Formidable Enemies* (Novato, Calif.: Presidio, 2001), 64.

5. Ronald Norley, 15539/2, IWMDS; see, e.g., John Dyer in *Forgotten Heroes,* BBC.

6. Large, *One Man's War,* 47. On other noises see, e.g., Herbert Spraggs, 11910/2, IWMDS.

7. See, e.g., John Dyer, 18474/3, IWMDS; Sebastian Mercer, 12605/5, IWMDS; M. N. S. McCord, 1991-05-1-1, NAM. Though there were persistent stories that troops did indeed get drunk on Kaoling brandy – see Jurgen Domes, *Peng Te-huai* (Stanford, Calif.: Stanford University Press, 1985), 62 – Lofty Large was probably correct in arguing against Chinese drug use: "For a start I'm quite sure there wouldn't have been enough dope to go around." Large, *One Man's War,* 73. On the soccer crowd analogy see Swatton quoted in Richard Lloyd Parry, "Forgotten heroes return to valley of nightmares," *The Independent,* 21 April 1997 ("It was like Wembley"); James Forward, 16078/3, IWMDS. On the film theater analogy see also Mervyn McCord, 21563/5, IWMDS.

8. Large, *One Man's War,* 72. On the prevalence of automatic weapons among

the Chinese at the Imjin see also, e.g., S. J. Davies, *In Spite of Dungeons* (London: Hodder and Stoughton, 1954), 28; Anthony Farrar-Hockley, *Edge of the Sword* (Stroud: Sutton, 1993), 7; Frank Carter memoir, 28, IWMDD (though see also David Holdsworth, 15428/3, IWMDS).

9. Kavanagh, *Perfect Stranger,* 93–94. The CofE chaplain, Sam Davies, certainly had no sense of an imminent battle. See Davies, *In Spite,* 16–17; Stanley Davies, 15475/1, IWMDS. On the Fusiliers preparing for St. George's Day see, e.g., Charles Mitchell letter, 22 April 1951, in Perrins, *'Pretty Rough,'* 112; Peacock, *Northumberland Fusiliers,* 103. On the Ulsters and the film show see, e.g., Albert Tyas, 18439/1, IWMDS.

10. Samuel Phillips, 17688/2, IWMDS.

11. 3d Infantry Division, Command Report, Narrative, p. 4, Box. 2898, RG 407, NARA. On British contacts see Farrar-Hockley, *British Part, Vol. II,* 113; Barclay, *First Commonwealth,* 60–61; Hamill, *Ulster Rifles,* 64; 29Bde History, App. G, p. 30, WO 308/42, TNA; 1RNF WD, 22 April 1951, WO 281/1160, TNA; Crahay narrative, p. 7, WO 308/49, TNA; 45FR narrative, p. 68, WO 308/44, TNA.

12. Patrick Weller, 12664/1, IWMDS; Large, *One Man's War,* 47; Cyril Papworth [in conversation with Pat Angier], 16618/3, TNA; Davies, *In Spite,* 15.

13. Carew, *Korea,* 182; Cutforth, *Korean Reporter,* 184. On expectations concerning the Chinese see Farrar-Hockley, *British Part, Vol. II,* 113–14; Hamill, *Ulster Rifles,* 64; Barclay, *First Commonwealth,* 61; Bryson and Coulcher, *Yorkshire Gunners,* 48; Harvey, *War in Korea,* 98.

14. T. V. Fisher-Hoch, "170 Independent Mortar Battery, R.A., in Korea," *Journal of the Royal Artillery* 78, no. 4 (1951): 250. On the Chinese having already identified their targets see, e.g., Robertson to Slim, 17 May 1951, Impression of the British Commonwealth part in the CCF Offensive on 22–26 April 1951 as seen by Lieutenant-General Sir H. C. H. Robertson, p. 1, WO 216/345, TNA.

15. Farrar-Hockley, *British Part, Vol. II,* 114–15.

16. Perrins, *'Pretty Rough,'* 116; 1RNF WD, 22 April 1951, WO 281/1160, TNA. A sentry going on night duty elsewhere in the Northumberland sector had dismissed the reports of his predecessor ("'somebody moving about there,' he said, 'and not squaddies'") as mere jumpiness ("'Oh, behave yourself,' I said, 'you're panicking'"). Denis Prout, 18775/2, IWMDS.

17. Major Farrar-Hockley of the Gloucesters and the Imjin River Offensive, http://www.thekoreanwar.co.uk/html/sound_bites.html (accessed 11 August 2007); see Guy Temple, 15557/1, IWMDS. On Carne worrying that the enemy force might be bigger than intelligence sources anticipated see Harvey, *War in Korea,* 98; Farrar-Hockley, *Edge,* 17. As one officer put it, "I think at this stage we weren't quite sure whether it was just a reconnaissance in force on their part or what it was." Sebastian Mercer, 1989-05-1-1, NAM.

18. Guy Temple, 15557/1–2, IWMDS; see Farrar-Hockley, *Edge,* 17–22; Carew, *Korea,* 184–85; Salmon, *Last Round,* 2–6.

19. David Holdsworth, 15428/2, IWMDS; Len Swatton in Richard Lloyd Parry, "Forgotten heroes return to valley of nightmares," *The Independent,* 21 April 1997; see Harvey, *War in Korea,* 99.

20. Gunst, Philips, and Vehaegen, *Saison,* 159; Crahay narrative, p. 7, WO 308/49, TNA.

21. Pauwels in Gunst, Philips, and Vehaegen, *Saison,* 172; see ibid., 159ff.

22. 1RNF WD, 22 April 1951, WO 281/1160, TNA; Perrins, *'Pretty Rough,'* 116.

23. Farrar-Hockley, *British Part, Vol. II,* 116.

24. Albert Tyas, 18439/1, IWMDS; M. N. S. McCord, 1991-05-1-1, NAM.

25. 1RUR WD, 22 April 1951, WO 281/1165, TNA; Hamill, *Ulster Rifles*, 64.

26. On the ambush see the account of the 2 i/c in Kavanagh, *Perfect Stranger*, 95–107; see also *Quis Separabit* 19, no. 2 (1951): 77; Salmon, *Last Round*, 140–41. On Craig's escape see his account in Philip D. Chinnery, *Korean Atrocity!* (Shrewsbury: Airlife, 2000), 144–45. On Craig losing his mind as a result of the ambush, see M. N. S. McCord, 1991-05-1-1, NAM.

27. De Kerpel in Gunst, Philips, and Vehaegen, *Saison*, 178; see ibid., 162ff.; Crahay narrative, pp. 8–9, WO 308/49, TNA.

28. Cubiss in Salmon, *Last Round*, 145; Kinne, *Wooden Boxes*, 16–18; see M. D. Young in *St. George's Gazette* 69 (1951): 105; 1RNF WD, 23 April 1951, WO 281/1160, TNA.

29. Roy Rees, 19854/1, IWMDS; Andrew Scott, 16855/1, IWMDS; Kinne, *Wooden Boxes*, 20; see Farrar-Hockley, *British Part, Vol. II*, 117; 1RNF WD, 23 April 1951, 281/1160, TNA; Perrins, *'Pretty Rough,'* 116.

30. Salmon, *Last Round*, 148–49.

31. See Farrar-Hockley, *Edge*, 25–27; 29Bde History, App. G, p. 2, WO 308/42, TNA; Carew, *Korea*, 186–88.

32. John Grosvenor, 16337/1, IWMDS; Ronald Norley, 15539/2, IWMDS; Whatmore, *One Road*, 69; William Clark, 18459/1, IWMDS; Frank "Nick" Carter, 18262/4, IWMDS; Walter Cleveland, 17348/3, IWMDS.

33. Hamill, *Ulster Rifles*, 64–65; Farrar-Hockley, *British Part, Vol. II*, 117.

34. Crahay narrative, p. 9, WO 308/49, TNA; see Farrar-Hockley, *British Part, Vol. II*, 117.

2. IMJIN: THE SECOND DAY

1. Davies, *In Spite*, 15.

2. Farrar-Hockley, *Edge*, 38–39.

3. On the Chinese actually fighting harder with the coming of daylight see Farrar-Hockley, *British Part, Vol. II*, 121.

4. See, e.g., Frank Cottam, 21729/4, IWMDS.

5. Harding, *Imjin Roll*, 13.

6. Carew, *Korea*, 189. The account of the conversation recorded by the adjutant of the Glosters is less abrupt but the same in essence. See Farrar-Hockley, *Edge*, 27.

7. Sebastian Mercer, 1989-05-1-1, NAM; see WO 32/15193, TNA; Salmon, *Last Round*, 155; Tim Carew, *The Glorious Glosters* (London: Leo Cooper, 1970), 73; Farrar-Hockley in Daniell, *Cap of Honour* (1975), 348; Frank Cottam, 21729/4, IWMDS; Cyril Papworth, 16618/3, IWMDS. According to a fellow junior officer, Curtis "didn't care whether he lived or died" since his wife had recently died of tuberculosis. Geoffrey Costello in *Forgotten Heroes*, BBC.

8. Farrar-Hockley, *Edge*, 29–30; see Farrar-Hockley, *British Part, Vol. II*, 117.

9. 29Bde History, App. H, Bde Log, 23 April 1951, WO 308/42, TNA; see Farrar-Hockley, *British Part, Vol. II*, 121.

10. Crahay narrative, p. 9, WO 308/49, TNA; P. Janssens in Gunst, Philips, and Vehaegen, *Saison*, 185. See also ibid., 203; Jean-Pierre Gahìde, *La Belgique et al guerre de Corée, 1950–1955* (Brussels: Musee Royal de l'Armee, 1991), 49–50; 29Bde History, App. H, Bde Log, 23 April 1951, WO 308/42, TNA.

11. Fus. J. Martin, AI9/K/BRIT/162, KB1073/11G Part 5, A2151, NAA.

12. Perrins, *'Pretty Rough,'* 116, 118.

13. Fitzroy, *Men of Valour*, 273.

14. 29Bde History, App. H, Bde Log, 23 Apr. 1951, WO 308/42, TNA; 1RUR WD, 23 April 1951, WO 281/1165, TNA.

15. See I U.S. Corps Command Report, April 1951, Section II, Narrative of Operations, p. 123, Box 1523, RG 407, NARA.

16. Farrar-Hockley, *British Part, Vol. II*, 118; 7th Infantry Command Report April 1951, Narrative, p. 4, Box 2950, RG 407, NARA. On the offensive from the division-level perspective, see Max Dolcater,

ed., *3d Infantry Division in Korea* (Paducah, Ky.: Turner, 1998), 196.

17. Farrar-Hockley, *British Part, Vol. II,* 121.

18. Peter Ormrod, 09863/2, IWMDS; Fitzroy, *Men of Valour,* 276–77. On thwarted hopes for artillery and air support see Farrar-Hockley, *Edge,* 30.

19. Harvey, *War in Korea,* 102; Whatmore, *One Road,* 72.

20. Whatmore, *One Road,* 73; see Harvey, *War in Korea,* 102–103.

21. Farrar-Hockley, *Edge,* 30.

22. Cyril Papworth, 16618/3, IWMDS. On A Company see also Sebastian "Sam" Mercer, 12605/4, IWMDS; William Clark, 18459/1, IWMDS.

23. Carne to Joslen, 24 July 1954, CAB 157/23, TNA.

24. Sebastian "Sam" Mercer, 12605/4, IWMDS; see Whatmore, *One Road,* 74–75; Harvey, *War in Korea,* 114–15; Farrar-Hockley in Daniell, *Cap of Honour* (1975), 349. The mortar battery, also coming under enemy fire, eventually withdrew as well. See citation for Capt. F. R. Wisbey, p. 56, K643, WO 373/119, TNA. It has been suggested in the VC citation for Philip Curtis that the failure to pursue A Company was also the indirect result of the Chinese having been cowed by his attack on the observation bunker. See Max Arthur, *Symbol of Courage* (London: Sidgwick and Jackson, 2004), 542.

25. On the problems of digging in see, e.g., Owen Smith, 18441/2, IWMDS. On the Korean porters see Farrar-Hockley in Daniell, *Cap of Honour* (1975), 349. On the meal see Farrar-Hockley, *Edge,* 31. On the deployment of the companies see ibid., 32.

26. Farrar-Hockley, *British Part, Vol. II,* 118; Bryson and Coulcher, *Yorkshire Gunners,* 51; 45FR narrative, p. 73, WO 308/44, TNA.

27. Salmon, *Last Round,* 171.

28. Grist, *Remembered,* 42–43. On other vehicle ambushes between F Echelon and Solma-ri see, e.g., Holles, *Now Thrive,* 152–54; 45FR narrative, p. 72, WO 308/44, TNA; Citation for 2/Lt. A. C. N. Preston, p. 58, WO 373/119, TNA; see also E. J. A. Hodgetts obituary, *The Wire,* October 2003, 512. Around two dozen Glosters were apparently able to make their way to safety that afternoon due to covering fire from the roving intelligence and reconnaissance platoon of the 1/7th RCT. See John C. McManus, *The 7th Infantry Regiment* (New York: Tom Doherty, 2008), 58–59.

29. Samuel Phillips, 17688/2, IWMDS; see Perrins, *'Pretty Rough,'* 117–18; 1RNF WD, 23 April 1951, WO 281/1160, TNA; Salmon, *Last Round,* 163–64.

30. Fus. Cyril Curling, p. 39, WO 71/1024, TNA.

31. 1RNF WD, 23 April 1951, WO 281/1160, TNA; 8RIH WD, 23 April 1951, WO 281/1142, TNA.

32. David Sharp, 17929/3, IWMDS; see 1RNF WD, 23 April 1951, WO 281/1160, TNA; Kinne, *Wooden Boxes,* 20–22. On 29Bde HQ losing communication with battalion HQs see, e.g., 3d Infantry Division, Command Report, 7th Infantry Regiment, April 1951, 7th Infantry Unit Journal, April 24, 1951, 05:00 hrs., Box 2950, RG 407, NARA.

33. Younger, *Blowing Bridges,* 199.

34. Though he did not mention the incident when interviewed by the Imperial War Museum (see 18544, IWMDS), Charles Sharpling, a lance-corporal in the Glosters during the battle, recalled in an interview with Andy Salmon that a radio conversation between Carne and Brodie took place in which Brodie seemed to question the accuracy of Carne's account of the numbers of Chinese crossing the Imjin (Salmon, *Last Round,* 170).

35. See E. J. Kahn, "No One But the Glosters," *New Yorker,* 26 May 1951, p. 68.

36. Farrar-Hockley, *British Part, Vol. II,* 119; Appleman, *Ridgway Duels,* 465; I U.S.

Corps, Command Report, April 1951, Section III, Narrative of Operations, p. 122, Box 1523, RG 407, NARA.

37. Gunst, Philips, and Verhaegen, *Saison,* 204.

38. William F. Long and Walter M. Turner, "Challenge Accepted," *Combat Forces Journal* 2 (1952): 14–15; see Farrar-Hockley, *British Part, Vol. II,* 119; Crahay narrative, p. 11, WO 308/49, TNA; 3d Division, Command Report, Apr. 1951, p. 16, Box 2898, RG 407, NARA; 3d Infantry Division, Command Report, 7th Infantry Regiment, 1st Bn Operational Order 23 April 1951, Box 2950, RG 407, NARA; 7th Infantry Command Report Narrative, April 1951, p. 4, Box 2950, RG 407, NARA.

39. Peter Ormrod, 09863/2, IWMDS.

40. Napier, *Horses to Chieftains,* 273–74.

41. On RUR observers thinking the American attack on Hill 257 had failed see O'Kane, *O'Kane's Korea,* 59; Hamill, *Ulster Rifles,* 66; see also Fitzroy, *Men of Valour,* 277; Farrar-Hockley, *British Part, Vol. II,* 120 [in which 257 is apparently mistyped as 287]. The chronicler of the 7th Infantry, however, suggests that the hill was indeed secured. See McManus, *7th Infantry,* 57. On the 1/7th attack see also Long and Turner, "Challenge Accepted," 15–16; 3d Infantry Division, 7th Infantry Command Report Narrative, April 1951, p. 4, Box 2950, RG 407, NARA.

42. Saenen and Derom in Gunst, Philips, and Verhaegen, *Saison,* 205–206; see Crahay narrative, p. 12, WO 308/49, TNA; Gahide, *Belgique,* 50; 3d Infantry Division, Command Report, Apr. 1951, p. 18, Box 2898, RG 407, NARA; 3d Infantry Division, Command Report, 7th Infantry Regiment, April 1951, 2nd Battalion Unit Journal, April 23, 1951, Box 2950, RG 407, NARA.

43. See Farrar-Hockley, *British Part, Vol. II,* 120; Barclay, *First Commonwealth,* 63; Hamill, *Ulster Rifles,* 67.

44. Farrar-Hockley, *British Part, Vol. II,* 124, 119. On 10BCT in the battle on 22/23 April see Juan F. Villasanta, *Dateline: Korea* (Bacolod City, Philippines: Nalco, 1954), 19–23.

45. Gordon Potts, 23213/7, 9, IWMDS; see Hamill, *Ulster Rifles,* 66–67; 1RUR WD, 24 April 1951, WO281/1165, TNA. On the effect of bazooka rounds see also Farrell in Salmon, *Last Round,* 185.

46. Perrins, *'Pretty Rough,'* 118; 1RNF WD, 24 April 1951, WO 281/1160, TNA; Kinne, *Wooden Boxes,* 22.

47. Frank "Nick" Carter, 18262/4, IWMDS; Large, *One Man's War,* 58; see Geoffrey Costello in *Forgotten Heroes,* BBC; see also Farrar-Hockley, *British Part, Vol. II,* 125; Holles, *Now Thrive,* 156; Harding, *Imjin Roll,* 16.

48. Green, *Captured,* 99–100; see David Kaye, 17468/1, IWMDS.

49. Davies, *In Spite,* 19; Farrar-Hockley, *Edge,* 39; see Farrar-Hockley, *British Part, Vol. II,* 125; Harding, *Imjin Roll,* 16. Andrew Salmon, contradicting the recollections of the adjutant, makes the case that the withdrawal of C Company was not ordered by Carne but was rather a semi-spontaneous action produced by the apparent absence of the company commander, Major Mitchell. See Salmon, *Last Round,* 160 footnote.

3. IMJIN: THE THIRD DAY

1. Harvey, *War in Korea,* 122.

2. Patrick Weller, 12664/2, IWMDS.

3. Large, *One Man's War,* 62, 60.

4. Costello in *The Independent,* 8 July 2003; Harding in Farrar-Hockley, *British Part, Vol. II,* 125.

5. Frank "Nick" Carter, 18262/4, IWMDS; see Farrar-Hockley, *Edge,* 45–46; Lt. A. Peal, AI9/K/BRIT/977, KB 1073/11G Part 6, A2151, NAA.

6. Harvey, *War in Korea,* 116; see Farrar-Hockley, *British Part, Vol. II,* 124, 126–27; 29Bde WD, 24 April 1951, WO 281/1157, TNA; Guy Temple, 15557/2, IWMDS.

7. Ronald Norley, 15539/2, IWMDS; Farrar-Hockley, *Edge*, 42. On Carne's inspiring leadership see also, e.g., R. F. Matthews, *No Rice for Rebels* (London: Bodley Head, 1956), 15; Sebastian Mercer, 1989-05-1-1, NAM; Carew, *Korea*, 218.

8. E. J. Kahn, "No One But the Glosters," *New Yorker*, 26 May 1951, 68.

9. Frank Cottam, 21729/4, IWMDS.

10. Farrar-Hockley, *Edge*, 47–48; Farrar-Hockley, *British Part, Vol. II*, 126; see also Anthony Eagles, 17283/3, IWMDS; Ronald Norley, 15539/2, IWMDS; Citation for F. G. Strong, p. 193, WO 373/119, TNA.

11. Cyril Papworth, 16618/3, IWMDS; Ronald Norley, 15539/2, IWMDS; see also Patrick Weller, 12664/2, IWMDS.

12. Green, *Captured*, 102; Holles, *Now Thrive*, 162; Sebastian "Sam" Mercer, 12605/5, IWMDS; see Matthews, *No Rice*, 10–12; Byron Murphy, 15338/4, IWMDS; Robert Hickey, 16061/1, IWMDS.

13. Crahay narrative, p. 13, WO 308/49, TNA; see Farrar-Hockley, *British Part, Vol. II*, 128.

14. Grist, *Remembered*, 44. Grist states that the plan was hatched with the brigade major, Ken Trevor. However, as Trevor was on leave during the battle (see Kenneth Trevor, 09784/2, IWMDS) it seems likely he and Watkin-Williams were in fact working with the acting brigade major, Jim Dunning.

15. Gilberto N. Villahermosa, *Honor and Fidelity: The 65th Infantry in Korea, 1950–1953* (Washington, D.C.: Center of Military History, U.S. Army, 2009), 128.

16. Grist, *Remembered*, 44; Farrar-Hockley, *British Part, Vol. II*, 126. On the Glosters rounded up by Grist for the attempt see James Forward, 16078/3, IWMDS.

17. Farrar-Hockley, *Edge*, 48; Harvey, *Korean War*, 120.

18. J. C. Gorman, "Korean Relief Column," *Stand-To* 4, no. 4 (1954): 2.

19. Ibid., 2–3; see Grist, *Remembered*, 44; Farrar-Hockley, *British Part, Vol. II*, 127.

20. Gorman, "Relief Column," 3; see Mossman, *Ebb and Flow*, 414.

21. Salmon, *Last Round*, 189.

22. Gorman, "Relief Column," 4, 2; see Farrar-Hockley, *British Part, Vol. II*, 127; Mossman, *Ebb and Flow*, 414; Charles Paul, "A Year in Korea 1950/51: Recollections of a Subaltern with the 8th KRI Hussars," p. 16, www.iccy.org.uk/vanguard/vanguard/page0016htm (accessed 19 June 2009). Huth was also evidently concerned that, with evening drawing on, his tanks would be easier targets for ambush. See 8RIH WD, 24 Apr. 1951, WO 281/1142, TNA; Huth to Goslen, 1 August 1957, CAB 157/23, TNA.

23. Milburn quoted in Braim, *Will to Win*, 251 (on the time of the meeting see Incl. 1, Commanding General's Journal, April 24, 14:15 hrs and Incl. 2, Assistant Division Commander's Journal, April 24, 14:45 hrs, 3d Infantry Division, Command Report, Box 2898, RG 407, NARA); Farrar-Hockley, *British Part, Vol. II*, 127; Mossman, *Ebb and Flow*, 413; 29Bde History, App. H, 29Bde Log, 24 April 1951, WO 308/42, TNA; G-3 Summary on 29th BIB Action, April 22–25, 1951, pp. 2–3, Incl. 3, Office of the AC of S of G-3, HQ 3d Infantry Division, Box 2898, RG 407, NARA. Soule was evidently not the only U.S. Army officer to misunderstand what was being said by Brodie; at 6:45 PM Soule received a message from his liaison officer at brigade HQ stating that the Glosters were "fairly safe." Villahermosa, *Honor and Fidelity*, 128.

24. Davies, *In Spite*, 21; see Stanley Davies, 15475/1, IWMDS.

25. General Brodie Orders the surrounded Glosters to hold, www.thekoreanwar.co.uk/html.sound_bites.html (accessed 11 August 2007); Farrar-Hockley, *Edge*, 49–50; see 29Bde History, App. H, Bde Log, 24 Apr. 1951, WO 308/42, TNA;

J. R. A. Smith, 18525/1, IWMDS. The assistant divisional commander had broken the news to Brodie in person shortly after 3:30 PM. 3d Infantry Division, Command Report, Apr. 1951, Incl. 2, Assistant Division Commander's Report, 24 Apr. 1951, Box 2898, RG 407, NARA.

26. Appleman, *Ridgway Duels*, 472; Gorman, "Korean Relief Column," 4.

27. Appleman, *Ridgway Duels*, 471–72; see Gorman, "Korean Relief Column," 4; Mossman, *Ebb and Flow*, 414; 29Bde History, App. H, Bde Log, 24 Apr. 1951, WO 308/42, TNA; 8RIH WD, 24 Apr. 1951, WO 281/1142, TNA; Eighth Army, Supporting Documents Section II, Book 4, Part 7, Incl. 31, Milburn to Van Fleet, 15 May 1951, pp. 2–3, Box 1184, RG 407, NARA. Abandoning the attempt to rescue the Glosters was probably made easier when Lieutenant-General Sir Horace Robertson of the Australian Army, the most senior Commonwealth officer in the theater and one who also happened to be visiting the two British-led brigades when the Chinese struck, called the I Corps Chief of Staff from IX Corps HQ that evening and "requested him not to endanger the remainder of the Corps if that would be the result of attempting to extricate the trapped Gloster Battalion." I Corps Command Report, Apr. 1951, Narrative of Operations, 24 Apr., p. 131, Box. 1523, RG 407, NARA.

28. Fitzroy, *Men of Valour*, 278.

29. Green, *Captured*, 102.

30. 29Bde History, App. H, 29Bde Log, 24 Apr. 1951, WO 308/42, TNA.

31. Grist, *Remembered*, 44–45; Davies, *In Spite*, 20; see Harding, *Imjin Roll*, 18; A. E. Younger, "Episodes from Korea," *Royal Engineers Journal* 65, no. 4 (1951), 347; Holles, *Now Thrive*, 156, 163; Whatmore, *One Road*, 77; Frank Cottam, 21729/4, IWMDS. On the problem of lack of aircraft recognition panels see Thomas Cunningham-Booth, 19913/3, IWMDS; Kahn, *"No One But the Glosters,"* 73. Though no other source mentions it, David Green of C Company recalled a botched parachute drop from USAF C-47s that day. "To our great anger and disappointment, they [the parachutes] drifted like dandelion seeds in the wind and fell outside the perimeter. The aircrews must have been on their first mission, utterly clueless and lacking any common sense. All we could do was shake our fists impotently at them, shouting all the names we could lay our hands on." Green, *Captured*, 101.

32. Davies, *In Spite*, 22; A. H. Farrar-Hockley, "Stories from Korea: The Last Day," *The Back Badge*, 4, no. 15 (1953): 227; Farrar-Hockley in Daniell, *Cap of Honour* (1975), 354; see Stanley Davies, 15475/1, IWMDS; David Holdsworth, 15428/2, IWMDS; Owen Smith, 18441/2, IWMDS; Patrick Weller, 12664/1, IWMDS.

33. Kinne, *Wooden Boxes*, 25; Andrew Scott, 16855/2, IWMDS; see Farrar-Hockley, *British Part, Vol. II*, 128; 1RNF WD, 24 Apr. 1951, WO 281/1160, TNA; Perrins, *'Pretty Rough,'* 119.

34. See Christopher Nixon's remarks in www.thekoreanwar.co.uk/html/sound_bites.html (accessed 11 August 2007); Farrar-Hockley, *British Part, Vol. II*, 128. On the porters see John Mole, 23221/5, IWMDS.

35. Denis Whybro, 20008/12, IWMDS; Younger, "Episodes from Korea," 349. On thinking that men suddenly encountered behind the lines were South Koreans when in fact they were Chinese see Denis Prout, 18775/3, IWMDS; Harvey, *War in Korea*, 122. On Chinese supposedly dressed as South Koreans being shot at see, e.g., Thomas Cunningham-Booth, 19913/3, IWMDS; M. N. S. McCord, 1991-05-1, NAM; Mervyn McCord, 21563/4, IWMDS; William Westwood, 19871/1, IWMDS.

36. Carew, *Korea*, 204; John Mole, 23221/5, IWMDS.

37. Farrar-Hockley, *Edge,* 53. On the Chinese giving themselves away through making too much noise see also Large, *One Man's War,* 48. On USAF efforts during the Fifth Phase Offensive see USAF Historical Division, *United States Air Force Operations,* 62. On night bombing on the 24/25 see Farrar-Hockley, *British Part, Vol. II,* 129. On USAF efforts in support of 29Bde on 23 and 24 April in the daylight hours see Carew, *Korea,* 205.

38. Carew, *Korea,* 195–202; 1RNF WD, 24–25 Apr. 1951, WO 281/1160, TNA; Perrins, *'Pretty Rough,'* 119. For his leadership Winn was awarded a DSO; some of his men thought he deserved the VC. Salmon, *Last Round,* 196, footnote.

39. Albert Tyas, 18439/1, IWMDS; see Hamill, *Ulster Rifles,* 68; No. 3, Notes from Korea, 27 March–26 Apr. 1951, p. 9, WO 308/46, TNA; 1RUR WD, 24–25 Apr. 1951, WO 281/1165, TNA.

40. Farrar-Hockley, *Edge,* 53; see also, e.g., Pte. W. Kear, AI9/K/BRIT/108, KB1073/11G Part 4, A2151, NAA.

41. Whatmore, *One Road,* 78; see Holles, *Now Thrive,* 165; Farrar-Hockley in Daniell, *Cap of Honour* (1975), 355. On Farrar-Hockley deliberately calling in bombardments very close to Gloster trenches see also David Holdswoth, 15428/2, IWMDS.

42. Farrar-Hockley, *Edge,* 52–55. On Gloster morale remaining quite solid through the battle see also, e.g., Large, *One Man's War,* 49; Stanley Davies, 15475/1, IWMDS; Sebastian Mercer, 12605/4, IWMDS; Cyril Papworth, 16618/1, IWMDS. On word about the air drop for the 25th spreading to the officers and men see, e.g., Frank Cottam, 21729/4, IWMDS; Whatmore, *One Road,* 77.

43. W. W. Harris, *Puerto Rico's Fighting 65th U.S. Infantry* (San Rafael, Calif.: Presidio, 1980), 182.

44. Younger, *Blowing Bridges,* 200–201. In fact Brodie, at age forty-seven, was only a few years older than J. P. Carne, CO of the Glosters, and Kingsley Foster, CO of the Northumberlands, but was still of course responsible for the lives of many times the number of men they were.

45. Younger, *Blowing Bridges,* 201; Harris, *Fighting 65th,* 182–83. The CO and staff officers from the 65th Infantry had cause to be grateful, had they known it, for British emotional restraint. "Small groups of the enemy had infiltrated and were operating all round and close to the Brigade HQ during the night," as the Royal Military Police historian recorded (A. V. Lovell-Knight, *The Story of the Royal Military Police* [London: Leo Cooper, 1977], 199). Some hours before they arrived at 29th Brigade HQ a friendly-fire incident had been narrowly averted when British soldiers guarding the perimeter had obeyed orders not to fire at a group of approaching foreigners who were initially thought to be Chinese but turned out to be wounded Puerto Ricans. See Davies, *Red Winds,* 98.

46. Younger, *Blowing Bridges,* 201; see Farrar-Hockley, *British Part, Vol. II,* 129.

47. Farrar-Hockley, *British Part, Vol. II,* 130–31.

48. Harris, *Fighting 65th,* 183; see 3d Infantry Division, Command Report, Apr. 1951, Incl. 2, Assistant Division Commander's Journal, 25 Apr., 07:30 hrs., Box 2898, RG 407, NARA. In the end, two attempts were made on the 25th to reach the Glosters, both quickly ending in failure. Eighth Army, Supporting Documents, Section II, Book 4, Part 7, Incl. 31, Milburn to Van Fleet, 15 May 1951, p. 3, Box 1184, RG 407, NARA.

49. Farrar-Hockley, *Edge,* 55–56; see Carew, *Korea,* 217. The Drum Major borrowed his instrument from another bugler. See P. E. Buss letter, *Soldier,* 22 July 1996, p. 12; Tony Eagles letter, *Soldier,* 2 September 1996, p. 29; Anthony Eagles, 12783/3, IWMDS.

50. Robert Hickey, 16061/2, IWMDS; Patrick Weller, 12664/1, IWMDS; Ronald Norley, 15539/3, IWMDS; Davies, *In Spite,* 23; Frank Cottam, 21729/4, IWMDS; Whatmore, *One Road,* 78 (Whatmore identified the private with the rifle as "Binman," but as there was no soldier of that name in the battalion it is likely that he was thinking of Bingham – see Harding, *Imjin Roll,* 48). See also W. J. Smyth, "RSM Smyth and the Gloster Bugle," www.thekoreanwar.co.uk/html/sound_bites.html (accessed 11 August 2007); Owen Smith, 18441/2, IWMDS; Guy Temple, 15557/2, IWMDS; Green, *Captured,* 103; Harvey, *War in Korea,* 125; Farrar-Hockley, *Edge,* 56.

4. IMJIN: THE FINAL DAY

1. Davies, *In Spite,* 23.
2. Ibid.
3. Carne quoted in *Daily Telegraph,* 2 September 1953, p. 1 (see also Carne to Joslin, 24 July 1957, pp. 4–5, CAB 157/23, TNA); Harris, *Fighting 65th,* 183; see Farrar-Hockley, *British Part, Vol. II,* 130; 29Bde History, App. H, Bde Log, 25 Apr. 1951, WO 308/42, TNA; 3d Infantry Division, Command Report with Annexes of the 65th RCT, April 1951, S-3 Journal, 25 Apr., Box 2963, RG 407, NARA; Villahermosa, *Honor and Fidelity,* 132–33.
4. 29Bde History, App. H, Bde Log, 25 Apr. 1951, WO 308/42, TNA; see Farrar-Hockley, *British Part, Vol. II,* 131. The drop may also have been canceled because it was thought that additional supplies would only weigh down the men when they tried to break out. See Eighth Army, Supporting Documents, Section II, Book 4, Part 7, Incl. 31, Milburn to Van Fleet, 26 May 1951, p. 3, Box 1184, RG 407, NARA.
5. K. Walters, http://members.tripod.com/~Glosters/kpow1.htm (accessed 18 April 2005); see K. V. Godwin, http://members.tripod.com/~Glosters/kpow1.htm (accessed 18 April 2005).
6. Carew, *Korea,* 213–15; Ronald Norley, 15539/3, IWMDS; see Farrar-Hockley, *Edge,* 57–58; Matthews, *No Rice,* 13; K. Walters, http://members.tripod.com/~Glosters/kpow1.htm (accessed 18 April 2005). The comment on the adjutant's bravery was made by Captain A. N. "Jumbo" Wilson to Private Tony Eagles (see Anthony Eagles, 17283/3, IWMDS). On Farrar-Hockley see also David Holdsworth, 15428/2, IWMDS; Sebastian Mercer, 12605/5, IWMDS; Frank Cottam, 21729/4, IWMDS; Henry Ponsford, 18456/1, IWMDS.
7. Farrar-Hockley, *Edge,* 58–59; Matthews, *No Rice,* 14. Along with Washbrook, Captain C. S. Dain of the Royal Artillery, though wounded, helped bring down accurate artillery fire while serving as a FOO with the surrounded Glosters. See Citation for Capt. C. S. R. Dain, f. 54, K-586, WO 373/119, TNA.
8. David Holdsworth, 15428/2, IWMDS (see also Davies, *In Spite,* 24; Andrew Salmon, *Last Round,* 214). On the adjutant's views concerning napalm see Farrar-Hockley, *British Part, Vol. II,* 130. On the Chinese drawing back after the napalm strike see Farrar-Hockley, *Edge,* 60–63; Whatmore, *One Road,* 79; Frank Cottam, 21729/4, IWMDS. On dislike of napalm see, e.g., Jack Arnall, 09972/1, IWMDS; Cutforth, *Korean Reporter,* 172; Davies, *Red Winds,* 74; Green, *Captured,* 103.
9. Harvey, *War in Korea,* 125; Farrar-Hockley, *Edge,* 63–65.
10. WO 308/42, 29Bde History, App. H, Bde Log, 25 Apr. 1951, TNA; Farrar-Hockley, *Edge,* 63–65; see Farrar-Hockley, *British Part, Vol. II,* 131. After this the 62 Set was destroyed in order to prevent it falling into enemy hands.
11. Carne to Joslen, 24 July 1957, p. 6, CAB 157/23, TNA.
12. Harvey, *War in Korea,* 128; Robert Hickey, 16061/2, IWMDS; Farrar-Hock-

ley, *Edge*, 64; see Davies, *In Spite*, 24–25; Patrick Weller, 12664/2, IWMDS. On Hickey letting the married men go but asking the single men among his staff to stay see also Cyril Papworth, 16618/3, IWMDS. On admiration among the wounded for the MO and his staff who remained with them see, e.g., Cpl. G. Elliott, AI9/K/BRIT/489, KB1073/11G Part 4, A2151, NAA.

13. Davies, *In Spite*, 26; Stanley Davies, 15475/2, IWMDS.

14. David Kaye, 17468/2, IWMDS; Frank Cottam, 21729/4, IWMDS (see also Sgt. F. W. Cottam, AI9/K/BRIT/875, KB 1073/11G Part 3, A2151, NAA); Green, *Captured*, 104; Matthews, *No Rice*, 19–20; see also, e.g., WOII G. E. Askew, AI9/K/BRIT/869, KB1073/11G Part 3, A2151, NAA; Pte. D. R. Butcher, AI9/K/BRIT/92, KB1073/11G Part 3, A2151, NAA; Gnr. J. C. Dabbs, AI9/K/BRIT/606, KB1073/11G Part 3, A2151, NAA.

15. Anthony Farrar-Hockley, 30102/1, IWMDS; William Westwood, 19871/1, IWMDS; see also Charles Sharpling, 18544/1, IWMDS; Patrick Weller, 12664/2, IWMDS.

16. Cyril Cunningham, *No Mercy, No Leniency* (Barnsley: Leo Cooper, 2000), 76. According to a U.S. account, Carne, like the MO, had elected to stay with the wounded. See Lieut. Colonel James P. Carne, British Army, f. 453, K-668, WO 373/119, TNA.

17. Harvey, *War in Korea*, 130; Whatmore, *One Road*, 80; see David Holdsworth, 15428/2, IWMDS.

18. Harvey, *War in Korea*, 131.

19. Ibid.; Whatmore, *One Road*, 81; Harding, *Imjin Roll*, 28. On men captured because they stayed with wounded mates see, e.g., Byron Murphy, 15338/4, IWMDS; Ronald Norley, 15539/3, IWMDS. On the wounded see also, e.g., Lt. T. Conneely, AI9/K/BRIT/954, KB1073/11G Part 3, A2151, NAA.

20. Whatmore, *One Road*, 83; Walter Cleveland, 17348/4, IWMDS; Harvey, *War in Korea*, 132–33; Harding, *Imjin Roll*, 28; Salmon, *Last Round*, 222–23; David Holdsworth, 15428/3, IWMDS; see Owen Smith, 18441/2, IWMDS; Donald Dickensen in *Daily Express*, 27 April 1951, p. 2. Six others, led by Lieutenant Bob Martin, who took a different route out of the valley, also survived. Salmon, *Last Round*, 223.

21. Harding, *Imjin Roll*, 23–26, 30–36, 80–81. On the Chinese making efforts to capture rather than kill parties of Glosters who were trying to make their way back to U.N. lines see, e.g., Cpl. W. K. Westwood, AI9/K/BRIT/157, KB1073/11G, Part 7, A2151, NAA; Anthony Farrar-Hockley, 30102/1, IWMDS.

22. On the Belgians see Crahay narrative, p. 13, WO 308/49, TNA. On the clearing force see Younger, "Episodes from Korea," 348; Maj. Allan [*sic*] E. Younger, f. 434, K-720, WO 373/119, TNA; George Cooper, *Fight, Dig, and Live* (Barnsley: Pen and Sword, 2011), 42.

23. Farrar-Hockley, *British Part, Vol. II*, 133; Perrins, *'Pretty Rough,'* 119–20; Cooper, *Fight, Dig, and Live*, 42. On the Oxfords, the Bofors guns, and tanks shedding tracks see Martin, *K Force*, 42–43.

24. Salmon, *Last Round*, 227; see O'Kane, *O'Kane's Korea*, 62; Hamill, *Ulster Rifles*, 69; Farrar-Hockley, *British Part, Vol. II*, 133.

25. 1RNF WD, 25 Apr. 1951, WO 281/1160, TNA; 1RUR WD, 26 Apr. 1951 [note that events for 25 April were wrongly listed as occurring on 26 April], WO 281/1165, TNA; Hamill, *Ulster Rifles*, 71.

26. A. Perrins, 19387/4, IWMDS. For a more detailed account of the withdrawal see Salmon, *Last Round*, chapter 10. On the accidental shelling of C Company see, e.g., Lt. J. M. C. Nicholls, p. 1, AI9/K/BRIT/42, KB1073/11G Part 3, A2151, NAA; Rfn. L. Jones and Rfn. H. O'Kane in Donald Knox, *The Korean War: Uncertain Vic-*

tory: An Oral History (San Diego, Calif.: HBJ, 1988), 173–74. Foster's low opinion of Rickord's textbook tactical withdrawal was not shared by higher authority, the U.S. Army being sufficiently impressed by his leadership during the Imjin battle – including the final withdrawal – to put him up for a Silver Star. Maj. Gerald P. Rickord, f. 434, K-719, HQ I Corps, WO 373/119, TNA.

27. Thomas Cunningham-Booth, 19913/3, IWMDS; Mitchell letter, 3 May 1951, in Perrins, *'Pretty Rough,'* 133; see ibid., 120; Hamill, *Ulster Rifles,* 70. On the friendly-fire incident with C Company and also the breakdown of communications and command and control among the Ulsters see, e.g., Vernon Whitamore, 19664/2, IWMDS; Gordon Potts, 23213/7, IWMDS; William Gibson, 16850/3, IWMDS; George Hobson, 16853/1, IWMDS; see also *Quis Separabit,* Winter 1951, p. 79. On 8 Platoon, Y Company getting pinned down – and then captured – see Sgt. D. McAnulty, AI9/K/BRIT882, KB1073/11G Part 5, A2151, NAA. On the breakdown of command and control among the Fusiliers see also, e.g., Dennis Matthews, 12729/2, IWMDS; William Bye, 20375/1, IWMDS; David Sharp, 17929/3, IWMDS.

28. William Gibson, 16850/4, IWMDS. On fighting on the saddle see, e.g., Peter Ormrod, 09863/2-3, IWMDS.

29. Kinne, *Wooden Boxes,* 26; 1RNF WD, 25 Apr. 1951, WO 281/1160, TNA; see Kingsley Foster obituary in *St. George's Gazette* 69, no. 821 (1951): 91. Foster had himself been strongly warned against going farther down the road by an Ulsters officer. See Winn, *Korean Campaign Supplement,* 17; Salmon, *Last Round,* 235.

30. Noble, *Shoot First,* 185. On 45FR coming under small-arms fire and firing over open sights see also 45FR narrative, p. 79, WO 308/44, TNA; *45 Field Regiment* RA *in the Imjin River Battle* pamphlet, p. 5, IWMDD (material drawn from *Garrison Herald* 2, no. 33 [1954]: 24–25); IWMDS John Smith, 18525/1, IWMDS. With the exception of C Troop, which was surrounded, 170 Mortar battery executed a similar fighting withdrawal. See citation for Maj. T. V. Fisher-Hoch, ff. 433–34, K-668, WO 373/119, TNA.

31. On Brigade HQ moving back, coming under fire, and getting support from 11LAA see, e.g., Davies, *Red Winds,* 99–102.

32. Dennis Matthews, 12729/2, IWMDS; Thomas McMahon, 18819/4, IWMDS; Thomas Cunningham-Booth, 19913/3, IWMDS; Holmes to Golsen, 2 Oct. 1957, p. 3, CAB 157/23, TNA. For NCOs rising to the challenge see, e.g., Cooper, *Fight, Dig, and Live,* 42–43.

33. Mervyn McCord, 21563/7, IWMDS (see also M. N. S. McCord, 1991-05-1-1, NAM). On giving Hamill the benefit of the doubt see Salmon, *Last Round,* 223, footnote.

34. Mervyn McCord, 21563/7, IWMDS; Gordon Potts, 23213/8, IWMDS; John Dyer, 18474/2, IWMDS. On individuals playing dead see, e.g., Thomas Cunningham-Booth, 19913/4, IWMDS; L. Jones in Knox, *Korean War,* 334. On other cases of men losing their nerve see, e.g., Alfred Gilder, 20057/2, IWMDS.

35. Peter Ormrod, 09863/3, IWMDS; Albert Tyas, 18439/2, IWMDS; see also Dennis Matthews, 12729/2, IWMDS; Fus. S. G. Bartell, AI9/K/BRIT/161, KB1073/11G Part 3, A2151, NAA.

36. M. N. S. McCord, 1991-05-1-1, NAM; Gordon Potts, 23213/7, IWMDS. On choosing the tank option see, e.g., David Sharpe, 17929/3, IWMDS; Albert Tyas, 18439/2, IWMDS.

37. John Dyer, 18474/2, IWMDS; Peter Ormrod, 09863/3, IWMDS; see, e.g., M. N. S. McCord, 1991-05-1-1, NAM; Denis Whybro, 20008/12-13, IWMDS; John Dyer quoted in *The Guardian,* 14 April 2001.

38. O'Kane, *O'Kane's Korea,* 64; Vernon [Peter] Whitamore, 19664/2, IWMDS; see also, e.g., Martin, *K Force,* 55; Thomas Cunningham-Booth, 19913/4, IWMDS; Denis Prout, 18775/3, IWMDS; David Sharp, 17929/3, IWMDS; Albert Tyas, 18439/2, IWMDS; Lt. S. W. Cooper, AI9/K/BRIT/955, KB1073/11G Part 3, A2151, NAA. On men on tank hulls making it difficult for the crews to operate effectively see, e.g., Denis Whybro, 20008/12, IWMDS. On thirty men to a tank see 8RIH WD, App. Q, p. 3, WO 281/1142, TNA. On the loss of the ambulance half-track see Douglas Patchett, 16795/1, IWMDS; Peter Ormrod, 09863/3, IWMDS. On placing wounded on tanks as a last resort see, e.g., Martin, *K Force,* 63. On the loss of six tanks (4 Centurions) see Farrar-Hockley, *British Part, Vol. II,* 134.

39. Roy Utting, 17568/4, IWMDS; Peter Ormrod, 09863/3, IWMDS; see Andrew Scott, 16855/2, IWMDS; Norman Sweetlove in Doherty, *Sons of Ulster,* 157–58; Hamill, *Ulster Rifles,* 71. The Centurions may have thought they were enemy troops who Huth had been warned were about to overtake the Ulsters. Fitzroy, *Men of Valour,* 284. On the Korean porters getting out see Gordon Potts, 23213/7, IWMDS.

40. Crahay narrative, pp. 15–16, WO 308/49, TNA; see Gunst, Philips, and Vehaegen, *Saison,* 209–15; Winn, *Campaign Supplement,* 18–19; Salmon, *Last Round,* 244–46, 252.

41. Pearson to Winn, 27 Apr. 1951 in Perrins, *'Pretty Rough,'* 125; Gordon Potts, 23213/8, IWMDS; Eighth Army, Supporting Documents, Section II, Book 4, Part 7, Incl. 31, HQ 3d Infantry Division, Office of the AC of S G-3, G-3 Summary on 29th BIB Action, 22–25 Apr. 1951, p. 4, Box 1184, RG 407, NARA. On Huth's parting shots see Fitzroy, *Men of Valour,* 285. On ammunition expenditure in 45FR, 23–25 April, see 3d Infantry Division, Artillery Command Report, April 1951, Unit Reports 143, 149, Box 2934, RG 407, NARA. When the 40-mm rounds of the light antiaircraft battery are included, the total artillery rounds expended were somewhere between 17,000 and 20,000. See Extracts from DO report dated 24 July 1951 by Lt.-Col. M. T. Young, p. 1, WO 308/50, TNA; HQ I Corps citation for Lt.-Col. Maris T. Young, f. 433, K-716, WO 373/119, TNA. On ammunition expenditure in 170 IMB, see Fisher-Hoch, "170 Independent Mortar Battery," 252. On Ellery appealing to Milburn see Miles Speer letter to John Winn and Charles Mitchell, 29 Apr. 1951, in Perrins, *'Pretty Rough,'* 128. On the Northumberland losses for 25 April see ibid., 342–60. On the strength of the Ulsters by the end see *North Irish Brigade Chronicle* 1, no. 4 (1952): 31. On the Belgians on 25 April see also J. Dargent, "Notes sur le combat de nuit: l'infiltration," *Bulletin Militaire* 65 (1953): 327.

5. KAPYONG: THE FIRST DAY

1. Gray, *Danger Close,* 51.

2. 16FR WD, 22 Apr. 1951, WA-K 1 DAK 1 2/1/7, ANZ.

3. M. Czuboka, p. 5, www.kvacanada.com/stories_czuboka.htm (accessed 28 February 2010); B. Ferguson in Bob Breen, *The Battle of Kapyong* (St. Georges Heights, N.S.W.: Headquarters Training Command, 1992), 22; see also, e.g., E. L. Eyre in Norman Bartlett, ed., *With the Australians in Korea* (Canberra: AWM, 1954), 90; Tom Muggleton, S02652, AWM; S. Connelly in *Kapyong,* Arcimedia. On 3RAR and "Sherwood Forest" – in fact an orchard – see P. J. Knowles, A Rifleman's View of 'The Battle of Kapyong', p. 1, PR83/154, AWM. On 2PPCLI and "Happy Valley" see Bishop, *King's Bishop,* 118.

4. O'Dowd, *Valiant Company,* 150; McGibbon, *New Zealand, Vol. II,* 121; Breen, *Battle of Kapyong,* 23; Gray, *Danger Close,* 142; Farrar-Hockley, *British Part, Vol. II,* 141; Robert Wellcombe, *All the Blue Bon-*

nets (London: Arms and Armour, 1980), 132–33; Anderson, *Argyll and Sutherland,* 226–27. 1MX would shortly be relieved by 1st battalion King's Shropshire Light Infantry, while 2PPCLI was transferred to the newly arrived 25th Canadian Infantry Brigade. On 28CB see Eaton, *Something Extra.* On Stone recovering from smallpox see Watson, "From Calgary to Kap'yong," 111.

5. Gordon, *Embarrassing Australian,* 153–54; Barry Reed, 2001-02-397, NAM; see also Gallaway, *Last Call,* 241; Van Fleet to Chung, 2 May 1951 and attachments, Box 86, James Van Fleet Papers, GCM. On problems with the 6th ROK Division and other units see Il-Song Park, "Dragon from the Stream," 112–13; Bryan Robert Gilby, "Fighting in the Korean War: The American Military Mission from 1946–1953" (PhD diss., Ohio State University, 2004), 174–75; Ja Jongman, "Making Cold War Soldiers: The Americanization of the South Korean Army, 1945–1955" (PhD diss., University of North Carolina at Chapel Hill, 2006), 94–95. The 6th ROK Division had no heavy machine-guns, no 4.2-inch mortars, and little ammunition for smaller mortars. James A. Van Fleet, "The Truth About the War in Korea: How We Can Win With What We Have," *Life,* 18 May 1953, p. 157.

6. Farrar-Hockley, *British Part, Vol. II,* 138. In the first quoted paragraph Farrar-Hockley attached the 40th Army to the 9th Army Group; in fact is was part of the 8th Army Group, though nevertheless assigned to take care of the eastern portion of 6th ROK Division. Mossman, *Ebb and Flow,* 381; Rottman, *Order of Battle,* 177–79.

7. James A. Van Fleet, "The Truth About Korea," 128.

8. That IX Corps was likely to be attacked on or after 22 April was known from prisoner interrogations, but not exact details as to enemy strength and axis of advance. See, e.g., Lynn Montross, Hubard D. Kuokka, Norman W. Hicks, *U.S. Marine Operations in Korea, 1950–1953: Volume IV, The East-Central Front* (Washington, D.C.: Historical Branch, G-3, HQ U.S. Marine Corps, 1962), 100. It has been suggested that General Ridgway expected the 6th ROK Division to collapse, but that under "Plan Audacious" he expected the U.S. divisions on the flanks to hold and funnel the Chinese into a salient that then could be pinched off by the 1st Cavalry Division waiting in army reserve, and that 27BCB only became involved because operations elsewhere necessitated the diversion of two-thirds of the 1st Cavalry Division to other trouble spots (see O'Dowd, *Valiant Company,* Appendix A). The records concerning Audacious, however, only indicate that Ridgway planned to withdraw to a series of prearranged defensive phase lines once the Chinese attacked and use his reserves – including 27BCB – when and where needed. The bulk of the 1st Cavalry Division, it should be noted, was not committed until the 25th (Appleman, *Ridgway Duels,* 440, 483).

9. Mossman, *Ebb and Flow,* 381–82; Korea Institute of Military History, *The Korean War, Vol. II* (Lincoln: University of Nebraska Press, 2000), 629.

10. *Mossman, Ebb and Flow,* 382; IX Corps Command Report, Book I, April 1951, Box 1797, RG 407, NARA.

11. Mossman, *Ebb and Flow,* 382; Farrar-Hockley, *British Part, Vol. II,* 139.

12. Hoge to Chang, 28 Apr. 1951, Box 12, James Van Fleet Papers, GCM; Sun Yup Paik, *From Pusan to Panmunjom* (Washington, D.C.: Brassey's, 1992), 144; Russell A. Gugeler, *Combat Actions in Korea* (Washington, D.C.: Office of the Chief of Military History, U.S. Army, 1970), 154–55; see Eighth Army Command Report: Section IV: After-Action Interviews: Book 2: Tanks Above Kapyong, Maj. Thomas A. Murphy, Asst. G3, IX Corps, p. 1, Box 56, RG 550, NARA; Mossman, *Ebb and Flow,*

382–83; Farrar-Hockley, *British Part, Vol. II,* 139; Korea Institute of Military History, *Korean War, Vol. II,* 630.

13. Mossman, *Ebb and Flow,* 383; see, e.g., 2nd Chemical Mortar Bn Command Report, 1 Sep. 1950–1 Aug. 1951, p. 16, Box 5030, RG 407, NARA.

14. McGibbon, *New Zealand, Vol. II,* 110.

15. Malcolm, *Argylls,* 84.

16. Wilson, *Sum of Things,* 187.

17. McGibbon, *New Zealand, Vol. II,* 111; 16FR WD, 22 Apr. 1951, WA-K 1 DAK 1 2/1/7, ANZ.

18. McGibbon, *New Zealand, Vol. II,* 111.

19. Ibid., 111–12.

20. T. Frazer in *Kapyong,* Arcimedia; see McGibbon, *New Zealand, Vol. II,* 111–12; 16FR WD, 22 Apr. 1951, WA-K 1 DAK 1 2/1/7, ANZ; Ralph Porter, "Battle of Kapyong – 16 NZ Fd Regt, 23–25 April 1951," *Duty First* 1, no. 4 (1992): 39. Stories of ROKs being bashed about and run over may have been exaggerated. See McGibbon, *New Zealand, Vol. II,* 432n28.

21. Van Fleet, "Truth About Korea," 128. On the 1st Marine Division in the Chinese spring offensive see Montrose, Kuokka, and Hicks, *U.S. Marine Operations,* 105ff.

22. Mossman, *Ebb and Flow,* 383.

23. William M. Hoge interview, p. 174, http://140.194.76.129/publications/eng-pamphlets/ep870-1-25/inter.pdf (accessed 25 January 2010).

24. Mossman, *Ebb and Flow,* 384.

25. Gray, *Danger Close,* 51–52.

26. 3RAR WD, 23 Apr. 1951, 4/28, Series 85, AWM; 2PPCLI WD, 23 Apr. 1951, Vol. 18318, RG-24-C-3, NLAC; see 27Bde WD, 23 Apr. 1951, WO 281/710, TNA. On the equipment losses of 6th ROK Division see Mossman, *Ebb and Flow,* 407.

27. See Petrie in Gray, *Danger Close,* 163; D. P. Laughlin, B Coy Report – Battle of Kapyong, 23–24 Apr. 1951, p. 1, 665/7/1, Series 114, AWM.

28. Malcolm, *Argylls,* 85; see also, e.g., Sim in Bjarnason, *Triumph,* 97.

6. KAPYONG: THE SECOND DAY

1. CBC Radio, *Five Nights,* 22 April 1976, archives.cbc.ca/war_conflict/korean_war/clips/782/ (accessed 27 August 2009).

2. Joe Vezgoff, www.australiansatwar.gov.au/ko_akh.html (accessed 7 October 2009).

3. 27Bde WD, 23 Apr. 1951, WO 281/710, TNA; 2PPCLI WD, 23 Apr. 1951, Vol. 18318, RG-24-C-3, NLAC; The Battle of Kapyong, p. 1, 145.2 P7013 (D4), DHH; O'Neill, *Australia, Vol. II,* 136–37. The suggestion that Burke planned to deploy 2PPCLI to Hill 677 and 3RAR to Hill 504 because the latter was more experienced and therefore in a better position to hold a lower and more approachable feature (see M. Edwards in *Kapyong,* Arcimedia) seems unlikely given that 1MX, though just as experienced as 3RAR, was supposed to hold the highest feature of all, Hill 794.

4. 16FR WD, 23 Apr. 1951, WA-K 1 DAK 1 2/1/7, ANZ; McGibbon, *New Zealand, Vol. II,* 114.

5. Farrar-Hockley, *British Part, Vol. II,* 141; McGibbon, *New Zealand, Vol. II,* 114; see also 27Bde WD, 23 Apr. 1951, WO 281/710, TNA; Denis Gavin, "Korea – The Battle of Kapyong," *RSA Review* 64, no. 5 (1988): 16.

6. McKeown, *Kapyong Remembered,* 17.

7. P. J. Knowles, A Rifleman's View of 'The Battle of Kapyong', p. 1, PR83/154, AWM; Harry Honner, "A Kiwi Opo with 3RAR Korea 1951," *Duty First* 1, no. 4 (1992): 33.

8. Breen, *Battle of Kapyong,* 27. On the "precautionary measure" nature of 27Bde thinking at this stage see Comments made on report of Capt. Gerke, n/d, 2 (a.), 665/7/1, Series 114, AWM. On the Chinese

as supposedly six to seven miles north of Hill 504 see Maj. D. P. Laughlin, B Coy Report – Battle of Kapyong, 23–24 Apr. 1951, p. 1, 665/7/1, Series 114, AWM.

9. O'Dowd, *Valiant Company,* 154 (see also O'Dowd in *Kapyong,* Arcimedia); Breen, *Battle of Kapyong,* 27; see Gallaway, *Last Call,* 241–42.

10. See 2PPCLI WD, 23 Apr. 1951, Vol. 18318, RG-24-C-3, NLAC.

11. 27Bde WD, 23 Apr. 1951, WO 281/710, TNA.

12. Farrar-Hockley, *British Part, Vol. II,* 141; Mossman, *Ebb and Flow,* 391; see 2nd Chemical Mortar Bn Command Report, 1 Sep. 50–1 Aug. 51, Part VII – Narrative Summary Period 1 to 30 April 1951, p. 17, Box 5030, RG 407, NARA. The tank company was missing its third platoon, which was guarding the IX Corps CP. Eighth Army, Command Report: Section IV: After-Action Interviews: Book 2: Tanks Above Kapyong, K. W. Koch, p. 1, Box 56, RG 550, NARA.

13. Maj. D. P. Laughlin, B Coy Report – Battle of Kapyong 23–24 Apr. 1951, p. 1, 665/7/1, Series 114, AWM.

14. Gray, *Danger Close,* 57; see Eighth Army Command Report: Section IV: After-Action Interviews: Book 2: Tanks Above Kapyong, Wade H. Padgett, Harold Burros, John L. Mazyck, Otho C. Bragg, Box 56, RG 550, NARA.

15. Arthur "Nick" Hutley, 18205/4, IWMDS; Capt. K. J. Carter, Kapyong – April 1951, 681.013, DHH; J. N. Shipster, ed., *The Die-Hards in Korea* (Middlesex: The Middlesex Regiment, 1983), 65; Hickey, *Korean War,* 212.

16. See Stone and Castonguay, *Korea 1951,* 16.

17. O'Neill, *Australia, Vol. II,* 138; Ferguson in Breen, *Battle of Kapyong,* 34.

18. Ferguson in Breen, *Battle of Kapyong,* 27.

19. See O'Neill, *Australia, Vol. II,* 138–39; Breen, *Battle of Kapyong,* 29–37.

20. See Watson, "From Calgary to Kap'yong," 23; Brown, "Loyal Edmonton Regiment," 91, 143, 167–68, passim.

21. Stone in McKeown, *Kapyong Remembered,* 20; Stone in Melady, *Korea,* 73–74.

22. Gray, *Danger Close,* 58.

23. See McGibbon, *New Zealand, Vol. II,* 115.

24. On 27Bde indicating "a quiet night" on Hill 504, see Gray, *Danger Close,* 57. On the intent to push up to Hill 794, as Burke had originally planned, see note following 1700 O Group, 2PPCLI WD, 23 Apr. 1951, Vol. 18318, RG-24-C-3, NLAC.

25. McGibbon, *New Zealand, Vol. II,* 116.

26. Tunstall, *I Fought,* 112; see also, e.g., Arthur Hutley, 18205/4, IWMDS; 1MX WD, 23 Apr. 1951, 1900 hrs., 1999-11-189-21, NAM.

27. McGibbon, *New Zealand, Vol. II,* 118–20; 16 FR WD, 23 Apr. 1951, WA-K 1 DAK 1 /2/1/7, ANZ; Shipster, *Die-Hards,* 65–66.

28. Ben O'Dowd, S02659, AWM; Joe Vezgoff, "Korea Remembered," p. 10, www.kmike.com/oz/kr/chapter1.htm (accessed 7 October 2009).

29. Some sources suggest 3RAR was in position as early as 5:30 PM (P. J. Knowles, A Rifleman's View of 'The Battle of Kapyong', p. 1, PR 83/154, AWM), or 6 PM (Maj. B. O'Dowd, A Coy Report – Battle of Kapyong, p. 1, 665/7/1, Series 114, AWM; Patrick Knowles, 19388/2, IWMDS; Bartlett, *With the Australians,* 92; James J. Atkinson, *The Kapyong Battalion* [Ryde, N.S.W.: NSW Historical Society, 1977], 17), while others indicate 8 PM (2PPCLI WD, 23 Apr. 1951, Vol. 18318, RG-24-C3, NLAC; O'Neill, *Australia, Vol. II,* 138–39). The 3RAR WD does not provide a time.

30. P. J. Knowles, A Rifleman's View of 'The Battle of Kapyong', p. 1, PR 83/154, AWM.

31. Joe Vezgoff, "Korea Remembered," p. 10, www.kmike.com/oz/kr/chapter1.htm (accessed 7 October 2009); also Joe Vezgoff, www.australiansatwar.gov.au/ko_akh.html (accessed 7 October 2009). On the improvised nature of the defenses on Hill 504 and the absence of wire and mines see Jack Gallaway, www.australiansatwar.gov.au/ko_akh.html (accessed 7 October 2009).

32. 2PPCLI WD, 23 Apr. 1951, Vol. 18318, RG-24-C3, NLAC.

33. Edwards in Gray, *Danger Close,* 58.

34. CBC Radio, *Five Nights;* see also Bishop, *King's Bishop,* 118.

35. Wanniandy in Gray, *Danger Close,* 61, 63.

36. Melady, *Korea,* 73 (see McKeown, *Kapyong Remembered,* 17; J. L. Granatstein and David J. Bercuson, *War and Peacekeeping* [Toronto: Key Porter, 1991], 116); see also, e.g., Crook in "Blood on the Hills," Breakthrough Films and Television; Edwards and Lapointe in Bjarnason, *Triumph,* 108; O. R. Browne, "Kapyong! What Is It?" *The Patrician* 20 (1967): 19.

37. LaPointe in Gray, *Danger Close,* 61; see Gray in *Kapyong,* produced by John Lewis (North Fitzroy, Vic.: Arcimedia, 2011). Major Jack George of C Company positioned his men atop Hill 677 but was due to go on leave to Japan; "and he was in tears when he left," a veteran recalled, "so we knew we were in for something bad." CBC Radio, *Five Nights.* Other groups of retreating ROKs were observed or heard still heading south in the valley overnight. See MacLeod in Gray, *Danger Close,* 68; Melnechuk in Hepenstall, *Find the Dragon,* 93.

38. Dicken in Bercuson, *The Patricias,* 259; see Petrie, Fouldes, Munro in Gray, *Danger Close,* 53–54, 63.

39. Munro in Hepenstall, *Find the Dragon,* 92.

40. 2PPCLI WD, 23 Apr. 1951, Vol. 18318, RG-24-C3, NLAC; Wood, *Strange Battleground,* 76. On half-track problems see Hurst and Hoffman in Gray, *Danger Close,* 62–63; McKeown, *Kapyong Remembered,* 20; Courtenay, *Patricias,* 188, 191.

41. Transcript of *Korea: Canada's Forgotten War,* produced by H. Clifford Chadderton (Ottawa: War Amps of Canada, 1989), p. 8, www.waramps.ca/military/korea.html (accessed 2 February 2010).

42. McKeown, *Kapyong Remembered,* 20–21; see Sim in Gray, *Danger Close,* 64.

43. Campbell in Hepenstall, *Find the Dragon,* 95; see, e.g., Reynolds in Bjarnason, *Triumph,* 119.

44. Gray, *Danger Close,* 54; Lynch in Bjarnason, *Triumph,* 120.

45. Munro in Bercuson, *Patricias,* 259.

46. Bishop, *King's Bishop,* 119; see Gray, *Danger Close,* 53.

47. See Cook in Hepenstall, *Find the Dragon,* 91; Cliff Chadderton, www.cliffchadderton.ca/blog/?page_id=15 (accessed 2 October 2009); Herst in Gray, *Danger Close,* 56, see also 118.

48. On 2PPCLI encounters with ROKs see, e.g., Bishop, *King's Bishop,* 121. On Chinese night patrols and 2PPCLI see Campbell in Hepenstall, *Find the Dragon,* 95. On the full moon see Maj. D. P. Laughlin, B Coy Report – Battle of Kapyong, 23–24 Apr. 1951, p. 4, 665/7/1, Series 114, AWM. On listening to the RAR fight over the radio link see Browne in Gray, *Danger Close,* 65. On watching what was going on across the valley see, e.g., Munro in Hepenstall, *Find the Dragon,* 93.

49. O'Dowd, *Valiant Company,* 162; Maj. D. P. Laughlin, B Company Report – Battle of Kapyong, 23–24 Apr. 1951, p. 6, 665/7/1, Series 114, AWM.

50. Farrar-Hockley, *British Part, Vol. II,* 143.

51. O'Dowd, *Valiant Company,* 162; O'Dowd in *Kapyong,* Arcimedia.

52. Breen, *Battle of Kapyong,* 45. O'Dowd himself had dismissed a report from 1 Platoon about an hour earlier that

suggested the Chinese were already below his positions. See P. J. Knowles, A Rifleman's View of 'The Battle of Kapyong', p. 1, PR83.154, AWM.

53. 2nd Infantry Division: Command Report, 72nd Tank Battalion, Apr. 1951, p. 6, Box 2729, RG 406, NARA. The time of the first attacks is given in this source as 11 PM. However, other sources suggest somewhere around 9:30–10:00 PM. See Eighth Army Command Report: Section IV: After-Action Interviews: Tanks Above Kapyong, Blumenson summary, p. 1, Box 56, RG 550, NARA; Farrar-Hockley, *British Part, Vol. II,* 143; Breen, *Battle of Kapyong,* 45; W. N. Gravener, D Company in the Battle of Kapyong, p. 1, 665/7/1, Series 114, AWM.

54. Eighth Army Command Report: Section IV: After-Action Interviews: Book 2: Tanks Above Kapyong, Kenneth W. Koch, p. 2, Robert B. Brown, p. 1, Box 56, RG 550, NARA; see ibid., Leroy W. Ritchotte, p. 1, Bert Tomlinson, p. 1; 2nd Infantry Division: Command Report, 72nd Tank Battalion, Apr. 1951, p. 6, Box 2729, RG 407, NARA; Farrar-Hockley, *British Part, Vol. II,* 143; O'Dowd, *Valiant Company,* 163.

55. Eighth Army Command Report: Section IV: After-Action Interviews: Book 2: Tanks Above Kapyong, Wilfred D. Millar, pp. 1–2, Box 56, RG 550, NARA.

56. Ibid., Wilfred D. Millar, pp. 1–2; see in ibid., Kenneth W. Koch, pp. 2–3, Robert B. Brown, p. 1, and Bert Tomlinson, p. 1; Young and Millar in Breen, *Battle of Kapyong,* 48–50; Young in Bartlett, *With the Australians,* 95; 2nd Infantry Division: Command Report, 72nd Tank Battalion, Apr. 1951, p. 6, Box 2729, RG 407, NARA.

57. O'Neill, *Australia, Vol. II,* 141; Maj. D. P. Laughlin, B Coy Report – Battle of Kapyong, 23–24 Apr. 1951, p. 5, 665/7/1, Series 114, AWM; ibid., Maj. B. O'Dowd, A Coy Report – Battle of Kapyong, 23–24 Apr. 1951, p. 1, 665/7/1, Series 114, AWM.

58. O'Neill, *Australia, Vol. II,* 142.

59. O'Dowd, *Valiant Company,* 164; McGibbon, *New Zealand, Vol. II,* 121. In fact a survey of the area had previously been carried out and was available (ibid.).

60. Ben O'Dowd, S02659, AWM; see also Eighth Army Command Report: Section IV: After-Action Interviews: Book 2: Tanks Above Kapyong, A. Argent, p. 1, Box 56, RG 550, NARA. The command report of the 2nd Chemical Mortar Battalion suggests that B Company did not withdraw until dawn on the 24th, admittedly without its weapons but in good order. See 2nd Chemical Mortar Battalion Narrative Report, 1 Sep. 1950–1 Aug. 1951, p. 18, Box 5030, RG 407, NARA. However, at around midnight a patrol from 3RAR Headquarters Company had come across its position already abandoned. O'Neill, *Australia, Vol. II,* 145.

61. Ben O'Dowd, S02659, AWM; see O'Dowd, *Valiant Company,* 166–67. On the Chinese having grenades and picking up rifles as they went see, e.g., O'Dowd in Breen, *Battle of Kapyong,* 52; Douglas H. Mancktelow, *Atsuko and the Aussie* (North Vancouver, B.C.: DMA, 1991), 35.

62. Breen, *Battle of Kapyong,* 53; see B. O'Dowd, A Coy Report – Battle of Kapyong, 23–24 Apr. 1951, p. 2, 665/7/1, Series 114, AWM.

63. B. O'Dowd, A Coy Report – Battle of Kapyong, 23–24 Apr. 1951, p. 2, 665/7/1, Series 114, AWM; O'Dowd, *Valiant Company,* 167; Ben O'Dowd, S02659, AWM; Patrick Knowles, 19388/2, IWMDS; P. J. Knowles, A Rifleman's View of 'The Battle of Kapyong,' p. 2, PR83/254, AWM; Bartlett, *With the Australians,* 98.

64. Patrick Knowles, 19388/2, IWMDS.

65. P. J. Knowles, A Rifleman's View of 'The Battle of Kapyong,' pp. 2–3, PR83/154, AWM.

66. O'Dowd, *Valiant Company,* 168.

67. B. O'Dowd, A Coy Report – Battle of Kapyong, 23–24 Apr. 1951, p. 3, 665/7/1,

Series 114, AWM; O'Dowd, *Valiant Company,* 169; Patrick Knowles, 19388/2, IWMDS.

68. Laughlin thought the artillery support did eventually arrive (D. P. Laughlin, B Coy Report – Battle of Kapyong, 23–24 Apr. 1951, p. 6, 665/7/1, Series 114, AWM) though the New Zealand official history seems slightly puzzled as to who provided it (McGibbon, *New Zealand, Vol. II,* 123) and O'Dowd was pretty certain that none could have been provided to B Company (O'Dowd, *Valiant Company,* 164–66).

69. Maj. D. P. Laughlin, B Coy Report – Battle of Kapyong, 23–24 Apr. 1951, pp. 7–8, 665/7/1, Series 114, AWM.

70. Ibid., 8–9; see Eighth Army Command Report: Section IV: After-Action Interviews: Book 2: Tanks Above Kapyong, Wilfred D. Millar, pp. 2–3, Paul W. Ragen, p. 1, Rudolph Triscik, p. 1. Mylas P. Moore, p. 1, Box 56, RG 550, NARA. On the importance of .50-caliber machine-gun fire from the tanks see Young in Bartlett, *With the Australians,* 99; Ray Parry, 225727/14-15, IWMDS.

71. See Capt. R. Saunders, C Coy Report – Battle of Kapyong, 23–24 Apr. 1951, p. 3, 665/7/1, Series 114, AWM; W. N. Gravener, D Coy Report – Battle of Kapyong, 23–24 Apr. 1951, pp. 1–2, 665/7/1, Series 114, AWM.

72. Stan Bushell, S03783, AWM.

73. Breen, *Battle of Kapyong,* 53; Capt. R. Saunders, C Coy Report – Battle of Kapyong, 23–24 Apr. 1951, p. 3, 665/7/1, Series 114, AWM.

74. Don Beard, S02687, AWM; see Breen, *Battle of Kapyong,* 36.

75. Fred From, S02649, AWM; see Phil Bennett, S02656, AWM; 3RAR WD, 23 Apr. 1951, 4/28, Series 85, AWM; A. Argent, "The Next Leader," in Butler, Argent, and Shelton, *Fight Leaders,* 105.

76. Eighth Army Command Report: Section IV: After-Action Interviews: Book 2: Tanks Above Kapyong, Kenneth W. Koch, p. 2, Box 56, RG 550, NARA; see Bartlett, *With the Australians,* 95–96; 3RAR WD, 23 Apr. 1951, 4/28, Series 85, AWM.

77. Fred From, S02649, AWM; see also From in Gallaway, *Last Call,* 151.

78. Breen, *Battle of Kapyong,* 53.

79. On the absence of radio communication see 27Bde WD, 24 Apr. 1951, WO 281/710, TNA. According to the CO's personal signaler, Ferguson did not even try to establish contact via radio. Gallaway, *Last Call,* 250. On the tearing up of telephone lines by vehicles see 3RAR WD, 23 Apr. 1951, 4/28, Series 85, AWM.

80. Jack Gallaway, S02651, AWM.

81. Breen, *Battle of Kapyong* 54 (see also Breen in the *Kapyong* documentary, Arcimedia); Gallaway, *Last Call,* 253; see 27Bde WD, 24 Apr. 1951, WO 281/710, TNA. Ferguson may in fact have originally intended only to go back to scout out a new position for his HQ. See Phil Bennett, S02656, AWM.

82. McGibbon, *New Zealand, Vol. II,* 125–27; 16 FR WD, 24 Apr. 1951, WA-K 1 DAK 12/2/1/7, ANZ.

83. See Eighth Army Command Report: Section IV: After-Action Interviews: Book 2: Tanks Above Kapyong, Kenneth W. Koch, p. 2, Box 56, RG 550, NARA; Breen, *Battle of Kapyong,* 55; McGibbon, *New Zealand, Vol. II,* 126.

84. 1MX WD, 24 Apr. 1951, 199-11-189-21, NAM; Eighth Army Command Report: Section IV: After-Action Interviews: Book 2: Tanks Above Kapyong, Kenneth W. Koch, p. 2, Box 56, RG 550, NARA; see 27Bde WD, 24 Apr. 1951, WO 291/1886, TNA.

85. Shipster, *Die-Hards,* 66; 1MX WD, 24 Apr. 1951, 1999-11-189-21, NAM.

86. Shipster, *Die-Hards,* 66–67; Kemp, *Middlesex Regiment,* 367; 1MX WD, 24 Apr. 1951, 1999-11-189-21, NAM; Barry Reed, 2001-02-397, NAM. The 3RAR war diary incorrectly reported that the 1MX

company had not in fact assaulted the position. 3RAR WD, 24 Apr. 1951, 4/28, Series 85, AWM.

87. Fred From, S02649, AWM. On the failure of radio communication see, e.g., Phil Bennett, S02656, AWM. On the failure of communications between 16FR and 3RAR HQ around 4 AM see McGibbon, *New Zealand, Vol. II,* 126.

88. Bartlett, *With the Australians,* 97; Fred From, S02649, AWM.

89. Breen, *Battle of Kapyong,* 57; see Bartlett, *With the Australians,* 97; Phil Bennett, S02656, AWM; "The Battle of Kapyong," *Australian Army Journal* 59 (1954): 17–18

90. Maj. D. P. Laughlin, B Coy Report – Battle of Kapyong, 23–24 Apr. 1951, p. 11, 665/7/1, Series 114, AWM; see Breen, *Battle of Kapyong,* 57–59.

7. KAPYONG: THE THIRD DAY

1. Maurice Gasson, *The Top of the Hill* (Wellington, N.Z.: M. Gasson, 2008), 9.

2. Don Hibbs interview, *The National Magazine,* 27 July 1999, archives.cbc.ca/war_conflict/korean_war/clips/684/ (accessed 27 August 2009).

3. Ben O'Dowd, S02659, AWM [see also Harris and O'Dowd in Breen, *Battle of Kapyong,* 65–66; Patrick Knowles, 19388/3, IWMDS]. On increased support from 16FR see McGibbon, *New Zealand, Vol. II,* 128.

4. B Coy Report – Battle of Kapyong, 23–24 Apr. 1951, p. 9, 665/7/1, Series 114, AWM; see Eighth Army Command Report: Section IV: After-Action Interviews: Book 2: Tanks Above Kapyong, Wilfred D. Millar, p. 3, Box 56, RG 550, NARA.

5. Breen, *Battle of Kapyong,* 67–68; O'Neill, *Australia, Vol. II,* 148.

6. O'Dowd, *Valiant Company,* 171.

7. Capt. W. N. Gravener, D Coy in the Battle of Kapyong, p. 1, 665/7/1, Series 114, AWM.

8. Ibid., pp. 1–2; McGibbon, *New Zealand, Vol. II,* 128.

9. See O'Neill, *Australia, Vol. II,* 146–48; Breen, *Battle of Kapyong,* 60–62; Eighth Army Command Report: Section IV: After-Action Interviews: Book 2: Tanks Above Kapyong, Kenneth W. Koch, pp. 3–4, Box 56, RG 550, NARA. Among the casualties was Bob Parker, Ferguson's dispatch rider, who did not receive word of the withdrawal and, trying to make his way south solo on his motorcycle, was injured and captured. See Breen, *Battle of Kapyong,* 60–61; A2151, AI9/K/AUST/490, 491, 527, 518, p. 3, KB1073/11G Part 6, NAA. Communication problems meant that a number of officers with the forward companies did not get advance word that Ferguson was withdrawing (see Breen in *Kapyong,* Arcimedia). "Where the hell he was . . ." Bob O'Dowd later commented, "I don't know. He certainly wasn't in the battle area" (O'Dowd in ibid.).

10. O'Neill, *Australia, Vol. II,* 148, gives the time as 7:15 AM. The 3RAR war diary lists the time as 8 AM (3RAR WD, 24 Apr. 1951, 4/28, Series 85, AWM). On the mortar round incident see O'Neill, *Australia, Vol. II,* 146; Dusty Ryan in Peter Thompson and Robert Macklin, *Keep Off the Skyline* (Milton, Qld.: Wiley, 2004), 67.

11. B Coy Report – Battle of Kapyong, 23–24 Apr. 1951, pp. 11–12, 665/7/1, Series 114, AWM; O'Neill, *Australia, Vol. II,* 148; Eighth Army Command Report: Section IV: After-Action Interviews: Book 2: Tanks Above Kapyong, Wilfred D. Millar, p. 3, Box 56, RG 550, NARA.

12. See Phil Bennett, S02656, AWM.

13. O'Dowd, *Valiant Company,* 173; Ben O'Dowd, S02659, AWM.

14. William M. Hoge interview, p. 174, http://140.194.76.129/publications/eng-pamphlets/ep870-1-25/inter.pdf (accessed 25 January 2010). The 5th Cavalry had been part of Eighth Army reserve, but as soon as

it was passed to IX Corps in the middle of the afternoon on 24 April it was attached to the Commonwealth Brigade. IX Corps Command Report: Book I, Apr. 1951, p. 37a, Box 1797, RG 407, NARA.

15. *The First Team* (Paduca, Ky.: Turner, 1994), 141.

16. B Coy Report – Battle of Kapyong, 23–24 Apr. 1951, p. 12, 665/7/1, Series 114, AWM; see O'Dowd, *Valiant Company,* 174.

17. Breen, *Battle of Kapyong,* 74–75.

18. Ibid., 75–77; see B Coy Report – Battle of Kapyong, 23–24 Apr. 1951, p. 13, 665/7/1, Series 114, AWM.

19. B Coy Report – Battle of Kapyong, 23–24 Apr. 1951, pp. 13–14, 665/7/1, Series 114, AWM; Breen, *Battle of Kapyong,* 80–81; MC citation for Lt. L. M. Montgomerie and MM citation for T/Cpl. D. B. Davie in Atkinson, *Kapyong Battalion,* 54–56.

20. Don Beard, S02687, AWM; see Eighth Command Report: Section IV: After-Action Interviews: Book 2: Tanks Above Kapyong, Wilfred D. Millar, p. 3, Box 56, RG 550, NARA; Breen, *Battle of Kapyong,* 82. Paradoxically, the 31 Set that Ferguson took with him now worked perfectly. Butler, Argent, and Shelton, *Fight Leaders,* 107n17.

21. Millar in Breen, *Battle of Kapyong,* 83.

22. *The 7.30 Report,* 25 April 2001, transcript p. 4, www.abc.net.au/7.30/content/2001/s283098.htm (accessed 28 January 2010); see Breen, *Battle of Kapyong,* 84.

23. O'Dowd, *Valiant Company,* 174–75; see Ben O'Dowd, S02659, AWM.

24. B Coy Report – Battle of Kapyong, 23–24 Apr. 1951, p. 16, 665/7/1, Series 114, AWM.

25. O'Neill, *Australia, Vol. II,* 148; Report on the Battle of Kapyong, C Company, 3RAR, pp. 4–5, 665/7/1, Series 114, AWM.

26. O'Dowd, *Valiant Company,* 175; AWM P. J. Knowles, A Rifleman's View of 'The Battle of Kapyong', p. 4, PR 83/154, AWM; Patrick Knowles, 19388/2, IWMDS.

27. D Coy in the Battle of Kapyong, p. 2, 665/7/1, Series 114, AWM; see O'Dowd, *Valiant Company,* 175.

28. Atkinson, *Kapyong Battalion,* 54.

29. Breen, *Battle of Kapyong,* 96–98; Bartlett, *With the Australians,* 103–104; O'Dowd, *Valiant Company,* 178; Ben O'Dowd, S02659, AWM; D Coy in the Battle of Kapyong, p. 4, 665/7/1, Series 114, AWM; Eighth Army Command Report: Section IV: After-Action Interviews: Book 2: Tanks Above Kapyong, A. Argent, p. 2, Box 56, RG 550, NARA; Mo Gwyther in Patsy Adam-Smith, *Prisoners of War* (Ringwood, Vic.: Viking, 1992), 574–75; see also Patrick Knowles, 19388/2, IWMDS; Len Opie, S02654, AWM. Argent, IO for 3RAR, and the 3RAR war diary give the time of the attack as 1:30 PM. O'Dowd and Breen both suggest it took place at about 3 PM. It is also unclear if a strike had been called in; various sources suggest Gravener called for air support (Bartlett, *With the Australians,* 103; "Battle of Kapyong," 24; Battle of Kapyong, 23–24 Apr. 1951, 3RAR, p. 4, 665/7/1, Series 114, AWM), but O'Dowd (*Valiant Company,* 178) denies this. Fifty percent of air support during the Fifth Phase offensive came from aircraft launched from the carriers of Task Force 77. See Allan R. Millett, "Korea, 1950–53," *Case Studies in the Development of Close Air Support,* ed. Benjamin Franklin Cooling (Washington, D.C.: Office of Air Force History, 1990), 379. Ironically, most of the USMC air sorties on the 24th were flown in support of I Corps farther west. See Montross, Kuokka, and Hicks, *Marine Operations, Vol. IV,* 116. As the 3RAR mortar platoon commander put it, air strikes at Kapyong were "few and far between." Phil Bennett, S02656, AWM.

30. Hawkins in Durney, *Far Side,* 117; see also Joe Vezgoff, "The Great Adventure

1950–1951," p. 10, www.kmike.com/oz/kr/chapter1.htm (accessed 7 October 2009).

31. Don Beard, S02678, AWM.

32. Len Opie, S020654; AI9/K/AUST/490, 491, 517, 518, p. 4, KB1073/11G Part 6, A2151, NAA; O'Dowd, *Valiant Company,* 185.

33. *The 7.30 Report,* 25 April 2001, transcript p. 1, www.abc.net.au/7.30/content/2001/s283098.htm (accessed 28 January 2010); Parry won an MM for this action (Atkinson, *Kapyong Battalion,* 56).

34. Goslen narrative, 27 Bde, April 1951, WO 308/36, TNA; Wood, *Strange Battleground,* 74–76.

35. Ben O'Dowd, S02659, AWM. Exactly when this conversation took place is unclear. Breen, *Battle of Kapyong,* 86, 91, suggests about 12:30 PM. The battalion war diary (3RAR WD, 24 Apr. 1951, 4/28, Series 85, AWM) indicates some point after 11:00 AM. O'Dowd claims that it was after USMC Corsairs struck 10 Platoon (O'Dowd, *Valiant Company,* 178), an event which the war diary lists as occurring at 1:30 PM and Breen (*Battle of Kapyong,* 96) after 3:00 PM. Decades later, Stone of 2PPCLI related that he overheard on the radio net Ferguson saying: "Withdraw as best you can to the Middlesex positions. I can no longer keep control." James Riley Stone, SC407_SJR_198, UVic.

36. See Breen, *Battle of Kapyong,* 54, 67.

37. P. J. Knowles, A Rifleman's View of 'The Battle of Kapyong', p. 4, PR 83/154, AWM.

38. O'Dowd in Breen, *Battle of Kapyong,* 92. On anticipating the order, see O'Dowd, *Valiant Company,* 179. O'Dowd also had to think about how to bring out the wounded as well as the unwounded, his men having made it clear that they should not be left behind in any withdrawal. See P. J. Knowles, A Rifleman's View of 'The Battle of Kapyong', p. 4, PR 83/154, AWM. Dead bodies, though, would be left where they lay. See Breen, *Battle of Kapyong,* 95.

39. O'Dowd, *Valiant Company,* 179–80; Ben O'Dowd, S02659, AWM; Breen, *Battle of Kapyong,* 92–93.

40. Ben O'Dowd, S02659, AWM; O'Dowd, *Valiant Company,* 183; see Breen, *Battle of Kapyong,* 99–100; McGibbon, *New Zealand, Vol. II,* 130. The exact time at which the withdrawal was supposed to and did start is not entirely clear, but it occurred somewhere between 3:00 PM and 5:30 PM. See Breen, *Battle of Kapyong,* 93; "The Battle of Kapyong," 24; O'Dowd, *Valiant Company,* 182. O'Dowd at first thought it too dangerous to take the forty-plus Chinese POWs along and considered having them shot, but in the end ordered Laughlin to take them with him. This decision turned out to have practical as well as moral advantages. "They did exactly as they were told," O'Dowd recalled: "In fact we used a few of them to carry the wounded out – mainly Gravener's burn cases from the American napalm." O'Dowd in Breen, *Battle of Kapyong,* 99; see O'Dowd, *Valiant Company,* 182.

41. O'Dowd, *Valiant Company,* 183; see McGibbon, *New Zealand, Vol. II,* 130; D Coy in the Battle of Kapyong, p. 3, 665/7/1, Series 114, AWM; Donald Scott, 16 Fd Regt and the 'Utah' Battalion at Kapyong, p. 1, www.riv.co.nz/mza/tales/scott.htm (accessed 27 January 2010); Eighth Army Command Report: Section IV: After-Action Interviews: Book 2: Tanks Above Kapyong, Blaine Johnson, p. 2, Box 56, RG 550, NARA; Porter, "Battle of Kapyong – 16 NZ Fd Regt 23–25 April 1951," 39; Hammond in *Kapyong,* Arcimedia.

42. O'Dowd, *Valiant Company,* 184; see O'Dowd in Breen, *Battle of Kapyong,* 102.

43. O'Dowd, *Valiant Company,* 184–85; Breen, *Battle of Kapyong,* 102–103; 3RAR WD, 24 Apr. 1951, 4/28, Series 85, AWM.

44. AWM Len Opie, S02654, AWM.

See, however, J. F. M. MacDonald, *The Borderers in Korea* (Berwick-upon-Tweed: Martins, 1978), 15.

45. CBC Radio, *Five Nights;* see also, e.g., MacLeod in Gray, *Danger Close,* 68.

46. Unidentified soldier in McKeown, *Kapyong Remembered,* 24; see also, with reference to refugees/infiltrators passing by the mortar platoon, Michael Czuboka, p. 6, www.kvacanada.com/stories_czuboka.htm (accessed 28 February 2010).

47. Mitchell in Barris, *Deadlock,* 84.

48. Gray, *Danger Close,* 69, 73–74; 2PPCLI WD, 24 Apr. 1951, Vol. 18381, RG-24-C3, NLAC. Loaded with extra ammunition, the men of B Company had arrived on Hill 504 carrying over sixty pounds of kit. They were, however, assisted by a platoon of Korean porters. Courtenay, *Patricias,* 200.

49. archives.cbc.ca/war_conflict/korean_war/clips/742/ (accessed 3 January 2010).

50. Mason in Gray, *Danger Close,* 78. Like those captured on the Imjin, prisoners taken at Kapyong noted the extent of this camouflage technique. "All around me were hundreds of Chinese with their own personal tree," Private Bob Parker (3RAR) remembered: "When they moved it was like a whole forest moving." Parker in Breen, *Battle of Kapyong,* 61.

51. Dave Crook in "Blood on the Hills," Breakthrough Films and Television; see William Chrysler, "Military Activities," p. 4, www.vac-acc.gov.ca/remembers/ (accessed 31 July 2009); Chrysler in *Kapyong,* Arcimedia.

52. archives.cbc.ca/war_conflict/korean_war/clips/742 (accessed 3 January 2010). This man was likely Ray Nickerson of A Company: see Ray Nickerson, "Were You scared?" www.veterans.gc.ca (accessed 10 July 2012). On fear see also McKeown, *Kapyong Remembered,* 39; Gerald Edward Gowing, "Waves of Screaming Enemy," www.veterans.gc.ca (accessed 10 July 2012); Hibbs in Bjarnason, *Triumph,* 118. The argument that A Company later gave way to semi-panic as battle raged around other companies (see Hepenstall, *Find the Dragon,* 92–93) is overstated (see Bishop, *King's Bishop,* 126; Browne in Gray, *Danger Close,* 80; Ray Nickerson, "To the Hills Near Kapyong," www.veterans.gc.ca [accessed 10 July 2012]).

53. Unidentified soldier in McKeown, *Kapyong Remembered,* 22. This may have been a Korean civilian refugee, but the assumption was that disguised Chinese were mixed in with both military and civilian Koreans and no chances were taken. See Barris, *Deadlock,* 84.

54. archives.cbc.ca/war_conflict/korean_war/clips/742 (accessed 3 January 2010).

55. 2PPCLI WD, 24 Apr. 1951, Vol. 18318, RG-24-C3, NLAC; Gray, *Danger Close,* 78.

56. Brian Munro in Hepenstall, *Find the Dragon,* 92.

57. Gray, *Danger Close,* 77.

58. Brent Watson, "Recipe for Victory: The Fight for Hill 677 During the Battle of the Kap'yong River, 24–25 April 1951," *Canadian Military History* 9, no. 2 (2000): 17.

59. 2PPCLI WD, 24 Apr. 1951, Vol. 18318, RG-24-C3, NLAC.

60. Bercuson, *Patricias,* 260; see Ulmer in Courtenay, *Patricias,* 218; Hibbs in Bjarnason, *Triumph,* 118–19; Gray in *Kapyong,* Arcimedia.

61. Bercuson, *Patricias,* 260; see Menard in Gray, *Danger Close,* 91; Gerald Edward Gowing, "Waves of Screaming Enemy," www.veterans.gc.ca (accessed 10 July 2012); Courtenay, *Patricias,* 219.

62. Reaume in Courtenay, *Patricias,* 220.

63. 2PPCLI WD, 24 Apr. 1951, Vol. 18318, RG-24-C3, NLAC; Lilley in G. R. Stevens, *Princess Patricia's Canadian Light Infantry, 1919–1957* (Griesbach, Alta,

Canada: Historical Committee of the Regiment, 1959), 301; Gray, *Danger Close,* 89–90, 95–96; Wood, *Strange Battleground,*76; McKeown, *Kapyong Remembered,* 24; Wayne Mitchell in transcript of *Korea: Canada's Forgotten War,* War Amps of Canada, p. 9.

64. Bishop, *King's Bishop,* 127.

65. James Riley Stone, SC407_SJR_198, UVic (hereafter J. Stone [UVic]).

66. Stone and Castonguay, *Korea 1951,* 20–21; see J. Stone (UVic); McKeown, *Kapyong Remembered,* 24–25. Lilley gives the time of this assault as 2 AM (Lilley in Stevens, *Princess Patricia's,* 301), but official sources suggest the attempted attack on battalion HQ took place before midnight. See 2PPCLI WD, 24 Apr. 1951, Vol. 18318, RG-24-C3, NLAC; The Kapyong Battle, p. 2, 145.2 P7013 (D4), DHH.

67. See Gray, *Danger Close,* 92–93; Michael Czuboka, p. 7, www.kvacanada.com/stories-czuboka.htm (accessed 23 August 2011); Bjarnason, *Triumph,* 126–27.

68. 2PPCLI WD, 24 Apr. 1951, Vol. 18318, RG-24-C3, NLAC.

69. Wood, *Strange Battleground,* 77; see Mitchell, transcript of *Korea: Canada's Forgotten War,* War Amps of Canada, pp. 9–10; Bjarnason, *Triumph,* 121–22; Waniandy in Bercuson, *Patricias,* 262.

70. Lilley in Wood, *Strange Battleground,* 79; see Gray, *Danger Close,* 95–96; Michael Czuboka, p. 6, www.kvacanada.com/stories_czuboka.htm (accessed 28 February 2010).

71. Lilley in Stevens, *Princess Patricia's,* 301; see Wood, *Strange Battleground,* 76, 79; The Kapyong Battle, p. 2, 145.2 P7013 (D4), DHH; Gray, *Danger Close,* 89.

72. Wood, *Strange Battleground,* 77; Gray, *Danger Close,* 94.

73. 2PPCLI WD, 24 Apr. 1951, Vol. 18318, RG-24-C3, NLAC [entries for the early hours of 25 April appear under 24 April]; The Kapyong Battle, pp. 2–3, 145.2 P7013 (D4), DHH; Mills in Wood, *Strange Battleground,* 77. The assertion that the Chinese were using the tubes abandoned by B Company, 2nd Chemical Mortar Battalion against the Canadians on the night of 24–25 April (see Gray, *Danger Close,* 87–88) seems unlikely given their recovery – along with the equipment abandoned by the 74th Engineer Combat Battalion – during the daylight hours of 24 April (see 2nd Chemical Mortar Battalion Command Report, 1 Sep. 1950 – 1 Aug. 1951: Part VII – Narrative Summary Period – 1 to 30 April 1951, p. 19, Box 5030, RG 407, NARA; RG 550, Eighth Army Command Report: Section IV: After-Action Interviews: Book 2: Tanks Above Kapyong, Wade H. Padgett, Harold Burros, John L. Mazyck, Otho C. Bragg, Haywood Butler, Frank Heard Jr., Box 56, RG 550, NARA).

74. See Stone in Hepenstall, *Find the Dragon,* 94.

75. 2PPCLI WD, 24 Apr. 1951, Vol. 18318, RG-24-C3, NLAC [entries for the early hours of 25 April appear under 24 April]; Mills in Wood, *Strange Battleground,* 77–78; McKeown, *Kapyong Remembered,* 25; Gray, *Danger Close,* 102. There is some question as to how bad the situation was with 12 Platoon. See ibid., 104.

76. Stone and Coombe in Gray, *Danger Close,* 104, 111; see Stone in Melady, *Korea,* 77; J. Stone (UVic); see also Notes on talk given by Lt.-Col. J. R. Stone, 5 June 1951, p. 4, 681.011 (D3), DHH. On the limits to vision even under the bright moonlight see, e.g., Bishop, *King's Bishop,* 124. Hub Gray, a mortar platoon officer, was convinced that the veteran Levy, in contrast to the comparatively un-blooded Mills, knew what he was doing at Kapyong. See Gray, *Danger Close,* xvi, 5, 7, 73, 115–16, 118, 214–25; Bjarnason, *Triumph,* 132–37. Others, however, suggest that Mills behaved quite professionally. See Courtenay, *Patricias,* 218, 228, 230–31, 237.

77. Stone and Castonguay, *Korea 1951,* 22; Stone in Melady, *Korea,* 77. The air drop was suggested to Stone by his IO, Lieutenant A. P. McKenzie. Courtenay, *Patricias,* 232; J. Stone (UVic).

78. See Notes on talk given by Lt.-Col. J. R. Stone, 5 June 1951, p. 4, 681.011 (D3), DHH; Report by Lt.-Col. J. R. Stone on activities of 2PPCLI in Korea, 23 Dec. 1950, p. 2, 145.2 P7013 (D6), DHH.

79. Gray, *Danger Close,* 104–106, 114; McGibbon, *New Zealand, Vol. II,* 134.

80. McKeown, *Kapyong Remembered,* 25; see also, e.g., Browne, "Kapyong! What Is It?" 21.

81. 16FR WD, 24/25 Apr. 1951, WA-K 1 DAK 1 2/1/7, ANZ; McGibbon, *New Zealand, Vol. II,* 134.

82. Campbell in Hepenstall, *Find the Dragon,* 96.

83. IX Corps Command Report, Book 1, Apr. 1951, p. 38, Box 1797, RG 407, NARA.

84. Campbell in Hepenstall, *Find the Dragon,* 96. On the barrage see also 16FR WD, 25 Apr. 1951, WA-K 1 DAK 1 2/1/7, ANZ.

85. 27Bde WD, 25 Apr. 1951, WO 281/710, TNA; see The Kapyong Battle, p. 4, 145.2 P7013 (D4), DHH; 16FR WD, 25 Apr. 1951, WA-K 1 DAK 1 2/1/7, ANZ.

86. William Chrysler, "Military Activities," www.veterans.gc.ca (accessed 10 July 2012). On expecting to be overrun see CBC Radio, *Five Nights;* Ray Nickerson, "To the Hills Near Kapyong," www.veterans.gc.ca (accessed 10 July 2012).

87. Bishop, *King's Bishop,* 126.

8. KAPYONG: THE FINAL DAY

1. Middleton in Gray, *Danger Close,* 120.

2. McKeown, *Kapyong Remembered,* 27.

3. Michael Czuboka, pp. 7–8, www.kvacanada.com/stories_czuboka.htm (accessed 28 February 2010); see Courtenay, *Patricias,* 245–46.

4. See Middleton in Hepenstall, *Find the Dragon,* 99. On the two helicopters see also 27Bde WD, 25 Apr. 1951, WO 281/710, TNA. The wounded were flown to the Indian Field Ambulance and then to a Commonwealth hospital in Japan. See Douglas in Gray, *Danger Close,* 121–22.

5. Gray, *Danger Close,* 118. On claims that no hatred was felt for the Chinese, see, e.g., archives.cbc.ca/war_conflict/korean_war/clips/742 (accessed 3 January 2010); John Kelanchey, 19386/2, IWMDS.

6. Bishop, *King's Bishop,* 126.

7. Stone and Castonguay, *Korea 1951,* 3.

8. McKeown, *Kapyong Remembered,* 40.

9. Welsh in Barris, *Deadlock,* 89; see Bill Lee in Gray, *Danger Close,* 122.

10. Bishop, *King's Bishop,* 126; Michael Czuboka, p. 8, www.kvacanada.com/stories_czuboka.htm (accessed 28 February 2010); William Chrysler, "Military Activities," www.veterans.gc.ca (accessed 10 July 2012); see 2PPCLI WD, 25 Apr. 1951, Vol. 18318, RG-24-C3, NLAC; McKeown, *Kapyong Remembered,* 27–28; Stone and Castonguay, *Korea 1951,* 22; James Riley Stone, SC407_SJR_198, UVic; Wood, *Strange Battleground,* 78. On the U.S. ammunition see Courtenay, *Patricias,* 246. On the redistribution of .303 ammunition see William Chrysler, "Military Activities," www.veterans.gc.ca (accessed 10 July 2012); McKeown, *Kapyong Remembered,* 26; Courtenay, *Patricias,* 245.

11. Gray, *Danger Close,* 122.

12. See ibid., 131–35, 233; McKeown, *Kapyong Remembered,* 26–27.

13. Gray, *Danger Close,* 123–24.

14. 2PPCLI WD, 25 Apr. 1951, Vol. 18318, RG-24-C3, NLAC; The Kapyong Battle, p. 3, 145.2 P7013 (D4), DHH. On sniper fire and grenades see Gray, *Danger Close,* 123.

15. See Gray, *Danger Close,* 118–19, 121; Cook in Hepenstall, *Find the Dragon,* 91–92; Douglas in Bjarnason, *Triumph,* 124–25. Douglas, who survived, was awarded an MM for his selfless action.

16. Pearson in Gray, *Danger Close,* 123; see 2PPCLI WD, 25 Apr. 1951, Vol. 18318, RG-24-C3, NLAC.

17. 2PPCLI WD, 25 Apr. 1951, Vol. 18318, RG-24-C3, NLAC.

18. IX Corps Command Report, Book 1, Apr. 1951, p. 37a, Box. 1797, RG 407, NARA; 27Bde WD, 25 Apr. 1951, WO 281/710, TNA.

19. Johnson in Hepenstall, *Find the Dragon,* 97; 2PPCLI WD, 25 Apr. 1951, Vol. 18318, RG-24-C3, NLAC. On artillery fire on the 25th see also 16FR WD, 25 Apr. 1951, WA-K 1 DAK 1 2/1/7, ANZ.

20. 3RAR WD, 25 Apr. 1951, 4/28, Series 85, AWM; Melnechuk in Gray, *Danger Close,* 125; see IX Corps Command Report, Book 1, Apr. 1951, p. 38, Box 1797, RG 407, NARA; Gray, *Danger Close,* 125, 127.

21. 27Bde WD, 25 Apr. 1951, WO 281/710, TNA.

22. 3RAR WD 25 Apr. 1951, 4/28, Series 85, AWM.

23. Bishop, *King's Bishop,* 127; see 2PPCLI WD, 25 Apr. 1951, Vol. 18318, RG-24-C3, NLAC.

24. 2 PPCLI WD, 25 Apr. 1951, Vol. 18318, RG-24-C3, NLAC.

25. 3RAR WD, 25 Apr. 1951, 4/28, Series 85, AWM; 27Bde WD, 26 Apr. 1951, WO 281/710, TNA.

26. Middleton in Gray, *Danger Close,* 135. In another version Middleton remembered the visitors included Ridgway himself; see Courtenay, *Patricias,* 248–49.

27. Gray, *Danger Close,* 127; 16FR WD, 26 Apr. 1951, WA-K 1 DAK 1 2/1/7, ANZ; 2PPCLI WD, 26 Apr. 1951, Vol. 18318, RG-24-C3, NLAC.

28. Michael Czuboka, p. 8, www.kvacanada.com/stories_czuboka.htm (accessed 28 February 2010).

29. McKeown, *Kapyong Remembered,* 29.

30. See 2PPCLI WD, 26–27 Apr. 1951, Vol. 18318, RG-24-C3, NLAC; 3RAR WD, 26–27 Apr. 1951, 4/28, Series 85, AWM.

31. Bishop, *King's Bishop,* 130; Munro in Gray, *Danger Close,* 127–29.

32. The 3RAR war diarist, after recounting some problems, admitted that: "Compared with the [U.N.] withdrawals of December [1950] and January [1951], the present just completed were orderly and well executed." 3RAR WD, 28 Apr. 1951, 4/28, Series 85, AWM. On confusion within the brigade during the withdrawal see, e.g., McKeown, *Kapyong Remembered,* 34; Middleton in Gray, *Danger Close,* 126–27.

33. Tunstall, *I Fought,* 113; see Notes on Talk by Lt.-Col. J. R. Stone, 5 June 1951, p. 4, 681.011 (D3), DHH; 2PPCLI WD, 27–28 Apr. 1951, Vol. 18318, RG-24-C3, NLAC; 3RAR WD, 27–28 Apr. 1951, 4/28, Series 85, AWM; 16FR WD, 27 Apr. 1951, WA-K 1 DAK 1 2/1/7, ANZ; 1KOSB WD, 27–28 Apr. 1951, WO 281/478, TNA. On the withdrawal not being liked in, e.g., 1MX, see Shipster, *Die-Hards,* 67; Kemp, *Middlesex Regiment,* 368.

EPILOGUE

1. Carne remark reported in *Daily Express,* 2 September 1953, p. 2.

2. McKeown, *Kapyong Remembered,* 39.

3. See Salmon, *Last Round,* 252.

4. Cubiss letter in Perrins, *'Pretty Rough,'* 123; see also, e.g., Alex Patterson in Doherty, *Sons of Ulster,* 158; Hamill, *Ulster Rifles,* 71; Mason, *Diplomatic Dispatches,* 71; R. S. Gill, letter 64, 26 April 1951, IWMDD.

5. Barclay, *First Commonwealth,* 67; Farrar-Hockley, *British Part, Vol. II,* 135. On the Gloster casualty figures see Harding, *Imjin Roll,* 46–77, 80–83. On the Northumberland casualty figures see Perrins, *'Pretty Rough,'* 342–60. On the Ulster

casualty figures see *Quis Separabit,* Winter 1951, p. 79. On the Belgian casualty figures see Gunst, Philips, and Vehaegen, *Saison,* 215.

6. Perrins, *'Pretty Rough,'* 157; Brodie to Steele, 29 April 1951, in *Quis Separabit* 18, no. 1 (1951): 9; see Mossman, *Ebb and Flow,* 429; Appleman, *Ridgway Duels,* 479, 630n48 (see also Appleman diary, September 10, 1951, Roy E. Appleman Papers, USAMHI). On Brodie blaming Soule, see Harris, *Fighting 65th,* 183; see also Brodie to Joslen, 19 July 1957, CAB 157/23, TNA.

7. Ridgway to Van Fleet, 9 May 1951, Folder T-Z, Box 19, Matthew B. Ridgway Papers, USAMHI.

8. Harris, *Fighting 65th,* 183.

9. Eighth Army, Command Conference held by Army Commander with Corps commanders, 30 April 1951, Box 1180, RG 407, NARA.

10. Van Fleet to Ridgway, 11 May 1951, File T-Z, Box 19, Matthew B. Ridgway Papers, USAMHI.

11. Matthew B. Ridgway, *The Korean War* (London: Cresset, 1968), xii. On the American view that the British had not called for help soon enough see also, e.g., oral history, Section III, p. 51, Harold K. Johnson Papers, USAMHI.

12. Ions, *Call to Arms,* 161; Perrins, *'Pretty Rough,'* 140; Matthew B. Ridgway, *The Korean War* (Garden City, N.Y.: Doubleday, 1967), 172; see Robertson to Slim, 17 May 1951, Impressions of the British Commonwealth part in the CCF offensive on 22–26 April 1951, p. 2, WO 216/345, TNA.

13. There were, however, occasional hints in the press that the South Koreans were to blame. See, e.g., *Washington Post,* 15 May 1951, p. 14.

14. *Daily Herald,* 30 April 1951, p. 1; *Guardian,* 27 April 1951, p. 5; see also, e.g., *The Times,* 27 April 1951, p. 6; 30 April 1951, p. 4.

15. *Daily Express,* May 2, 1951, p. 1; *Daily Telegraph,* 28 April 1951, p. 1.

16. Statement by the Minister of Defence on Operations in Korea – 2 May 1951, PREM 8/1405, TNA.

17. *Parliamentary Debates, House of Commons,* 5 Series, 2 May 1951, cols. 189–90.

18. *Daily Herald,* 3 May 1951, pp. 1–2; *Guardian,* 3 May 1951, p. 6; *The Times,* 3 May 1951, p. 5; *Daily Telegraph,* 3 May 1951, p. 4.

19. R. S. Gill letter 69, 9 May 1951, IWMDD.

20. *The Times,* 9 May 1951, p. 6. The full Milburn tribute was reproduced in *St. George's Gazette,* 31 May 1951, p. 104. Van Fleet was also "full of praise" for the Glosters when interviewed privately about the Imjin battle several months later. See Appleman diary, 15 Sep. 1951, Roy E. Appleman Papers, USAMHI.

21. On the citation and its presentation see Harding, *Imjin Roll,* 95–96; Barclay, *Commonwealth Division,* 67; *The Times,* 12 May 1951, p. 5.

22. *Daily Telegraph,* 9 May 1951, p. 1; *Daily Herald,* 9 May 1951, p. 2. On audiences cheering see *The Back Badge* 3, no. 11 (1951): 226.

23. *The Times,* 4 June 1951, p. 4; 21 May 1951, p. 4; 16 May 1951, p. 4; see, e.g., *Washington Post,* 15 May 1951, p. 14.

24. Kahn, *The Gloucesters.* On enthusiasm for Kahn's article see, e.g., *The Back Badge* 3, no. 11 (1951): 226.

25. *The Back Badge* 3, no. 11 (1951): 227–28.

26. Noble, *Shoot First,* 185–86; Holles, *Now Thrive,* 173; Grist, "Korean Campaign," 44.

27. Frank Cottam, 21729/4, IWMDS [see also, e.g., Charles Sharpling, 18544/1, IWMDS]. On captured officers feeling guilty see Cunningham, *No Mercy,* 76; see also Anthony Farrar-Hockley, 30102/1,

IWMDS; though see also David Holdsworth, 15428/3, IWMDS. Other ranks might have similar feelings. See, e.g., Large, *One Man's War,* 71.

28. Gordon Potts, 23213/8, IWMDS (also on the platoon commander who had to be replaced); Denis Prout, 18775/4, IWMDS; Whatmore, *One Road,* 85; M. Harvey quoted in news.bbc.co.uk/2/low/uk_news/1288010.stm (accessed 14 August 2007); see also Roy Rees, 19854/2, IWMDS; Grist, *Remembered,* 46; Kavanagh, *Perfect Stranger,* 111.

29. Kavanagh, *Perfect Stranger,* 122 (see also, e.g., Thomas Cunningham-Booth, 19913/3, IWMDS). On the men recovering quickly see, e.g., Dennis Matthews, 12729/2, IWMDS; *North Irish Brigade Chronicle* 1, no. 4 (1952): 32; H. G. Martin, "With the 27th and 29th Brigades," *Daily Telegraph,* 30 April 1951, p. 4.

30. Younger, *Blowing Bridges,* 208.

31. On a mutiny in 9 Platoon of the Fusiliers see WO 71/1024, TNA. On bitterness in the RNF see also Cpl. W. K. Westwood, p. 2, AI9/K/BRIT/157, KB1073/11G Part 7, A2151, NAA. On the court-martial cases for desertion in the aftermath of the Imjin see list in WO 93/59, TNA. On breaking down under fire post-Imjin, see, e.g., description by Adams in Walker, *Barren Place,* 21.

32. "Korea 1951," *Journal of the Northamptonshire Regiment* 15, no. 2 (1953): 20; Scott to Blackett-Orde, 1 May 1951, in Perrins, *'Pretty Rough,'* 131. On replacing signals equipment see Robertson to Slim, 17 May 1951, p. 3, WO 216/345, TNA. On officer replacements being flown out see, e.g., Ions, *Call to Arms,* 148–53. Other ranks also might find themselves aboard aircraft for at least part of the journey. See, e.g., Ronald Wells's narrative, pp. 7–8, IWMDD.

33. Harvey, *War in Korea,* 136; Grist, *Remembered,* 42; see "Korea 1951," *Journal of the Northamptonshire Regiment* 15, no. 2 (1953): 20; Major Boris J. Eastwood, f. 442, K-671, WO 373/119, TNA.

34. *The Telegram* [Toronto], 27 April 1951, p. 6; *The Age* [Melbourne], 27 April 1951, p. 1; *Sydney Morning Herald,* 28 April 1951, p. 2; see, e.g., *Sydney Morning Herald,* 27 April 1951, p. 1; *The Globe and Mail* [Toronto], 26 April 1951, p. 1; *The Telegram* [Toronto], 26 April 1951, p. 1; *The Gazette* [Montreal], 26 April 1951, p. 1.

35. See "Unique," by Harry Hall – himself an ex-Gloster – in *The Telegram,* Toronto, 14 June 1951, p. 6; see also www.glosters.org.uk/collection (accessed 15 March 2010). For a rare British report on the Kapyong battle – made in conjunction with a report on the Imjin fighting – see *Daily Telegraph,* 30 April 1951, p. 4.

36. WO 32/14250, TNA.

37. On national coverage of the PUC see, e.g., *Globe and Mail* [Toronto], 27 June 1951, p. 6; *The Telegram* [Toronto], 26 June 1951, pp. 1–2; *Toronto Daily Star,* 26 June 1951, pp. 1–2; *Sydney Morning Herald,* 27 June 1951, p. 1.

38. The casualty figures are from Bartlett, *With the Australians,* 106. On fatigue see, e.g., Young in Bartlett, *With the Australians,* 105; Patrick Knowles, 19388/2, IWMDS; Tim Holt in Thompson and Macklin, *Keep Off,* 70. On morale see Ben O'Dowd, S02659, AWM.

39. Stone and Castonguay, *Korea 1951,* 23; see Notes on talk by Lt.-Col. J. R. Stone, 5 June 1951, p. 4, 681.011 (D3), DHH. The casualty figures are those listed in Stevens, *Princess Patricia's,* 303.

40. McKeown, *Kapyong Remembered,* 39.

41. See, e.g., Jack Gallaway, http://www.australiansatwar.gov.au/ko_akh.html (accessed 7 October 2009); Tom Muggleton, S02652, AWM; William Chrysler, "Military Activities," www.veterans.gc.ca (accessed 10 July 2012).

42. Doherty, *Sons of Ulster,* 158; see Owen Smith, 18441/3, IWMDS. On the

grim business of identifying remains see Sean Fitzsimons in Doherty, *Sons of Ulster,* 159; Grist, *Remembered,* 51; Harvey, *War in Korea,* 144; Whatmore, *One Road,* 92–98; Thomas Cunningham-Booth, 19913/5, IWMDS; Denis Whybro, 20008/13, IWMDS.

43. Keith Taylor, 1989-05-257-1, NAM.

44. Samuel Phillips, 17688/3, IWMDS; Andrew Scott, 16855/2, IWMDS; on strengthening defenses see also, e.g., Grist, *Remembered,* 52; 1GLOS WD, 29 June 1951, WO 281/1244, TNA; Gordon Potts, 23213/9, IWMDS; Anthony Perrins, 19387/3, IWMDS; Hamill, *Ulster Rifles,* 77; Gregory Blaxland, *The Regiments Depart* (London: Kimber, 1971), 183.

45. Linklater, *Year in Space,* 108; see also, e.g., Cassels, "The Commonwealth Division," 367. Prior to its departure for Hong Kong, 1MX, as part of 28Bde, had also dug in with a will. See Shipster, *Die-Hards,* 68.

46. Keith Taylor, 1989-05-257-1, NAM; see, e.g., Taylor to Slim, 21 July 1951, WO 216/741, TNA.

47. Minute 3, RAC1 to FVA2, 25 May 1951, WO 32/14418, TNA.

48. On, e.g., 8RIH officers trading whisky for Browning machine-guns see Salmon, *Last Round,* 266; see also Gray in Walker, *Barren Place,* 75; George Forty, *At War in Korea* (Shepperton: Ian Allan, 1982), 141.

49. Ions, *Call to Arms,* 177; see, e.g., Maj. R. Leith-Macgregor Battle Experience Questionnaire, p. 1, WO 231/89, TNA; Martin, *K Force,* 147–48.

50. On Major Wilson and the grenades see Dare Wilson, *Tempting the Fates* (Barnsley: Pen and Sword, 2006), 173. On wearing helmets post-Imjin, see, e.g., Keith Taylor, 1989-05-257-1, NAM.

51. Taylor letter, 9 Oct. 1951 in Perrins, *'Pretty Rough,'* 207; see also Thomas Cunningham-Booth, 19913/4, IWMDS; Samuel Phillips, 17688/3, IWMDS. On Operation Commando see Farrar-Hockley, *British Part, Vol. II,* 218–29. On the part played by the Ulsters see also Hamill, *Ulster Rifles,* 91–94. The Northumberlands, it seems clear, were far from happy to find themselves attacking only six days before they were due to leave (see Perrins, *'Pretty Rough,'* 206, note).

52. Barclay, *Commonwealth Division,* 204; 45FR would go home in November, 8RIH in December. Many of the Belgians had already returned home in August. 16FR stayed in Korea, but, as with 3RAR, most officers and men were replaced in the course of 1951.

53. Appleman diary, September 10, 1951, Roy E. Appleman Papers, USAMHI; see Brigadier Thomas Brodie, f. 454, K-664, WO 373/119, TNA; www.unithistories.com/officers/Army_officers_B04.html (accessed 27 June 2009). On the replacing of Brigadier Taylor see Hickey, *Korean War,* 264. On Burke see www.generals.dk/general/Burke/Brian_Arthur/Great_Britain.html (accessed 17 March 2010).

54. See Barclay, *Commonwealth Division,* 223; Farrar-Hockley, *British Part, Vol. II,* 135. On the static phase of the war, 1951–53, see, e.g., Hastings, *Korean War,* chapter 16.

55. 339 Australian and 516 Canadian servicemen died between 1950 and 1953.

56. Grist, *Remembered,* 61; see *The Times,* 22 December 1951, p. 2; Holles, *No Rice,* 174–75; Ronald Wells narrative, p. 12, IWMDD.

57. *The Times,* 22 December 1951, p. 2; 21 December 1951, p. 6.

58. "US General Ridgway and the Glosters battle," www.thekoreanwar.co.uk/html/sound_bites.html (accessed 11 August 2007).

59. *Daily Telegraph,* 24 April 1952, p. 5; *The Times,* 24 April 1952, p. 3; see *The Times,* 27 March 1952, p. 6; 28 April 1952, p. 4; 1 May 1952, p. 3. On the Imjin POWs in Chinese hands see S. P. MacKenzie, *Brit-*

ish Prisoners of the Korean War (Oxford: Oxford University Press, 2012), chapter 5.

60. Linklater, *Our Men*, 61. The Imjin narrative was covered on pp. 55–61, while Kapyong was covered on pp. 61–64. On the development of *Our Men in Korea* see AIR 2/11509, BW 83/17, INF 12/602, TNA.

61. VC Citation in Harding, *Imjin Roll*, 89–90. On the DSC see *The Times*, 19 November 1953, p. 5. On press interest in the return of Carne and the Glosters see, e.g., *Daily Express*, 2 September 1953, p. 2; *Daily Telegraph*, 15 August 1953, p. 7; 29 August 1953, pp. 1, 8; 31 August 1953, pp. 1, 8; 1 September 1953, p. 1; 14 October 1953, pp. 1, 5.

62. See Farrar-Hockley, *Edge*; Davies, *In Spite*; Kinne, *Wooden Boxes*; Matthews, *No Rice*.

63. Historical Section, General Staff, Army Headquarters, *Canada's Army in Korea* (Ottawa: Queen's Printer, 1956), 14–18; Barclay, *First Commonwealth*, 58–70.

64. See, e.g., Eagle's comment, "Korean Veterans Remember Fallen Comrades," 20 April 2001, news.bbc.co.uk/2/low/uk_news/1288010.stm (accessed 14 August 2007). The "forgotten" theme is also plugged in the titles of various programs and films; see, e.g., *Korea: Canada's Forgotten War*, produced by H. Clifford Chadderton (Ottawa: War Amps of Canada, 1989), www.waramps.ca/military/korea.html (accessed 2 February 2010); "The Forgotten Battle in the Forgotten War," *The 7.30 Report*, ABC Television, 25 April 2001, www.abc.net.au/7.30/content/2001/s283098.htm (accessed 28 January 2010).

65. One popular British writer went even further, suggesting that it was the stand of 29th Brigade that not only halted the enemy drive on Seoul but also first brought the Chinese to the negotiating table. See Perrett, *Last Stand*, 213. This was also the implication – with the Glosters very much at center stage – in Newbould and Beresford, *Glosters*, 126–27. On Canadian and Australian claims to have saved Seoul compare, e.g., the statements made in two television programs: Ben Evans in *The 7.30 Report*, ABC Television, 25 April 2001, www.abc.net.au/7.30/content/2001/s283098.htm (accessed 28 January 2010); Dan Bjarnason in *The National Magazine*, 27 July 1999, archives.cbc.ca/war_conflict/korean_war/clips/684/ (accessed 27 August 2009). Compare also the claims made on behalf of the two brigades for the South Korean official history: Ministry of National Defense, *United Nations Forces II*, 179, 623.

66. See Notes on Talk by Lt.-Col. J. R. Stone, 5 June 1951, p. 4, 681.011 (D3), DHH; Odgers, *Remembering Korea*, 91.

67. See Dolcater *3d Infantry*, 205; Hickey, *Korean War*, 235. For the patriotic habit of associating the figure of 10,000+ enemy casualties with the efforts of 29Bde on the Imjin see, e.g., Newbould and Beresford, *Glosters*, 126–27; www.remuseum.org.uk/on_line/rem_online-korea3.hm (accessed 10 March 2009); Charles Whiting, *Battleground Korea* (Stroud: Sutton, 1999), 168; Ministry of National Defense, *United Nations Forces, Vol. II*, 623 (the official South Korean account drafted by British authorities – see Hickey, *Korean War*, 382). British accounts of the Korean War almost always place greater emphasis on the Battle of the Imjin than American accounts. It is notable that in the latter the halting of the Chinese Fifth Phase offensive is explained as a collective effort in which the Battle of the Imjin played only a part and which did not culminate until 29 April. See, e.g., Mossman, *Ebb and Flow*, chapters 21–22; Appleman, *Ridgway Duels*, 458–97; Clay Blair, *The Forgotten War* (New York: Times Books, 1987), chapter 26.

68. On the 10,000 figure as accepted but rather arbitrary see Hastings, *Korean War*, 270.

69. Salmon, *Last Round*, 260, second footnote. It is also commonly repeated that the Chinese 63rd Army was so badly

mauled by the brigade that it had to be withdrawn from the war. This was not in fact the case. Ibid., first footnote.

70. On the Glosters dodging amalgamation as a result of their battle honors from Korea see, e.g., Blaxland, *Regiments Depart,* 336, 482; see also Salmon, *Last Round,* 329. On public awareness of the war in Britain centering on the Imjin battle see, e.g., BBC News, "Korea veterans return to scene of battle," 22 April 2001, news.bbc.co.uk/1290593.stm (accessed 29 February 2008); "Veterans Return to Pay Their Respects," *Soldier,* 26 May 1997, pp. 17–19. A battlefield memorial was unveiled in 1957 when the last British soldiers left the Republic of Korea. See *Soldier* 13 (1957): 19. A memorial to 3RAR at Kapyong did not appear until 1963 (rebuilt 1988), and the Commonwealth Monument at Kapyong – along with a full-scale Imjin monument – only appeared in 1967, followed by a Canadian monument in 1975 and a New Zealand monument in 1988. 1st Peace Camp for Youth, youth-peace-camp .blogspot.com (accessed 17 March 2010).

71. Younger, *Blowing Bridges,* 205 ("severe setback"). For the designation of each battle as a "separate engagement" see War Office, *The Official names of the Battles, Actions & Engagements fought by the Land Forces of the Commonwealth during the Australian Campaign in the "South-West Pacific 1942–1945" and the "New Zealand Campaign in the South Pacific 1942–1944" and the "Korean Campaign 1950–1953"* (London: HMSO, 1958), 16–17.

72. See Stone in William Johnston, *A War of Patrols* (Vancouver: UBC Press, 2003), 105.

CONCLUSION

1. John Mole, 23221/5, IWMDS; see also Thomas Chadwick, 1653727/27, IWMDS.

2. Stone and Castonguay, *Korea 1951,* 23; see also James Stone, "Some Commonwealth Men," *Duty First* 1, no. 4 (1992): 37.

3. Unidentified 29Bde HQ officer quoted in Hastings, *Korean War,* 261. Tom Brodie in fact used this phrase in reference to the Glosters only, and to the divisional rather than the corps commander.

4. See Grey, *Commonwealth Armies,* 82.

5. On the Chinese having to conduct improvised reconnaissance at Kapyong (in contrast to the detailed picture built up before the attack across the Imjin started) see, e.g., Browne, "Kapyong! What Is It?" 20. As one Canadian historian has noted, "the Chinese were initially slow to exploit the ROK collapse." Johnston, *War of Patrols,* 91. This may have been because the enemy was expecting to encounter and fight it out with 27Bde. McGibbon, *New Zealand, Vol. II,* 111.

6. On blaming the 1st ROK Division see Ridgway, *The Korean War* (Doubleday), 172; *Washington Post,* 15 May 1951, p. 14; Robertson to Slim, 17 May 1951, Impressions of the British Commonwealth Part in the CCF Offensive on 22–26 April 1951, p. 2, WO 216/345, TNA; Ions, *Call to Arms,* 161; Perrins, *'Pretty Rough,'* 140.

7. Anthony Farrar-Hockley, 30102/1, IWMDS. On the 1st ROK Division fighting well at the Imjin see Appleman, *Ridgway Duels,* 468–69; see also Salmon, *Last Round,* 260, third footnote.

8. Hepenstall, *Find the Dragon,* 103 ("morale problem"); Phil Bennett, S02656, AWM ("no esprit"); Ben O'Dowd, S02659, AWM ("not very good"). On Australian complaints about D Coy 1MX withdrawing at Kapyong and their unfairness see Barry Reed, 2001-02-397, NAM. Reed himself, as noted, won an MC. Compare also the award totals for the Patricias and Australians on the one hand and the Fusiliers and Glosters on the other for actions between 22 and 25 April 1951: 2PPCLI garnered an MC, a DSO, a DCM, and two MMs (Gray, *Danger Close,* 146, 225), while 3RAR received an MC, a DSO, a DCM, and two MMs (Atkinson, *Kapyong Bat-*

talion, 53–57). 1RNF, meanwhile, received two MCs, two DSOs, and two DCMs (Perrins, *'Pretty Rough,'* 362–90) while 1GLOS got two VCs, three MCs, and eight MMs (Harding, *Imjin Roll,* 86–87).

9. On the steepness of the slopes making it hard for attackers – or tourists – to quickly ascend Hill 677 see, e.g., Norm Christie's comments in "Blood on the Hills," Breakthrough Films and Television.

10. Pearson in Gray, *Danger Close,* 73; see also, with reference to the Lee-Enfield rifle, e.g., Ben O'Dowd, S02659, AWM; Large, *One Man's War,* 46.

11. On the increase in MMGs see Taylor to Slim, 21 July 1951, WO 216/741, TNA. On the hunt for U.S. weapons see, e.g., Martin, *K Force,* 147–48.

12. See Eighth Army Command Report: Section IV: After-Action Interviews: Book 2: Tanks Above Kapyong, Box 56, RG 550, NARA; Winn, *Korea Campaign Supplement,* 12–21.

13. See Watson, "Recipe for Victory," 18, 21.

14. Reliable communication between D Company and Battalion HQ allowed for the calling in of the massed artillery that saved the 2PPCLI position in the early hours of 25 April. "We had telephone lines to each company," Stone recalled, "and by good fortune they remained intact." He also had unusually good reception on the brigade radio net. Stone, "Commonwealth Men," 37. Other units, as noted in previous chapters, suffered communication breakdowns at various stages. See with reference to 3RAR, e.g., Peter Londey, "Feeling Like an ANZAC: The Battle of Kapyong, April 1951," *Wartime* 9 (2000): 22.

15. Grey, *Commonwealth Armies,* 85.

16. Lieutenant Michael G. Levy, according to another junior officer in 2PPCLI, functioned far more competently than Captain J. G. Mills at Kapyong, though it was the latter who was awarded an MC. See Gray, *Danger Close,* passim.

17. Grey, *Commonwealth Armies,* 85.

18. Korea Institute of Military History, *Korean War, Vol. II,* 635–36. Stone argued that "they could have overrun us" but did not because "our area was the limit of their operation." Stone, "Commonwealth Men," 37. Even if the Chinese had pushed harder, though, 2PPCLI was unlikely to have suffered the same fate as the Glosters. See Johnston, *War of Patrols,* 105.

19. Grey, *Commonwealth Armies,* 84.

20. On the Americans blaming the British and vice versa see Epilogue. On the Belgians blaming the British see, e.g., Gunst, Philips, and Vehaegen, *Saison,* 145ff.

21. Douglas Johnson-Charlton, 1525/6, IWMDS; see also, e.g., Hepenstall, *Find the Dragon,* 104.

22. Appleman, *Ridgway Duels,* 471.

23. See Watson, "Recipe for Victory," 20.

24. Salmon, *Last Round,* 314. There is also a question mark surrounding Carne's decision not to try to break out southward on the 24th in order to link up with the 10BCT/8RIH force, which before being stopped was only a couple of thousand yards from Gloster Hill. This arises, however, with the advantage of hindsight, that is, the knowledge – denied to Carne at the time – that this would be the closest any rescue effort would come in light of the dispersion of the relief forces on the 25th. If Carne had struck out on the 24th, there might well have been fewer overall Gloster casualties than was ultimately the case, but the likelihood is that while fewer prisoners would have fallen into Chinese hands, the number of dead and wounded would have been higher than was ultimately the case. What would actually have happened if Carne had chosen to gamble rather than exercise prudence on Tuesday afternoon? "The answer, of course," as Andrew Salmon rightly points out, "can never be known." Ibid., 308.

25. Andrew Salmon argues that the "sticky" misunderstanding on Tuesday afternoon was essentially irrelevant, since the Glosters did indeed hold out through the night and – if they had not been redeployed due to other pressing needs – the American units originally allocated for the counter-attack on Wednesday were strong enough to have broken through. Ibid., 309–10. This does, however, overlook the possibility that if Brodie had used more forceful, American-style language, then Soule, perhaps with help from Milburn, might have been able to gather forces sufficient to reinforce the 10BCT/8RIH force that had failed and make a second, more powerful, and ultimately successful attempt to push up Route 57 before darkness fell on Tuesday. On the other hand, it is very unlikely that such a second task force would have been able to escort the Glosters back before nightfall; in other words, the end result might well have been an even larger U.N. force (the Glosters plus the rescuers) surrounded and facing either ultimate extinction or a "death ride" southward, and of a worse kind than the rest of 29th Brigade experienced at the same time as all U.N. forces were pulling back on Wednesday. See Huth to Joselen, 8 Aug. 1957, CAB 157/23, TNA.

26. See Grey, *Commonwealth Armies,* 85.

27. The adjutant of the Glosters, Tony Farrar-Hockley, remembered asking himself repeatedly, after the Glosters were ordered not to withdraw, what was the point of having prepared positions to fall back on? Hastings, *Korean War,* 261. Farrar-Hockley probably was referring to Line Delta, which Eighth Army had prepared earlier, rather than to positions dug by the Glosters, which explains why no references to a Gloster-created fall-back line could be found by Andrew Salmon (*Last Round,* 311, first footnote).

28. Appleman diary, September 15, 1951, Roy E. Appleman Papers, USAMHI.

29. On Van Fleet privately thinking the loss of the Glosters had been worth it see Van Fleet to Ridgway, May 11, 1951, Folder T-Z, Box 19, Ridgway Papers, USAMHI. On Van Fleet not wanting to withdraw too hastily see Braim, *Will to Win,* 248, 251. Andrew Salmon argues: "Had the Glosters pulled out on the 23rd or 24th, they would have left a gap some four miles wide in Line Kansas, which would have opened the floodgates . . ." Salmon, *Last Round,* 313–14. This argument does seem to assume, however, that the Glosters would have been unable to establish effective defensive positions farther south during a fighting retreat – an understandable position in light of what happened when the rest of the brigade withdrew from Line Kansas – and that no U.S. reserve forces could have been made available to help plug the gap.

30. Paik, *Pusan to Panmunjom,* 144.

31. See Salmon, *Last Round,* xiv; McKeown, *Kapyong Remembered,* 40; Bishop, *King's Bishop,* 118.

32. Tom Brodie, www.thekoreanwar.co.uk/html_sound_bites.html (accessed 11 August 2007).

Select Bibliography

GOVERNMENT ARCHIVAL SOURCES

Australia

Australian War Memorial, Canberra
AWM Series 85, 4/28; AWM Series 114, 665/7/1

National Archives of Australia, Canberra
A2151, KB1073/11G

Canada

Directorate of History and Heritage, Department of National Defence, Ottawa
111.41 (D22); 145.2 P7013 (D4); 145.2 P7013 (D6); 314.009 (D464); 681.011 (D3); 681.013

National Library and Archives of Canada, Ottawa
RG 23-C-3

Great Britain

National Archives, Kew
AIR 2; AIR 20; BW 83/17; CAB 157; DEFE 11, 12; FCO 21; FO 369; INF 12; PREM 8; WO 32, 71, 93, 208, 216, 231, 281, 291, 308, 373

New Zealand

Archives New Zealand, Wellington
WA-K 1DAK 1 2/1/7

United States

National Archives and Records Administration, Archives II, College Park, Md.
RG 407, RG 550

UNPUBLISHED MEMOIRS, DIARIES, LETTERS, ETC.

Angier, P. (IWMDD); Appleman, R. (USAMHI); Barrett, D. (NAM); Beckerley, E. (IWMDD); Bermingham, E. (NAM); Black, A. (IWMDD); Carter, F. (IWMDD); Chaderton, C. http://www.cliffchadderton.ca/blog/?page_id=15 (accessed October 2, 2009); Coad, B. (IWMDD); Cook, G. http://www.cliffchadderton.ca/blog/?page_id=15 (accessed October 2, 2009); Czuboka, M. http://iwvpa.net/willbondwhat/heroes-u.php (accessed September 25, 2009); http://www.kvacanada.com/stories_czuboka.htm (accessed August 23, 2011); Ferguson, S. http://www.thekoreanwar.co.uk/html/s_ferguson.html (accessed May 12, 2006); Holtham, J. http://www.riv.co.nz/rnza/tales/holtham1.htm (accessed January 27, 2010); Gasson, M. http://www.riv.co.nz/rnza/songs/gasson.htm (accessed January 28, 2010); Gill, R. (IWMDD); Godwin, K. http://members.tripod.com/~Glosters/kpow1.htm (accessed April 18, 2005); Green, C. http://iccy.org.uk/vanguard/page 0014.htm (accessed June 19, 2009); Jacobs, J. (IWMDD); Jaunal, J. http://www.korean-war-educator.org/memoirs/jaunal_jack/

index.htm (accessed January 11, 2011); Jones, P. http://www.britains-smallwars.com/korea/Jones.htm, (accessed May 7, 2006); Knowles, P. (AWM); Man, A. (IWMDD; NAM); Matthews, S. http://www.riv.co.nz/rnza/tales/dli.htm (accessed February 8, 2010); Potter, J. (IWMDD); Ridgway, M. (USAMHI); Scott, D. http://www.riv.co.nz/rnza/tales/scott.htm (accessed January 27, 2010); Stowe, E. (IWMDD); Taylor, G. (IWMDD); Vezgoff, J. http://www.kmike.com/oz/kr/chapter1.htm (accessed October 7, 2009); Van Fleet, J. (GCM); Walters, K. http://members.tripod.com/~Glosters/kpow1.htm (accessed April 18, 2005); Wells, R. (IWMDD); Whatmore, D. (IWMDD); "The White Circle: Acceleremus: A Short History of 29 Independent Infantry Brigade Group, July 1940–August 1950," K02/1934 (IWMDB); Wilson, A. http://britains-smallwars.com/korea/Pachon.htm (accessed May 7, 2006); "Battle of the Imjin, 22/25 Apr 51," 84/2280K (IWMDD).

INTERVIEWS/ADDRESSES

Arnall, J. (IWMDS); Bartlett, B. http://www.thekoreanwar.co.uk/html/bert_bartlett.html (accessed May 7, 2006); Beard, D. (AWM); Beckerley, E. (IWMDS); Bennett, P. (AWM); Bombell, S. (AWM); Bone, D. (IWMDS); Boydell, S. (NAM); Brodie, T. http://www.thekoreanwar.co.uk/html.sound_bites.html (accessed August 11, 2007); Brodie, F. (IWMDS); Bruford-Davies, R. (NAM; IWMDS); Butler, D. (AWM); Bye, W. (IWMDS); Cameron, J. (BLDS); Carter, F. (IWMDS); Chadwick, T. (IWMDS); Choi, Y. (AWM); Chrysler, W. (VAC); Church, J. (AWM); Clark, W. (IWMDS); Cleveland, W. (IWMDS); Connolly, G. (IWMDS); Cottam, F. (IWMDS); Cunningham-Booth, T. (IWMDS); Davies, S. (IWMDS); Dixon, G. (VAC); Dyer, J. (IWMDS); Eagles, A. (IWMDS); Eberle, M. (AWM); Ellis, E. (IWMDS); Erricker, R. (IWMDS); Farrar-Hockley, A. (IWMDS; http://www.thekoreanwar.co.uk/html/sound_bites.html [accessed August 11, 2007]); Forward, J. (IWMDS); French, J. (NAM); From, F. (AWM); Gallaway, J. (AWM); Gibson, W. (IWMDS); Gilder, A. (IWMDS); Gower, G. (VAC); Green, E. http://www.thekoreanwar.co.uk/html/interview/html (accessed May 7, 2006); Grosvenor, J. (IWMDS); Harvey, M. http://news.bbc.co/uk/2/low/uk_news/1288010.stm (accessed August 14, 2007); Hawkins, A. (IWMDS); (AWM); Hibbs, D. http://archives.cbc.ca/war_conflict/korean_war/clips/684/ (accessed August 27, 2009); Hickey, R. (IWMDS); Hill, E. (IWMDS); Hobson, G. (IWMDS); Hoge, W. http://140.194.76.129/publications/eng-pamphlets/ep870-1-25/inter.pdf (accessed January 25, 2010); Holdsworth, D. (IWMDS); Hutley, A. (IWMDS); Johnson-Charlton, D. (IWMDS); Johnson, H. (USAMHI); Kaye, D. (IWMDS); Knowles, P. (IWMDS); Kolanchey, J. (IWMDS); Knowles, A. (IWMDS); Lang, G. (AWM); Man, A. (IWMDS; BLSA); Matthews, D. (IWMDS); McCord, M. (NAM; IWMDS); McMahon, T. (IWMDS); Mercer, S. (IWMDS; NAM); Miles, C. (BLDS); Mole, J. (IWMDS); Moreton, L. (IWMDS); Muggleton, T. (AWM); Murphy, B. (IWMDS); Newall, J. (AWM); Nickerson, R. (VAC); Nixon, C. http://www.thekoreanwar.co.uk/html/sound_bites.html (accessed August 11, 2007); Norley, R. (IWMDS); O'Dowd, B. (AWM); Opie, L. (AWM; Ormrod, P. (IWMDS); Papworth, C. (IWMDS); Parry, R. (IWMDS); Patchett, D. (IWMDS); Perrins, A. (IWMDS); Pfeifer, R. (VAC); Phillips, S. (IWMDS); Pilbeam, E. (IWMDS); Ponsford, H. (IWMDS); Portner, W. (AWM); Potts, G. (IWMDS); Prout, D. (IWMDS); Quinn, P. http://www.britiains-smallwars.com/korea/pq.htm (accessed May 7, 2006); Reed, B. (NAM); Rees, R. (IWMDS); Reitsma, S. (VAC); Rickord, G. http://www.thekoreanwar.co.uk/html/sound_bites.html (accessed August 11, 2007); Ridgway, M. http://www.thekoreanwar

.co.uk/html/sound_bites.html (accessed August 11, 2007); (AWM); Scott, A. (IWMDS); Sharp, D. (IWMDS); Sharpling, C. (IWMDS); Shaw, J. (IWMDS); Smith, J. (IWMDS); Smith, O. (IWMDS); Smyth, W. http://www.thekoreanwar.co.uk/html/sound_bites.html (accessed August 11, 2007); Spraggs, H. (IWMDS); Stewart, R. (AWM); Stone, J. (UVic); Taylor, K. (NAM); Temple, G. (IWMDS); Trevor, K. (IWMDS); Tyas, A. (IWMDS); Utting, R. (IWMDS); Watts, A. (IWMDS); Weller, P. (IWMDS); Westwood, W. (IWMDS); Whitamore, V. (IWMDS); Wiseman, J. (IWMDS); Whybro, D. (IWMDS).

NEWSPAPERS, MAGAZINES, JOURNALS

The Age [Melbourne]; The Back Badge [Journal of the Gloucestershire Regiment]; Christian Science Monitor; Daily Express; Daily Herald; Daily Telegraph; The Die-Hards [Journal of the Middlesex Regiment]; Globe and Mail [Toronto]; [Manchester] Guardian; Illustrated London News; New York Times; North Irish Brigade Chronicle; Quis Separabit [Journal of the Royal Ulster Rifles]; Soldier; St. George's Gazette [Journal of the Royal Northumberland Fusiliers]; Sydney Morning Herald; The Gazette [Montreal]; The Independent; The Telegram [Toronto]; The Times; Toronto Sun; Washington Post.

TELEVISION DOCUMENTARIES

"Blood on the Hills." *In Korea: With Norm Christie.* Produced by Paul Kilback and Peter Williamson. Toronto: Breakthrough Films and Television, 2006.

Forgotten Heroes. Produced by Alastair Lawrence. London: BBC, 2001.

Kapyong. Produced by John Lewis. North Fitzroy: Arcimedia, 2011.

Korea: Canada's Forgotten War. Produced by H. Clifford Chadderton. Ottawa: War Amps of Canada, 1989. [transcript at http://www.waramps.ca/military/korea.html (accessed February 2, 2010)].

Korea: The Unknown War. Produced by Michael Dorner. London/Boston: Thames Television/WGBH, 1988.

PUBLISHED PRIMARY SOURCES

"45 Field Regiment RA in the Imjin River Battle." *Garrison Herald* 2, no. 33 (1954): 24–5.

"Korea 1951." *Journal of the Northamptonshire Regiment* 15, no. 2 (1953): 20.

Parliamentary Debates, House of Commons, 5th Series.

Aandahl, Frederick, ed. *Foreign Relations of the United States 1951, Volume VII, Part 1.* Washington, D.C.: USGOP, 1983.

Anderson, Ellery. *Banner Over Pusan.* London: Evans, 1960.

Bartlett, Norman, ed. *With the Australians in Korea.* Canberra: Australian War Memorial, 1954.

Berton, Pierre. *My Times: Living with History, 1947–1995.* Toronto: Doubleday, 1995.

Billière, Peter de la. *Looking for Trouble: SAS to Gulf Command: The Autobiography.* London: HarperCollins, 1994.

Bishop, John R., with G. W. Stephen Brodsky. *The King's Bishop: A Canadian Corporal in Korea 1950–51.* Duncan, B.C.: Mossy Knoll, 2000.

Briton, John. *Shapes of War.* Leamington Spa: Korvet, 1999.

Brown, Andrew Wilkie. *A Memoir: From Music to Wars.* Aberdeen: A. W. Brown, 2001.

Browne, O. R. "Kapyong! What Is It?" *The Patrician* 20 (1967): 17–21.

Cameron, James. *Point of Departure: An Attempt at Autobiography.* New York: McGraw-Hill, 1967.

Cassels, James H. "The Commonwealth Division in Korea." *Journal of the Royal United Services Institution* 98 (1953): 362–72.

Coad, B. A. "The Land Campaign in Korea." *Journal of the Royal United Services Institution* 97 (1952): 1–15.

Crahay, Albert. "La battaille de l'Imjin, 22–25 avril 1951." *L'Armée [et] la nation* 9 no. 5 (1954): 2–13.

Cushing, Thomas "Red." *Soldier for Hire.* London: Calder, 1962.

Cutforth, René. *Korean Reporter.* London: Allan Wingate, 1952.

Dargent, J. "Notes sur le combat de nuit: l'infiltration." *Bulletin Militaire* 65 (1953): 323–29.

Davies, Norman "Taff." *Red Winds From the North.* Knebworth: Able, 1999.

Davies, S. J. *In Spite of Dungeons: The Experiences as a Prisoner-of-War in North Korea of the Chaplain to the First Battalion, the Gloucestershire Regiment.* London: Hodder and Stoughton, 1954.

Dicker, Snow. "My Korean Adventure." *Wartime: The Official Magazine of the Australian War Memorial* 9 (2000): 26–29.

Farrar-Hockley, Anthony. *The Edge of the Sword.* Stroud: Sutton, 1993.

———. "Stories from Korea: The Last Day." *The Back Badge,* 4, no. 15 (1953): 227.

Fisher-Hoch, T. V. "170 Independent Mortar Battery, R.A., in Korea." *Journal of the Royal Artillery* 78, no. 4 (1951): 249–53.

Gabriel Dumont Institute. *Remembrances: Métis Veterans.* Regina, Sask.: Gabriel Dumont Institute of Metis Studies, 1997.

Gasson, Maurice. *To The Top of the Hill.* Wellington, N.Z.: M. Gasson, 2008.

Gorman, J. C. "Korean Relief Column." *Stand To: Journal of the Australian Capital Territories Branch, Returned Soldiers and Airmen's Imperial League of Australia* 4, no. 4 (1954): 1–5.

Granfield, Linda. *I Remember Korea: Veterans Tell Their Stories of the Korean War, 1950–53.* Markham, Ont.: Fitzhenry and Whiteside, 2004.

Green, David. *Captured at the Imjin River: The Korean War Memoirs of a Gloster, 1950–1953.* Barnsley: Leo Cooper, 2003.

Grist, D. B. A. "The Korean Campaign as a Soldier Sees It." *The Back Badge* 14, no. 12 (1952): 42–45.

Grist, Digby. *Remembered with Advantage: A Personal Account of the Korean Campaign, August 1950–December 1951.* Gloucester: The Gloucestershire Regiment, 1976.

Harris, W. W. *Puerto Rico's Fighting 65th U.S. Infantry: From San Juan to Chorwan.* San Rafael, Cal.: Presidio, 1980.

Harvey, M. G. *The War in Korea: The Battle Decides All.* Eggleston: Raby, 2002.

Holles, Robert O. *Now Thrive the Armourers: A Story of Action with the Gloucesters in Korea (November 1950–April 1951).* London: Harrap, 1952.

Honner, Harry. "A Kiwi Opo with 3RAR Korea 1951." *Duty First* 1, no. 4 (1992): 33–35.

Hopton, L. J. "Maintenance of the Australian Infantry Battalion in Korea." *Australian Army Journal* 25 (1951): 5–15.

Ions, Edmund. *A Call to Arms: Interlude with the Military.* Newton Abbot: David and Charles, 1972.

Kavanagh, P. J. *The Perfect Stranger.* Saint Paul, Minn.: Graywolf, 1988.

Kinne, Derek. *The Wooden Boxes.* London: Muller, 1955.

Knox, Donald. *The Korean War: Uncertain Victory: An Oral History.* San Diego, Calif.: Harcourt Brace Javanovich, 1988.

Large, Lofty. *One Man's War in Korea.* London: Kimber, 1988.

Li, Xiaobing, Allan R. Millett, and Bin Yu, eds. and trans. *Mao's Generals Remember Korea.* Lawrence: University Press of Kansas, 2001.

Linklater, Eric. *A Year in Space: A Chapter in Autobiography.* London: Macmillan, 1953.

Long, William F., Jr., and Walter M. Turner. "Challenge Accepted." *Combat Forces Journal* 2 (1952): 12–16.

Man, A. M., John Smallridge, and Don Barrett. "The Middlesex Regiment 'The

Diehards' 1st Battalion Korea 1950–51." *Duty First* 1, no. 4 (1992): 18–19.
Mancktelow, Douglas H. *Atsuko and the Aussie*. North Vancouver, B.C.: DMH, 1991.
Martin, John. *K Force: To the Sharp-End*. Leamington Spa: Korvet, 1999.
Mason, John. *Diplomatic Dispatches: From a Son to his Mother*. Canberra: National Library of Australia, 1998.
Matthews, R. F., as told to Francis S. Jones. *No Rice for Rebels: A Story of the Korean War*. London: Bodley Head, 1956.
Maxwell, Peter. *Home and Abroad: Some Memories of a Very Lucky Man*. Cronulla: P. Maxwell, 2005.
Monks, Noel. *Eyewitness*. London: Muller, 1955.
Napier, Richard. *From Horses to Chieftains: With the 8th Hussars, 1934–1959*. Bognor Regis: Woodfield, 2002.
Newcombe, Michael. *Guns and the Morning Calm*. Newcastle: Minden, 1999.
Noble, Ronnie. *Shoot First! Assignments of a Newsreel Cameraman*. London: Harrap, 1955.
O'Dowd, Ben. *In Valiant Company*. St. Lucia: University of Queensland Press, 2000.
O'Dowd, Bennie. "The Australian Battle of Kapyong: From the Inside." *Duty First* 1, no. 4 (1992): 41–51.
O'Kane, Henry. *O'Kane's Korea: A Soldier's Tale of Three Years of Combat and Captivity in Korea, 1950–53*. Kenilworth: Henry O'Kane, 1988.
Paik, Sun Yup. *From Pusan to Panmunjom*. Washington, D.C.: Brassey's, 1992.
Peng, Dehuai. *Memoirs of a Chinese Marshal: The Autobiographical Notes of Peng Duhuai (1894–1974)*, trans. Zheng Longpu. Beijing: Foreign Languages Press, 1984.
Perrins, Anthony, ed. *'A Pretty Rough Do Altogether': The Fifth Fusiliers in Korea, 1950–1951: An Aperçu*. Alnwick: Trustees of the Fusiliers Museum of Northumberland, 2004.
Porter, Ralph. "Battle of Kapyong – 16 NZ Fd Regt 23–25 April 1951." *Duty First* 1 (1992): 39.
Raschen, Dan. *Send Port and Pyjamas!* London: Buckland, 1987.
Ridgway, Matthew B. *The Korean War*. Garden City, N.Y. / London: Doubleday/Cresset, 1967/1968.
———. *Soldier: The Memoirs of Matthew B. Ridgway as told to Harold H. Martin*. New York: Harper, 1956.
Rose, David. *Off the Record: The Life and Letters of a Black Watch Officer*. Staplehurst: Spellmount, 1996.
Shipster, John. *Mist on the Rice Fields: A Soldier's Story of the Burma Campaign and the Korean War*. Barnsley: Leo Cooper, 2000.
Shipster, J. N., ed. *The Die-Hards in Korea*. Middlesex: The Middlesex Regiment, 1983.
Stone, James. "Some Commonwealth Men." *Duty First* 1, no. 4 (1992): 37–39.
Stone, James R., and Jacques Castonguay. *Korea 1951: Two Canadian Battles*. Ottawa: Canadian War Museum/Balmuir, 1988.
Thompson, Reginald. *An Echo of Trumpets*. London: Allen and Unwin, 1964.
———. *Cry Korea*. London: Macdonald, 1951.
Thomas, Graham, and Ronald Hutchinson. *Turn by the Window*. London: Cassell, 1959.
Tunstall, Julian. *I Fought in Korea*. London: Lawrence and Wishart, 1953.
Tyler, William. *L/Cpl Bill Tyler's Letters from Korea: The Thoughts of a Socialist Worker about the War which He Opposed and which Cost Him His Life*. London: Labour Publishing Society, 1951.
Van Fleet, James A. "The Truth About Korea: From a Man Who Now Speaks his Mind." *Life*, 11 May 1953: 127–42.
———. "The Truth About Korea: How We Can Win With What We Have." *Life*, 18 May 1953: 157–72.

Villasanta, Juan F. *Dateline: Korea: Stories of the Philippine Battalion*. Bacolod City: Nalco, 1954.

Vivario, B. E. M. "Quelques aspects de la guerre en Corée." *L'Armée, Le Nation* 8, no. 8 (1953): 3–4, 6.

Warner, Denis. *Out of the Gun*. London: Hutchinson, 1956.

Whatmore, D. E. *One Road to Imjin: A National Service Experience, 1949–1951*. Cheltenham: Dew Line, 1997.

Whicker, Alan. *Within Whicker's World: An Autobiography*. London: Elm Tree, 1982.

Wilson, Arthur, ed. *Korean Vignettes: Faces of War: 201 Veterans of the Korean War Recall That Forgotten War*. Portland, Oreg.: Artwork, 1996.

Wilson, Dare. *Tempting the Fates: A Memoir of Service in the Second World War, Palestine, Korea, Kenya, and Aden*. Barnsley: Pen and Sword, 2006.

Wilson, David. *The Sum of Things*. Staplehurst: Spellmount, 2001.

Winn, Roland. *Korean Campaign Supplement to "The Crossbelts," 1950/1, Journal of the VIII King's Royal Irish Hussars*. Luneberg: Hoppe, 1952.

Worthington, Peter. *Looking for Trouble: A Journalist's Life . . . and Then Some*. Toronto: Key Porter, 1984.

Younger, A. E. *Blowing Our Bridges: The Memoirs of a Young Officer Who Finds Himself on the Beaches at Dunkirk, Landing at H-Hour on D-Day and then in Korea*. Barnsley: Pen and Sword, 2004.

———. "Episodes from Korea." *Royal Engineers Journal* 65, no. 4 (1951): 338–55.

UNPUBLISHED DISSERTATIONS AND THESES

Brown, Shaun R. G. "The Loyal Edmonton Regiment at War, 1943–1945." MA thesis, Wilfrid Laurier University, 1984.

Gilby, Bryan Robert. "Fighting in the Korean War: The American Advisory Mission from 1946–1953." PhD diss., Ohio State University, 2004.

Jongman, Ja. "Making Cold War Soldiers: The Americanization of the South Korean Army, 1945–1955." PhD diss., University of North Carolina at Chapel Hill, 2006.

Jordan, Kelly C. "Three Armies in Korea: The Combat Effectiveness of the United States Eighth Army in Korea, July 1950–June 1952." PhD diss., Ohio State University, 1999.

Park, Il-Song. "The Dragon from the Stream: The ROK Army in transition and the Korean War, 1950–1953." PhD diss., Ohio State University. 2002.

Watson, Brent Byron. "From Calgary to Kap'yong: The Second Battalion, Princess Patricia's Canadian Light Infantry's Preparation for Battle in Korea, August 1950 to April 1951." MA thesis, University of Victoria, 1993.

PUBLISHED SECONDARY SOURCES

The First Team: First Cavalry Division in Korea, 18 July 1950–18 January 1952. Paducah, Ky.: Turner, 1994.

"The Battle of Kapyong." *Australian Army Journal* 59 (1954): 14–24.

"Guerre en Corée." *VICE*, 154 (1953): 5–8.

Adam-Smith, Patsy. *Prisoners of War*. Ringwood: Viking, 1992.

Anderson, R. C. B. *History of the Argyll and Sutherland Highlanders: 1st Battalion, 1939–1954*. Edinburgh: Constable, 1956.

Appleman, Roy E. *Ridgway Duels for Korea*. College Station: Texas A&M University Press, 1990.

———. *Disaster in Korea: The Chinese Confront MacArthur*. College Station: Texas A&M University Press, 1989.

———. *United States Army in the Korean War: South to the Naktong, North to the Yalu*. Washington, D.C.: Office of the Chief of Military History, Department of the Army, 1961.

Arthur, Max. *Symbol of Courage*. London: Sidgwick and Jackson, 2004.

Atkinson, James J. *The Kapyong Battalion: Medal Roll of the Third Battalion, The*

Royal Australian Regiment, Battle of Kapyong, 23–24 April 1951. Ryde: New South Wales Historical Society, 1977.

Barclay, C. N. *The First Commonwealth Division: The Story of the British Commonwealth Land Forces in Korea, 1950–1953*. Aldershot: Gale and Polden, 1954.

Barris, Ted. *Deadlock in Korea: Canadians at War, 1950–1953*. Toronto: Macmillan, 1999.

Bercuson, David J. *The Patricias: The Proud History of a Fighting Regiment*. Toronto: Stoddart, 2001.

———. *Blood on the Hills: The Canadian Army in the Korean War*. Toronto: University of Toronto Press, 1999.

Berton, Pierre. *Marching as to War: Canada's Turbulent Years, 1899–1953*. Toronto: Doubleday, 2001.

Bjarnason, Dan. *Triumph at Kapyong: Canada's Pivotal Battle in Korea*. Toronto: Dundurn, 2011.

Blair, Clay. *The Forgotten War: America in Korea 1950–1953*. New York: Times Books, 1987.

Blaxland, Gregory. *The Regiments Depart: A History of the British Army, 1945–1970*. London: Kimber, 1971.

Bowers, William T., ed. *Striking Back: Combat in Korea, March–April 1951*. Lexington: University Press of Kentucky, 2010.

———, ed. *The Line: Combat in Korea, January–February 1951*. Lexington: University Press of Kentucky, 2008.

Braim, Paul F. *The Will to Win: The Life of General James A. Van Fleet*. Annapolis, Md.: Naval Institute Press, 2001.

Breen, Bob. *The Battle of Kapyong: 3rd Battalion, The Royal Australian Regiment, Korea 23–24 April 1951*. Georges Heights: Headquarters Training Command, 1992.

Bryson, Richard, and Blane Coulcher. *The West Yorkshire Gunners: Forty Years of 45 Field Regiment Royal Artillery*. Tiverton: 45 Field Regiment RA, 1991.

Butler, D. M., A. Argent, and J. J. Shelton. *The Fight Leaders: A Study of Australian Battlefield Leadership: Green, Ferguson and Hassett*. Loftus: Australian Military History Publications, 2002.

Carew, Tim. *The Glorious Glosters*. London: Leo Cooper, 1970.

———. *Korea: The Commonwealth at War*. London: Cassell, 1967.

Catchpole, Brian. *The Korean War*. London: Constable, 2000.

Chinnery, Philip D. *Korean Atrocity!* Shrewsbury: Airlife, 2000.

Cooper, George. *Fight, Dig, and Live: The Story of the Royal Engineers in the Korean War*. Barnsley: Pen and Sword, 2011.

Corbally, M. J. P. M. *The Royal Ulster Rifles, 1793–1957*. Glasgow: Paramount, 1960.

Courtenay, Vincent R. *Patricias in the Korean War: A Tribute*. Windsor: North American Heritage, 1999.

Cowper, J. M. *The King's Own: The Story of a Royal Regiment, Volume III, 1914–1950*. Aldershot: Gale and Polden, 1957.

Crahay, Albert. *Berêts Bruns en Corée, 1950–1953*. Brussels: J. M. Collet, 1985.

———. *Les Belges en Corée, 1951–1953*. Brussels: Renaissance du Livre, 1966.

Cunningham, Cyril. *No Mercy, No Leniency: Communist Mistreatment of British Prisoners of War in Korea*. Barnsley: Leo Cooper, 2000.

Daniell, David Scott. *Cap of Honour: The Story of the Gloucestershire Regiment (the 28th/61st Foot) 1694–1975*. London: Harrap, 1951. Reprint: London: White Lion, 1975.

Dennis, Peter, and Jeffrey Grey, eds. *The Korean War: A 50 Year Retrospective*. Canberra: Army History Unit, Department of Defence, 2000.

Doherty, Richard. *The Sons of Ulster: Ulstermen at War from the Somme to Korea*. Belfast: Appletree, 1992.

Dolcater, Max W., ed. *3d Infantry Division in Korea*. Paducah, Ky.: Turner, 1998.

Domes, Jurgen. *Peng Te-huai: The Man and the Image.* Stanford, Calif.: Stanford University Press, 1985.

Dunstan, Simon. *Centurion Universal Tank.* Oxford: Osprey, 2003.

Durney, James. *The Far Side of the World: Irish Servicemen in the Korean War 1950–53.* Naas: Leinster Leader, 2005.

Dutton, John. *The Forgotten Punch in the Army's Fist: Korea 1950–1953, Recounting REME Involvement.* Edited by Peter Gripton. Arborfield: kenandglen.com, 2004.

Eaton, H. B., comp. *Something Extra: 28 Commonwealth Brigade, 1951 to 1974.* Durham: Pentland, 1993.

Farrar-Hockley, Anthony *The British Part in the Korean War,* 2 vols. London: HMSO, 1990–1995.

———. "The Post-War Army 1945–1963." In *The Oxford Illustrated History of the British Army,* edited by David Chandler and Ian Beckett, pp. 329–56. Oxford: Oxford University Press, 1994.

Firkins, Peter. *The Australians in Nine Wars: Waikato to Long Tan.* London: Hale, 1972.

Fitzroy, Olivia. *Men of Valour: The Third Volume of the History of the VIII King's Royal Irish Hussars.* Liverpool: Tinling, 1961.

Fletcher, David, and Tony Bryan. *Universal Carrier 1936–48: The 'Bren Gun' Carrier Story.* Oxford: Osprey, 2005.

Forty, George. *At War in Korea.* Shepperton: Ian Allan, 1982.

French, David. *Raising Churchill's Army: The British Army and the War against Germany 1919–1945.* Oxford: Oxford University Press, 2000.

Gahide, Jean-Pierre. *La Belgique et la guerre de Corée, 1950–1955.* Brussels: Musée Royal de L'Armee, 1991.

Gallaway, Jack. *The Last Call of the Bugle: The Long Road to Kapyong.* St. Lucia: University of Queensland Press, 1994.

Gardam, John. *Korea Volunteer: An Oral History From Those Who Were There.* Burnstown: General Store, 1994.

Gaston, Peter. *Thirty-Eighth Parallel: The British in Korea.* Glasgow: Hamilton, 1976.

Gavin, Denis. "Korea – The Battle of Kapyong." *RSA Review* 64, no. 5 (1988): 16.

Giesler, Patricia. *Valour Remembered: Canadians in Korea.* Ottawa: Veterans Affairs, 1990.

Gordon, Harry. *The Embarrassing Australian: The Story of an Aboriginal Warrior.* Melbourne: Lansdowne, 1962.

Granatstein, J. L., and David J. Bercuson. *War and Peacekeeping: From South Africa to the Gulf – Canada's Limited Wars.* Toronto: Key Porter, 1991.

Gray, Hub, with Grania Litwin. *Beyond the Danger Close: The Korean Experiences Revealed: 2nd Battalion Princess Patricia's Canadian Light Infantry.* Calgary: Bunker To Bunker, 2003.

Green, Olwyn. *The Name's Still Charlie.* St. Lucia: University of Queensland Press, 1993.

Grey, Jeffrey. *A Military History of Australia.* Melbourne: Cambridge University Press, 1999.

———. *Australian Brass: The Career of Lieutenant-General Sir Horace Robertson.* Oakleigh: Cambridge University Press, 1992.

———. *The Commonwealth Armies and the Korean War: An Alliance Study.* Manchester: Manchester University Press, 1988.

Gugeler, Russell A. *Combat Actions in Korea.* Washington, D.C.: Office of the Chief of Military History, U.S. Army, 1970.

Gunst, Petra, Armand Philips, and Benoît Vehaegen. *Une Saison en Corée: Du "Kamina" à l'Imjin.* Brussels: Racine, 1999.

Hamill, Hugh. *The Royal Ulster Rifles in Korea.* Belfast: Mullan, 1953.

Harding, E. D. *The Imjin Roll*. Gloucester: Southgate, 1981.

Hastings, Max. *The Korean War*. London: Michael Joseph, 1987.

Hayhurst, Fred. *Green Berets in Korea: The Story of 41 Independent Commando Royal Marines*. Cambridge: Vanguard, 2001.

Henry, Chris, and Mike Fuller. *The 25-pounder Field Gun*. Oxford: Osprey, 2002.

Hepenstall, Robert. *Find the Dragon: The Canadian Army in Korea 1950–1953*. Edmonton: Four Winds, 1995.

Hickey, Michael. *The Korean War: The West Confronts Communism*. New York: Overlook, 2000.

Hickman, Tom. *The Call-Up: A History of National Service*. London: Headline, 2004.

Historical Section, General Staff, Army Headquarters. *Canada's Army in Korea: The United Nations Operations, 1950–53, and Their Aftermath*. Ottawa: Queen's Printer, 1956.

Horner, David. *Duty First: The Royal Australian Regiment in War and Peace*. North Sydney: Allen and Unwin, 1990.

Johnston, William. *A War of Patrols: Canadian Army Operations in Korea*. Vancouver: UBC Press, 2003.

Kahn, E. J. "No One But the Glosters." *The New Yorker*, 26 May 1951.

———. *The Gloucesters: An Account of the Epic Stand of the First Battalion, The Gloucestershire Regiment in Korea*. London: Central Office of Information, 1951.

Kemp, P. K. *The Middlesex Regiment (Duke of Cambridge's Own), 1919–1952*. Aldershot: Gale and Polden, 1956.

Korea Institute of Military History. *The Korean War*. 3 vols. Lincoln: University Press of Nebraska, 2000–2001.

Li, Xiaobing. *A History of the Modern Chinese Army*. Lawrence: University Press of Kansas, 2007.

Linklater, Eric. *Our Men in Korea*. London: HMSO, 1952.

Londey, Peter. "Feeling Like an ANZAC: The Battle of Kapyong, April 1951." *Wartime: Official Magazine of the Australian War Memorial* 9 (2000): 16–25.

Lovell-Knight, A. V. *The Story of the Royal Military Police*. London: Leo Cooper, 1977.

MacDonald, J. F. M. *The Borderers in Korea*. Berwick-on-Tweed: Martins, 1978.

MacKenzie, S. P. *British Prisoners of the Korean War*. Oxford: Oxford University Press, 2012.

Madsen, Chris. *Another Kind of Justice: Canadian Military Law from Confederation to Somalia*. Vancouver: UBC Press, 1999.

Mahony, Kevin. *Formidable Enemies: The North Korean and Chinese Soldier in the Korean War*. Novato, Calif.: Presidio, 2001.

Malcolm, G. I. *The Argylls in Korea*. Edinburgh: Thomas Nelson, 1952.

Manera, Brad. "Kapyong Captured." *Wartime: Official Magazine of the Australian War Memorial* 34 (2006): 34

Marr, Andrew. *A History of Modern Britain*. London: Macmillan, 2007.

Masters, John, and Paddy Baxter. *Fusilier Geordie: Tales from The Fifth (Royal Northumberland) Fusiliers 1944 to 1968*. Durham: Pentland, 1997.

McGibbon, Ian. *New Zealand and the Korean War*. 2 vols. Auckland: Oxford University Press, 1992–96.

McKeown, Michael G. *Kapyong Remembered: Anecdotes from Korea: Second Battalion, Princess Patricia's Canadian Light Infantry, Korea 1950–1951*. Ottawa: M. G. McKeown, 1976.

McManus, John C. *The 7th Infantry Regiment: Combat in the Age of Terror: The Korean War through the Present*. New York: Tom Doherty, 2008.

Melady, John. *Korea: Canada's Forgotten War*. Toronto: Macmillan, 1983.

Meulstee, Louis. *Wireless for the Warrior, Vol. 1: Wireless Sets No. 1–88*. Broadstone: G. C. Arnold, 1995.

Millett, Allan R. *The War for Korea: They Came from the North*. Lawrence: University Press of Kansas, 2010.

———. *The Korean War*. Washington, D.C.: Potomac, 2007.

———. *The War for Korea: A House Burning*. Lawrence: University Press of Kansas, 2005.

———. "Korea 1950–1953." In *Case Studies in the Development of Close Air Support*, edited by Benjamin F. Cooling, pp. 345–410. Washington, D.C.: USAF Office of Air Force History, 1990.

Ministry of National Defense. *The History of the United Nations Forces in the Korean War*. 6 vols. Seoul: Ministry of National Defense, 1972–77.

Montross, Lynn, Hubard D. Kuokka, and Norman W. Hicks. *U.S. Marine Operations in Korea, 1950–1953: Volume IV, The East-Central Front*. Washington, D. C.: Historical Branch, G-3, HQ, U.S. Marine Corps, 1962.

Mossman, Billy C. *United States Army in the Korean War: Ebb and Flow, November 1950–July 1951*. Washington, D.C.: Center of Military History, United States Army, 1990.

Moyse-Bartlett, H. *The King's African Rifles: A Study in the Military History of East and Central Africa, 1890–1945*. Aldershot: Gale and Polden, 1956.

Newbould, Christopher, and Christine Beresford. *The Glosters: An Illustrated History of a County Regiment*. Stroud: Sutton, 1992.

Odgers, George. *Remembering Korea: Australians in the War of 1950–53*. Sydney: Landsdowne, 2000.

O'Neill, Robert. *Australia in the Korean War, 1950–53*, 2 vols. Canberra: AWM/AGPS, 1981–1985.

Peacock, Basil. *The Royal Northumberland Fusiliers: (The 5th Regiment of Foot)*. London: Leo Cooper, 1970.

Pears, Michael, and Fred Kirkland, comps. *Korea Remembered: The RAN, ARA and RAAF in the Korean War of 1950–1953*. Georges Heights: Doctrine Wing, Combined Arms Training and Development Wing, 1998.

Peate, Les. *The War That Wasn't: Canadians in Korea*. Ottawa: Esprit de Corps, 2005.

Perrett, Bryan. *Last Stand! Famous Battles Against the Odds*. London: Arms and Armour, 1991.

Rees, David, ed. *The Korean War: History and Tactics*. London: Orbis, 1984.

Rottman, Gorden L. *Korean War Order of Battle: United States, United Nations, and Communist Ground, Naval, and Air Forces, 1950–1953*. Westport, Conn.: Praeger, 2002.

Salmon, Andrew. *Scorched Earth, Black Snow: Britain and Australia in the Korean War, 1950*. London: Aurum, 2011.

———. *To the Last Round: The Epic British Stand on the Imjin River, Korea 1951*. London: Aurum, 2009.

Sealey, D. Bruce, and Peter Van De Vyvere. *Thomas George Prince*. Winnipeg: Peguis, 1981.

Smith, Neil C. *Home By Christmas: With the Australian Army in Korea 1950–56*. Gardenvale: Mostly Unsung, 1990.

Smurthwaite, David. *Project Korea: The British Soldier in the Korea 1950–53*. London: National Army Museum, 1988.

Steel, Nigel. "Getting the Measure of Kapyong." *Wartime: Official Magazine of the Australian War Memorial* 39 (2007): 56–59.

Stevens, G. R. *Princess Patricia's Canadian Light Infantry, 1919–1957*. Griesbach: Historical Committee of the Regiment, 1959.

Suthren, Victor, ed. *The Oxford Book of Canadian Military Anecdotes*. Toronto: Oxford University Press, 1989.

Sutton, D. J., ed. *The Story of the Royal Army Service Corps and Royal Corps of*

Transport, 1945–1982. London: Leo Cooper and Secker and Warburg, 1983.

Taylor, Barry. "Open Road Barred." *Military History* 7 (1991): 47–52.

Thomas, Peter. *41 Independent Commando Royal Marines: Korea – 1950 to 1952.* Portsmouth: Royal Marines Historical Society, 1990.

Thompson, Peter, and Robert Macklin. *Keep Off the Skyline.* Milton: Wiley, 2004.

Trembath, Richard. "'But to this day I still ask myself, why did I serve in Korea?': The Formation of K Force." In *The Korean War, 1950–53: A Fifty Year Retrospective,* edited by Peter Dennis and Jeffrey Grey, pp. 104–35. Canberra: Army History Unit, Department of Defence, 2000.

USAF Historical Division, Air University. *United States Air Force Operations in the Korean Conflict, 1 November 1950–30 June 1952.* USAF Historical Study No. 72. Washington, D.C.: Department of the Air Force, 1955.

United States Army, 24th Division. *24th Infantry Division, a Brief History: The Story of the 24th Division's actions in the Korean Conflict.* Tokyo: Japan News, 1954.

Villahermosa, Gilberto N. *Honor and Fidelity: The 65th Infantry in Korea, 1950–1953.* Washington, D.C.: Center of Military History, U.S. Army, 2009.

Walker, Adrian. *A Barren Place: National Servicemen in Korea, 1950–1954.* London: Leo Cooper, 1994.

War Office. *The Official names of the Battles, Actions & Engagements fought by the Land Forces of the Commonwealth during the Australian Campaign in the "South West Pacific 1942–1945" and the "New Zealand Campaign in the South Pacific 1942–1944" and the "Korean Campaign 1950–1953."* London: HMSO, 1958.

Watson, Brent Byron. *Far Eastern Tour: The Canadian Infantry in Korea, 1950–1953.* Montreal and Kingston: McGill-Queen's University Press, 2002.

Watson, Brent. "Recipe for Victory: The Fight for Hill 677 During the Battle of the Kap'yong River, 24–25 April 1951." *Canadian Military History* 9, no. 2 (2000): 7–24.

Wood, Herbert Fairlie. *Strange Battleground: The Operations in Korea and Their Effects on the Defence Policy of Canada.* Ottawa: Queen's Printers, 1966.

Woollcombe, Robert. *All the Blue Bonnets: The History of the King's Own Scottish Borderers.* London: Arms and Armour, 1980.

Zaloga, Steven J., and Peter Sarson. *M3 Infantry Half-Track, 1940–73.* Oxford: Osprey, 1995.

Zhang, Shu Guang. *Mao's Military Romanticism.* Lawrence: University Press of Kansas, 1995.

Index

Page numbers in italics indicate illustrations.

S. P. MacKenzie is Caroline McKissick Dial Professor of History at the University of South Carolina and author of *British Prisoners of the Korean War; Bader's War; The Battle of Britain on Screen; British War Films, 1939–1945; The Colditz Myth; Revolutionary Armies in the Modern Era; The Home Guard;* and *Politics and Military Morale.*